Muslims, Dalits, and
the Fabrications of History

Muslims, Dalits, and
and the Fabrications of History

EDITED BY

SHAIL MAYARAM
M. S. S. PANDIAN
AJAY SKARIA

LONDON NEW YORK CALCUTTA

Seagull Books
Editorial offices:
1st Floor, Angel Court, 81 St Clements Street
Oxford OX4 1AW, UK

1 Washington Square Village, Apt 1U, New York
NY 10012, USA

26 Circus Avenue, Calcutta 700 017, India

Published in arrangement with Permanent Black, India

ISBN 1 9054 2 212 1

British Library Cataloguing-in-Publication Data
A catalogue record for this book is available from the British Library

Typeset by Seagull Books, Calcutta, India
Printed in the United Kingdom by Biddles Ltd, King's Lynn

Contents

Note on Contributors

Shahid Amin is Professor of Modern History at the University of Delhi. He is the author of *Event, Metaphor, Memory: Chauri Chaura 1922–1992* (Delhi: Oxford University Press, 1995), and editor of *Concise Encyclopedia of North Indian Peasant Life* (Delhi: Manohar, 2004).

M.T. Ansari is Reader at the Centre for Comparative Literature, University of Hyderabad, and has edited a volume entitled *Secularism, Islam and Modernity: Selected Essays of Alam Khundmiri* (New Delhi: Sage, 2001). He is revising his thesis as a book, *In the Interstices of India: Islam and the Processes of Nation-formation.*

Prathama Banerjee teaches history at Lady Sri Ram College, Delhi. Her doctoral dissertation is titled 'The Politics of Time: "Primitives" and History-writing in a Colonial Society', SOAS, London University.

Rashmi Dube Bhatnagar is revising her dissertation on Jonathan Swift. **Renu Dube** teaches rhetoric at the Communication Department of Boise State University and is currently revising her dissertation on Aristotle. **Reena Dube** teaches film at the English Department of Indiana University in Pennsylvania. Her book on Satyajit Ray and the differential value of cultural labour is in press. Rashmi Dube Bhatnagar, Renu Dube, and Reena Dube have coauthored *In the Name of Woman: A Feminist History of Female Infanticide and the State in India, 1800–2003* (New York: SUNY, 2005).

Faisal Devji is the Dr Malathy Singh Senior Lecturer, Department of History, Yale University.

Praveena Kodoth is a research associate at the Centre for Development Studies, Trivandrum.

Shail Mayaram is Senior Fellow at the Centre for the Study of Developing Societies, Delhi. She is the author of *Against History, Against State: Counterperspectives from the Margins* (New York/Delhi: Columbia University Press/Permanent Black, 2003) and *Resisting Regimes: Myth, Memory and the Shaping of a Muslim Identity* (Delhi: Oxford University Press, 1997).

M.S.S. Pandian is currently a visiting Fellow, Sarai Programme, Centre for the Study of Developing Societies, Delhi. He was earlier on the faculty of the Centre for the Study of Social Sciences, Calcutta, and Madras Institute of Development Studies, Madras. His publications include *Image Trap: M.G. Ramachandran in Films and Politics* (New Delhi: Sage, 1992).

Anupama Rao is Assistant Professor of South Asian History at Barnard College, Columbia University, and is working on a book titled *The Caste Question: Untouchable Struggles for Rights and Recognition*. She has recently authored *Gender and Caste: Contemporary Issues in Indian Feminism*.

Ajay Skaria teaches history at the University of Minneapolis. He is the author of *Hybrid Histories: Forests, Frontiers and Wildness in Western India* (Delhi: Oxford University Press, 1999).

Milind Wakankar teaches English at SUNY, Stony Brook, and is working on a manuscript titled 'Prehistory of the Popular: Caste and Canonicity in Indian Modernity'.

CHAPTER 1

Representing the Musalman

Then and Now, Now and Then*

SHAHID AMIN

'Our people should be exposed to the reality of history very carefully.'—Letter to the Editor, on the controversy regarding the screening of Bhisham Sahani–Govind Nihalani's tele-serial *Tamas* on Doordarshan, *Times of India*, 30 January 1988

There has been a steady rise in majoritarian politics and majoritarian history in India since the mid-1980s. Over the past years, these two notions have moved from the margins of popular discourse to the centre of political deliberations. The descriptive phrase 'India has a majority of Hindus' has now been fashioned into the battering ram of Hindu nationalism—an aggressive ideological tool aimed at redrawing the basic contours of an avowedly secular nation-state. Its logic is to enforce the majoritarian idea of a singular national history whereby the enactment of historical vendetta against the Muslim conquest of pre-colonial India becomes simultaneously the condition for the 'realization' of Indian history as well as for demarcating the 'natural' citizens of India. In this view, all Indian citizens have at the very least to assent to the forging of a 'New Hindu History'—the continuous journey of a Hindu national history whose

*I dedicate this essay to Arvind Narayan Das (1949–2000), for whom I wrote an earlier draft. I also wish to acknowledge the friendship of Shobhit Mahajan, which began with a discussion of this essay. For exceptional bibliographic help I am beholden to Shabana Mahmud, Graham Shaw, Dipali Ghosh and Leena Mitford of that great offshore repository of our subcontinental past, the India Office Library, London.

positivist base is alloyed crucially with Hindu religious belief and with nuggets dug out from the seams of a supposedly single collective memory. This essay is an intervention in the debate on nation-building and the contest over India's medieval past.

The sense of belonging—belonging to the present nation—involves the creation and replication of a sense of 'them' and 'us' through icons, stories, and narratives. This siring of communities and narratives about long-existent collectivities often takes place simultaneously. And this pair has a duplex—both 'twin' and 'duplicitous'—claim to history and to particularistic remembrances of times past. There has developed in India, especially since the mid-1980s, a tendency that freezes all public discourse with the caveat: 'That may be your history, but this is my/our past.' Extant histories of the Indian land mass, in this stridently insistent view, don't answer to present needs. In order to counter this tendency we cannot, in my view, merely confront it with definitive, historical records. History-writing, I argue, needs additionally to allow place for the ways in which pasts are remembered and retailed, and for the relationship of such pasts to people's sense of belonging. As a practising historian, one must then pose afresh the relationship between memory and history, the oral and the written, the transmitted and the inscribed, and between stereotypicality and lived history. A 'true history of communalism', to use a slightly tendentious phrase, would be one that sets out not just to unravel what happened between India's two, or three, or four largest communities, but also to show how these communities remember, understand, explain and recount pasts and presents to themselves. We could well replace the term 'nation' for 'community' in the above statement, and my argument would, in relation to history-writing, remain the same. The periodic struggle over the writing of history primers in our country should, in my view, be located within this general problematic.

I do not wish to analyse the relationship between popularly fabricated pasts and professionally constructed histories in detail: that requires a book. Rather, I take as an example here, and as my point of reference, the Musalmans of Hindustan and the way they are remembered. My concern in this essay is with the expressive category 'Musalman'. What constitutes common sense about the North Indian Musalman? What are the distinguishing elements of their otherness? What is the relationship, in this context, between the recognition of everyday difference between communities and their attachment to different pasts, such that the antagonist communities are believed to be the the carriers of two violently different histories? What is the nature of this mix of history, memory, ideas of innate difference, and the changed context of India's present within statements about resident Indian Muslims as 'resident outsiders'? My essay seeks to address this clutch of related questions. My argument stretches over long patches of time, with an emphasis on the late nineteenth century, when, as is well known, community definitions became particularly sharp in North India. The essay's first two sections are concerned with stereotypes of the Musalman in contemporary India. Subsequent sections deal with a variety of texts—literary, linguistic, agricultural, ethnological—from the late nineteenth century. They address the relationship between popular remembrance and standardized accounts of the past, as well as the manner in which a generalized Hindu/Musalman past is frequently fabricated in accounts other than the overtly historical. This then allows me to query the notion of a supposedly authoritative representation of popular remembrance.

1. The Topoi of a Topi; or the Contours of the Indian Muslim Cap

A major problem confronting the Indian nation today is this: How can difference be represented without stereotyping the group concerned? That this is not usually the subject of editorials suggests the refusal of our serious journalists to step outside the self-inflicted *lakshman-rekha* of what comprises Indian nationhood.[1] The same question of the representation of difference is equally elided in scholarly endeavours to put 'secularism in its place'. The main concern of such academic

[1] This section is based on an article that I wrote for the *Times of India*, 16 October 1988 (special issue on culture). The context was the Ramjanmabhumi movement. I have not tried to cover the journalistic origins of this section, nor change its rhetoric.

writers is to shake the modernist minority out of its secularist trance. Political democracy and a secular society, they argue, are incompatible in India: the westernized *neelkanth* Indian is therefore advised to gulp this bitter truth for the greater health of the body politic. However, the contrast between the 'extra-ordinary' secularist and the ordinary Hindu/Muslim is painted in such terms that the problem of how the nation represents its people to itself loses its poignance.[2] The question has, all the same, tremendous immediacy in contemporary India because the issue of difference relates to the basic Nehruvian axiom of 'unity in diversity'.

How is this diversity to be represented on a billboard framed, for instance, by the unifying rectangle of the nation-state? (See Illustrations 1, 2, and 3.) The question is not just rhetorical, it stares us in the face. I am referring to the ubiquitous national integration poster that underlines the slogan 'We are One' by painting a beard and a Turkish cap on to a common visage in order to make it that of a Musalman. This is the visual shorthand by which difference is officially advertised.[3]

I do not wish to enter the debate on whether a beard (of whatever sort) is a requirement for representing Muslim fellow-citizens in India;

Illustration 1: An Official Poster: 'We are all Indians . . . Let no one divide us now.'

[2] See T.N. Madan, 'Secularism in its Place', *Journal of Asian Studies*, February 1988; Ashis Nandy, 'An Anti Secularist Manifesto', *Seminar*, 314 (October 1985).

[3] For a perceptive engagement with some of these issues, see Patricia Uberoi, ' "Unity in Diversity": Dilemmas of Nationhood in Indian Calendar Art', *Contributions to Indian Sociology* (n.s.), 36:1–2 (2002), pp. 191–232.

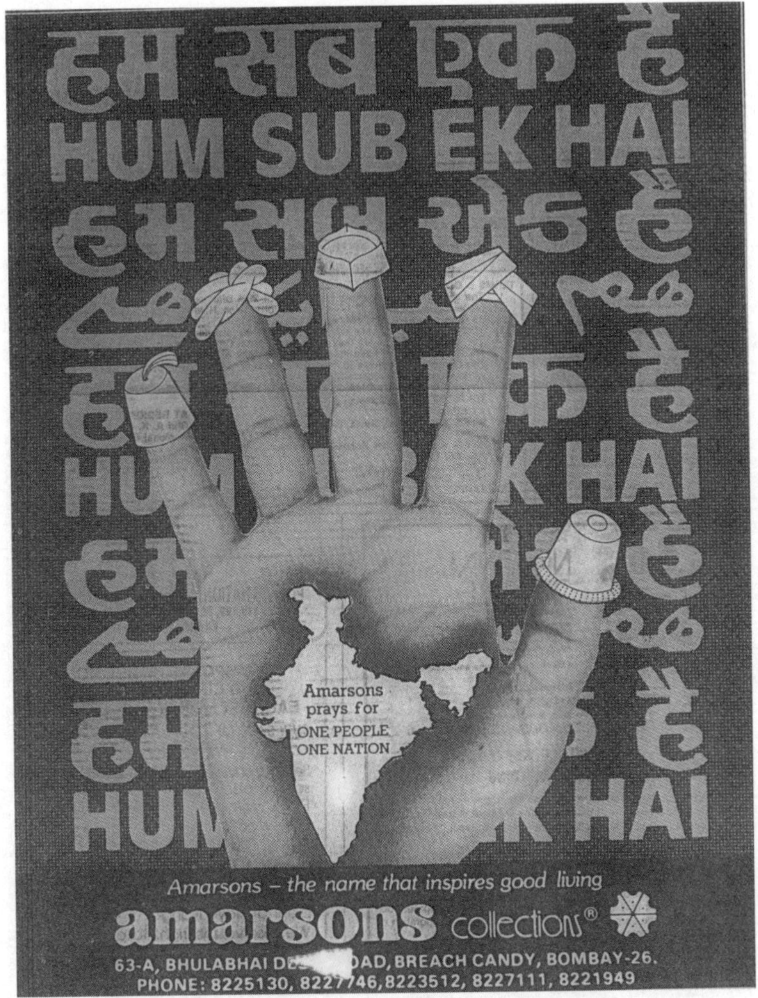

Illustration 2: 'We Are One': Advertisement of a Bombay Clothing Firm

let us pass over the beard. But what about the Turkish cap, the fez? Who put it there? The answer is that it does not belong to any truly representative Musalman. It has been put in there by the advertisers of our multi-religious nation-state. The Turkish cap as a marker of Muslim distinctiveness is in fact quite nonsensical. One hardly encounters a *Turki-topiwalla* outside publicity posters and handouts. Indeed it would be as difficult to procure a dozen Turkish caps in the average Indian town as it would be to purchase period costumes for a Shakespeare play. Yet that miniature upturned waste-paper basket with its tail sits neatly on that abstract Musalman head.

This stereotypical image on the billboard is not a real-life image: it is officially reproduced on such posters in the supposed interests of

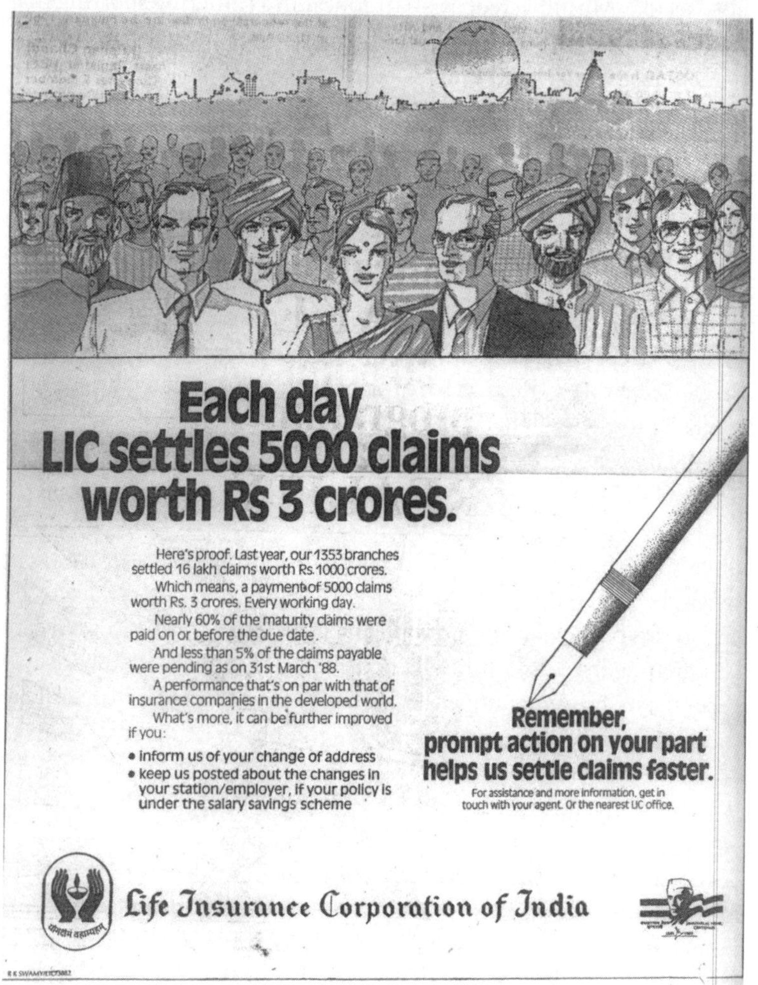

Illustration 3: The Turkish-capped Musalman as Part of an Image of Indian Diversity

nation-building. The result is a paradox: although Indians are not used to a Turkish cap in their midst, it is a prominent sign of the Indian Muslim in national integration posters. In other words, the national advertisement asks us to recognize an image which we do not encounter within the geographical confines of our nation-state.

Let us follow this paradox a bit further. Were people with impeccable 'secular Muslim' credentials to appear in a gathering sporting that particular headgear, they would be seen to be making a sectarian, fundamentalist, and—who knows—even anti-national statement! If all those who could afford it donned that headgear in public, the effect would be electrifying. A gratuitous and unsavoury gesture, a politics of looking different, would be seen as coming into being. This in turn would be queried from a national viewpoint. The *Hum ek hain* billboard would have fallen flat on its fez!

But let us put the billboard up once again and peer at it a bit more closely. Don't we find the fez in other representations of twentieth-century Musalmans as well? In a sketch in his recent Raj series, M.F. Husain portrays a 'Retired Khan Bahadur' with a veiled lady, an umbrella, and the fez. The Muslim League functionary in the television serial *Tamas* is distinguished by his beard, chaste Urdu, and that topi once again.

If one were to try historicizing this topi as Indian topoi, it would be obvious at the outset that the Turks did not bring the cap with them when they arrived here in the thirteenth century. In fact, as late as the 1910s this particular topi was known as the *Rumi topi*, or Roman cap. Originating in Constantinople, or the second Rome, our topi came to carry the name of that imperial city![4] It was only with the dismemberment of the Ottoman empire and the rise of the Khilafat movement

[4] 'Very often, in ancient times, the word *Rom* meant Constantinople and not *Rome*'. Gopinath Kaviraj, 'The Tantra-Vartika and Its Author', in Ganganath Jha, ed., *Kumarilla Bhatta, Tantra Vartika* (*c.* 1923, rpt., Delhi: 1983), vol. I, p. xvi (emphasis in original). The confusion persisted down to modern times. Mullas in some Mymensingh villages asked Muslims to burn 'fez' caps (Rumi topi) in protest against the Italian invasion of Tripoli in 1913. See Tajul Hashmi, 'Peasants and Politics in East Bengal, 1920–47' (University of Western Australia, Ph.D. thesis, 1986), p. 67. That in the late-nineteenth and early-twentieth centuries the Muslim gentry in towns and country wore the 'fez' does not affect my argument about the incongruity of the Turki topi in national integration posters today.

in the post-First World War years that the fez became a sign of anti-colonialism in India. Do our collective memories and history primers aid us in appreciating the value of this sign within its historical context? Does the topi tell us anything of the camaraderie between the followers of Gandhi and those of the Ali brothers, a coming together that challenged colonial rule in the early 1920s? I doubt it very much. Rather, the topi is made to stand in as an essential marker of the otherness of things Muslim, as witness the following digression on the Turkish cap in a discussion of the influence of Persian on the Hindi language:

> Just as Sanskrit, Persian etc. are Aryan languages, so are Arabic, Assyrians . . . called Semitic. . . . Arabic and [Hebrew] have had a great influence on Persian, and that perhaps is the reason why, despite the fact that it [Persian] is an Aryan language from within, it appears to be an un-Aryan or Semitic language. Just as a Hindu wearing a tasselled Unani fez cap is mistaken by the people for a Musalman, similarly, seeing Persian dressed in Arabic garb, those of mediocre intellect think it is a Semitic language.

And then follows this footnote:

> Some years ago, seeing Sarojini Naidu's son wearing this kind of a cap, it was published in newspapers that he had converted to Islam. But the Hindus of Hyderabad also wear such a cap and the late Vitthalbhai Patel wore it as well. Vitthalbhai was chairman of the reception committee at the Special Congress held in Bombay under the chairmanship of Hasan Imam in 1918. Those days, he sported a long beard and the fez, and so appeared a full-fledged [*pakke*] Musalman.[5]

The faces on the national integration poster are not burdened with particular histories, they try vainly to capture 'innate' differences. They therefore end up with stereotypical projections. The face on the poster does not match that of the man in the street. To be sure, the man in the street is no less an abstraction than the one stuck on the billboard. What we have specifically, however, are real-life men and women with distinct class positions, social backgrounds, and individual dispositions. So the problem of the stereotypical image refuses to go away in everyday chance encounters. With the widespread dissemination and social acceptance of such images we find biography and

[5] Pandit Ambika Prasad Vajpayee, *Hindi par Farsi ka Prabhav* (3rd edn, Prayag: Hindi Sahitya Sammelan, 2100 *samvat*), p. 24. My translation.

history being left behind, and ourselves recognizing and interpreting those different from us largely through these hegemonic visible signs, as if such humans belonged to a different species altogether. It is such stereotypical sightings that cause an Azim Premji, a Rohinton Mistry, or a Mahmood Mamdani to be isolated by the racial profiling regime of post-September 11 American airports.

Let us take a common example from nearer home. Unless a Musalman announces her or his presence by acceptable and well-recognized signs—these could be speech, appearance, or mode of address—the possibility is not normally entertained that one of the ten per cent out there could be in our midst. So, if a person is asked the routine question: *Aap ki caste kya hai?*—with which chance meetings on a train are still rendered meaningful in the Hindi belt—and the reply is that he/she is a 'Muslim', the polite response is often: *Acchha! Aap lagte to nahin* (Oh, I see! But you don't look it). This is no mere provincialism. The probing query and the stock reply offer us an insight into the majoritarian view of a minority.

Within this worldview, a Muslim should either be stereotypically so, or he should be found only within a particular locality—in his habitat. This special area is normally around the major mosque of the town, which can then be pejoratively deemed a ghetto. Here, of course, anyone can be a Musalman; no outward signs are required of a species in its proclaimed habitat. If this is a social fact, as I believe it to be, then we are back to the paradox of the national integration poster. No diversity is countenanced unless 'they' appear different to 'us' in the way 'we' expect them to.

Stereotypical images by which we recognize the Musalman are elements of a larger process of 'fabrications' of the past. Groups, large and small, simultaneously 'construct, manufacture, invent and forge' (*Concise Oxford English Dictionary* definition of 'fabricate') their identities. The urge to define ourselves *vis-à-vis* the other is no respecter of a systematic narration of things past—of history, in short. The urge manifests itself in picking out past events, no doubt, but it is equally a product of belief, memory, and imagination. This imagination thrives on 'facts' without contexts and events without history, and it soars ahead, usually unchallenged, unruffled by contradictions.

It is in this light that the strange and ridiculous slogan about taking revenge against the '*santān* of Babur', heard during the *masjid–bhoomi* turmoil and beyond, becomes intelligible. By what stretch of imagination can a young citizen of India be conceived of as the offspring of the founder of the Mughal empire? The point needs to be pressed further. Those who believe in such historic vendetta also maintain (and ironically rightly so, this time) that the majority of Muslims in India are converts to Islam: Indian Muslims are not a race apart. Raja Todar Mal was surely closer to the scions of the adventurer from Farghana than an Abdullah Churihar from Gorakhpur district. Therefore, the irrational slogan '*Badla lenge Babur ki santanon se*' flies in the face of facts. But that matters little; it is the belief that the Musalman is recognizably different that counts and endures. That many Muslims of the subcontinent also fabricate exotic Arab, Central Asian, and Irani lineages only goes to prove my point that imagined pasts clutter and distort subcontinental minds, Hindu and Muslim alike.

2. Hindus' Hindi

Let us look at this process of the fabrication of a community past within some representative literary and non-literary writings of late-nineteenth-century North India. In his sensitive discussion of the development of Hindi literature in the late nineteenth century, Sudhir Chandra has drawn attention to the semantic freewheeling of the terms 'Hindus' and 'Hindustan', such that within these terms (i) Hindustani = Hindus minus the Muslims; and (ii) Hindus = Hindus plus Muslims. He provides us with an illuminating analysis of this two-way fabrication of a unified Hindu–Hindustani past in late-nineteenth-century Uttar Pradesh (UP). In his play *Bharat mein Yavan Raj* (Muslim Rule in India) the author, Radhacharan Goswami, has Vamdev thank an Englishman thus: 'Victory to Huzoor. Huzoor has saved us Hindustanis from the jaws of death. These Musalmans have for some centuries not permitted us any respite. Today the uprooting of their raj has given us great happiness. May God ever perpetuate your raj.' [6]

[6] Sudhir Chandra, *The Oppressive Present: Literature and Social Consciousness in Colonial India* (New Delhi: Oxford University Press, 1992), p. 123. All references in parenthesis in the main body of my essay are to this work.

In a public lecture delivered at the Dadri mela at Ballia in 1877, Bharatendu Harishchandra stated: 'He who inhabits Hindustan, whatever be his colour or caste, is a Hindu. Help the Hindu. Bengali, Maratha, Punjabi, Madrasi, Vedic, Brahmo, Musalman, also should hold each others hands' (p. 125).

As the above extracts make clear, in the first the semantic range of the term 'Hindustani' is contracted so as to exclude not only Muslim kings, but, by analogy, the author's Muslim contemporaries as well. In the second the meaning of the term 'Hindu' is extended to incorporate Musalmans. Sudhir Chandra notes that these early modern Hindi writers, located largely in eastern Uttar Pradesh (and Banaras in particular)—men such as Bharatendu Harishchandra, Balkrishna Bhatt, Radhacharan Goswami, Pratap Narayan Mishra—were not Hindu exclusivists; rather, they were fully aware of the 'urgent need to bring about Hindu–Muslim unity' as part of an 'organized national effort to deal with political subjection' (p. 119). Yet the paradox—one should say the paradox constitutive of the formation of Hindi as a modern language—was [is?] that these very authors 'could be perfectly venomous against Muslims, cutting at the root of their efforts' (p. 119).

A demarcation was worked out in their writings by attributing diametrically opposite traits to each and every individual member of the two religious communities. Goswami harangued the Musalmans of Hindustan thus in his powerful Hindi prose (1885):

> You were baptized with blood, and we with milk. Discord is the seed of your religion, and ours is rooted in peace. We, therefore, never offer the first provocation. When you nettle us needlessly, our policy, too, is 'Do evil unto evil' . . . Be that as it may, in the end we implore Musalmans once again to give up their Nadirshahi temperament. Such tyranny and obduracy will not last long. The government has understood your character through and through. The rest is up to you (p. 133).

Amplifying on this theme, Goswami turned to his Hindu readers: 'That the Muslim community is aggressive and strife-loving all over the world is not hidden from anyone. Mischief-making courses through their every vein. Quarrelling, rioting, causing harm unto others are, for them, normal acts, and oppressing the oppressed and persecuting the poor constitute their daily routine . . .' (p. 133). Thus, a year before the ruling of the Allahabad High Court on cow slaughter,[7] and a couple of years before the proliferation of *gaurakshini sabhas*, leading Hindi litterateurs were laying the foundation of early modern Hindi prose even as they were classifying the population of India through their journalistic writings, welding an account of the past and an explanation of the present into a demotic diatribe.

In such writings, a persistent, specific, oppressive, tyrannical, bigoted memory of the Musalman through historic time, *c.* 1000–1900, alongside accredited 'facts' of history, snuggled nicely, and this in turn set two processes at work. On the one hand an 'authentic' Hindu experience of 'Muslim rule' could be located simultaneously in an unhistoricized past even as it could be buttressed by a singular Hindu memory of defeat and subjection. And on the other the hard historical fact of Muslim conquest could enable these Hindi writers to fill in the space of this Hindu past with historical statements which had no verifiable anchorage other than the fact of their placement within the time of a tyrannized Hindu India's 'Muslim past'.

For Sudhir Chandra, this view of a 'general decline of the country . . . [from] the beginning of Muslim rule . . . fulfilled certain collective needs, this belief was not dependent [for these writers] on historical evidence'. He believes that 'It possessed sufficient vitality to defy the facts that undermined it' (p. 116). Within this 'communally-oriented construction of the past', specific social evils, such as the practice of sati, purdah and child marriage, all 'emerged as a consequence of Muslim rule. . . . (T)he practice of sati, in keeping with the ascription of nearly every social evil to Muslim rule was explained as a consequence of the lecherous nature of Muslim rule' (p. 129). Lodged within a collective memory wherein 'repression and make belief' sustained it as axiomatic, this perspective on the correlation of Muslim rule and Hindu decline was 'projected even in situations where blaming Muslims strained the limits of plausibility'. Such, for example, was the case of the ascription of 'something so nebulous as the loss of good

[7] The Provincial Court of UP ruled in 1886 that a cow was not an 'object' as defined under section 295 of the Indian Penal Code, and 'that Muslims who slaughtered them could not be held to have violated the legal provisions against incitement to religious violence.' C.A. Bayly, *The Local Roots of Indian Politics: Allahabad 1880-1920* (Oxford: Clarendon Press, 1975), p. 111.

taste', by the Marathi writer Vishnu Krishna Chiplunkar in 1874, to Muslim rule! (pp. 130–2)

If I have cited Sudhir Chandra at such length it is because, of all the historians of North India's 'communal pasts', it is he who has wrestled most deftly with the problem of how to contextualize these late-nineteenth-century remembrances of the Musalman. Chandra has cautioned us against hearing in excess of what was heard by the contemporaries of Harishchandra and Goswami, or indeed against reading in excess of that which was written by these Hindi writers (p. 136). In 'the oppressive present' of these late-nineteenth-century Hindi writers, he has located the proximate contexts of such 'violent outbursts' in the immediacy of certain public issues or events, be they a communal riot or the widespread feeling that the Hunter Education Commission (of the 1880s) was favouring Urdu at the expense of Hindi. He also makes the interesting point that, 'traditionally, religious antagonisms and religious polemics were articulated in a rabidly offensive language' : ribald ridicule of the ideas of Buddhists, Jains, Charvaks and Kapaliks—as in the popular eleventh-century Sanskrit play *Prabodhachandrodaya*—was a popular model much available to Hindi litterateurs such as Harishchandra, who in fact authored one of the five nineteenth-century translations of this text under the evocative title *Pakhand Vidambana*. Sudhir Chandra is quick to acknowledge that to provide a context for the articulation of such hostility 'is not to condone it, for such hostility also created a context: it could not but have affected communal relations adversely' (p. 136). He adds that, as 'exaggeration and fantasy were characteristic features of popular Indian modes of perception and articulation . . . there was considerable mismatch between the force of this articulation and the effect intended and created (p. 136).

Several questions may be posed to Sudhir Chandra's perceptive account of the essentializing prose of nineteenth-century Hindi writers. Important though the question of virulent speech is, I think concentration on the 'excessive' aspects of these various Hindi texts underplays the issue of typecasting within language, and this tendency to sterotype can be seen in several other writings that lack the characteristic venom picked out by Sudhir Chandra for extended comment. Again, while the zealous advocacy of Hindi against Urdu was no doubt occasioned by the question of a second official language, the elision of Hindi/Hindu and Urdu/Musalman evoked a clutch of essentialist features in relation to Musalmans, harking back to their supposedly obvious, commonsensical, and quotidian differences with Hindus throughout history.

Inasmuch as Urdu, from the days of the language controversy of the 1870s, came to stand for the Gangetic Musalman, the historical power of Pratap Narayan Mishra's 'Hindi, Hindu, Hindustan' lay not solely in its brevity and lucidity, 'help[ing] others move towards some clarity with regard to the problem of competing loyalties' (p. 141). Rather, it was on the constant reference to history and to a memory of Musalmans as rulers and as a single social group that the question of Hindi/Urdu was, and is, based. Indeed this marks the emergence and prevalence of what could be called the linguistic commonsense of Hindustan, and it had far-reaching consequences. The consequences are still with us, well over a hundred years after the campaign for Hindi found its haiku in Pratap Narayan's alliterative cementing of language, community, nation. (I shall return to this notion of linguistic commonsense later in this esssay.) In fact, the question of Hindi as the (national/official) language of the Indian republic, which arose from the very first day of the Constituent Assembly, had less to do with a resolution to the 'problem of competing loyalties' than with according this commonsense with the necessary attributes of majoritarian power within the newly emergent nation-state.[8]

[8] See Jyotindra Das Gupta, *Language Conflict and National Development* (Berkeley: University of California Press, 1970). The debate in the Constituent Assembly on the language issue is best analysed in Ralph H. Retzlaff, 'Constituent Assembly and the Problem of Indian Unity: A Study of the Actions taken by the Constituent Assembly of India to Overcome the Divisive Forces in Indian Social and Political Life During the Drafting of the Indian Constitution', Unpublished Ph.D. thesis, Cornell University, 1960, esp. pp. 363–9. For the change in positions by several North Indian leaders on the language issue, see the contributions by Purshottam Das Tandon, Bhagwan Das, and Kaka Kalerkar, in Z.A. Ahmad, ed., *National Language for India: A Symposium* (Allahabad: Kitabistan, 1941), and the discussion in the Constituent Assembly. See also the important contemporary polemic by Ravishankar Shukla, written in August 1946, *Hindiwalon Savdhan!* (Lucknow: 2004 *samvat*). See also Alok Rai, 'The Persistence of Hindustani', *IIC Quarterly*, Winter 2002–Spring 2003; and Alok Rai, *Hindi Nationalism* (New

3. Remembrances: Oral and Printed

To return to the point of our departure: a question relating to the virulence of these writings that cannot be solved for us is the relationship of such writings to earlier, pre-print remembrances, both elite and popular, of the Musalmans. Within his monograph, Sudhir Chandra modifies his earlier suggestion that Bharatendu and others in the 1870s 'gave expression to what could have been the prevailing pattern of popular Hindu remembrance of Muslim rule'.[9] This idea seems to have been replaced partly by his suggestion that 'exaggeration and fantasy were characteristic features of popular Indian modes of perception and articulation'. The search for a historical context to the virulence of nineteenth-century Hindi writings seems to have led Sudhir Chandra towards two distinct possibilities. Either these litterateurs were merely grasping and transcribing what was already in the air, or they were following a traditional mode of adversarial writing characterized by excess. Both these suggestions have the effect of denying creative agency to these Hindi authors, who were certainly responsible for laying the foundations of modern Hindi prose as we know it—and siring, concomitantly, an authoritative popular Hindu remembrance of the Musalman.

My quest is for a more clearly grounded history of remembrances of the Musalman. This is a question easier posed than answered, but that does not lessen its importance for history-writing and politics in present-day India. The basic fact is that the tension between popular remembrances of the Musalman and their authorial inscription is a theme which needs further exploration. I would like to argue that unless it can be reasonably established that these Hindi litterateurs

Delhi: Orient Longman, 2001). There is an extended discussion of these issues between Alok Rai, Sanjay Sharma, Shahid Amin, and Palash Mehrotra: 'Yeh Khalish Kahan se hoti . . .' and 'Jo Jigar ke Paar hota', in Ravi Kant and Sanjay Sharma, eds, *Diwan-i-Sarai 01: Media Vimarsh://Hindi Janpad* (New Delhi: CSDS/Sarai & Vani Prakashan, 2002), pp. 112–33. See http://hindi.sarai.net/deewan/deewan01.html

[9] Sudhir Chandra, 'Communal Consciousness in Late 19th Century Hindi Literature', in Mushirul Hasan, ed., *Communal and Pan-Islamic Trends in Colonial India* (Delhi: Manohar, 1981), p. 173.

relied heavily on ballads, folktales, adages, proverbs, etc., it would be premature to assume that the 1870s witnessed the simple transcription of popular memory into literary texts. It seems to me more likely, in the absence of evidence to the contrary, that popular Hindu remembrance was in fact being *fabricated* by these writers in the late nineteenth century. The combination of journalism and literature, the conscious cultivation of a standard Hindi, the desire to catch up with the established Urdu press—all these developments created preconditions for the widespread appreciation of a common glorious Hindu past on the part of the literati.

We know very little, in fact, about popular remembrances of 'Muslim rule' and of the Musalman. There is a good case for suggesting that these memories would have been particularistic as well as generalized, i.e., referring to discrete social groups in particular localities as well as to Hindus in general. What were the ways in which a particular community's dealings with the Musalmans were cast as data from a common Hindu past? Representations of Rajput–Mughal matrimonial alliances in Rajasthani folklore and court histories, and their recasting in North Indian literature from the late nineteenth century onwards, could be one such exercise of mapping the specific inscription of the medieval popular into the colonial Hindi textual. Pratap Narayan Mishra upbraided Hindus for these marriages as follows:

Jahan rajkanya ke dola Turkan ke ghar janya
tahan dusari kaun bat hai jehman log lajanya
bhala in hinjaran te kuch hona ah.

To quote Sudhir Chandra's translation of this:

> Where the princesses in their palanquins are carried to the houses of the Turks,
> What else can happen that can make these people blush?
> Can these eunuchs be good for anything? (p. 123 and endnote 24)

'These eunuchs', are of course the author's contemporaries, 'who are being asked to avenge past humiliations, recover courage, and become warriors of a proud Hindu identity' (p. 123). The historical reference is to Rajput–Mughal matrimonial alliances, which Mishra considers a blot on the virility of all manly Hindu society. Here, clearly, we see a particular 'fact' of history being transformed into an important datum postulating a common Hindu past—from Rajputana to Rajshahi. And this is achieved without having to contest and contextualize the Rajput houses' view of themselves as wife-givers to the Mughal court.[10] From now on, it is being suggested via this unsubtle transformation, certain localized 'facts' of India's medieval history can induce only one pan-Hindu feeling—of shame and impotent rage; the *actual* history of such a remembrance within Rajasthani manly and feminine lore, and in royal chronicles, is being cut short and pasted into a broader picture outside Rajputana so as to construct what Hindu India felt under 'Muslim Rule'. We need to know more about such fresh constructions and radically modified representations of a supposedly singular and common past.

There seems to me a reasonably strong case, then, for arguing that the Goswamis, the Mishras, the Harishchandras, and their ilk in UP were for the first time extolling the virtues of British rule while condemning their Muslim contemporaries alongside the erstwhile Musalman kings. And they were creating afresh this ideology within an idiom easily comprehensible to the Hindi-knowing intelligentsia of the muffasil.[11] The *Kaithi*-using mahajan; the landlord who may have had his *amla* keep the state accounts in *shikasta*-Urdu but had *Ramcharitmanas* for his religious text; the schoolmaster; the *patwari* and the *qanungo*—all would have comprised the readership of journals

[10] For perceptive discussions of Muslim kings as Rajput wife-takers during the Sultanate and Mughal period, see Norman P. Zeigler, 'Marvari Historical Chronicles: Sources for the Social and Economic History of Rajasthan', *Indian Economic and Social History Review* (*IESHR*), 13:3 (1976), pp. 219–50; and Ramya Sreenivasan, 'Alauddin Khalji Remembered: Conquest, Gender and Community in Medieval Rajput Narratives', *Studies in History*, 18:2, n.s. (2002), pp. 274–96.

[11] For an argument that the Sanskritists did not provide an effective critique of Muslim rule during the medieval period, see Devraj Chanana, 'The Sanskritists and Indian Society', *Enquiry* (Monsoon, 1965), pp. 49–67. For the contexts in which the terms *tajika, turushka, hammira, mleccha*, etc. were used in *mahakavya, charits* and land grants during the eleventh–fourteenth centuries, see Brajadulal Chattopadhyaya, *Representing the Other? Sanskrit Sources and the Muslims* (Delhi: 1998).

like *Hindi Pradip* and *Bhartendu*, in which Goswami and Harishchandra were standardizing both language and history.[12]

The 'striking feature of the *gaurakshini* movement in Azamgarh', officials reported, is 'the favour it finds among the lower subordinate Hindu officials'. To the Azamgarh District Magistrate this fact was an indication of the 'Brahman schoolmasters', sub-postmasters and *naib tahsildars* having been educated beyond their means. One could argue that it was equally their acquaintance with Hindi literature and journalism, as much as the expensive lifestyle induced by a smattering of English, that made them 'discontented with their lot'.[13] In 1892 Pratap Narayan Mishra had exhorted all the 'children of Bharat' to chant the mantra of 'Hindi, Hindu, Hindustan'. Direct and militant action for *gauraksha* amounted to a semantic welding of the terms Hindu and Hindustan. A long, demotic, warring poem, *Hindi Urdu ki Larai*, published from Gorakhpur in 1884, had the following last 399th couplet (*doha*) for its end: '*Hindi daftar mein basai, gau ghat ho band; tehi chin chamkai Hind jas chamkat ravichand.*' This, in prose,

[12] For evidence on the standardization of language, i.e. the rejection of Braj Bhasha poetry, and the rejection of the prevalent Kaithi script in favour of Devnagari, see Christopher R. King, ' Forging a New Linguistic Identity: The Hindi Movement in Banaras, 1860–1914', in Sandria Freitag, ed., *Culture and Power in Banaras: Community, Performance and Environment 1800–1980* (Berkeley: University of California Press, 1989), pp. 179–202, and Christopher R. King, *One Language, Two Scripts: The Hindi Movement in Nineteenth Century North India* (Delhi: Oxford University Press, 1994). On the Kaithi script and its orthographic differences with Devnagari, see Chandi Prasad Singh, *Kaithi Varnmala, Pahila Khand* (3rd edition, Bankipore: Khadagvilas Chapakhana, 1884), and *Kaithi Patramala, arthat Urdu Maktub Ahmadi ka Tarjuma, Jise Shriyut Vidvaan, buddhimaan J.C. Nesfield sahib bahadur* [*Suba*] *Awadh ke madrason ke Inspector ke hukum se zila Lucknow ke madrason ke Deputy Inspector, Ambika Prasad ne Kaithi Aksharon aur Desh ke roz-roz ke bol-chal mein likha* (Lucknow: Nawal Kishore Chapakhana, 1880). See also G.A. Grierson, *A Handbook of Kaithi Characters* (Calcutta: Thackrey, Spink & Co., 1881). I am grateful to Pratap Bhanu Mehta for making a copy of this last text available to me.

[13] The Officiating District Magistrate of Azamgarh wrote to the Commissioner of Gorakhpur during the cow-protection riots (7 July 1893): 'The education this sort of men have received has rendered them discontented with their lot. Their average pay is some twenty pounds a year and this though sufficient for the need of a native official of the old stamp is inadequate for a man whose very education has created needs that only money can buy'. File xiv–37 (1898–1900), Gorakhpur Records.

translates to the view that the ban on cow slaughter and the recognition of Hindi in the colonial offices will, without a moment's ado, add lustre to India.[14]

While arguing that a common past was being specifically fabricated at this time in Hindi literary texts, I do not wish to suggest that the Musalman was cast as a radically different type in the adages and folktales of North India. '*Til-gur bhojan, Turk mitai; age meeth, pache karvai*'—i.e., 'eating *gur* and linseed *laddus* is like a Musalman's friendship: sweet first and bitter afterwards.[15] Yet such was the presence of Musalmans as the stereotypical other in late-nineteenth-century North India that it could make an individual Musalman's refined literary or critical sensibility quite uncharacteristic of his tribe. Consider the manner in which Babu Baijnath, bookseller of mohalla Raja Darwaza, Banaras, advertised a book titled *Hamari Paristhiti* (Our Difficult Situation). The advertisement starts with the well-known couplet of Bharatendu Harishchandra in praise of devotional Muslim poets of the past: '*In Musalman harijanan pae kotin Hindun variye.*' And then we read: 'It is indeed marvellous [that] despite the fact that

[14] *Hindi-Urdu ki Larai* by Sohan Prasad (1884, 3rd, edn., Gorakhpur: Bhainsa Bazar, 1929). I am quoting from the third edition of this controversial booklet. Veer Bharat Talwar has followed the career of Sohan Prasad's scurrillous tract in Hindi journals like *Bharat Jeevan*, where the author disingenuously garnered support against the Gorakhpur Muslims for unnecessarily moving court against his innocent versifying on behalf of mother-tongue Hindi. See Veer Bharat Talwar, *Rassakashi: 19veen sadi ka Navjagran aur Paschimottar Prant* (Nai Dilli: Saransh Prakashan, 2002), pp. 263–75. Commenting on the widespread tendency to link cow protection and Hindi promotion in the same statement, of which the subject was a regenerate Hindu jati, Talwar states: '*Apni kitab mein Sohan Prasad gae ke uddhar ke liye raja-maharajaon ki or usi tarah dekhte hain jaise us zamane mein Hindi ke uddhar ke liye unki or dekha jata tha.*' This translates roughly as: 'In his pamphlet Sohan Prasad looked up to the Raja-Maharajas for cow-protection as it was then customary to crave their patronage for the progress of Hindi.' Talwar cites Sohan Prasad as ending his booklet (1st edition, 1884?) with the following lines:

Mohi poorn vishwas hai jo das-bees naresh
Ekmat hoi ubariheen Hindi, Gae wa Des
Yahi chinta chit vyaapi go jhankat ho din-raat
Kab Hindi uddhar ko, kab band hoi go ghat.

See Talwar, ch. 4: 'Hindi, Nagari aur Goraksha', esp. p. 353, from where all the quotations in this note are taken.

[15] R.C. Temple, 'Agricultural Folklore Notes', *Folk Records*, v (1882), p. 49.

the author is a Musalman, the simple, lucid and lively manner in which he has collated and expounded on the complex problems of human existence is verily indescribable.'[16]

4. *Kajli*, or the Recollection and Forgetting of Muslim Oppression

In many instances of popular remembrance, Musalmans figure as defilers of various sorts. These mnemonic forms have to be studied, their locale identified, and questions on the interaction between the oral and the written, memory and history, explicitly posed. I take, as my present example, stories about the origin of the popular song form *kajli/kajri*. In his 1883 essay on 'Hindi Bhasha' Bharatendu wrote as follows about the origin of this 'destroyed' song form:

> *Kajli* poetry is indeed very strange. Before giving an illustration of this genre, we shall say something about the origin of this destroyed [*nasht*] song-form. In Kantit country there once was a Gaharwar Kshatriya king named Dadu Rai. He ruled over Mara, Bijaipur, etc. Remnants of his ruined fort can still be detected at the *nala* [drain] near the Vindhyachal Devi temple. He had made his fortress [*garh*] in the middle of four *mairag* and he would not allow Musalmans to touch Gangaji in his raj. The rains failed in his kingdom and he performed many a religious deed; and then it rained. On his death and his rani Nagmati committing sati, the women of Kantit sang their glory [*kirti*] in ragas and *dhuns* of their own composition. That's how it came to be called *kajli*. The reasons for this are twofold. First, there was a forest owned by the raja and it was called *kajli*. Second, the third day [*tritiya*] on which *kajli* is sung is called *kajli-teej* in the Puranas.
>
> The rustics composed this *chand* during that time to the glory of the king—'*Kahan gaye Dhandhooraiyya bin jag soon; Turkan Gang jhutara bin Arjun*' . . . Women normally compose this destroyed [*nasht*] *kajli* on their own, but there are *kajli* poets even among men. Sanprat, a *punkhawalla*, has composed many *kajlis*, but the best are compositions by a Brahmin named Veni Ram.[17]

[16] Advertisement on the back of *Krishi Kahavat Darpan* [*Bharitya Kisanon ka Krishi Sambandhi Prakritik Bhaugolik Gyan* by Thakur Rajeshvari Prasad Sinha (Banaras Siti: Babu Baijnath Bukseller, Sri Bisesvar Press, Bula Nala Kashi Mein Mudrit, 1938)].

[17] '(ka): Hindi Bhasha', *c.* 1883, Krishna Datt Paliwal, ed., *Bharatendu Harishchandra ke Shreshtha Nibandh* (The Essential Essays of Bharatendu Harischandra) (New Delhi: Sachin Prakashan, 1987), pp. 68–9. Emphasis added. My translation.

This notice, which forms part of one of Bharatendu's two essays on the Hindi language, is intriguing. We learn that Dadu Rai 'would not allow Musalmans to touch Gangaji', but the Musalman-as-Ganga-defilers trope captured here, and in the phrase '*Turkan Gang jhutara*' somehow gets lost in the welter of other facts about this Kshatriya king.

This motif is central to Ram Gharib Chaube's description of the customs and ceremonies of the Hindus of eastern UP, *c.* 1890: '*Kajli*, as everyone knows, is a kind of song sung best and particularly [*sic*] in the District of Mirzapur. The name of the festival derives from the name of the song which is sung in every Hindu household in the eastern districts of NWP near Mirzapur.' Having given the provenance and popularity of *Kajli teej* (lunar third of the month of Sravan), and indicated that the origin of the song was disputed 'among the learned natives', Chaube provides the following story, as told by the people of Mirzapur:

> Once upon a time there was a king in the Mirzapur District named Dadu Rai. He was so strict a Hindu that he never allowed a Musalman even to touch the Ganges. On his death the Musalmans touched the Ganges and troubled the Hindus of the Raj in various ways. *It seems that the Musalmans particularly outraged his harem.* Those who could manage, fled to a dense forest in the vicinity of his capital with all the female attendants, whose number was very great. They sang the trouble and indignities that befell them at the hands of the Musalmans in a gloomy strain. The same songs were afterwards named *Kajli*, from their gloomy nature and the name of the forest in which they were sung. The following couplet is common among the educated natives of the Mirzapur District:
>
> *Barwai Chand*
>
> *Kanhan gaye Dadu Raiya jeh bin sab jag soon;*
> *Turkan gang jhutara bin Arjun*
>
> *Tr.* 'Where is gone Dadu Ray to? Without whom the world is gloomily silent. The Turks have sacrileged the Ganges without Arjun (Dadu has been compared to Arjun, the famous archer of antiquity in respect of might').[18]

[18] 'Customs and Ceremonies of the Natives of Eastern NWP', MS. One of the classical Awadhi *chands*, the Barwai meter is ideally suited to convey a sense of pain and loss. Its origins located in the popular, the 'originary' Barwai chand is said to have been composed by the wife of a servant of Abdur Rahim Khan Khana so as

After this awkward and barely adequate translation, Chaube provided further details on kajlis sung in eastern UP. While women 'everywhere in [east] NWP sing kajli at night on Nag Panchami . . . and [on] *kajli tij*', it was in Mirzapur, near the ruins of Dadu Rai's fort, that a major kajli event took place every year. The location was the shrine of Ashtbhuja Devi near Vindhyachal and the Kajirahwa Pokhra (the kajli pond), 'where the entire gentry, common people, officials and dancing girls repair' on two Tuesdays in Sravan, 'solely devoted to singing and hearing *kajli*'.

Both these texts, one a part of a larger statement on the Hindi language by Harishchandra and the other a near-contemporary account of the culture of the Hindus of eastern UP by one of its most accomplished ethnographers, refer to an identical popular remembrance: namely, the time-honoured rapacity of Hindustan's medieval Muslim conquerors. However, it is not this remembrance but the context of the kajli's annual articulation in the sensuous monsoon month of Savan (or Sravan)—a well-established, feminine erotic, musical genre associated with such master practitioners as Girja Devi and Naina Devi—that has reached us in the present.

---

to convey the delicate tissue of love and separation that was the lot of newly wedded wives separated from husbands serving distant masters. The first-ever Barwai is said to be the following: '*Prem pirit ka birwa chalev lagai; seenchan ki sudhi leejau, murajhi na jaay*': i.e.: 'Away you go planting the tender sapling of love and desire; beware it needs watering else it might dry up.' The Khan Khana's servant put his turban containing this Barwai written by his forlorn wife at the feet of Rahim to explain his tardiness in answering the summons of the master. The great poet is said to have been so taken by the beauty of this chand of 12 matras in *visham charan* and 7 matras in the *sam charan* that he took two immediate decisions. First, to send the servant back to his wife, and second to begin composing in Barwai chand himself. I am grateful to Professor Namvar Singh for readily answering my queries about Barwai chand. This episode, along with the specimen of the originary Barwai, is to be found in Ramnaresh Tripathi, ed., *Nawab Abdul Rahim Khan Khana ka Jivan Charitra aur unki Hindi Kavitaen* (Hindi Mandir, Prayag: 1978 *samvat* [1922]), pp. 7–10. See also Rev. E. Greaves, London Mission, Banaras Cantt., and Pandit Sham Behari Misra, Deputy Collector, Bulandshahr (comp.), *Hindi Final Reader: Larkon ke Vernacular Madrason ki Saatveen Jamat ke Vaste* (revised edition, Ilahabad: Indian Press, 1918), pp. 15–16, for a brief view of the technical specificities of Barwai chand.

The theme of Musalmans as defilers of the Ganges, and as lustful creatures who heap indignities on Hindu women is central to the late-nineteenth-century Mirzapur story about kajli. What is remarkable is that city folk have no inscribed recollections of the connection between Muslim lasciviousness and the pleasures of this sensuous musical form, which was malleable enough to incorporate political comment from the somewhat forced '*swatantra* kajli' of Madan Mohan Malaviya (about the victory of Indian liberals and the flight of Lord Lytton) to the latter-day idealized nationalist desire of women following the *hukum* (order) of Gandhi to ply the spinning wheel.

The reason for the disappearance of the Muslim context of kajli seems to lie in the contingent fact that subsequent to the writings of Harishchandra and Ram Gharib Chaube in the 1880s, this connection was not written up as a datum of popular Hindu memories of the Musalman. Rather, a detailed notice on kajli published in 1913 by a prominent Hindi aesthete (*rasik*) of east UP concentrates on highlighting the low-caste and feminine nature of this folk form so as to denounce its debasement at the hands of city-based male singing troupes.[19] 'Kajli is that which is composed by village women, filled

[19] Upadhyay Badri Narayan Sharma 'Premghan' virachit, *Kajli Kutuhal, arthat kajli ka tyohaar, uske mele aur kajli ke geeton ka tatva, bhed, vibhed, utpatti aur tat sambandhi itihas aadi ka varnan* (Meerjapur: Vikrami Samvat 1970, *c.* 1913). The information about the 'independence kajli' by Malaviya in the previous paragraph is taken from here. For an ethnographic description of the feminine nature of the kajli festival, omitted in most standardized accounts of 'Hindu festivals' because of its absence in Puranic literature and in 'known texts', see *Ritiratnakar, Jisko Shriman Bharatkhand, Vartaragan, Samuday Viravants nayak Sir William Muir sahib Lt. Governor, Government Paschimottar Deshadhikari ki Agyanusar, tatha cha Shriman Vidyagunanidhan Shikshaprakarnnayak, Gunijan Vishramdayak Campeson sahib bahadur ki shiksha se Prayag Panch Krosh madhyagat Lehra grambasi Pandit Ram Prasad Tiwari ne nirmit karke ukt shriman ke sanmukh nivedan kiya* (Ilahabad: Government Chapakhana, 1872), pp. 118–20. Again, there is no mention of kajli in the monthly listing (*jantri* = almanac) of the various festivals of Hindustan, prepared specially for H.M. Elliot in the 1830s. The festival is noticed in a supplementary list under Bhadon, Krishna Pakh, 3rd day, but the column 'Kaifiyat written by Pandit according to Shashtras' is left blank, testifying to the non-Shastric and historically more contingent origin myth of kajli. See OR MS 2031, Folios 1–84, Oriental and India Office Collections (OIOC), British Library, London.

with their unique feelings, current and propagated through time by them, in their very own language and tone, and which is not to be heard outside the rustic *dhundhuniya* play [i.e. band of women bending and encircling while singing to the snapping of fingers].'[20] Nowhere in Premghan's detailed exposé on the 'origins and characteristics of kajli' is there any reference to Dadu Rai and the prohibition on Musalmans touching the holy Ganges; Premghan's entire effort is to establish kajli as an authentic, rustic, women's folk form, as against a whole range of male folk creations. Premghan repeatedly stresses that what the singing of *holi* is to men, kajli is to the women of eastern UP. Though concerned largely with *prem* and *shringar*, kajlis were women's 'very own comment on the present, on noteworthy events of the immediate past or even the history of the last one hundred years or so.' An index of the sexual banter shared by low-caste women in their dhundhuniya play, kajli, for Premghan, excluded very largely women belonging to the higher castes:

> I shall give twenty rupees to the *thanedarwa*, and five rupees to the *jamadarwa*;
> These two breasts I shall offer [my lover] *sipahiya*;
> And to the [lowly, but higher than the *sipahi*] *dafadarwa* I shall give my thumb [i.e., nothing],
> Oh my darling *sanwaliya*.[21]

Whether a parallel low-caste culture of kajli existed alongside the memory of the lustful invasive Musalmans, as highlighted by Bharatendu and Chaube in the 1890s, we do not know at present. What is clear is if the Musalmans figure at all in Premghan's account, it is as *Musalmanis*: Muslim women who, ventures Premghan, might have agreed to come out and sing and play kajli with *Hindunis* on condition that they break the widespread interdiction against uttering the name of their husbands. Quoting the lines—'*Khilawe moke Hinduni, main khel na jaanon Hinduni!*': i.e. I don't know how to play; it is the

[20] Premghan, p. 39. For examples of 'dhundhuniya kajlis' composed by Premghan, see *Premghan Sarvasva, Pratham Bhag*, edited by P.P. Upadhyay and D.N. Upadhyay (Prayag: Hindi Sahitya Sammelan, 1884 *shak samvat*), pp. 524–7.

[21] बीस रूपैया थानेदरवा के देबै, पांच रुपया जमादरवा के रे;
ई दुनो जोबना सिपाहिया के देबै, अंगूठा चटाय दफादरवा के रे संवलिया. Ibid., p. 40.

Hinduni who is making me play—Premghan proffers the information that low-caste Hindu women end their kajli play by singing these lines and naming their husbands to each other. This leads him to conjecture that by 'making the Hindunis break a very strict interdiction of their dharma, the Musalmanis perhaps agreed to break their own *dharmic niyam* and begin participating in their [common] festive kajli play'.[22]

5. The Battle of Stereotypes

Another stereotypicality lurks in Premghan's suggestion that Muslim wives have no compunction lettering their husband's name. Both Hindu and Muslim peasant and low-caste urban women refrain largely, as a matter of course, from naming their husbands: '*hamaar prani*' (lit. 'my life/partner') was, and is, one common Bhojpuri euphemism. The alternative for women with children is to refer to husbands as 'the father of Shakur or Ramchanner', as the case may be. Among the middle class this oblique naming of husbands is replaced by such occupational sobriquets as 'Doctor Sahib', 'Vakil Sahib', etc. There seems to be no evidence of Indian Islam changing a prevalent Hindu taboo on husband-naming, as Premghan implies, even if he is not explicit on the matter.

The image of both Musalman and low-caste Hindu women breaking their respective dharmic injunctions to tell each other tales of their husbands maintains the difference between Hindus and Muslim women, but only to underscore the breach of this etiquette in the kajli play of the sensuous rainy season. This is a far cry from the Ganges/women defilement motif by male Musalmans, a motif which had the potential to become part of current commonsense but failed to do so. A major recent study of kajli in Banaras, and specially Mirzapur, attests to the growing importance of male kajli competitions (kajri *dangal*, with identifiable *akharas*). While it touches upon the popularity of kajli singing by women in groups on the occasion of Anant Chaturdashi (in the town), and in rice fields and during *jhula* (swinging time) in Savan, it gives no indication of the connection of kajli with a local folk memory of Muslim oppression.[23]

[22] Ibid., p. 14. My translation.

[23] See the important collection by the novelist Abdul Bismillah, *Lok kavya-Vidha: Kajri* (Delhi: 2000), esp. pp. 12–16.

The 'Ganges-polluted' motif appears nevertheless to have been a highly charged one, for it also figures as a 'well-known episode' in the saga of Ghazi Miyan, the legendary and hugely popular Muslim warrior-saint of the Gangetic corridor. A late-nineteenth-century version has the following counter-account:

> King Danu's castle was at Kantit, overhanging the Ganges, across the Mirzapur border. His tyranny and bigotry were such that he forbade all believers to bathe in the sacred river. To effect this purpose, he ordered every believer to be ferried over with his hands and feet pinioned. The Warrior Saint was strolling about the river bank, and quietly began to wash his feet and rinse his mouth in the water. 'Mi! Mi!' cried the watchman, 'is this dog spitting on the breast of Mother Ganges?'
>
> They hurried him off into the castle before King Danu. 'Away with him,' cried the tyrant, 'cut off his hands and feet, that he may never again pollute the hallowed river.' The Warrior Saint breathed the Opening Prayer. At the first words, his fetters were unloosed. At the second, every charger fell dead in the stables. At the third, the host was destroyed. At the fourth, the castle tumbled, thundering down in ruin. King Danu fled in terror to Bijaypur, where his line still continues . . .[24]

Women are absent from this narrative: an ingenious reversal of the women-capturing theme is played out in another Ghazi Miyan story, but on that later. In the above episode, King Danu's edict maintaining the purity of the Ganges is shown to be cruel and unjust. Ghazi Miyan is apprehended while engaged merely in the ablutionary ritual preparatory to prayers. It is the injustice of Dadu Rai (here called Danu, or Demon King) towards believers which brings about his downfall.

In the story about King Danu, the highly charged purity–pollution encounter gets reduced to a just, spiritual contest between Ghazi Miyan and yet another cruel, unjust (deceitful in some other episodes) 'unbeliever' raja. This mythic contest, predicated on a clash of differing popular remembrances, takes place in terms of accepted stereotypes of the Musalman. I say 'accepted stereotypes' because a popular ballad about the victory of Islam in North India would necessarily have to invert existing stereotypes about 'the believers'; it can afford to ignore these only at the risk of becoming a sectarian saga.

[24] *The Heroes Five* (Allahabad: The Pioneer Press, 1898), p. 100. My translation.

It is this tension within the local battles between stereotypes (usually conducted in Awadhi, Bhojpuri, or Braj) on the one hand, and the generation of a common view of the Hindu past on the other (increasingly so in an emerging standard, Khari Boli), that requires further analysis.

6. A Hindu Agrarian Past?

The fabrication of a standardized past was not limited in late-nineteenth-century Hindustan to Hindi poets and publicists alone; it appears in cognate efforts to take social science and the 'science of agriculture' to the people. In 1899 Ram Gharib Chaube, the senior clerk in Grierson's Linguistic Survey of India, whom we met earlier in this essay, published a popular tract, *Bhashavigyankur*, for the benefit of the 'children of the country' (*nij desh ke balakon ke labh ke liye*). A learned pamphlet on the languages of India, *Bhashavigyankur* set out, *inter alia*, to prove the linguistic unity of India. Chaube informed his readers that 'the different dialects and speeches [*boli*]' of 'the different provinces of Bharatvarsha are closely related to each other, and must have emerged out of one language in days gone by [*kisi samay mein*]'. The reasons advanced for this linguistic sameness were self-evident: 'When the residents of every part of Hindustan follow one religion with minor variations; when they regard basically the same type of *granths* as *their dharm granth*; when they are sub-divided into the same type of groupings or jatis, then surely their ancestors must have spoken one common language in days gone by.'[25]

This common past was not just a linguistic past, it was every other kind of past as well; according to *Krishi Karm Sudharan* (1874) there was even a common Hindu agrarian past. A translation in easy Hindi (*sugam bhasha*) of the Urdu *Kimiyazirayat* (The Alchemy of Agriculture, written by Maulvi Ulfat Husain of Normal School, Delhi), this fifty-page booklet was subsidized by the Inspector General of Public Instruction, Madhya Pradesh, and published from Nagpur 'for the benefit of peasants'. *Krishi Karm Sudharan* is full of interesting advice on how to improve upon existing methods of cultivation. The

[25] *Bhashavigyankur: was kuch bayan apne desh ki juban ka jise Pandit Ram Gharib Chaube, Assistant Linguistic Survey of India [ne] nij desh ke balakon ke labh ke liye likha* (Patna: Khadagvilas Press, Bankipur, 1899), pp. 11–12.

climate—the 'fearless age' of opportunity ushered in by *pax Britannica*—was now, after a long time, conducive to agricultural progress. All that was now required for the peasants was to be educated, or at the very least pay heed to the new, improved methods of agriculture advocated by the author on behalf of the Raj. Peasants 'should realize that *kisani* is not a matter of following [an immutable] *dharma*'.[26] There was no point in continuing with traditional agricultural practices, for these were not the product of an unchanging agricultural past. Rather, traditional practices were historical adjustments made by North Indian peasants to the negative conditions prevailing during India's medieval past. Now was the time for change, for in the Victorian colonial present '*Sarkar ka jo kuch hai de do, phir apne ghar ke raja ho*', i.e. after paying what you owe the state, you are masters of your destinies![27]

Chapter 2, 'On Cultivating Interest in Agriculture', places the decline of *kheti* and the hold of 'traditional peasant practices' (e.g. using seed from one's own field, putting a large area under 'inferior' food-grains, peasant conservatism, preponderance of wooden implements, etc.) within a historical context. Apparently, the 'Muslim invasions' had caused a decline in agricultural productivity and peasant ingenuity alike. Since then, peasants remained in the thrall of an asinine helplessness (*bebasi ka nikamma dhang*). Here is the agricultural history of medieval North India according to *Krishi Karm Sudharan*:

> Farming [*kisani*] was much advanced in an earlier time. In those ancient times very few countries will have attained such heights as were reached by agriculture in Hindustan. All the implements and methods of cultivation are the product of that very age.
>
> Different sorts of fine grain were produced. Hindustan was verdant, like a garden. The little wealth that remains to this day in this fearless age [*nirbhay kaal*] was generated then, and has continued somehow until now.
>
> During the heyday of that prosperous, ancient time, this fertile soil, aided by the labour of *kisans*, yielded gold and silver. Because of the internecine quarrels and squabbles among Hindu rajas, the wealth of Hindustan began to decline.
>
> Since then, agriculture has been gradually imperilled by disturbances and injustice. The gazelle of creativity lost its stride [*buddhi ka mrig sab*

[26] *Krishi Karm Sudharan* (Nagpur: 1874), p. 8.
[27] Ibid., p. 7. My translation.

chaukri bhul gaya]. There was little chance for peasants to improve agriculture. Peasants lost touch with the finer points of their craft even in that ancient time—this partially accounted for the decline. And then, because of the Muslim invasions, it became difficult to keep body and soul together, not to mention agriculture and commerce. The little subsistence agriculture that was possible (under the circumstances) was undertaken in nearby fields.

Roads and highways were unsafe because of robbers. It was impossible for peasants to procure seeds from outside, sow them, and sell the crop. The system of farming was adversely affected; techniques and practices lost their edge. Otherwise, would not the same Hindustanis who developed the techniques of agriculture in that earlier time [*poorva kal*] not have improved upon them in the subsequent period? Had they been happy then, they would [surely] have done something to improve agriculture.

Agriculture as practised today is mindlessly imitative [*bher chal*]. Whatever [peasants] see each other do, or what they have heard from their forefathers about the conditions during that age of injustice, they follow mindlessly. Peasants today are the prisoners of a pathetic mentality . . .

To tell the truth, for some reason, and especially because of disturbances, peasants have become unthinking and emulative—they don't apply their mind and profit from it. That's why they go on planting *juar, mot, matar, gojai* and *kankun* [all inferior foodgrains] that they cultivated in the past. They don't realize that the times and the age have changed. Earlier, when our peasant ancestors planted such unprofitable crops, there were good reasons: it was difficult to go out of the village; there were innumerable disturbances; water was not available; bullocks and agricultural implements could not be taken to outlying fields for fear of robbers. Peasants somehow eked out a living and counted themselves lucky.

Now you have all sorts of Freedoms . . .

Now *rahat* is also a good instrument [dating back to *poorva kaal*]. It has 360 wooden parts, but practically no iron. Iron was perhaps not used because it would have been difficult to guard it in the distant fields.[28]

It can be argued that the colonial presence is crucial to this ordering of a tripartite agricultural history: Ancient/Muslim/Modern. I would not deny that the context is important. What is significant, though, is the manner of argument about the country's medieval *longue durée*. That both the original Urdu text and the Hindi translation were authored by Muslims is not what interests me most; it is these authors'

[28] Ibid., pp. 9–12, 34. My translation.

subordinate position within the colonial educational bureaucracy as advocates of agricultural change, and the strong plea to make up for medieval India's lost time, that are important for my argument. North Indian agricultural time is here divided into the fearless present (*nirbhay kal*) and a distant, ancient past (*adi kal/poorva kal*), with an unbearable interlude in between. The truth content of individual statements about this interlude is not the issue here; they are reorganized and given meaning by the operation of a generalized principle—the oppression and otherness of Musalmans.

If *Krishi Karm Sudharan* suggests a heightened portrayal of such oppression, the 1870 Hindi text of *Khet Karm* reveals an equally cussed notion of linguistic apartheid. Its short history is as follows. With the definition of Hindi as a separate language from the 1870s, the speech of peasants began to be typecast in increasingly shallow moulds, wherein the opposition Urdu/Hindi (and Musalman/Hindu) got superimposed on to a historical understanding of the separate linguistic domains of urban elites and rural subalterns. In 1841 Munshi Kali Rai 'Tameez' published a Hindustani tract in the Persian script, with several agricultural terms replicated in the Nagari alphabet. Written at the behest of the Lieutenant Governor of NWP, Kali Rai's *Khet Karm*—a compendium of agricultural practices and modes of assessment and revenue payment—went through several editions.

In 1870 a Hindi translation appeared from Lahore. The need for translation and transcription from Hindustani and the Arabic/Persian script was justified in terms which were to become the staple of the Hindi/Urdu controversy soon after.[29] What is equally interesting is

[29] Namely, that Urdu in Persian script, even if the local idiom is used, is difficult to comprehend; that the Devnagari alphabet is easier to master, etc. For a taste of the contemporary polemic, see *Court Character and Primary Education in the N.W.P. and Oudh* (Allahabad: 1897), and *A Defence of the Urdu Language and Character* (Allahabad: 1900). See also *Hindi kya hai: Anek granthon ki sahayta se Jaipur-niwasi Mister Jain Vaidya Sansklit aur Kashi Nagari Pracharini Sabha ke adhikar se prakashit* (Banaras: 1900), which reproduces the arguments of 'court characters', and supplements these with a 98-couplet poem, 'Hindi Lekchar' by Bharatendu Harishchandra. Harishchandra's lecture in verse is available in *Bharatendu Samagya* (3rd edn, Kashi: 1989), pp. 228–30; for a good discussion of this important statement, see Vasudha Dalmia, *The Nationalization of Hindu*

that the Hindi translator chose to demarcate the Urdu/Arabic/Persian words from the main body of the text by underlining them. The bowdlerization is revealing: *akhtiyar, sailab, jazira, abi, baz, auzar; siway, chal-chalan, khaki, do tarah, kam; kabristan*, even *zamindar* and, of course, *Musalman* get typecast as foreign, and in a sense outside the text proper. In the very first sentence, not only 'Deputy Collector' (Kali Rai), an English word, but also 'Farukhabad', the district that he served, is italicized on the grounds that both 'abad' and 'Farrukhsiyar' who populated it had nothing to do with things Indian.[30] The 1870 Hindi text of *Khet Karm* reveals, then, a peculiar understanding of linguistic practice as applied to Indian fields, farms, and places.

A remarkable glossary of agricultural terms prevalent in Aligarh district—published more recently and by far the best such work for North India—is similarly marked by the strong desire to establish a pure ancient genealogy for India's peasant past. As a result, an otherwise excellent linguistic exercise gets invested with a strong sense of ethnicist history. The philological aim of Amba Prasad Suman's *Krishak Jeevan Sambandhi Brajbhasha Shabdavali* (1960–1) is to build a picture of Sanskritic indigenous peasant culture within which Arabic and Persian words associated with seven centuries of Muslim 'foreign' rule have a negligible presence.[31] As Amba Prasad's mentor says in his foreword to the book:

> It is worth remarking that agricultural terms in the Hindi language hardly bear the impress of foreign words. Arabic and Persian words were restricted [in India] to things associated with the court, with pomp and splendour, with the world of pleasure. The tradition of peasant words associated with tillage, sowing, weeding and watering, etc. is in a large measure traceable to Vedic times.[32]

Traditions: Bharatendu Harishchandra and Nineteenth-century Banaras (Delhi: Oxford University Press, 1997), pp. 201–6.

[30] *Khet Karm* (3rd edn, Lahore: 1870).

[31] Amba Prasad Suman, *Krishak Jeevan Sambandhi Brajbhasha Shabdavali (Aligarh Kshetra ki Boli ke Adhar par)*; 2 vols (Ilahabad: Hindustani Academy, 1960–1).

[32] Vasudev Sharan Agarwal, Preface in ibid., p. 2. My translation. Friedrich Max Müller expected to find in Grierson's *Bihar Peasant Life* 'the houses and carts

In highlighting an indigenous uncorrupted Sanskritic root of present-day agricultural terminology, this view of popular culture is based on the unstated assumption—which is larger than the sheer limitation or otherness (linguistic and social)—of 'foreign' rule. For, in electing to sidestep large-scale peasantization of Arabo-Persian official, legal, judicial and agricultural terms, it ends up constructing a technicist view of rural and peasant life. This is a world without 'masters' (*hakim*), without offerings to superiors (*nazar*), without rumours (*goga*), and without life imprisonment (*damal* = from *dayam-ul-habs*) for 'riotous' peasants.

We have here an essentialism of the categories agricultural and rural which leaves very little room for peasants' dealings with their superordinates, or indeed the world outside. The purity of the category 'Hindu agricultural' is predicated in Suman on a particularistic view of rural and linguistic history, a 'history' which makes no allowance for the ability of peasants to appropriate the terms of their own domination.[33]

7. Ethnography and the Deteriorated Ways of Indian Musalmans

Perhaps the most revealing insight into the way community identities were being thought out in terms of essential historic differences—of speech, dress, and most importantly, religion—comes from the notice on *dupattas* sent by that master-informant Ram Gharib Chaube to William Crooke in late 1900. Chaube is here discussing the *dupatta* basically as a part of formal male attire. 'In reality,' he tells Crooke (now in retirement) '*dupattas* are special favourites of Pandits in general and Bengalis in particular.' He then mentions their dimensions and price, and comments on the way the dupatta is put across the shoulder, a style captured in Tulsi Das's lines, '*piyaar dupatta kankha soti*'.

---

and utensils of the people very much as they are described in the Vedas . . .' Max Müller to G.A. Grierson, 5 January 1896, MS Eur E. 226/xi, no.77(6), OIOC, British Library.

[33] For a fuller discussion, see Shahid Amin, 'Cataloguing the Countryside: Agricultural Glossaries from Colonial India', *History and Anthropology*, vol.8, nos. 1–4 (1994), pp. 35–53.

After these ethnographic and literary insights we get the following disquisition on the Musalmans of India, across space and time:

> In ancient times high-caste Hindus used dupattas universally. Now I find people of Benares and Bengal using dupattas universally as part of their suit. NWP men, influenced as they are by Moslems, have generally forgotten their ancient Aryan ways. Persians are said to be Aryans, but Indian Musalmans seemed to have availed of the praiseworthy ways of Persians very little, though they study Persian poems with a tenacity which is simply wonderful. Their religion (i.e. the religion of the Prophet of Mecca) is responsible to a great degree for their deteriorated ways and manners. They prefer Persian poems because Persian poets of comparatively modern times wrote generally on 'love' of the inferior kind, and they have their special relish for this theme.[34]

These 'deteriorated ways and manners' of Indian Muslims were in evidence in almost every aspect of their social existence—there was little point in dating this process, for it was a function of their religion. The task was merely to underscore the shortcomings in their dietary habits, their aesthetics, their language . . .

In his racy poem, 'Urdu Stotra', *c.* 1890, Shiv Nath Sharma identifies the darling of the 'Muslim-male (*miyan-priya*) Urdu' with a set of characteristics which were as much descriptions of the *miyan sahibs* as of Urdu *sahiba* herself! The paean of praise (*stotra*) to Urdu/Farsi—an albatross round the necks of Hindus—includes Urdu as the opium-eating one; the meat-and-kabab devourer; the describer of Aryas-as-kafirs, and so on. This play on words and rhymes ends with an allusion to an abusive, demotic appellation of the Musalman as 'the circumcised one'.

> *Nimau Urdu Farsi Hinduan kanth madhya har si . . .*
> *Darbadhu satyasangha dayini*
> *Mans wa kabab nitya khayani*
> *Jarr sarr arr phrr bolini*
> *post wa afim nitya gholini . . .*
>
> *twam namamiantaram miyan-priya*
> *haulvi lakuwatasu garjani*
> *Arya nam kafira kutarjani*

[34] Appendix B in William Crooke, *A Glossary of North India Peasant Life*, ed. Shahid Amin (Delhi: Oxford University Press, 1989).

mucch shikha shudh kesh mundani
utsave napuns chinh khandani.[35]

And when Begum Urdu comes out to defend herself in a *svang* court-drama, she has this to say for herself:

This is my work-passion I'll teach,
Tasks of your household we'll leave in the breach
We'll be lovers and rakes, living for pleasure
Consorting with prostitutes, squandering our treasure . . .[36]

There is an aggressive ascription of meaning in this 'Urdu Stotra' by Shiv Nath Sharma which is partially lost in the *natakiya andaaz* (theatricality) of Begum Urdu Sahiba. As another powerful illustration of this lexical positional warfare, one could turn to the Gorakhpur Hindi monthly *Gyan Shakti* of 1916. In its very first issue, Shiv Kumar Shastri, the editor, writes: 'One who really desires the welfare [*hit*] of Bharatvarsha or Hindustan, one who considers its gain to be his own gain, and who regards himself a Hindustani or a Bharatiya, he is to be called Hindu. "Hindu" does not signify "Kafir" or "Ghulam". The Persian lexicons [*loghat*] might have given this word whatever meaning they wished, but what has that got to do with us?'[37] Persian lexicons had indeed saddled the word 'Hindu' with the cumulative weight of paradoxical meanings—'thief' and 'beloved' being two such connotations.[38] In the late nineteenth and early twentieth centuries an unsuccessful attempt was made to distend the term 'Hindu' so as to encapsulate all Hindustanis within its expansive folds.

The failure to encapsulate 'Hindustani' within the folds of 'Hindu' is an important datum of community and national consciousness in

[35] Shiv Nath Sharma, 'Urdu Stotra', *Bharatvarsha* (Vitur), 1 December 1890, cited in Ram Ratan Bhatnagar, *The Rise and Growth of Hindi Journalism* (*1826–1945*) (Allahabad: 1948?), pp. 218–19.

[36] Cited in King, 'Forging a New Linguistic Identity', p. 181.

[37] *Gyan Shakti* (Baisakh, 1972, *samvat* 1916), pp. 268–71.

[38] '*Bakhal-e hinduash baksham Samarkand-o-Bukhara ra*' (Hafiz Shirazi). This translates as: For the mole on the beloved I sacrifice the fiefdom of Samarqand and Bukhara / For her black mole I sacrifice the fiefdom of Samarqand and Bukhara. See Anne Marie Schimmel, 'Turk and Hindu: A Poetical Image and Its Application to Historical Facts', in Speros Vryonis Jr., ed. *Islam and Cultural Change in the Middle Ages* (Wiesbaden: Otto Harrasowitz, 1975), pp. 107–26.

twentieth-century North India. Over the years, Hindustani became the semantic opposite of an overtly religious Hindu. This denouement was partly written into the campaign script for the propagation of the term Hindu: the territorial and cultural connotations of Hindustani were not easily amenable to the sort of redefinitions that were attempted from the 1880s. In the post-Partition decades, Hindustani came in fact to stand for all North Indians/Indians. The emphatic phrase 'Hum Hindustani', as in a popular film song of 1960, was meant to evoke a New Age Nehruvian consensus: it was an exhortation to non-sectarian nation-building. In fact, in that particular rendition, it followed from an invitation to forget the 'recent old past':

> *Chhoro kal ki baten, kal ki bat purani:*
> *Nai daur mein likhenge, mil ke nai kahani,*
> *Hum Hindustani! Hum Hindustani!*[39]

[39] From the film *Hum Hindustani* (1960), lyrics Prem Dhavan, music Usha Khanna, playback singer Mukesh, direction R. Mukherji.

CHAPTER 2

Refiguring the Fanatic
Malabar 1836–1922

M.T. Ansari

> On the outbreak of the [1921] rebellion he became king, celebrated his accession by the murder of Khan Bahadur Chekkutti, a Moplah retired Police Inspector . . . He styled himself Raja of the Hindus, Amir of the Mohammedans and Colonel of the Khilafat Army. He wore a fez cap, wore the Khilafat uniform and badge and had a sword in his hand. He enjoyed absolute Swaraj in his kingdom of Ernad and Walluvanad: he announced that he was aware that the inhabitants have suffered greatly from robbing and looting, that he would impose no taxation on them this year (1921) save in the way of donations to the Ayudha Fund and that next year the taxes must be forthcoming. He ordered numbers of agricultural labourers to reap and bring in the paddy raised on the ['upper' caste] Thirumulpad's lands, the harvesters being paid in cash and the grains set apart to feed the Haji's forces. He issued passports to persons wishing to go outside his kingdom and the cost of the pass was a negligible figure, according to the capacity of the individual concerned. His swaraj commenced about the 22nd of August 1921 and lasted until 6th January 1922 on which day he was captured . . . and sentenced . . . [and was shot on] . . . 20th January 1922.[1]

While the Jallianwala Bagh massacre of 13 April 1919 (in which, according to official sources, 379 people were killed) and the Chauri Chaura incident of 5 February 1922 (in which

[1] The rebel leader Variamkunnath Kunhamed Haji, a bullock-cart driver by profession, as described in *The Moplah Rebellion, 1921* (Calicut: Norman Printing Bureau, 1923), pp. 77–8, by C. Gopalan Nair, a retired Deputy Collector.

23 policemen were burnt alive by angry peasants) find their place in the history of the Indian nationalist struggle for independence, the 1921 Malabar rebellion is often reduced to a mere footnote.[2] The final toll of the 1921 rebellion, according to official sources, was 2,337 rebels killed, 1,652 wounded and 45,404 imprisoned—unofficial sources put the figures at about 10,000 dead, 50,000 imprisoned, 20,000 exiled and 10,000 missing. These figures, and the fact that the Mappila rebels had virtual control of—in fact they 'governed'[3] for about five months—an area in which 40,000 'Hindus' resided, and which is now distributed among at least four districts, gives an idea of its magnitude. The national imaginary, however, seems more captivated with the (Arya Samajist) figures of 600 'Hindus' killed and 2,500 forcibly converted.

The 1921 rebellion has been customarily situated with 'uprisings' in this area from 1836 to 1919. These uprisings (referred to as 'outbreaks' or 'outrages'[4]) by the Mappilas of Malabar were directed against

[2] History textbooks, invariably highlight the 'Wagon tragedy' of 20 November 1921 (if they write about the Mappilas at all) in which 67 Mappila and 3 Hindu prisoners died due to suffocation. The rest were mutilated and barely alive while being transported by rail from Tanur to Coimbatore in a wagon without ventilation.

[3] See, for instance, Variamkunnath Kunhamed Haji's letter published in *The Hindu*, 18 October 1921, reproduced in K.N. Panikkar (ed.), *Peasant Protests and Revolts in Malabar* (New Delhi: Indian Council of Historical Research and People's Publishing House, 1990), p. 417. This is a collection of various documents and is hereafter abbreviated as *PPRM*.

[4] For a detailed list, see Stephen Dale, *Islamic Society on the South Asian Frontier: The Mappilas of Malabar, 1498–1922* (Oxford: Clarendon Press, 1980), appendix, pp. 227–32; and Conrad Wood, *Moplah Rebellion and its Genesis* (New Delhi: People's Publishing House, 1987), pp. 11–14. Apart from the 29 actual rebellions, there were also 12 putative outbreaks, with a total participation of 70, in which the insurgents were not, reportedly, inclined towards martyrdom. There was also an incident when a Mappila, due to a dispute over family property, attacked his own relatives: see Wood, appendix 2, pp. 246–7. The number of Mappila participants in the 29 'uprisings' varied from 1 to 20; 3 uprisings, however, of 1849, 1894 and 1896, had 65, 34 and 99 participants, respectively. Also, there is some justification in labelling an event involving a single Mappila as 'insurgency', since the insurgent had the full backing of the community and often underwent rituals similar to those before a pilgrimage.

both Hindu landlords and Christian overlords.[5] Of the 352 Mappila peasants who actively participated in these 29 uprisings, only 24 (of them 12 in one instance) were captured alive. As against these Mappila casualties, one British District Magistrate (H.V. Conolly) and 82 Hindus were killed, of which 63 were members of the 'high' castes, presumably Namboodiris. These 'outbreaks' came to be ascribed to the 'fanatical' character of the Mappila community and the logic of fanatic causation was invoked during the 1921 rebellion as well.

The fanatic is commonly defined, 'normed', as a person excessively or abnormally religious; s/he needs to be controlled. The fanatic looks backward to the 'heathen', or to the 'pagan'—one who believes in a different and 'primitive' religion—with the implication that s/he ought to have been better educated. The figure of the fanatic also looks forward to the 'fundamentalist' or the 'terrorist'; s/he can only be confined or killed. The fanatic, the fundamentalist, and the terrorist constantly appear in contemporary discourses representing attitudes that have to be condemned outright. However, the slow dissolve of 'heathen' and 'pagan' brings into relief the image of a refurbished terrorist, pointing to a metonymic displacement within the metaphoric. Metaphors for the non-modern 'other' seem to have undergone a substitution whereby they have acquired an exclusive 'Islamic' tenor. Examining the figure of the fanatic, as it evolved through colonial procedures and continues in various nationalist discourses is, hence, a necessity in our 'secular-modern' times. As part of such an endeavour, I focus in the first section on Logan's monumental project of endowing Malabar with a history which is also an intrusion of History into Malabar; an ethno-history that also produces the excessive figure of the fanatic. The second section attempts a contrasted reading of two narratives of the uprising of November 1841. The colonial records pertaining to this event are read against the grain as well as in juxtaposition to a pamphlet written by the insurgent-martyrs. The third section analyses nationalist phrasings of the 1921 rebellion in juxtaposition to the report of the Superintendent of Police, in order to examine the afterlives of the 'fanatic'.

[5] Isolated rebellions have been traced as far back as 1796–1800, and even earlier; see especially entry under serial no. 429 in records stored by Herman Gundert, *Tuebingen University Library Malayalam Manuscript Series*, vol. 5, published as *Tellicherry Records*, (ed.) Joseph Zacharia (Kottayam: DC Books, 1996), 245 F & G, p. 114.

I

The Mappilas[6] are geographically located in Malabar, the northern part of present-day Kerala. Their ancestry is often traced to Arab traders/settlers and converts to Islam from among the native population of Malabar. Arab trade dates back to the fourth century CE, and most records accept that Islam was a significant presence in Malabar at least by the ninth century, if not earlier.[7] Islam thus came to present-day Kerala, unlike in north-western India, through traders and pilgrims, and its place in the region was firmly established by the last of the all-'Kerala' kings, Cheraman Perumal. It was believed that Perumal, entrusting his land to various chiefs, secretly left for Mecca in 822 CE and met the Prophet.[8] Reaching the Arabian coast, he changed his name to

[6] Variously spelled as Mappilla, Mapilla, Maplah, Moplah, Mopla, Moplar and Moplaymar. Etymologically it has been glossed as a contraction of *Maha-pilla* ('big child', a title of honour conferred on immigrants) or as *ma-pilla* ('mother's child') implying a foreign, if not unknown, paternity, or as *mappila*, meaning 'bridegroom' or 'son-in-law'.

[7] Andre Wink stresses the 'brahmanization' of the social order in Malabar around the eight century, which, apart from contributing to the effacement of Buddhism, seems to have 'adversely affected the still relatively open maritime orientation of Malabar'; *Al-Hind: The Making of the Indo-Islamic World* (2 vols; Leiden: E.J. Brill, 1990; New Delhi: Oxford University Press, 1999), vol. 1, p. 72. 'It is no coincidence', notes Wink, 'that the implantation of Muslim communities becomes better visible the more caste prohibitions against trans-oceanic travel and trade seem to obtain a hold on the Hindu population and turns it to agrarian pursuits and production, away from trade and maritime transport.' Thus, Jews and Muslims came to monopolize the market; the latter settled down in Malabar and contracted marriages with women of 'low' fishermen and mariner castes. Their offspring, the Mappilas, became 'the privileged intermediaries of trade with the Islamic world' (vol. 1, p. 72). In the words of Ibn Battuta, the fourteenth-century traveller, 'the Muslims are the people who are most respected in this country, but the *natives* do not eat with them and don't allow them to enter their houses.' Cited by Wink, vol. 1, p. 74, from C. Defremery and B.R. Sanguinetti (eds and transl.), *Voyages d'Ibn Batoutah* (4 vols; Paris, 1853–8), vol. IV, p. 75, emphasis added. In contrast to the Hindus, marked by 'stereotype ritual isolation and the unusually rigid caste barriers and concepts of pollution' (vol. 1, p. 72), the Mappilas, 'assimilating converted Hindus from early on, became ethnically quite diverse. They spoke Malayalam and dressed like the [Nairs], from whom they often took over the matrilineal kinship organization as well' (vol. 1, p. 75).

[8] M.Q. Ferishta notes that 'all the materials of the history of the Mahommedans

Abdul Rahman Samiri—a name that appears on a tomb in Shahr or Zuphar on the Arabian coast. Legend has it that his plan of returning to his kingdom was interrupted by ill health. He thus implored his companions to return to Malabar on his behalf and gave them undertakings in Malayalam for various princes/chiefs. These companions were permitted by local princes/chiefs to build mosques at Kodungallur, Kollam, Chirackal, Srikandapuram (this is debated), Darmapattanam, Pantalayini-Koolam in Kurumbranad, and Chaliyam in Ernad. Other traditions maintain that the king returned and was called the Zamorin (*as-Samuri*, 'mariner').

William Logan,[9] pioneering the history of the 'Malayali race' (p. v), says: 'There is good reason to believe that [the] account of the introduction of Muhammadanism into Malabar is reliable' (p. 195). Logan, the Collector of Malabar and, later, the District Magistrate of Malabar, also takes note of the impact of trade rivalry among the Portuguese, Dutch, French and British powers in Malabar: 'if *foreign* peoples and *foreign* interventions had not intervened it might, with almost literal truth, have been said of the Malayalis that happy is the people who have no history' (p. vi). Logan elaborates on this:

> A people who throughout a thousand and more years have been looking longingly back to an event like the departure of Cheraman Perumal for Mecca, and whose rulers even now assume the sword or sceptre on the understanding that they merely hold it 'until the Uncle who has gone to Mecca returns', must be a people whose history presents few landmarks or stepping stones, so to speak,—*a people whose history was almost completed*

---

of the Malabar coast that I have been able to collect are derived from the Tuhafat-ul-Mujahideen': *History of the Rise of the Mahomedan Power*, trans. John Briggs (4 vols; London: Longman, 1829), vol. 4, p. 531. The reference here is to Shaik Ahmad Zein-ud-Din (d. 1581) whose *Tuhfat al-Mujahidin* (An Offering to Jihad Warriors) was directed against the Portuguese, cited from Roland E. Miller, *Mappila Muslims of Kerala: A Study in Islamic Trends* (Hyderabad: Orient Longman, 1976; revised edition 1992), p. 48. See also Francis Buchanan, *A Journey from Madras through the Countries of Mysore, Canara and Malabar* (London: T. Cadell and W. Davies, 1807).

[9] William Logan, *Malabar* (2 vols; New Delhi: Asian Educational Services, 1989). Known as the *Malabar Manual*, it was first published in 1887 and reprinted in 1906 and 1951. All my references are to the first volume.

> *on the day when that wonderful civil constitution was organized which endured unimpaired through so many centuries*. The Malayali race has produced no historians simply because there was little or no history in one sense to record. (p. vii, emphasis added)

Logan's orientalist formulation of 'a people whose history was almost completed' around the eighth century without any historians is in sharp contrast to the teleology that he has the fortune to inaugurate. He wishes nostalgically that a history existed, written by some other hand, and is almost apologetic that he has been entrusted with the responsibility and burden of writing such a history. He would rather wander along 'some of the *many fascinating vistas of knowledge which have been disclosed in the course of its preparation*' (p. v, emphasis added).

Logan is called upon to render an account of Malabar, to insert Malabar into History, and his narrative is marked by violent resistance of the militant Mappilas and Nairs during the Portuguese period (1498–1663), during the rivalry for trade supremacy between European powers (1663–1766), during the Mysorean conquest (1766–92), and during the British supremacy (1792 onwards). The 700-odd pages of the history he compiles from diverse sources in the first volume and the 400-odd pages of appendices in the second volume underline the fact that historical resources, in fact histories, did exist. What Logan laments, then, is the lack of a usable/readable past, where a specific consciousness amasses information and orders it into readily accessible data, a past that would lend itself to the processes of colonization/modernization. The intervention of the colonizer playing the role of modernizing agency is significantly linked to the insertion of 'traditional' societies into History. The ethnographic task structuring William Logan's *Malabar* is brought out by his division of the first volume into four sections, entitled 'The District', 'The People', 'History', and 'The Land'. Such ethnographic undertakings clearly point to the political imperatives behind institutionalizing History. Logan's project is driven by the colonial context, indeed derives its meaning and function from the administrative exigencies of a colonial set-up. He acknowledges as much in his analysis of the English Company's decision to dispatch several officials to Malabar in 1663 to look after its investments: 'It would be difficult to over-estimate the benefits of the experience thus obtained . . . for the factors had perforce to study native character and to adapt themselves to it; and in so doing this they were unconsciously fitting themselves to become the future rulers of the empire' (p. 339).

What emerges out of Logan's account is a picture of a heterogeneous region with different religions and races, in vibrant interaction with peoples of various countries on account of Malabar's importance to trade routes. It is against such a backdrop that Malabar becomes a battleground of European rivalry for trade monopoly, and here Logan makes a distinction between the policies and practices of other powers and those of the British: 'the Portuguese [did not] content themselves with suppressing Mohammadan trade; they tried to convert the Moslems to Christianity and it is related that, in 1562, they seized a large number of Moorish merchants at Goa and forcibly converted them. Of course these converts reverted to their religion at the first convenient opportunity' (p. 331). His ability to perceive the manner in which trade and religion were enmeshed in this episode does not, however, inform his account of British interventions in the region. For example, when the Company factors, as per instruction, tried to stop Mappilas from trading in pepper—

> In retaliation . . . Mappilas took to committing outrages. In March 1764 two of them entered a church on Darmapattanam Island, where a priest was saying mass, and murdered one man and severely wounded several. They were shot by the garrison 'and spitted'. A few days afterwards another Mappila came behind two *Europeans* while walking along one of the narrow lanes leading to Fort Mailan and cut one of them through the neck and half way through the body with one stroke of his sword. The other was mangled in such a way that his life was despaired of. After this the Mappila picked a quarrel with a [Nair] and was subsequently shot by the ['lower' caste Tiya] guard. His body was 'spitted' along with those of the others, and then thrown into the sea, to prevent their *caste* men from worshipping them as saints for killing Christians. (p. 403; emphases added)

Logan's objective description of events is structured around the race/religious/caste denominations of the actors, despite his acknowledgement that these 'outrages' were the result of the English Company's attempts to delimit the Mappila pepper trade.

It is in this context of the 'history' of Mappila 'outrages' that it would be useful to locate Logan's characterization of the inhabitants.

He observes that learned Arab settlers, who are described as 'Malayali Arabs' (p. 191), belong to an order different, indeed superior, from the other inhabitants of the region:

> Genuine Arabs, of whom many families of pure blood are settled on the coast, despise the learning . . . imparted [by the 600-years' old Muhammadan college in Ponnani] and are themselves highly educated in the Arab sense. Their knowledge of their own books of science and of history is very profound, and to a sympathetic listener who knows Malayalam they love to discourse on such subjects. They have a great regard for truth, and in their finer feelings they approach nearer to the standard of English gentlemen than any other class of persons in Malabar. (p. 108)

The few Christians in the area, Logan notes, are divided among themselves into the four main sects of Syrians, Romo-Syrians, Roman Catholics, and Protestants of all denominations (pp. 199–214). Since, according to him, they seem to have played no significant role in local affairs, he does not discuss them in any detail; all he does is provide an inventory of the number of churches and priests in each parish. Of Hindus—'[o]f the strange medley of cults and religions which goes by the name of Hinduism, it is very difficult to give any adequate idea . . .' (p. 179). Examining caste and occupations among them, he notes that 'Brahmans had a monopoly of learning for many centuries, and doubtless this was one of the ways in which they managed to secure such commanding influence in the country' (p. 108). Logan traces their eminence to the preservation of their Aryan heritage: 'There can hardly be a doubt that the high degree of civilization to which the country had advanced at a comparatively early period was due to Aryan immigrants from the North.'[10] A significant part of this enduring 'wonderful civic constitution' (p. vii) is caste, a concept, word and practice alien, Logan acknowledges, to the inhabitants, but one which was 'readily adopted

[10] See, footnote 7 above. The parallel between the Aryan 'immigrants' and the timely British intrusion need not be belaboured. Elsewhere, Logan refers to the Mysorean conquest of Malabar in 1766 as the 'Muhammadan invasion' and colonization as 'British occupation' (p. 109). He writes: 'the origin of the caste system is to be sought . . . in the ordinary everyday system of civil government imported into the country by Aryan *immigrants*, and readily adopted by the *alien* peoples among whom the immigrants came, not as conquerors, but as peaceful citizens . . .' (p. 112, emphases added).

by the alien peoples' (p. 112), which enabled 'easy and rapid development', and which 'accounts for the advanced state of the people in early times' (p. 113). Consequently, 'custom' became paramount and caste norms became rigid and ceased to be a cohesive force, so much so that they had now reached a point of stasis, and seemed to call for *another* such intervention. The evil ways of caste would, according to Logan, continue to multiply 'till British freedom evokes, as it is sure to do in good time, a national sentiment, and forms a nation out of the confusing congeries of tribal guilds at present composing it' (p. 113).

In contrast to the divided Hindu community, the Mappilas are, the 'indigenous Muhammadan[s]' (p. 108) who 'as a class pull well together', so much so that 'he is a daring Hindu indeed who dares now-a-days to trample on their class prejudices or feelings' (p. 198). They are 'frugal and thrifty as well as industrious', 'serviceable on ordinary occasions, and the most reliable in emergencies'. They become attached to those who treat them 'with kindness and consideration' but must be controlled with a firm hand since 'leniency is an unknown word, and is interpreted as weakness, of which advantage [will] be taken at the earliest possible moment' (p. 198). They are also 'illiterate', and 'as a class, being thus ignorant, are very easily misled by designing persons, and they are of course as bigoted as they are ignorant'. From the promise held out during his survey of the people, '[o]f their fanaticism and courage in meeting death enough will be said further on' (p. 198), it seems clear that the Mappilas are firmly fixed in the frame of a religion of which they are largely ignorant.

The 'mixed race' of Mappilas, in whom 'the Arab element . . . is now very small indeed', and their 'fanaticism' are even more worrisome as their 'race is rapidly progressing in numbers' (p. 197). Logan observes that the 'country would no doubt have soon been converted to Islam either by force or by conviction, but [for] the nations of Europe' (p. 294). Duarte Barbosa, who was in Malabar during 1500–16, had estimated the 'evil generation' of Mappilas to be 20 per cent and growing, and noted, in Stephen Dale's phrasing, that 'they were so influential in trade and navigation that Kerala would have had a "Moorish King" if the Portuguese had not discovered India.'[11] Logan explains

[11] Longworth M. Dames (ed. and transl.), *The Book of Duarte Barbosa* (2 vols; London: Hakluyt Society, 1918–21), vol. 2, p. 75; Dale, p. 24.

Islam's influence as an effect of the Calicut Zamorin raja's policy enjoining 'Hindu' fishermen families to bring up at least one of their sons as Muslims so that the raja would have skilled persons ready to risk their lives and man his navy. Logan also acknowledges that the spread of Islam in Malabar was significantly on account of voluntary conversions from 'lower' castes. A case in point was the Cherumar caste. Citing the Presidency Census (1881 Report, paragraph 151), Logan notes that this caste, characterized by their degraded position and humiliating disabilities, numbered 99,009 in Malabar at the census of 1871, but were returned at only 64,725 in 1881. This is a loss of 34.63 per cent instead of the gain of 5.71 per cent observed generally in the district. Logan wryly observes that the District Officer of that time attributes this to 'some disturbing cause' which 'is very well known to the District Officer to be conversion to Muhammadanism.' (p. 197) The District Officer notes that the 'honour of Islam' enabled 'lower' caste Hindus to move, at one spring, several places higher socially, a fact corroborated by what had actually been observed in the district. Figures show that nearly 50,000 Cherumars and other Hindus availed themselves of the opening (p. 197). Logan adds in a footnote that since the Cherumars numbered 187,758 in 1856, 'the decrease in 25 years has been over 65 percent' and that the District Officer's comments were 'written before *Mappilla* outrages exalted this community so greatly in the district' (p. 197). He also takes note of the fact that the 'Hindu is very strict about such matters now' (p. 198) than when the District Officer was writing; there had been more conflicts between Nairs and Mappilas, particularly 'in consequence of the complete subversion of the ancient friendly relations' (p. 478) by the introduction of new colonial policies. Leaving aside, for now, the question of whether this bigotry is narratively construed as an attribute of Islam, I merely point out that other categories through which the Mappila might be identified—peasant, working class and 'lower' caste—are overwritten through an emphasis on religion.

Over a period of seventy years, from 1851 to 1921, the Mappila population increased by 8 per cent in spite of a high (especially, infant) mortality rate. Though, according to the 1921 census, Mappilas comprised only 33 per cent of the population of Malabar, as against 66 per cent Hindus, the concentration of Mappilas in the three taluks

(Ernad, Walluvanad and Ponnani) of Malabar was as high as 60 per cent. These taluks were delineated in administrative records as the heart of the 'fanatical zone'. An overwhelming majority of Mappilas were poor and middling peasants (cultivating tenants, landless labourers, petty traders, and fishermen),[12] while the landlords were mostly Namboodiri Brahmins or Nairs. British land reforms, aimed at righting the 'wrongs' done by Tipu Sultan,[13] made it all the more easy for the better-equipped Hindu landlords to resort to evictions, and the Mappila peasantry was soon reduced to penury.[14]

A significant change in the pattern of Mappila 'uprisings' occurs at around the turn of the century. Logan was appointed Special Commissioner on 5 February 1881 because of the increasing number of anonymous petitions received by the British. Logan himself received about 2,200 petitions from 4,021 individuals, of whom 2,734 (over 67 per cent) were from Mappilas complaining against unjust evictions. The evictions were a consequence of a new system of fixing a standard rent as against the customary practice of sharing each year's produce

[12] K.N. Panikkar, *Against Lord and State: Religion and Peasant Uprisings in Malabar, 1836–1921* (New Delhi: Oxford University Press, 1989), pp. 50–3. I am not elaborating on the stratification among Mappila peasantry since, in contrast to the historians' focus on presenting as 'objective' a picture as possible by digging for more 'facts' to write a more 'true' and 'accurate' account, I am more interested in the blurring that occurs in narratives and the framing/phrasing of the Mappila insurgencies.

[13] The period of Mysorean invasion 1766–92 is one of rivalry and alliances between European and native powers. Tipu Sultan ascended the throne of Mysore in 1782 on the death of his father, Hyder Ali. The latter had invaded Malabar, with varying degrees of success, many times over ten years, the first time in 1766. He also had designs on Travancore, the princely state, but was defeated by the British in 1780. However, in 1784, as per a British treaty, Malabar was returned to Tipu Sultan, only to be taken back in 1792.

[14] Wood traces the problem to the return of Hindu landlords from their exodus to Travancore during Tipu's reign: 'In 1792, in the wake of victorious British arms, the Hindu [janmis] returned to Malabar from exile eager to reclaim their rights in their ancient landed estates' (p. 100). The British, who had drawn on Hindu support to defeat Tipu favoured the landlords and decreed that all usurpations after 11 September 1787 were illegal. Further, legal and police persecution of Mappilas continued, thereby lending conviction to the theory of Hindu–British collusion (p. 106).

as per a fixed ratio. In effect, the new system replaced the traditional relationship between landlord and tenant with that of ownership—instituting thereby the landlords' 'right' to evict tenants.[15] Logan notes that the 'British authorities mistook [the landlord's] real position and invested him erroneously with the Roman *dominium* of the *soil*' (p. 582).[16] It is possible to read, as Conrad Wood does, the pattern of Mappila uprisings at the turn of the century as a gradual falling off, consequential to Logan's reforms. However, it would perhaps be more productive to read the shift in the nature of later uprisings—from the heavy casualty in 1896, the surrender of all insurgents in 1898, the targeting (after 1855) of a British magistrate in 1915, and the equal ratio of insurgents and targets in 1919[17]—as not so much due to the success of Logan's reforms as the result of the emergence of a 'modern'

[15] See D.N. Dhanagare, 'The Moplah Rebellions', in *Peasant Movements in India, 1920–1950* (New Delhi: Oxford University Press, 1983, 1994), p. 67. For a discussion of the background of the colonial assessment of native ownership of land, see, Ranajit Guha, *A Rule of Property for Bengal: An Essay on the Idea of Permanent Settlement* (New Delhi: Orient Longman, 1982).

[16] The failure of the administration to redress Mappila grievances can be deduced from the following: 'Whereas the Mappilas of the village of Cundooty have represented to us that they have heretofore been greatly oppressed by the Nairs in so much that they were obliged to take up arms in their own defence. We hereby warn all persons whatever from molesting them in any shape in future, and the said Mappilas are hereby required to apply themselves to their former occupations and if they meet any oppressions from the Nairs they must come to Calicut and represent the same to us, when speedy redress shall be given them, Given under our hands and the seal of the Honourable Company in Calicut, this 26th day of June 1792, Sd/- W.G. Farmer and Alexander Dow', in William Logan, *A Collection of Treaties, Engagements and Other Papers of Importance Relating to British Affairs in Malabar* (1951; rpntd New Delhi and Madras: Asian Educational Services, 1989), p. 152.

[17] The 'uprising' on 25 February 1896 in which 99 Mappila insurgents were involved (94 were killed, 5 were captured alive) had the highest toll ever. The next uprising—barring the one on 1 April 1898 in which all the 12 participants who killed a *janmi* surrendered because they were urged by other Mappilas to give in—was on 28 February 1915 (Dale puts it on 2 November 1915) and targeted the District Magistrate, C.A. Innes, who escaped narrowly. However, in the uprising of 6 February 1919, Mappila martyrs were 7, as were the number of 'upper' caste Hindu victims. It is also significant that no putative uprisings are recorded between 1894 and 1915.

consciousness; a consciousness that takes stock of the futility of waging war against a better-armed adversary and is attuned to the wider significance of the anti-imperialist struggle in the context of a nascent nationalist aspiration. Read in this manner, the seventeen-year hiatus that Wood attributes to Logan's reform initiatives could equally be attributed to the decimation or perhaps reconstitution of existing Mappila leadership. The resurgence of Mappila resistance should also be viewed in the light of the colonial government's sluggishness in implementing Logan's suggestions for reform. Logan's 'primitive socialist'[18] ideas were not implemented because the colonial authorities feared the landed class turning against them (Wood, pp. 26, 34–9). The obverse of such British inertia would be that, overall, the landed classes were content with colonization, were in fact its collaborators and supporters, and, hence, could not have been convinced of any anti-imperialist or nationalist manoeuvres, peaceful or otherwise.

According to Logan, from 1834 onwards 'the administration [in Malabar] entered upon a period of disturbance, which unhappily continues down to the present time. The origin and causes of this are of so much importance' that Logan proposes to treat the subject 'with a view not only to exhibit the difficulties with which the District Officers had to deal, but to elucidate the causes from which such difficulties have sprung' (p. 554). After about forty pages of summarizing various 'outbreaks', Logan marks his disagreement with earlier repressive measures adopted by the administration which were also 'a departure from the policy of wise and just neutrality in all matters of religion' (p. 572). Logan advocates measures by which fanaticism can be administered out of existence: 'Fanaticism . . . flourishes only upon sterile soil. When the people are poor and discontented, it flourishes apace like other crimes of violence' (p. 594). With increased security by means of settled homelands and an assured income, he predicts, 'fanaticism would die a natural death'. Logan underlines the importance of measures to ameliorate the economic condition of peasants by stating that he disagrees with others who advocate education as the

[18] An offhand remark of J.C. Griffiths on 16 April 1976. As M. Gangadhara Menon pointed out to Dale, Logan was more a capitalist influenced by utilitarianism than a socialist; see Dale, p. 170 and footnote 48, p. 255. See also M. Gangadhara Menon, *The Malabar Rebellion* (Allahabad: Vohra Publishers, 1989).

primary strategy. He astutely observes that 'starving people are not easily taught, and, if taught, it would only lead to their adopting more effectual measures to obtain for themselves that security and comfort in their homesteads which it would be much wiser to grant at once' (p. 594). What emerges from Logan's formulation of fanaticism is an understanding of the economic hardships of Mappilas that remain a stumbling block in the progress of colonization and the accumulation of capital.

With characteristic objectivity, Logan cites himself:

> Mr. Logan finally formed the opinion that Mappila outrages were designed 'to counteract the overwhelming influence, when backed by the British courts, of the *janmis* in the exercise of the novel powers of ouster and of rent raising conferred upon them. A *janmi* who, through courts, evicted, whether fraudulently or otherwise, a substantial tenant, was deemed to have merited death, and it was considered a religious virtue, not a fault, to have killed such a man, and to have afterwards died in arms fighting against an infidel Government which sanctioned such injustice'. (p. 584)

Logan's imperatives are clearly laid out. His concern is with laying the foundations for 'civilizing' procedures. It is almost as if the 'fanaticism' exemplified by the 'outbreaks' has become generic. The repetition of 'outbreaks' and the religious sanction accorded to them calls, in Derrida's view, for a nomenclature with which 'to order the manifold'. What constitutes a genre is the repetition and reiteration of a distinctive trait, and the figure of the 'fanatic', as if in accord, emerges in Logan's teleological ordering of history. Fanaticism is the only 'identifiable recurrence of a common trait'[19] in outbreaks as diverse as those caused by economic hardships, mere criminality, and madness.[20] It is as if the fanatic, born at the moment of History, exceeds its norm and

[19] Jacques Derrida, 'The Law of Genre', *Critical Inquiry* 7.1 (Autumn 1980), pp. 57, 61, 63. Subsequent references on this issue below are to the same source.

[20] The slippage between 'outbreaks' with and without any justification is brought out when Logan, in his own voice, notes: 'While Pulikkal Raman was cleaning his teeth . . . on 31st October 1883, Asaritodi Moidin Kutti . . . attacked him from behind with a sword. . . . Raman fled pursued by Moidin Kutti, who held the sword in one hand and a book in the other' (p. 584). Moidin Kutti used 'unintelligible expressions as he ran. After dancing about on a rock for sometime, brandishing his sword and striking the back of his neck with it . . . on the

becomes its remainder. Fanaticism, in Logan's history of Malabar, is also an instance of the excess of genre in relation to itself in that, at the moment of ordering (to quote Derrida again) 'lodged within the heart of the law itself [is] a law of impurity or a principle of contamination'. It is at such moments that the law of the genre (and the genre of law) becomes problematic in Logan's text, and its sources are those moments when the categories of 'race' and 'caste' become unviable.

One of the crucial nodes in Logan's text is his confusion whether the Mappilas are a race or a caste. At times referred to as a race and at other times as a caste, this 'mixed race' seems to combine the worst of Islam and India. While Logan understands and respects Arab settlers and Hindu inhabitants, the mix of races and castes as embodied by Mappilas presents a methodological problem which arises because community formations do regroup, as evident in the spate of conversions at the time. The Mappila, as a sub-genre, seems to exceed the law of genre itself. Faced with the incessant, insistent, and inexplicable acts of rebellion that threaten his norms and terms of reference, Logan nonchalantly ignores all that opens, inside out, his ideas of civilization and progress. His proposals to the colonial authorities underline the need to provide material conditions in order to facilitate the processes of humanizing Mappilas, so that they can be assigned their appropriate role in the procedure of Progress. As against earlier repressive measures, Logan recognizes that Mappilas have to be reconstituted as colonial subjects so that they can be ruled by History.

---

intervention of [other Mappilas, he] threw the sword and book down and surrendered. He was afterwards tried and acquitted on the grounds of insanity' (p. 585). Another instance: 'A Hindu . . . [K. Raman] who had several years previously embraced and subsequently renounced Islam . . . was waylaid and attacked in a most savage manner by two Mappillas. . . . [He managed to escape and later] denounced . . . the men [responsible]. These men had intended to run the usual fanatical course, but their courage failed them at the last moment and they were in due course arrested, brought to trial [and transported for life]. Three other persons were also deported in connection with this case. . . . The Acting District Magistrate . . . proposed to fine [the village to the tune] of Rs. 15,000, [later reduced to Rs. 5,000 because of the poverty of Mappilas] of which he proposed to assign a sum of Rs. 1,000 to K. Raman as compensation for his wounds' (p. 585). The award of money to the apostate 'rankled in the minds of the Mappilas generally [since] they held the perverted view that an apostate should suffer death' (p. 586).

The 'fanatic' was enforced and administered into existence. A construct first deployed by the colonial administrator for the political control of a people, this label puts together a particular kind of 'individual', an anthropological object, and in doing so conceals the machinery of control exerted on the Mappila peasant body. The violence involved is erased; colonialism and the processes of counterinsurgency come to be represented as the impartial rule of the enlightened over a primitive people. The designation 'fanatic' is of immense use to the colonialist since it institutes 'disciplinary control and the creation of docile bodies [both] unquestionably connected to the rise of capitalism'.[21] This kind of tag is designed to control the insurgent Mappila body and at the same time excuse the resort to counterviolence. What is required is an endeavour to extricate the Mappila peasant 'from the state and from the type of individuation which is linked to the state'.[22] After all, who is a fanatic? A fanatic is among other things 'a dangerous individual', that is, inversely, an individual dangerous to the nation-state. In fact, the metaphors commonly employed—'outbreak', 'outrage', 'fanatical eruptions', 'madness' (the latter two from Gandhi[23])—conjure up the picture of an uncontrollable violence and extreme irrationality. In so far as these metaphors are employed in order to master the people, they also testify to a lack of control on the part of the state over the peasant body. This is brought out by the fact that the Mappila community not only celebrated the insurgents through songs, but can also be said to have sanctioned such 'madness'. Such 'madness' is dangerous in that it is directed against the social body symbolized by the colony and later the nation-state.

Working against the idea of the natural stupidity of a peasant, I would interpret 'martyrdom' as a religio-political strategy. It was, after all, not an easy task to risk an insurrection against a well-armed adversary. Having everything to lose[24] yet confronted with the sheer

[21] Hubert L. Dreyfus and Paul Rabinow, *Michel Foucault: Beyond Structuralism and Hermeneutics* (Sussex: Harvester, 1982), p. 134.

[22] Michel Foucault, 'The Subject and Power', Afterword in Dreyfus and Rabinow, p. 216.

[23] M.K. Gandhi, *The Collected Works of Mahatma Gandhi* (New Delhi: Publication Division, Ministry of Information and Broadcasting, Govt. of India, 1976), vol. 21, p. 321; hereafter *CW*.

[24] The move from everything-to-lose to nothing-to-lose is the first step in insurgency. Frantz Fanon writes: 'In the colonial countries peasants alone are

impossibility of continuing as before, peasant-insurgents had to be aware of the implications of their deed. Once the peasants' decision to become 'martyrs' is reconfigured as a political choice, it is possible to see how such a decision is strategic, taken after careful consideration of the available options. In 1507, when the Portuguese withdrew into their fortress and teased the might of the Zamorin and his Muslim troops, Logan says a '[n]umbers of Moors took oath to die as [shahids]' (Logan, p. 314). 'Fanaticism' is not invoked here; trade interests visibly structure Muslim action, and Logan and his sources commend the courage and determination of the Arabs. Though Logan, in contrast to less sensitive analyses, acknowledges that the Mappilas were driven to rebellion due to economic and cultural oppression, it is fanaticism which eventually provides him with the frame with which to understand the peasant-subaltern. The inadequacy of 'fanaticism' as an explanatory category is amplified by the fact that members of 'lower'-caste communities either voluntarily espoused Islam or resorted to banditry.[25] That caste (and gender) was always just beneath the surface of the various revolts is particularly evident in the documentation of the 19 October 1843 uprising. H.V. Conolly, the Magistrate, records that some Mappilas had complained against the village headman dishonouring Islam 'by forcing a hindoo woman of one of the lower castes [Tiya] to apostatize from the mussulman faith to which she had lately converted, probably, tho' I am not certain of the fact, by the zeal of the *Hal Yerikum* party'.[26] This merits a footnote:

---

revolutionary, for they have nothing to lose and everything to gain. The starving peasant, outside the class system, is the first among the exploited to discover that only violence pays. For him there is no compromise, no possible coming to terms; colonization and decolonization are simply a question of relative strength,' *The Wretched of the Earth* (Harmondsworth: Penguin, 1971), p. 47.

[25] During the 1790s, that is before the period of 'outbreaks', when the breach between Nairs and Mappilas was very wide, 'on the outskirts of this lawless country there dwelt a tribe of what were in those days called "jungle" Mappillas, who were banded together under chiefs and who subsisted on the depredations committed on their neighbours': Logan, p. 485. Logan's *history* is littered with 'fanaticism', which occurs as many as six times on a given page (p. 588).

[26] *PPRM*, p. 114. In January 1844 Conolly adds: 'About 5 months ago I received intimation from Shernaad tahsildar, that a sect of enthusiasts had sprung up among the lower orders of moplahs in his talook who professed an intention of

> The woman, a bold and disrespectable looking person, had taken advantage of her new position to be insolent to her master, as the [Tiya] of the day before she only approached within 12 paces of him and called him by the peaceful title of Lord or Master as the mussulmans. On the next day she came close to him and called him by his proper and familiar name, a peculiar insult in this country, from an inferior to a superior. The *adigharee* was naturally very angry, and ordered her with abusive language to take off the dress which had led to her change of behaviour. She was cowed and did so but on going abroad reported what had taken place. (p. 114)

This conflict[27] is temporarily resolved, impartially, by replacing the headman, though when a Mappila 'refused to pay the tax demanded of him and was insolent in his demeanour, *refusing to take off his slippers*' (p. 115, emphasis added), it 'flares up' again.

II

Broadly, it is possible to discern two distinct perspectives in the writings on the Mappila insurgencies: the colonial and the nationalist/marxist. T.L. Strange, the Special Commissioner appointed by the Madras government on 17 February 1852, exemplifies a colonialist mode of analysis and explanation that found renewal in wave after

---

living in a manner more suited (as they declared) to the spirituality of their religion. . . . They met together in small bodies for the purpose of devotion many times a day, and pressed on all around them the desirableness of joining them in this practice and of becoming parties to what was called the *Hal Yerikum*. . . . I sent for an Arab priest . . . [who] assured me that it was the work of a few insignificant men . . . [and] priests of note in Shernaad . . . would do their best to discourage it and make it die away quietly' (*PPRM*, pp. 112–13). Many such sects with short lives seem to have sprouted in various places.

[27] Not much evidence is available about the extent and nature of participation by women in the 'uprisings', though R.H. Hitchcock's report (first published in 1925 as *A History of the Malabar Rebellion, 1921*) mentions (citing Fawcett) the active participation of women in the 'uprising' of 25 February 1896. Hitchcock also notes that it was women who incited the men in Pukkotur and he takes note of the participation by women during the 1921 rebellion, especially of the 'fanatical cruelty' of one Chetali Biyumma; see, section B, 'Part Taken by Women and Children in the Rebellion', *Peasant Revolt in Malabar: A History of the Malabar Rebellion, 1921, by R.H. Hitchcock*, Introduction by Robert L. Hardgrave, Jr. (New Delhi: Usha Publications, 1983), pp. 150–2; hereafter cited as Hitchcock.

wave of administrative and political commentary. His conclusion was that ' "the Mappila outrages have been one and all marked by the most decided fanaticism" fostered by a "selfish, ignorant and vicious priesthood" in the minds of the illiterate Mappilas who were "grasping, treacherous and vindictive" in character' (cited from Panikkar, *Against Lord*, p. 95). The Mappilas are depicted by the British not only as ignorant and bigoted, but as 'rabid animals . . . possessing no spark of reason' (*PPRM*, p. 110). The most liberal colonial voices under this category, like that of Logan, acknowledge economic hardship as a contributory factor, though in the final analysis 'fanatic' causation remains. It is obviously possible to examine the colonial logic of these 'outrages' from the perspective of the insurgents. There is not much written material left behind by the rebels; 'evidence' of Mappila voices are mostly the typescripts of police interrogations of captured rebels. I will therefore illustrate my counter-arguments by examining a pamphlet left behind by Mappila insurgents. This pamphlet relates to the uprising of 13–14 November 1841 at Koduvayur in Ernad taluk, and we also have the taluk administrative records[28] of this uprising. This year indicates a definite increase in the number of insurgents as well as insurgencies,[29] and it is through reports of this event that we can perceive a significant shift in the colonial perception.

The Magistrate, H.V. Conolly, in his report dated 22 November 1841, traces the origins of the event that has disrupted his government. He characterizes the 14 November 1841 outbreak as one in a larger series: 'a similar outbreak, attended with similar results' had occurred earlier in a different place in which 'nine mopla criminals met their death' (p. 94). In the present instance, an upper-caste landlord had complained that Mappila peasants had encroached upon his land and built a mosque. The tahsildar sent a peon to summon the peasants

[28] *PPRM*, pp. 94–105; Logan, p. 556. All citations are from the former, unless mentioned otherwise, and the pagination is incorporated within parenthesis.

[29] In the three separate uprisings in April, November and December of 1841, the rebel/victim ratio was 9:3, 11:2 and 8:2. The first recorded uprising on 26 November 1836 and the next one on 15 April 1837 had a ratio of 1:1. While the next on 5 April 1839 had a ratio of 2:1, the one in the same place on the very next day had a ratio of 1:1. The only other uprising before 1841 was on 19 April 1840 with a 1:1 ratio; Wood, p. 11; Logan, pp. 554–5.

concerned. The peasants killed the peon and the landlord who had accompanied the peon. Subsequently the peasants, along with some associates, took refuge in a small mosque. Conolly's account stops here; the rest of the story unfolds in an enclosure, a report written by the official I.L. Platel who had rushed to the spot (pp. 100–4).

Platel, apart from emphasizing the fact that they had to travel from 10 p.m. to 3 a.m. and had little rest since they reached the mosque where the insurgents had taken refuge at about 6 a.m. tells us that the insurgents were seen walking around a mosque. 'People' were sent to induce the insurgents to surrender, though Platel does not specify who these people were. The 'infatuated' Mappilas are then reported to have 'shouted back taunting answers, such as "you are not enough to capture us—not one of you shall return alive, we have been waiting for you these three days, give us [50 minutes'] time so that we may take our [gruel], and then we will come down and meet you, but we will not lay down our arms", or words to this effect'. The last message calling for surrender meets with the following response: 'If you are men, come up here, we are ready for you. We will not surrender ourselves, the sirkar [government] will hang us. We wish to kill and die that we may become [shahid*s*]' (p. 100). Platel remarks that the peasant rebels must have been bent on forfeiting their lives since they had sufficient time to escape capture, 'for a time', before the troops arrived. About 200 to 300 villagers are reported to have remained near the mosque throughout the time. The tahsildar is helpless because the villagers are no longer on his side, and the officials decide to use the peons to flush out the insurgents.

Platel writes: 'Great was indeed the difficulty experienced in prevailing upon the peons and villagers to do this, at length after much persuasion and promise and instant support on the part of the military, they resolved to go'. Seeing the advancing party the Mappila peasant insurgents prayed loudly, and then 'rushed out like *mad men* with their knives, shields and spears' (p. 101; emphasis added). Two or three of the insurgents were immediately shot down, and Platel adds as an afterthought in a footnote, almost as if to underscore the 'irrationality' of the rebels, that even now the rest of them could have escaped through the jungle lying to the south-west of the mosque. But they did not. Within minutes, all eleven insurgents were killed. On the official side only two or three were wounded. Platel recounts the 'fanatical' preparations to ensure that the relatives of the deceased did not take the bodies away. Though the authorities 'would have liked to have made an example of the rebels by burying their bodies with a dog or some other unclean animal and by escheating their property' (Panikkar, *Against Lord*, p. 70), they were unceremoniously buried.[30]

An interesting detail emerges when the narrative lets slip that '[a]mong the villagers assembled there was not a single mopla nor could the presence of the [chiefs] of that caste [*sic*] be procured' (p. 103). This surely suggests that the assembled non-Mappila villagers, irrespective of religious and caste affiliations, supported the insurgents. Platel also notes that the only musket that the insurgents had between them was recovered from the road leading from the mosque, and that a boy was seen carrying away the musket while the insurgents were rushing out so as to prevent 'the discovery of its owner'. Such forethought demonstrates that Platel's narrative clearly runs counter to his characterization of the peasants as 'mad' and 'infatuated'. Rather, the whole episode can be read as a carefully planned operation on the part of the Mappilas. Conolly's report also stresses that the tahsildar was right in requesting reinforcements since the 'criminals' would 'meet with sympathy and assistance from the surrounding mopla populations' (p. 94). The desperation of the Mappilas, concludes the Magistrate, 'is explainable only by the unhappy feeling prevalent among the ignorant and bigoted mussulman population of Malabar, that revenge is no crime, and that they are secure in paradise if they die fighting against an infidel power, whatever be the reason that has caused the use of their arms' (p. 95). What punctuates this representation by both the officials is their desperate need to explain to the higher authority, in this case the Chief Secretary to Government, Fort St George, why they were not able to comply with the instructions to capture the peasants alive. On the peasants' side, it does not require much imagination to figure out why they dreaded being taken prisoners.

[30] Logan adds: 'On the 17th of the same month a large band of Mappillas, estimated at 2,000, set at defiance a police party on guard over the spot where the . . . criminals had been buried, and forcibly carried off their bodies and interred them with honours at a mosque. Twelve of these were convicted and punished' (p. 556).

The *warola* or pamphlet was written on 14 November 1841 by Pathyl Valia Kunholan, one of the 'martyrs', and was found at the gate of the mosque where the eleven insurgents met their death. This short pamphlet frames the event in terms quite different from the colonial account. It narrates how the disputed land had been leased by one Mappila, enumerates the improvements made by him on the land, and stresses that the rights over this land were purchased from the landlord.[31] Thereafter a mosque, and later a mud wall around it, were constructed. The landlord, this narrative continues, 'went and made a false representation' (p. 99) to the court; and the tahsildar, 'without any consideration of the state of things', dispatched a peon to summon the accused. Accompanied by four or five people, the peon 'with directions to seize and drag the nine of us' reached the mosque 'before sunset of the 28th day of our fast' and 'abused and called us out'. When the peasants 'told him that we would go with him after we shall have broken our fast' (p. 99), the peon and the others abused and 'laid hold of the right hand' of one of them, the 'owner of . . . [another] mosque', dragged him to a nearby well and began to tie him up. Then the 'eight of us, with the weapon . . . kept ready' for the landlord when he returned, had done 'what has been done' (p. 99). The *warola* concludes by noting that they had been trying 'to get hold of the useless' tahsildar and another person who was 'the instigator of the complaint' (p. 100).

Similar 'records' left by Mappila peasants, few as they are, are not often part of the archive. Athan Gurukkal—whose ancestors reportedly rebelled against Tipu Sultan in 1784–5 and the British in 1800–2 (Panikkar, *Against Lord*, pp. 71–2) and who was the leader of the 'uprising' on 25 August 1849 in which 64 Mappilas were killed and one captured, left behind in the temple (where the rebels made their last stand) a very illuminating record addressed to the collector. Pointing out the colonial government's ignorance of the real state of affairs,

[31] This was also a period of competition among agrarian farmers and peasants for procuring land on lease for cultivation; a result was that landlords kept hiking up the rent every year and evicting those who could not pay the revised rent. The colonial government made a policy decision that in cases of eviction the landlord must pay for any improvements on the land. However, this only resulted in more and more litigation because, with the help of lawyers, landlords argued that they had to pay only the actual cost of the improvements and not its considerably higher market value.

Gurukkal writes that the collusion between the landlords and the Hindu public servants has resulted in their

> preferring false and vexatious complaints in the *adalat* and police, against several wealthy Mussalman who held land on mortgage . . . which were the means they had of supporting themselves and family, which complaint, the *sirkar* without knowing the real merits of the case, decreed against them, upon the arguments [false pleas] brought forward in support of them, and afterwards thus passed, were enforced . . . the consequence of all these has been, that many Mussalman have been reduced to a state of beggary, so much so, that they find themselves unable to represent, and prove to the *sirkar*, the real state of matters, with the view of putting a stop to such practices. Hence, the cause of the events which took place before this, in this part of the country, when some of the landed proprietors and their adherents were cut down and put to death, the perpetrators of which, after setting the public authority at defiance, were punished by Government.[32]

K.N. Panikkar delineates the reasons behind Gurukkal's action in the following manner: he was 'neither influenced by the desire for martyrdom nor by the lure of the pleasures of paradise . . . [since Gurukkal had] emphatically asserted that "nobody will throw away their life, unless forced to it by unendurable grievance and dishonour" ' (Panikkar, *Against Lord*, pp. 72–3). However, such a distinction only reinforces the 'fanaticism' of other Mappilas; and moreover it is doubtful, in this context, if we can refer to personal insult and dishonour, the supposed motives behind Gurukkal's desperate attempt, as 'secular' concerns, since the personal and the public worlds are deeply intermeshed.

Similar pamphlets and petitions, however, did not deter the colonial authorities, who insisted on framing the Mappila uprisings as fanatical, so much so that by 25 September 1852 T.L. Strange, after analysing thirty-one separate instances, concludes: 'It is apparent thus that in no instance can any outbreak or threat of outbreak that has arisen be attributed to the oppression of tenants by landlords.'[33]

[32] Cited by Panikkar (*Against Lord*, p. 73) from *Correspondence on Moplah Outrages in Malabar* (2 vols; Madras: 1863), vol. 1, p. 52.

[33] Report of T.L. Strange, Special Commissioner, to T. Pycroft, Secretary to Government, Judicial Department, Fort St. George, *Correspondence on Moplah Outrages*, vol. 1, pp. 399–477; *PPRM*, p. 175.

Among the numerous such representations found in colonial administrative records, one very chilling anonymous document is the 'Petition Purporting to be Addressed by Certain Mussulmans, [Nairs], [Tiyas] and Men of Other Castes'.[34] Submitted on 14 October 1880, this petition points to the reason why it was mostly Mappilas who resorted to violence:[35] 'That the mussulmans are the people committing riots; all the hindu officials and landlords impress this fact upon the European officers of the district; that there are no mussulmans holding high offices or acquainted with English; that this accounts for the mussulmans being declared the principal offenders' (p. 186). The petition delineates the complicity of the Travancore native state in securing land for 'upper' caste Hindus returning and also newly migrating to Malabar, and goes on to add:

> That the people having, therefore, conspired to create a disturbance are advised by some wise men to wait until a representation of the popular grievances has been made to government and orders received thereupon.
>
> That whatever enactments may be passed, before all such suits have been decided and all such decrees executed, disturbances and bloodshed of a kind unknown in Malabar will take place; and that this should not be construed into a vain threat held out to deceive. By the Almighty God who has created all, petitioners swear that this will be a fact. (p. 187)

Though this petition could possibly be the work of a single individual in the name of a collective, a number of anonymous petitions were continually made alongside other overt and physical means of resistance, even if this led to death.[36] The anxiety caused by these 'outbreaks'

[34] Though unsigned, it was purportedly written by E. Thompson, the Malayalam translator to the government. See Judicial Department, G.O. no. 281, dated 5 February 1881; *PPRM*, pp. 185–8.

[35] Stating that 'demolition of mosques, religious persecution, cruel oppression and ejectment of mussulmans by landlords are the causes that have led to moplah outbreaks', the petition even tries to placate the authorities by blaming earlier Mappila rebels: 'That the assassination of Collector Conolly was committed by some moplahs of bad character whose continued imprisonment made them despair of being liberated from jail' (*PPRM*, p. 187).

[36] I reproduce another anonymous petition, Judicial Department, G.O. no. 884, dated 19 May 1896 (*PPRM*, pp. 245–7), to strengthen the possibility of reading these uprisings in terms of counter-narratives: 'To, The Honourable

is exemplified by the studied parallel drawn by the colonial authorities between Malabar and Ireland, whereby they try to 'understand' the Mappila 'outbreaks' as caused by 'a real grievance' (p. 189).

The manner in which the magistrate's report on the 14 November 1841 uprising commences frames the event as 'a similar outbreak, attended with similar results', where 'nine mopla criminals met their death' by killing two landlords (p. 94). Though he frames the event of 14 November as similar to the earlier 'uprising' of 5 April, he himself acknowledges in the report made at that time that the two Brahmins who were murdered had acted with 'great duplicity' towards a Mappila who, with eight others, attempted to redress the 'great injustice' done to him (pp. 92–3). The earlier outbreak is recharacterized—reinterpreted as 'fanatical' despite prior recognition of the non-religious

---

Governor-in-Council, Madras. We, numbering not less than 363 rioters belonging to an area extending from Calicut eastwards up to Palghat, and from Cochin northwards up to Wynad, who have held ourselves in readiness, with the help of god, for an outbreak in the month of ramzan to government as follows: After the close of the enquiries, which were made by the commissioner Mr. Logan, under the pretense of securing redress of the grievances of the tenants oppressed by the *janmis*, the tenants have been all the more ground down by the *janmis* and reduced to indigent poverty, destitute of any means of obtaining a livelihood. . . . Owing to the present levy of punitive fines it has been rendered absolutely impossible for us to live in the country with our children weeping on account of intolerable hunger. In the recent outbreak at Pandikad, mothers and sisters, after being stripped of their clothes, were severely tortured by painful pressure being applied to their breasts, and by introducing into their eyes, nostrils and anal and urinary orifices, thorny sticks . . . smeared over with ground chilly, sulphate of copper and similar terrible materials. By inflicting such terrorising cruelties in the manner described, head constables Kumaran Nair, Krishnan Nair, and others extorted and amassed large fortunes and reduced us and our sorrow-stricken family and children to poverty. As these miseries were too hard for us to bear any longer, we have been forced to make preparations and to hold ourselves in readiness for an outbreak. So long as the *janmis* continue to oust their tenants and so long as the government refuse to institute any enquiries whatever into the grievances of these mussalmans such as we are, we, the petitioners, are prepared to fight until the whole lot of us perish in the struggle'. After suggesting eight immediate measures that the government can carry out, the petition continues: 'Instead of protecting the subjects by these means, if the sovereign should abandon true justice . . . we the rioters do hereby particularly announce that we are determined to die in the

causes of it. The earlier 'uprising', devoid of details, now has a new function; it determines the new event, and in the process is itself rewritten as fanatical. And the next uprising on 27 December 1841 is unhesitatingly represented as '*another* outbreak among the moplahs, of a *more outrageous and extraordinary character*' (p. 106; emphases added). So much so, that in this new event, unlike the earlier two events that 'had some intelligible cause . . . the sole wish of the insurgents seems to have been to kill some one and then die themselves. Their conduct indeed was more like that of rabid animals' (p. 110).

In the earlier report we see the magistrate hesitating between 'criminality' and 'fanaticism': the Mappilas of the region have 'dangerous habits' and they have been 'gang robbers' and 'general disturbers of the district'. The switch from 'crime' to the 'criminal' is part of the shift from the 'act' to the 'individual' which, Foucault has shown, occurred in the West during this period.[37] If crime and insanity can coincide, that is, if insanity manifests itself in a crime, is the criminal legally responsible and hence punishable for the crime? In attempting to resolve this problem, judicial and medical (psychiatric) institutions shifted the focus from the event to the individual. Confronted with people whose lives could not be contained within the accepted definitions of individuation, the colonial administration reinvented native communities (the Thuggees are an obvious example) in whom 'fanaticism' aided and abetted an inherent 'criminality' allied to insanity. Consequently, it also changed its stance from the 'sympathetic and conciliatory' attitude of attributing the '"Mappila turbulence" to the "political

---

struggle, rather than give government any respite. Should government . . . still proceed on to levy punitive fines, we are determined to become [shahids] of our cause; and have also arranged with certain hindu friends of ours to chop off the heads of such of those and others as so found with the accounts to levy the said punitive fines. Believing that these particulars will receive special attention we, the rioters, proceed to assume the role of [shahids]. In vain, have many representations been, on several occasions, made to subordinate officials; but on the present occasion we believe that similar negligence and indifference will not be shown. In conclusion, remember well that a due reply to this will be demanded of you at the *srathpalam*'.

[37] Michel Foucault, 'The Dangerous Individual', in Lawrence D. Kritzman (ed.), *Michel Foucault: Politics, Philosophy, Culture: Interviews and Other Writings, 1977–1984* (New York and London: Routledge, 1988), pp. 125–51.

misfortunes of the country" ', that is, the oppression by the Hindu landlords, to the 'inherent aggressive character and lack of civilization among the Mappilas' (cited in Panikkar, *Against Lord*, pp. 56–7). Mappila 'acts' of rebellion were then determined as more than criminal since the individuals volunteered their lives in accordance with the needs of a 'fanatical' community. As a measure to cure this 'mad' community, the Moplah Outrages Acts (1854) were enforced to curb fanaticism among its members and police them into individuality. In the report about the earlier uprising the magistrate had complacently written: 'I can see no reasonable fear of a similar excess occurring, especially, as this one has been so summarily repressed' (p. 92). Though one 'uprising' by the native peasant population has been 'summarily repressed', the Mappilas were not completely crushed; in fact, they came back with greater dedication and better organization. Unable to perform its 'civilizing mission', its very foundation under threat, the British administration invented a new category, the fanatic: the cause of the local resistances to the imperial government would henceforth be organized around this new appellation. Answers to problematic questions (such as: How could the victimized Mappila get associates with such ease? Why were they ready to sacrifice their lives when they were offered possibilities of escape?) could now be confidently sought in fanaticism.

'The Mappilas of the interior Malabar have always been a troublesome and dubious description of subjects' (p. 92), wrote H.V. Conolly to the Chief Secretary to the British government on 30 April 1841. The subjecthood of the Mappila is indeed a dubious one. Colonial representations of the fanatic involve a twofold reduction: a reduction to religion as well as a reduction of religion. Most of the records emphasize their religious fervour and excitability, especially at the time of yearly fasts, their desire for death and martyrdom, their ignorance, criminality, blind faith in rumours and rituals, their inability to comprehend the virtues of non-violence and the politics of the national movement, their lack of patriotism, their hatred of Hindus, their proneness to believe what their religious priests 'wrongly' interpret for them, their readiness to murder or attack without provocation or cause, the ease with which they can be incited and often made tools in the local power struggles of which they have no inkling—all these make up the Mappila fanatic. It is not that all these contribute and determine a fanatic; on the other hand, the concept of fanatic determines the attributes. A well-fed Mappila, in Logan's later formulation, would be a more amenable subject and perhaps processes of subjectification would replace fanaticism—which denotes a pre-political[38] 'communal' mode of subaltern consciousness. But severe repressive measures adopted during the 1921 rebellion show that direct control or suppression almost always displaces ideological control. The very term 'subject' is understood to have two meanings: subject to someone else by control and dependence, and tied to his/her own identity by a conscience or self-knowledge. Foucault reminds us that '[b]oth meanings suggest a form of power which subjugates and makes subject to'.[39] The notion of subject is linked to a particular norm of the individual. Hence, the very term fanatic suggests it has its logic and life as resistance to the colonial-modern. More importantly, the making of the Mappila fanatic is also a marking of the Muslim body so as to locate the rupture outside the liberal ideology that sustains colonialism/nationalism. The sweep of this appellative covers the stark contradictions within the colonialist project of being the ideal civilizing force in the expansion of world capital. Guha states that 'in a pre-capitalist culture, prior to the emergence of any clear distinction between the sacred and the secular in the affairs of the state, politics, one would have thought, was so thoroughly mingled with religion as to permit of no categorical separation between the two'.[40]

Hence, unable to accept or understand or grasping only too well the idiom of the subaltern who revolts at an immediate as well as at a symbolic level, the colonialist is left with no choice and has to name the act

[38] Eric J. Hobsbawm defines the pre-political people as those 'who have not yet found, or only begun to find, a specific language in which to express their aspirations about the world', and 'their movements are thus in many respects blind and groping, by the standards of modern times', in *Primitive Rebels: Studies in Archaic Forms of Social Movements in the 19th and 20th Centuries* (New York: W.W. Norton, 1959), p. 2, and also Eric J. Hobsbawm, *Bandits* (Harmondsworth: Pelican-Penguin, 1969).

[39] Dreyfus and Rabinow, p. 212.

[40] Ranajit Guha, 'Dominance without Hegemony and its Historiography', in David Arnold and David Hardiman (eds), *Subaltern Studies VI* (New Delhi: Oxford University Press, 1989), p. 302. For an elaborate treatment of peasant consciousness, see Ranajit Guha, *Elementary Aspects of Peasant Insurgency in Colonial India* (New Delhi: Oxford University Press, 1983).

'fanaticism' in order to explain away the act as well as to disavow responsibility for it. The British policy of neutrality in matters of religion ties in with an ethno-historiography that produces the Mappila as outside History, as one who has to be controlled, coerced, confined, or killed.

III

The fanatic also has afterlives in nationalist discourses, diverse as they are, in which the insurgent Mappila seems to be produced as a not-yet, not full-fledged, citizen-subject. This is underscored by the spate and intensity of efforts to *sanitize* (clean as well as cure) the 'fanatical zone' by *shuddhi* or purification initiatives.[41] In this section, I read various sources, some of them written during the aftermath of the rebellion and others (re)written after the 1947 incidence of independences in the subcontinent. I will not, however, be examining in detail the 1921 rebellion in terms of a chronology of events. Rather, my interest is limited to its narrative construction.

Malabar in the 1920s was politically vibrant with triangular anticolonial initiatives. The Mappilas seem to have, by now, reconfigured their strategies as a result of their growing awareness of the larger scale of the anti-imperial struggle. The Tenancy[42] and Khilafat movements[43] provided a public platform to address their problems. It was in this context that Congress launched a campaign for Non-cooperation in September 1920. These triangular initiatives and the Congress'

[41] Gail Minault notes that the 'new Shuddhi effort . . . was directly inspired by the Mappilla rebellion and renewed communal tensions, and the Muslims—especially the ulama—were alarmed', leading to the Tabligh initiative; *The Khilafat Movement: Religious Symbolism and Political Mobilization in India* (New Delhi: Oxford University Press, 1982; rpntd 1999), p. 193.

[42] Grievances of the tenants were the central theme of the debates in Malabar so much so that tenancy reform became a debate unavoidable even in the District Congress conferences. Though 'the Congress avoided taking a clear-cut stand on the issue in deference to the wishes of the *janmis*' (Panikkar, *Against Lord*, p. 120), by 1916 there had evolved a Tenancy Movement that focused on unjust evictions, over-leasing and illegal rent collections.

[43] The first Khilafat conference, chaired by Gandhi, was held in November 1919 in Delhi, and resulted in the formation, in February 1920, of a Central Khilafat Committee at Bombay.

mass mobilization drive energized nationalist aspirations. The whole of Malabar, literally, responded to the nationalist call, but not the princely states. The tension between diverse movements with different agendas was accentuated by Mappila grievances that were often side-lined amidst larger concerns, and a volatile situation prevailed. In order to defuse the situation the authorities decided to arrest Ali Musaliyar[44] and searched, unsuccessfully, the Mambram mosque on 20 August 1921. A rumour that he was arrested and the shrine destroyed drew people from various places towards the town. Mappila anger was further exacerbated when British forces engaged a crowd, reportedly of 3,000 Mappilas, killing seven and arresting several. In another instance Mappilas, by now pouring into the town, killed two British officers. Consequently, various leaders (according to one report, Ali Musaliyar and his followers also emerged from hiding and) tried to reach a compromise. Led by a local Mappila leader, a large number of Mappilas approached the British camp to negotiate the release of prisoners. 'They were ordered to sit on the ground, and, after obeying, were fired upon by soldiers'. (Miller, p. 137) After this incident, Mappilas in groups dispersed to different locations leading to attacks on janmis and guerilla-type skirmishes with the police and the military.

[44] Ali Musaliyar, a venerated priestly figure among the Mappilas, had tried to follow the Gandhian path, but finally lost patience when the police repression intensified and the Congress leaders were nowhere to be seen. The Secretary of the Kerala Congress Committee, K.P. Keshava Menon, did meet Ali Musaliyar at the Mambram mosque on 26 August 1921. He was welcomed by two boats packed with Mappilas waving the Congress and the Khilafat flags: see *Kazhinja Kalam* (1957, Calicut: Mathrubhumi, 1986), pp. 106–8. When he asked the sixty-five-year-old Ali Musaliyar what he intended to do thereafter, Ali Musaliyar posed the question back and was told to surrender. Ali Musaliyar agreed to do so, though some of his followers would not have that, reasoning that Ali Musaliyar's presence at the mosque would deflect bullets. The Congress leaders' incomprehension of the causes and nature of the rebellion is apparent in Keshava Menon's advice to Ali Musaliyar, the most significant leader who could perhaps have single-handedly changed the course of the rebellion, to turn himself in. Ali Musaliyar surrendered on 30 August, was sentenced on 5 November 1921 and was hanged to death on 7 February 1922. The rebels' resolve is further indicated by the fact that the struggle continued, with a strategic resort to guerilla warfare, for more than four months after Ali Musaliyar surrendered.

The impact of the rebellion on the struggle for independence at the national level is sidelined by nationalist histories. Gandhi had set the trend when he examined the rebellion as the primary cause of Hindu–Muslim tension, only to dismiss it: the 'Malabar happenings undoubtedly disquieted the Hindu mind. What the truth is no one knows . . . it is impossible to arrive at the exact truth and it is unnecessary for the purpose of regulating our future conduct'.[45] Examining the series of 'riots' which followed year after year—for example, thirty-nine different instances documented between 1921 and 1931—Gandhi acknowledged the possibility that a 'vital connection' exists between them since 'a peaceful Tehsil at the foot of the Himalayas will be affected by a violent hamlet situated near the Cape Comorin'.[46] At the same time, Gandhi tried to distance the Congress from the Malabar rebellion, not allowing it 'to affect any of our plans'. Gail Minault, taking note of the distorted form in which the Khilafat movement reached the Mappilas, argued that Hindu–Muslim understanding had been irrevocably violated by the Malabar rebellion. She comments that a Calcutta newspaper testified precisely to such a sentiment on 27 October 1921: 'The Muslim lion and the Hindu lamb will lie down together, but the lamb will be inside the lion'.[47] However, it was not so much the rebellion itself as the representations generated by the Congress nationalist perception and persuasion of the causes of the Mappila 'uprisings' and the character of the Mappilas that affected this change. Accounts by Congress leaders in Kerala were significant in disseminating these ideas.[48]

[45] 'Hindu–Muslim Tension: Its Cause and Cure', in *CW*, vol. 24, pp. 137–8.

[46] *CW*, vol. 23, pp. 2–3.

[47] Minault, p. 148.

[48] I examine, briefly, the local Congress leader K. Madhavan Nair's memoir, *Malabar Kalapam* (Kozhikode: Mathrubhumi, 1993; serialized during early 1920s and first published 1971; hereafter abbreviated as KMN) in conjunction with M.P.S. Menon's biographical *Malabar Samaram: M.P. Narayana Menonum Sahapravarthakarum* (Malappuram: M.P. Narayana Menon Memorial Committee, 1992; hereafter abbreviated as MPSM). All translations from these texts are mine. I read these texts in juxtaposition to the report of R.H. Hitchcock, the District Superintendent of Police. For more detailed analyses of these and M.B. Namboodiripad, *Khilaphathu Smaranakal* (Thrissur: Kerala Sahitya Akademi, 1993; short version published in 1930, full version in 1965), see my Ph.D. dissertation, 'In the Interstices of India: Islam and the Processes of Nation-Formation' (especially, chapter 3, CIEFL, Hyderabad, 2003).

The nationalist framing of the rebellion seems to emerge most clearly when K. Madhavan Nair, Secretary of the Calicut Congress Committee, met the sixty-year-old Variamkunnath Kunhamed Haji. 'Kunhamed Haji, holding on to my hands, requested: "What should we do next, please advise us" ' (p. 170). Madhavan Nair felt the question was sincere and wondered at the trepidation he had felt before the meeting, for he was not sure, though they were not enemies, whether Kunhamed Haji would receive him like a friend. Now he was thoroughly nonplussed by the question since he believed that the Mappilas who had resorted to *lahala*[49] in spite of his advice to the contrary would never listen to him. However, Madhavan Nair, for whom non-violence was a matter of faith, had no difficulty in answering:

> Everything has gone wrong. The whole country has been destroyed. Now what can I say to you. Nonetheless if you are even now ready to take my advice, I will tell you, 'Throw away all your weapons and go home, stop your attacks and advice others to remain calm. You may not like my words, but that's the only advice I have for you'. I thought my words would anger Haji, but in a calm voice Haji said: 'There is no use telling that now, I started out like this, and have already done some things; there is no way I can withdraw now. Moreover, Ali Musaliyar is in danger. I have to help him. What other advice have you to offer?' After considering awhile, I replied: 'I have nothing else to say. But did you see the outrages committed by Mappilas? Is there any Hindu home which has not been robbed? What injustice is this? Is this what your religion professes? If you have strength and willingness, you should stop this robbery.'
>
> Immediately Haji rolled his eyes and told me: 'I came here with that purpose. I have already publicly declared the same at the Manjeri crossroads. I will cut the right hand off any Mappila who dares to steal. Let there be no doubt about that. I came here now because I heard there was some robbery afoot here'.
>
> 'Cutting off a hand is too much, don't do that. But it's imperative that the robbery is stopped somehow', I replied.
>
> Haji whispered in my ear: 'They will be frightened only if I say things like that'.
>
> About to turn back, Haji asked me: 'When will we meet again?' I replied: 'We will never meet again. Our paths are different and there is nothing to be gained by our meeting', and returned home. (pp. 170–1)

[49] Though Madhavan Nair's title uses the term *kalapam* (revolt), throughout the text he refers to the rebellion as *lahala* (outbreak or uprising).

In Madhavan Nair's own account of the rebellion, there were no serious attacks on Hindus in the first phase (20 to 31 August 1921), yet we find him asking Kunhamed Haji on 26 August 1921 about the horrors committed by the Mappilas, forcing one to review the anger felt by the Mappilas towards the Congress leaders for blowing isolated incidents of forced conversion and looting out of proportion.

Apart from the obvious disjuncture between the Khilafat movement and the Mappila peasant response, what becomes evident in this account of the meeting is the reluctance of the Congress leaders to associate with the Mappila insurgents. Yet, other events, which Madhavan Nair himself acknowledges, show that at some points the paths of the nationalists and the rebels were not so different. Madhavan Nair recounts that on 15 February 1921, local Congress leaders had met Yakub Hasan—called from Madras with the express purpose of calming down the Mappilas and (re)gaining their trust in the Congress (p. 71)—and had decided to conduct a meeting, thereby disobeying the government order. This was despite a perceptive Madhavan Nair pointing out that once a leader like Yakub Hasan has disobeyed the government it might not thereafter be possible to restrain the 'ignorant people' from following suit (p. 73). The very next day, most of the Congress Khilafat leaders, including Yakub Hasan and Madhavan Nair, were arrested. Madhavan Nair was released on 17 August 1921 and may not have been cognizant of the various events and preparations taking place all over Malabar. However, he acknowledges that the imprisoning of the Congress leaders 'suddenly awakened a hither to sleeping Malabar' (p. 77). The government notices as per section 144, bail cases, and punishments shook the whole of Kerala: 'The *khaddar* dress spread over the land . . . officials panicked'. (p. 78) He writes of the Congress Khilafat cadre swelling and of many Khilafat meetings; one in which over 20,000 people participated was the first sign of things going wrong. In that meeting, Mappilas who attended from distant places were armed and they attacked, but failed to provoke, a police force that was, strangely, very patient (p. 81). Madhavan Nair is critical of the Khilafat workers for forming about 200 Congress committees without properly finding out whether the leaders thus selected were imbued with the non-violent spirit (p. 82). He rationalizes that though evictions may have played a part, albeit minor, in the earlier Mappila uprisings, the true reason behind them was that 'In the competition between the desire to live and the bitterness at poverty, fanaticism supports the bitterness and uproots the fear of death' (p. 15). He presents a picture in which the Tenancy movement and the Khilafat movement gradually elude the control of Congress. He writes that prior to the repressive measures and arrests as per section 144, it was possible to restrain Mappilas by convincing them that they could have recourse to legal measures; he talks of many cases where the Mappilas have repented for their revolt against the janmis. However, the arrest of leaders and the prohibition of public meetings resulted in depressing the Mappilas so much that they lost faith in non-violent methods (p. 92).

Hitchcock, the architect of the colonial government's response to the rebellion, details the specific link between the Congress and the Mappila rebels. Contrary to Madhavan Nair's disowning of any Congress–Khilafat association with Kunahmed Haji, Hitchcock states that in May 1920 Kunhamed Haji was appointed to collect subscriptions, though he lost interest and ceased to do so immediately (Hitchcock, p. 55). He also asserts that 'Variamkunnath Kunhamath Haji and Chembrasseri Thangal had started out with the idea of obtaining in the only practical way what the supporters of Non-cooperation and *Khilafat* had promised would be obtained on a fixed date by prayer and spinning' (Hitchcock, p. 79). Kunhamed Haji's participation in the Congress–Khilafat movement is further underlined by Chembrasseri Thangal's statement to the police that he was inducted by Kunhamed Haji into the Khilafat (Hitchcock, p. 100). Moreover, Karat Moideen Kutti Haji, a twenty-eight-year-old literate rebel who could write in Arabic as well as English, when captured 'by chance' on 27 January 1922, stated that he was persuaded to join the Khilafat by Madhavan Nair himself (Hitchcock, pp. 112, 190–1). Although his statements were issued to the police under duress—for example, he describes Ali Musaliyar, with whom he had gone on Haj as a lad of eighteen, as 'a religious fanatic [who] had the hope of obtaining *Khilafat* Government' (Hitchcock, pp. 112, 190), the detailed information provided about various political meetings that he had attended supports the perception that Madhavan Nair indeed played an active role in mobilizing the Mappilas. Hitchcock also stresses the influence of outside events on the rebellion:

> Three times it had seemed that matters would right themselves but each time it was something outside the district, over which the District officers had no control which upset the hope—in February 1921 the Nagpur Conference, followed by Yaqub Hasan's visit to Calicut—in April 1921 Muhammad Ali's speech in Madras and at the end of July 1921 the Karachi *Khilafat* Conference resolutions. Both these last were printed in Malayalam and circulated. There was no other organization. By August 1921 the result was inevitable and it was merely a question of the amount of force which might be required. (Hitchcock, p. 164)

These events, Hitchcock argued, had specific effects in Malabar: 'A speech in Calicut would rouse the local Mappila audience to such a pitch that they would offer their clothes to be burnt: the same speech in Ernad would send the audience away quietly to the making of swords' (Hitchcock, p. 178). Apart from the famous inflammatory speech by Gandhi, where he stressed the particular duty of all Muslims to rebel against the British government in the light of the Khilafat issue and pointed out that all Muslims were enjoined by their religion to follow their religious scholars in the ways they chose and to wipe away the shame facing Islam,[50] several similar speeches were directed at the Muslims from various local Congress–Khilafat platforms. Therefore it is not difficult to believe that Ali Musaliyar ardently believed in the Khilafat, as reported in Moideen Kutti Haji's police statement. Hitchcock attests to the influence and hope that Congress–Khilafat held out to the Mappilas when he writes: 'Refugees, Hindu and Mappila, who escaped after being kept with gangs for some days at this time, reported from different places that the rebels were holding out in the expectation of the whole of India rising as a result of the Ali brothers' trial which was fixed for the 18th October 1921' (Hitchcock, p. 71). Hitchcock's report also provides a glimpse into the careful manner in which the rebellion was organized by the Mappilas: looting to boost key supplies, and using terror, as in the murder of the Mappila policeman Khan Bahadur K.V. Chekkuti in August 1921 (Hitchcock, p. 63),

[50] Speech made at the Khilafat meeting in Bombay on 19 March 1920, cited in MPSM, p. 43.

to prevent police from acquiring informants, thus 'making it impossible to get messengers and informants anywhere beyond Manjeri' (Hitchcock, p. 66). Belying the idea of 'fanaticism' and a grandiose dream of an actual Khilafat kingdom, during interrogation Kunhamed Haji remarks: 'They were collecting money for "Swayabharanam" [self-rule]. There is no *Khilafat* here. *Khilafat* is a Turkey matter' (Hitchcock, p. 186).

The significant point here is that neither the national nor the local leaders protested or worked towards influencing the government decision to deal summarily with the rebels. Rather, the colonial government and nationalist leaders worked hand in glove at different levels and in different ways to quell the rebellion. No nationalist support accrued even to M.P. Narayana Menon, though he was Secretary of the Ernad Congress Committee and a leader of no mean stature. Unlike other Congress leaders who sought to distance themselves from the rebellion and downplay the effect of the Khilafat movement on the Mappila peasants, Narayana Menon openly allied with the rebel leaders.[51] But he stood by the Mappilas and sought to prevent the violence that he had foreseen; he had warned Gandhi, during his visit to Malabar in August 1920, about the danger of disseminating the Khilafat cause among the Mappilas who, traditionally, are known to war against

[51] Whether it was out of personal conviction or, since he lived right amidst the 'fanatic zone', out of fear is beside the point. He seems to have been actively involved with the Mappilas for which he was often scoffed at by other leaders. During his trial he is said to have defended his actions of wearing Mappila dress and eating with them by pointing out that such dress was common in Kerala, Burma and Ceylon and that he did not eat or cohabit according to the dictates of caste or religion but those of friendship alone; cited in MPSM, p. 163. Most Congress leaders from Madras and the North preferred to stay at Keshava Menon's house, where Mappilas were not allowed to enter, than at Narayana Menon's house (MPSM, pp. 28, 38, 45). We also have Gandhi's response: 'To the questions whether he would bless his own daughter if she wanted to marry a Muslim, and whether he would sit beside a Muslim and eat the food prepared by a Muslim, Gandhi's answer is interesting: "If daughter desires to marry a Muslim I will advise her against it. But if she is adamant, she would have no place in my house. Eating food prepared by a Muslim beside a Muslim doesn't occur at all. My eating habit is my own personal matter" '. Reported by Narayana Menon on 10 October 1962 (MPSM, p. 38).

all injustices, even to the extent of embracing a heroic death. But 'big leaders like K.P. Keshava Menon, K. Madhavan Nair and C. Rajagopalachari were against [restraint]. Gandhi accepted their suggestion' and probably thought that Mappilas would listen to the Muslim scholars and the Ali brothers (MPSM, pp. 40, 56). Narayana Menon was arrested in September 1921 for waging war against the king, transported for life, and released after fourteen years. He was offered conditional freedom if he pleaded guilty, asked for mercy and agreed not to set foot in Malabar for a couple of years. (MPSM, p. 175) His refusal to do so perplexed Congress; Gandhi conveyed his helplessness[52] to Narayana Menon's wife because her husband was not ready to apologize; in fact Gandhi requested her to convince him to do so (MPSM, p. 188).

[52] The local leaders did try to help him. K. Keshava Menon, a lawyer, was scheduled to represent Narayana Menon, but failed to turn up (MPSM, p. 161) and another advocate had to argue the defence; K. Madhavan Nair, also a pleader of Manjeri court, was the chief witness. The judge, in summation, discredits Madhavan Nair's attempt to disown the rebels—in his memoirs as well—because of his statement that when he met Kunhamed Haji the latter was accompanied by thirty men with guns, of whom some were in uniform and bore the Khilafat flag. 'D.W. 8 [that is defence witness no. 8, K. Madhavan Nair] makes desperate and useless efforts to explain away the words "Uniform and Khilafat flag" but it is clear that they were Khilafat uniforms and Khilafat flags.' (Hitchcock, p. 223). Madhavan Nair's attempt to provide an alibi for Narayana Menon during the time of a meeting when the latter reportedly spoke against the king is also exposed by the judge. Madhavan Nair had stated that they were 'elsewhere'—symbolic of the Congress position regarding the rebellion—during the 'inflammatory' speech at the meeting. But this collapses in the face of Narayana Menon's own admission that he participated in Kunhamed Haji's prevention of a bank robbery and the return of ornaments to their rightful owners. Indeed, the judge is reported to have remarked later that if one had friends like Madhavan Nair and Keshava Menon, there was no need for enemies (MPSM, p. 171). The judgement of Ali Musaliyar and 37 other rebels also categorically states that though '[i]n the past [murderous outrages by the Mappila community] may have been due to fanaticism' (Hitchcock, p. 245), the 1921 rebellion was the result of the Congress–Khilafat initiative and that '*Khilafat* volunteers must, we should think, be unpaid soldiers, who are meant to fight, when occasion arises, in support of the cause for which they are enrolled. This would be the ordinary interpretation of the word "volunteers". Such volunteers have certainly been enrolled in large numbers in this district and have in due course fought exceedingly' (Hitchcock, p. 246).

Gandhi, at the helm of Congress when news of the rebellion first reached him, wrote: 'our Moplah brethren', 'undisciplined . . . all these years', have now '*gone mad*'.[53] As Gyanendra Pandey puts it, Gandhi, 'reflecting in his own speech the discourse of public order', can only exclaim: 'All that [the Mappilas] know is fighting. They are our ignorant brethren. The Government of course has done nothing to reform them but neither have we done anything'.[54] Gandhi's rhetoric re-lives the stereotypical character-construct of the Muslim: 'The Moplahs are Muslims. They have Arab blood in their veins. It is said that their forefathers came from Arabia many years ago and settled in Malabar. They are of a fiery temperament, and are said to be easily excitable. They are enraged and resort to violence in a matter of seconds. They have been responsible for many murders. . . . They always set out for fighting with a pledge not to return defeated. . . . It is not clear as yet what led to their present outburst'.[55]

'The Moplahs are Muslims' sounds more like an indictment than information. The adjectives and statements which follow, 'fiery', 'excitable', 'enraged', 'resort to violence in a matter of seconds', 'responsible for many murders', 'fighting with a pledge not to return', merely reiterate those of the colonial administration. Gandhi, who had been to Malabar in August 1920 as part of his mobilization drive for the Non-cooperation and Khilafat movements, had pressed the Mappilas to oppose the British government over the Turkish question. The speech by this 'semi-lunatic' (as Gandhi was described by the police, cited in Panikkar, *Against Lord*, p. 125) was attended by about 20,000 people, of whom a large number were Mappilas. Shaukat Ali, who had accompanied Gandhi, exhorted his Malabar audience: 'If you are strong and capable then it is your bounden duty, so long as one Musalman breathes, to fight the unjust king, the unjust government that proved to be an enemy to your faith and to your God. If you are weak and could not cope physically with your opponents then it is incumbent for you to go, migrate, to another country and leave that unjust

[53] M.K. Gandhi, *CW*, vol. 21, p. 120; emphasis added.

[54] Gyanendra Pandey, 'The Prose of Otherness', in David Arnold and David Hardiman (eds), *Subaltern Studies VIII* (New Delhi: Oxford University Press, 1994), p. 203; *CW*, vol. 21, p. 204.

[55] M.K. Gandhi, *CW*, vol. 21, pp. 47–8.

kingdom and that unjust tyrant and king.' (cited, Panikkar, *Against Lord*, p. 125) Though there are isolated voices that speak of police repression or of the dream of a Khilafat Raj as principle causes for the massive outbreak, nationalists at that time tended to view the 'uprising' as nationalism driven into the communal channel. Gandhi's remark: 'It is not clear yet what led to their present outburst', underlines the essentialized 'communality' thrust on the Mappila peasantry. What could be more symptomatic and disturbing than the readiness to judge the Mappilas without even bothering to find out 'what led to their present outburst'! Gandhi, much like Conolly, frames the 'present outbreak' as another event in a series, and 'Muslimness' seems to be sufficient explanation for their action. Gandhi interprets the Malabar rebellion as a blow against nationalist aspirations:

> Thus, for the time being progress has been arrested in Malabar and the Government has had its way. It is well versed in the art of suppressing such revolts. Many innocent men must have been, and more will be, killed. Who will come forward to blame the Government? And even if anyone does, what is the chance of the Government paying attention to him?
>
> That is a Government which prevents or stops violence. . . . A Government to be worthy of its name should be able to get the people under control.[56]

Yakub Hasan wrote to Gandhi from Malabar to inform him that:

> Moplahs as a class have always been poor. . . . The oppression of the [*janmis*] is a matter of notoriety and a long-standing grievance of the Moplahs that has never been redressed by means of legislation. . . . Something has to be done and immediately if the Moplah community is to be saved from moral, even physical, destruction. In spite of all his faults and shortcomings, the Moplah is a fine man. He has the bravery, the pluck and the grit of his Arab father, and the gentleness and the industry of his Nair mother. His religious zeal is more misunderstood than appreciated. He is as a rule peaceful, but he brooks no affront to his honour or religion. Unfortunate circumstances, the causes of which I need not enter into on this occasion, forced him into the position of a rebel. He has done what anyone, Hindu, Muslim or Christian, under the same circumstances and in the same emergency, would have done in self-defence and self-interest. He has suffered

[56] *CW*, vol. 21, p. 48.

> the consequence of his deeds. Should the society also visit his sins on his wife and children?[57]

Yakub Hasan's letter and Gandhi's response were published in *Young India* (1 May 1924) where Gandhi pointedly picks on Yakub Hasan's 'sweeping assertion' that anybody else would have done the same and says: 'We may not remember against posterity the sins of its forefathers. The Moplahs sinned against God and have suffered grievously for it. Let the Hindus also remember that they have not allowed the opportunity of revenge to pass by'.[58] Writing to Congressman U. Gopala Menon, in the context of a report in *Naveena Keralam*, Gandhi says: 'How to reach the Moplahs as also the class of Hindus whom you would want to reach through your newspaper is more than I can say, but I know that Hindus should cease to be cowardly. The Moplahs should cease to be cruel. In other words, each party should become truly religious'.[59] Elsewhere he notes: 'A verbal disapproval by the Mussulmans of Moplah madness is no test of Mussulman friendship. The Mussulman must *naturally feel the shame and humiliation* of the Moplah conduct about forcible conversions and looting, and they must work away *so silently and effectively* that such things might become impossible even on the part of the most fanatical among them.'[60] The thrust of Gandhi's argument, unlike mainstream nationalism, seems not to be directed against fanaticism as such, but against a 'loud' (ineffectual, even inhuman) manifestation of it. What was unforgivable for Gandhi was that they 'sinned against God', which poses questions about Mappila understandings of the sacred/secular. Apart from the ease of his own position of being secular by being truly religious, a position unviable for the Muslim,[61] Gandhi is also completely taken over by the notion of a non-violent, even sacred, struggle for independence, eliding over the fact that non-violence is only a strategy worked out for a particular purpose. He condemns violence in absolute, pietist

57 Cited from 'The Starving Moplah', *CW*, vol. 23, pp. 512–13.

58 *CW*, p. 524.

59 *CW*, pp. 81–2.

60 *CW*, vol. 21, p. 321; emphases added.

61 This point is elaborated in my 'Mohamed Ali's Autobiographical Fragment and the Genre of a Nation', forthcoming.

terms. There is an outright ruling out of alternative modes of struggle, and, later, this approach ensures a categorical writing out of local struggles that do not fit into this devised Indian history.

If nationalist/marxist[62] thought failed to understand peasant insurgency, it could not even begin to comprehend the religious aspect of the subaltern Mappila. In the nationalist discourse, the 'fanatic' produced as the other of the secular modern, served to define the boundaries of belonging. Islam presents a different picture.[63] From the position of Islam, one could argue that the communal mode of consciousness exists in postcolonial worlds alongside a bourgeois mode of power. In fact, it could be that the communal mode is a critique—especially so with Islam, which does not seem to brook a private/public division—of the bourgeois secular modern. It is this sense of community that, perhaps, enabled the Mappila insurgents to see connections between their local situation and the national, even global, context.

[62] The case of marxist historiography has not been, in the larger context, very different. Put schematically, instead of a theory of 'fanatic' causation, the marxist version assumes that economic grievances are *the* major determining factor. It was E.M.S. Namboodiripad who took note of the wider participation, even leadership, of 'Hindus', at least during the early stage of the rebellion. He argued for the redesignation of the 1921 Mappila rebellion as Malabar rebellion or Malabar freedom struggle, *The National Question in Kerala* (Bombay: People's Publishing House, 1952), p. 121. He notes, in *Kerala Society and Politics*, that '*spontaneous* peasant actions . . . started developing in Malabar' (p. 90). However, the national bourgeois leadership 'abandoned the vanguard to the tender mercies of the British troops. Had it not been for this disgraceful betrayal by the leadership at the crucial moment, the history of the glorious rebellion of 1921 would have been different' (p. 114). Nonetheless, 'at a subsequent stage of the movement, i.e., at the stage when British troops had started their depredations and when British rulers and their Hindu stooges had spread the canard of Muslim fanaticism being the source of the militancy of the peasants, the movement acquired a communal colour' (p. 114). The marxist explanation draws on the notion of the 'pre-political peasant rebel' in order to analyse peasant insurgencies which were to a great extent influenced/informed by religion.

[63] The inverse of Chatterjee's postulation of moments of departure, manoeuvre and arrival of the Indian nation, in *Nationalist Thought and the Colonial World: A Derivative Discourse?* (New Delhi: Oxford University Press, 1996), would be the Muslim response to post-Enlightenment thought, which then would involve a moment of arrival (an arrival at modernity, viz. Syed Ahmad Khan), a moment of

The Mappila insurgents were not, could not, be reclaimed and renamed as martyrs of the independence struggle. Gandhi, in a letter dated 3 March 1922 to Konda Venkatappayya, expresses his late realization:

> I can still distinguish between Malabar and Gorakhpur [Chauri Chaura]. The Moplahs themselves had not been touched by the non-co-operation spirit. *They are not like the other Indians nor even like the other Mussulmans* . . . The Moplah revolt was so different in kind that it did not affect other parts of India, whereas Gorakhpur was typical, and therefore, if we had not taken energetic steps, the *infection might easily have spread to other parts of India*. (*CW*, vol. 23, p. 3; emphases added)

While the peasant violence at Chauri Chaura is redeemable, the 1921 Malabar rebellion cannot be. What is the difference evoked by Gandhi here, if not the difference of Islam? The casual conjunction of 'other Indians' and 'other Mussulmans' in Gandhi's comment underlines this point: Indians and Muslims are separate, if not contradictory, categories. Ironically, what Gandhi had hoped to achieve by his alliance with Muslims was 'a three-fold end—to obtain justice in the face of odds with the method of satyagraha . . . to secure Mahomedan friendship for the Hindus and thereby internal peace also, and last but not least to transform ill-will into affection for the British and their constitution.'[64] What was achieved was the remainder outside as well as inside the destiny of the Indian nation. Islam continues to be a spectre that holds the nation together by virtue of a familiar interplay of haunting.

---

manoeuvre (mobilization; Ali brothers), and a moment of departure (out of the Indian nation; Jinnah).

[64] Cited by Dale, p. 183, from Judith Brown, *Gandhi's Rise to Power* (Cambridge: Cambridge University Press, 1972), p. 194.

CHAPTER 3

A Practice of Prejudice

Gandhi's Politics of Friendship

FAISAL FATEHALI DEVJI

He wanted to be the friend of many men, but no man's brother.—
Hannah Arendt

These words, from an essay on the political language of Lessing, oppose the virtue of friendship to the vice of brotherhood.[1] The bond of friendship, claims Arendt, entails by its differentiation the activity of choice, while that of brotherhood implies a passive commonality that enters politics only to destroy the differentiation of such choice.[2] The point here being that while friendship must think its condition in terms of discrimination as such, the condition of brotherhood is thought a false unity that can only destroy itself.

While they enter modern politics together, as equal relations between men that are no longer regulated by a paternal hierarchy, friendship and brotherhood here exist at cross purposes. Indeed they represent two perhaps contradictory conceptions of egalitarian relations between men: those based on choice and those based on nature. Both these conceptions being jeopardized by the very presence, not to mention inclusion, of women, whose formal relations with men as sexual beings might well limit if not put into question any order based

[1] It is appropriate at the mention of friendship to thank Dipesh Chakrabarty and Uday Mehta for the conversations that made this essay possible.

[2] Hannah Arendt, 'On Humanity in Dark Times: Thoughts About Lessing', *Men in Dark Times*, trans. Clara and Richard Winston (San Diego: Harcourt, 1983), pp. 3–31.

on friendship or brotherhood.[3] In this discussion women remain precisely the jeopardy for all masculine relations based on friendship or brotherhood. The jeopardy acknowledged but not discussed.

Historically, the terms friendship and brotherhood become politically imperative at a particular moment in the history of Western Europe, that of the emergence of liberalism out of an old paternal order. A moment when the unequal contract of interests which liberalism inherits from its feudal past has to account for the novel totality of national mobilization with some egalitarian universality such as brotherhood, although it can only do so in a highly contradictory way.[4] Rather than acting as ideological masks for the particular reality of interest, therefore, terms like brotherhood become imperative precisely in order to overcome the political limits of liberal interest with the universal mobilization of nationalism.

The universality of brotherhood, then, both accommodates and contradicts the particularity of liberal interests in nationalism. Liberalism here being defined, minimally, as a social order based on the contractual freedom of ownership (of things as well as selves), one that makes a regime of interests possible or identifiable. The universality of friendship, however, exists in a different sort of relationship with the particularity of interest because it presupposes the differentiation of choice. Unlike a brotherhood that is based in nature and can be flouted a hundred times without ceasing to remain brotherhood, the choice upon which friendship is based is remarkably fragile. More than this, it subsists in a strange intimacy with interest, itself defined as a choice from which friendship differs precisely because it must be disinterested.

How is choice without interest to be defined in a regime of interests? I will argue that it is defined here as discrimination and as prejudice if only because it does not partake of the rationality of a liberal political order. My object in this essay is to describe this discrimination of friendship as it operates in one of Gandhi's boldest experiments, his

[3] For a discussion of the gendered implications of a language of brotherhood , see Carole Pateman's *The Sexual Contract* (Stanford: Stanford University Press, 1988).

[4] For the classic statement on this contradiction, see Carl Schmitt's *The Crisis of Parliamentary Democracy*, trans. Ellen Kennedy (Cambridge: M.I.T., 1992).

attempt to rethink political relations in the colonial context of liberalism. A context in which illiberal relations can neither be fully destroyed, nor liberal interests fully developed, so that such contractual relations as exist increasingly come to occur only through the mediation of the state as a contract of interests. A context, then, of effective de-politicization as far as the everyday relations of Indians are concerned, since in the absence of state mediation these relations between Indians arise out of juxtaposition alone.[5]

What I contend is that Gandhi approaches this voiding of politics at the everyday level by developing the prejudice which is the only thing that remains between Indians here into a basis for friendship. For if prejudice constitutes a relation that is not reasoned into interest through the state and its politics of contract, if it in fact constitutes such a regime of interests as its leftover or outside, then, Gandhi seemed to think, it could also be made to produce friendship as the very emblem of disinterest. And this was important because prejudice might be the only thing that stood in the way of brotherhood as a depoliticization of everyday life. Brotherhood as a false unity that can only sustain itself by trivializing if not destroying the difference upon which prejudice and friendship rely. Brotherhood, finally, as a hatred of the citizen, who must inevitably betray his fraternity to a contract of interests mediated by the state. After all only an ideology of brotherhood makes possible the language of betrayal and revenge that was in Gandhi's time coming to mark relations among Indians, and especially between Hindus and Muslims, with an increasingly ferocious violence.

Now the colonial state in India, despite its naturalist claims (those having to do with race or civilization, for example) and paternalist hierarchies, did not make much use of the language of brotherhood to describe its subjects. Perhaps because all positive claims of a natural sort were to be reserved for the state (its subjects being defined only by the bad nature of racial or civilizational inferiority), colonial rhetoric tended to stress friendship as the preferred relation among natives and between natives and their rulers. However, friendship was conceived

[5] This de-politicization is discussed by Karl Marx in his 'Critique of Hegel's Doctrine of State', *Early Writings*, trans. Rodney Livingstone and Gregor Denton (London: Penguin, 1992), p. 20.

by it not as an ideological universality but like interest itself as the essence of the particular. And no matter how interested such friendship without the possibility of national mobilization might be, it did contain within itself another kind of possibility, that of an ethical imperative. One has only to think of the importance of friendship, even as an incantatory word, in texts like Forster's *Passage to India* to realize the seriousness of such an imperative in the imperial imagination. The colonial order might therefore be described, by contorting Pateman's thesis, as paternalism without brotherhood.

It is nationalism that introduces the modern language of egalitarian brotherhood to Indian politics. And while Gandhi is often ambiguous about the difference between friendship and brotherhood, I am reading him here, in light of the peculiar colonial history of these terms, as an advocate of the former. In other words I am looking at Gandhi as a spoiler within the rhetoric of colonial India. One who launched criticisms of colonial and national liberalism both by re-reading and making productive the very terms of imperial rhetoric. In this essay I am claiming that Gandhi took up the colonial idea of friendship as an ethical imperative and made it productive for an anti-colonial politics. And just as in its colonial variant, friendship for Gandhi was not a universal concept of national mobilization but a very particular attitude that might be applied politically only to certain people, in this case the British and the Muslims. And these two, we shall see, were linked not so much as the former and current conquerors of Hindu India, but, in a typically Gandhian rereading of the trope of conquest, as possessors of imperial imaginaries that had productive political uses.[6]

The occasion for Gandhi's experiment in the friendship of prejudice, or the prejudice of friendship, was Khilafatism, the first manifestation of mass politics in the history of India. This extraordinary movement began in the aftermath of the First World War as a Muslim attempt to force upon Britain the protection of the defeated Ottoman empire, whose sultan claimed also to be caliph, the fount of Islamic authority worldwide. The sudden devotion of Indian Muslims to this

[6]The particularistic use of friendship, among other Gandhian terms of political identity, is discussed in Ajay Skaria's rich and remarkably suggestive essay 'Gandhi's Politics: Liberalism and the Question of the Ashram', *South Atlantic Quarterly*, vol. 101, no. 4, Fall 2002, pp. 955–86.

titular authority has never ceased to confound historical explanation, so that at most we are treated to analyses accusing the disenfranchised Muslims of India of a fantastically vicarious identification with the freedom of their co-religionists abroad, and the disenfranchised Hindus of India who join them of an opportunistic desire to unify India for the ulterior motive of independence.

While an analysis of the Khilafat movement falls outside the scope of this essay, it will at least dispose of explanations based on psychology or opportunism to point out another possible reading of its combination of a disparate Muslim elite never in control of the movement, and a Muslim mass galvanized for the first time by an extra-Indian issue. Might this combination not suggest a class compromise leading to a pan-Islamist mobilization whose numerous local effects were purposefully not based upon that bourgeois form of property that has as its arena, guarantor, and apotheosis the state and its politics of interest? Whatever the reasons were for the emergence of the Khilafat movement, its very originality elicited an equally original response from Gandhi, one we may explore through the speeches and articles published in his journal *Young India*. I shall begin, then, with an analysis of Gandhi's views on liberalism, move on to the challenge posed by the Khilafat Movement to its regime of interest, and end with Gandhi's working out of a practice of prejudice in response to this challenge.

The Khilafat movement, so often and contradictorily judged as nationalist or pan-Islamist in its politics, was nevertheless loyal and liberal, because it petitioned the colonial government as an association of interested subjects: 'The preservation of the Khilafat with such guarantees as may be necessary for the protection of the interests of the non-Muslim races living under Turkish rule and the Khalif's control over Arabia and the Holy Places with such arrangement as may be required for guaranteeing Arab self-rule, should the Arabs desire it.'[7] Insofar as these Levantine demands were addressed to the British government by an Indian movement, they were of course imperial demands and neither national nor pan-Islamist ones, because their terrain was the terrain of the British empire. But more than mere territory, this empire was for Gandhi also the terrain where a liberal

[7] M.K. Gandhi, 'The Khilafat', 28 January 1920, *Young India 1919–1922* (New York: B.W. Huebsch, 1923), p. 144.

regime of interests—such as the nation with its bounded authenticity could never be—approached universality: 'What is this British Empire? It is as much Mahomedan and Hindu as it is Christian. Its religious neutrality is not a virtue, or if it is, it is a virtue of necessity. Such a mighty Empire could not be held together on any other terms. British ministers are, therefore, bound to protect Mahomedan interests as any other.'[8]

In other words the virtue of neutrality, which made the liberal arbitration of interests possible in contract, was necessary only in and as an empire where political relations could not be based on terms like brotherhood or friendship.[9] And it was because he sought to fulfill the universality of liberalism in empire, or of empire in liberalism, that Gandhi argued with the British on the basis of contractual interest:

> If India is to remain equal partner with every other member of the Empire, India's voting strength must be infinitely superior to that of any other member. . . . Thus, the centre of equilibrium must shift to India rather than remain in England, when India has come into her own. That is my meaning of Swaraj within the Empire. . . . To-day we are striving for Swaraj within the Empire in the hope that England will in the end prove true, and for independence if she fails. But when it is incontestably proved that Britain seeks to destroy Turkey, India's only choice must be independence.[10]

Indeed Gandhi's celebrated loyalty to the empire should be taken seriously precisely because he saw in it the possibility of a liberal universality whose order was worthy of loyalty despite being in no sense a moral order:

> My duty to the Empire to which I owe my loyalty requires me to resist the cruel violence that has been done to the Mussalman sentiment. So far as I am aware, Mussalmans and Hindus have as a whole lost faith in British justice and honour. . . . In these circumstances, the only course open to one like me is either in despair to sever all connection with British rule, or, if

[8] Ibid.

[9] The complicated relations between liberalism and empire are examined by Uday Singh Mehta in *Liberalism and Empire* (Chicago: The University of Chicago Press, 1999).

[10] Gandhi, 'The Turkish Question', 29 June 1921, *Young India 1919–1922*, p. 181.

> I still retained faith in the inherent superiority of the British constitution to all others presently in vogue, to adopt such means as will rectify the wrong done, and thus restore confidence. I have not lost faith in such superiority and am not without hope that somehow or other justice will yet be rendered. . . . Indeed, my conception of that constitution is that it helps only those who are ready to help themselves. I do not believe that it protects the weak. It gives free scope to the strong to maintain their strength and develop it. The weak under it go to the wall.[11]

Now defending an empire in which one's own country is to dominate may be disingenuous, if not hypocritical, but it is exactly prejudice of this sort, after all, that belongs at the heart of liberalism as interest. The problem then is not prejudice as such, but prejudice that is not translated into an interest to be managed contractually; prejudice that inevitably exceeds a regime of interests to form its limits. These limits to a liberal order might or might not be exceptional, but they are certainly produced by such an order in a logic whose end is often violent, and, what is worse, unsurprisingly so. Thus Gandhi describes the violence of one possible outcome in the dismemberment of the Ottoman empire quite flatly, as if it followed naturally from a liberalism that constituted interests in such a way that, once disconnected from the arbitration of the state, they could only become enemies:

> Britain has made promises to the Zionists. . . . The Jews, it is contended, must remain a homeless wandering race unless they have obtained possession of Palestine. I do not propose to examine the soundness or otherwise of the doctrine underlying the proposition. All I contend is that they cannot possess Palestine through a trick or a moral breach. Palestine was not a stake in the war. The British Government could not dare have asked a single Muslim soldier to wrest control of Palestine from fellow-Muslims and give it to the Jews. Palestine, as a place of Jewish worship, is a sentiment to be respected, and the Jews would have a just cause of complaint against Musulman idealists if they were to prevent Jews from offering worship as freely as themselves.
>
> By no canon of ethics or war, therefore, can Palestine be given to the Jews as a result of the war. Either Zionists must revise their ideal about Palestine, or, if Judaism permits the arbitrament of war, engage in a 'holy

[11] This excerpt from a letter to the viceroy, dated 22 June 1920 inaugurating non-cooperation, is included in *Young India 1919–1922*, pp. 198–9.

> war' with the Muslims of the world with the Christians throwing in their influence on their side.[12]

If Gandhi argued with the British not only on their terms, but also for their terms, he did so with a realization of the limits of these terms. And faced with British recalcitrance, it was to these limits that Gandhi turned when arguing with Indians for a cause whose very pan-Islamism allowed him to espouse for the first time an issue beyond the particularity of their interests: 'The Khilafat question has now become a question of questions. It has become an imperial question of the first magnitude.'[13]

Indeed Gandhi was adamant enough about the importance of this issue as international enough to grapple with the empire in its entirety, refusing even to compare it to something as local as the British massacre of civilians at Jallianwala Bagh. This latter event, after all, did not arise out of the terms of the peace, which could only be imperial–international. Only the Khilafat movement, and by extension Islam, raised Indian concerns to imperial or international heights because it had political implications that extended beyond the would-be borders of a national state. Here is one way in which Gandhi transformed colonial and nationalist anxieties about pan-Islamism into a productive if still ambivalent political idea:

> However grievous the wrong done in the Punjab, it is after all a domestic affair and it would show on our part a want of sense of proportion to bring in the Punjab grievances to justify our non-co-operation in the Imperial celebration. The Punjab grievance does not arise out of the peace terms as does the Khilafat question. We must isolate the Khilafat question if we wish to give it its proper place and value. In my humble opinion, it is not open to us to refuse to share the peace celebrations on grounds other than those that arise directly out of the peace and that touch the vital parts of our national existence. The Khilafat question alone satisfies these two tests.[14]

Indeed pan-Islamism seems to have provided Gandhi with something of an alternative model to the British empire. Even in his earliest work,

[12] Gandhi, 'The Khilafat', *Young India*, 23 March 1921, pp. 178–9.

[13] Gandhi, 'The Question of Questions', *Young India*, 10 March 1920, p. 145.

[14] Gandhi, 'All-India Khilafat Conference', *Young India*, 13 December 1919, pp. 140–1.

Hind Swaraj (Indian Self-Rule), Gandhi had as it were reconstituted the very geography of the empire by his use of the Arabic word *Hind*, which had become archaic both in Gujarati and English, to designate India. *Hind*, of course, not only has no specifically nationalist connotations, but also exists in an imaginative geography that belies the official territoriality of the British empire, including instead the more amorphous spaces of a traditionally Muslim geographical imagination. *Hind*, in other words, cannot exist on the same map as the Aden Protectorate or the Dominion of South Africa.

And all this is completely unsurprising given Gandhi's own curious navigation of British imperial space as if he were using an astrolabe from older Muslim imaginings of the area. So we know that *Hind Swaraj*, itself replete with Arabic and Persian terminology, was written in South Africa, whence Gandhi had gone in search of employment, following not the abstract routes of colonial capital so much as the traditional ones of Muslim trade in the Indian Ocean. It is important to point out in this respect that in choosing to follow the international trade routes, of which Gujarat was such an integral part, Gandhi had in effect ignored the India of a nationalist imagination as a source of livelihood, and this because the Indian presence and struggle in South Africa seemed for him to exist in the same imperial–international (or Muslim–Gujarati) world as the Indian presence and struggle in India itself. But more was at stake in the international character of the Khilafat movement than some antiquated geographical imaginary that I am for the purposes of this essay calling Muslim. For the Khilafat movement was not international because of the extent of its constituency so much as because it revealed itself in a millennial struggle between Christianity and Islam: 'The Great Prelates of England and the Mahomedan leaders combined have brought the question to the fore. The Prelates threw down the challenge. The Muslim leaders have taken it up.'[15]

Gandhi seemed to suggest that whatever the interests were of the parties concerned, the dismemberment of the Ottoman empire could only play itself out structurally as a prejudice outside the bounds of state arbitration, and despite the efforts of the League of Nations to

[15] Gandhi, 'The Question of Questions', *Young India*, 10 March 1920, p. 145.

reinstate a forum for such arbitration following the collapse of the Concert of Europe: 'Oppose all Turkish misrule by all means, but it is wicked to seek to efface the Turk and with him Islam from Europe under the false plea of Turkish misrule. . . . Was the late war a crusade against Islam, in which the Mussalmans of India were invited to join?'[16]

And again: 'I do say that the affront such as has been put upon Islam cannot be repeated for a century. Islam must rise now or "be fallen" if not for ever, certainly for a century.'[17]

Indian Muslims, therefore, were engaged in an imperial-international struggle that could not be appropriated or translated by the state into any contractual interest, but had to manifest itself in a novel way as a religious ideal:

> In my opinion, if the demands of the Muslims of India are conceded, it will not much matter whether Turkey's are satisfied or not. And this for two reasons. The Khilafat is an ideal and when a man works for an ideal, he becomes irresistible. The Muslims, who represent the ideal, have behind them the opinion of the whole mass of the Indian people.[18]
>
> What I venture to commend to . . . Christians . . . is to join the defence of the Khilafat as an ideal, and thus recognize that the struggle of Non-co-operation is one of religion against irreligion.[19]

It was on the basis of this prejudice in the form of religion, then, that Gandhi tried to make the Khilafat movement into a denial of that politics of interest characterizing the Peace of Versailles: 'If India—both Hindu and Mahomedan—can act as one man and withdraw her partnership in this crime against humanity which the peace terms represent, she will soon secure a revision of the treaty and give herself and the Empire at least, if not the world, a lasting peace.'[20]

The idealism of the Khilafatist cause provided Gandhi with a position from which to focus on the everydayness of Indian relations

[16] Gandhi, 'The Meaning of the Khilafat', *Young India*, 8 September 1921, p. 190.

[17] Gandhi, 'At the Call of the Country', *Young India*, 21 July 1920, p. 212.

[18] Gandhi, 'The Khilafat', *Young India*, 23 March 1921, pp. 177–8.

[19] Gandhi, 'The Meaning of the Khilafat', *Young India*, 8 September 1921, p. 190.

[20] Gandhi, 'Pledges Broken', *Young India*, 19 May 1920, p. 161.

in general, and so to develop them politically. He did this first by insisting upon the irreducibility of prejudices, which could not be negotiated into interests amenable to a reason that is always a reason of state. Thus his description of the Muslim claim:

> If the Muslim claim was unjust apart from the Muslim scriptures, one might hesitate to support it merely on scriptural authority. But when a just claim is supported by scriptures, it becomes irresistible.[21]
>
> I cannot regulate the Mahomedan feeling. I must accept his statement that the Khilafat is with him a religious question in the sense that it binds him to reach the goal even at the cost of his own life.[22]

Without reasoning, of course, there is no interest, so that even the famous pledge to Muslims (regarding the preservation of the Ottoman empire) which the British prime minister was supposed to have broken, can be spoken of not as a breach of contract, but as a violation of prejudice:

> (T)he people must not be party to a wrong—a broken pledge—a violation of deep religious sentiment.[23]
>
> In my opinion Hindu India is solidly on your side, for your cause is not merely scripturally true, but it is morally just, and presently England will be on our side when . . . Englishmen learn that *British honour is at stake. . . .*[24]

Perhaps Gandhi's most spectacular avowal of prejudice, however, and so also his denial of that whole mutuality of compromise characteristic of liberal contract, comes with his refusal to make Hindu participation in the Khilafat movement conditional, whether upon Muslim support for Indian political reforms, or upon Muslim abstention from cow slaughter. Cow slaughter itself being, like the Khilafat, an issue seemingly intractable to the rationality of liberal interests, precisely a prejudice of the sort that the liberal Hindu found embarrassing:

[21] Gandhi, 'The Question of Questions', *Young India*, 10 March 1920, p. 145.

[22] Gandhi, 'Khilafat: Further Questions Answered', *Young India*, 2 June 1920, p. 170.

[23] Gandhi, 'How to Work Non-co-operation', *Young India*, 5 May 1920, p. 191.

[24] This excerpt from a telegram addressed to the Khilafatist leader Shaukat Ali on 31 January 1920 is included in *Young India*, p. 145.

> I trust that the Hindus will realize that the Khilafat question overshadows the Reforms and everything else.[25]
>
> The test of friendship is assistance in adversity, and that too, unconditional assistance. Co-operation that needs consideration is a commercial contract and not friendship. Conditional co-operation is like adulterated cement which does not bind. It is the duty of the Hindus, if they see the justice of the Mahomedan cause, to render co-operation. If the Mahomedans feel themselves bound in honour to spare the Hindus' feelings and to stop cow-killing, they may do so, no matter whether the Hindus co-operate with them or no. Though, therefore, I yield to no Hindu in my worship of the cow, I do not want to make the stopping of cow-killing a condition precedent to co-operation. Unconditional co-operation means the protection of the cow.[26]

This last sentence, which makes the protection of the cow audaciously depend upon the lack of agreement between Hindus and Muslims, negates even a relation among Indians that is based on the contract of recognition. For what structures a friendship founded upon prejudice is not the abstract recognition of Hindus as Hindus and of Muslims as Muslims, but rather an everyday neighbourliness, whose particularistic contiguity overrides all the implicitly universal rights of liberal recognition:

> I am sorry to have to confess that the ordinary Mahomedan entertains today no affection for Englishmen. He considers, not without some cause, that they have not played the game. But if I am friendly towards Englishmen, I am no less so towards my countrymen, the Mahomedans. And as such they have a greater claim upon my attention than Englishmen.[27]

> I have already stated that, if I were not interested in the Indian Mahomedans, I would not interest myself in the welfare of the Turks any more than I am in that of the Austrians or the Poles. But I am bound as an Indian to share the sufferings and trials of fellow-Indians.[28]

[25] Gandhi, 'The Question of Questions', *Young India*, 10 March 1920, p. 145.

[26] Gandhi, 'Khilafat and the Cow Question', *Young India*, 10 December 1919, p. 141.

[27] Gandhi, 'How to Work Non-co-operation', *Young India*, 5 May 1920, p. 191.

[28] Gandhi, 'Khilafat: Further Questions Answered', *Young India*, 2 June 1920, p. 171.

Now neighbourliness, while it does imply some form of proximity, by no means presupposes a place, however constituted, as its arena of occurrence. Indeed the duties of neighbourliness extend unproblematically outside any place, so that even a threat to the neighbourliness of such a place can be contemplated with understanding, if also with regret:

> Let Hindus not be frightened by Pan-Islamism. It is not—it need not be—anti-Indian or anti-Hindu. Mussalmans must wish well to every Mussalman state, and even assist any such state, if it is undeservedly in peril. And Hindus, if they are true friends of Mussalmans, cannot but share the latter's feelings. We must, therefore, co-operate with our Mussalman brethren in their attempt to save the Turkish Empire in Europe from extinction.[29]

> The Mahomedan speakers gave the fullest and frankest assurances that they would fight to a man any invader who wanted to conquer India, but they were equally frank in asserting that any invasion from without undertaken with a view to uphold the prestige of Islam and to vindicate justice would have their full sympathy if not their actual support. It is easy enough to understand and justify the Hindu caution. It is difficult to resist the Mahomedan position.[30]

The fact that Gandhi will not posit some third entity as a ground for relating, of course, means that he will not countenance the unifying character of any ground apart from the relation of neighbourliness itself. Ground here being a universal that as concept, state, or territory, provides a place for the particularity of political relations; the kind of universality that we have seen reaches its consummation in liberalism. But how is neighbourliness as proximity to be determined apart from particularity, and without such a universal? One way in which we can think of Gandhi's valorization of proximity beyond place is by invoking the work of Emmanuel Levinas. In an essay titled 'Language and Proximity', for example, Levinas ties neighbourliness to the terms obsession and hostage. An obsessive relationship, writes Levinas, is one in which the neighbour cannot be placed through the mediation of universality, but remains ungraspable in his very proximity, both as an infinite presence, and as an infinite absence.[31] This presence, then,

[29] Gandhi, 'The Turkish Question', *Young India*, 29 June 1921, pp. 180–1.

[30] Gandhi, 'The Mahomedan Decision', *Young India*, 9 June 1920, p. 194.

[31] E. Levinas, 'Language and Proximity', *Collected Philosophical Papers*, trans. Alphonso Lingis (Dordrecht: Kluwer, 1993), p. 120.

which is also an absence from the universal, holds its neighbour hostage to the un-chosen demand for a relationship out of place.[32] According to Levinas, it is precisely the obsessiveness of this hostage, his voiding of subjecthood in the form of an ability to place things *qua* concept, state, or territory, that makes him capable of ethics in the form of altruistic virtues like pity or compassion.[33]

It should be clear how this ethics might relate to Gandhi's practice of prejudice. In both cases, the very discomfort, and even violence, of an ungraspable neighbourly presence as absence, would make for an everyday friendship beyond the inherently antagonistic politics of liberal universality. As a ground for, or grounding of, political relations, of course, this universality constitutes an origin as much as a place; an origin whose commonness, as God, father, or country, produces a fraternity. In defying ground as origin, therefore, Gandhi defied the kind of historical determinism that both united people in, and divided them by, lineages of causality. Thus he refused to accept responsibility even for the genealogies of his own actions, instead manufacturing an independence from such causality out of sheer irresponsibility:

> It is perfectly true that I am assisting and countenancing the union between Hindus and Moslems, but certainly not with 'a view of embarrassing England and the Allied Powers in the matter of the dismemberment of the Ottoman Empire.' It is contrary to my creed to embarrass Governments or anybody else. This does not however mean that certain acts of mine may not result in embarrassment. But I should not hold myself responsible for having caused embarrassment when I resist the wrong of a wrong-doer by refusing assistance in his wrong-doing.[34]

> But I must refuse to be deterred from a clear course, because it may be attended by violence totally unintended and in spite of extraordinary efforts that are being made to prevent it. At the same time I must make my position clear. Nothing can possibly prevent a Satyagrahi from doing his duty because of the frown of the authorities. I would risk, if necessary, a million

[32] Ibid., p. 123.

[33] Ibid., p. 124.

[34] Gandhi, 'Why I Have Joined the Khilafat Movement', *Young India*, 28 April 1920, pp. 152–3.

> lives so long as they are voluntary sufferers and are innocent, spotless victims.[35]

It is easy, and even profitable, to read Gandhian irresponsibility in the celebrated terms of Soren Kierkegaard's essay *Fear and Trembling*, according to which the realm of ethics actually denies individual responsibility by its very universality.[36] In other words the universally communicable claims of this ethical realm create communities of moral sentiment that rob the responsible act of its interiority, and so of its absolute character as well.[37] All of which means, of course, that only an irresponsible act, such as Abraham's willingness to sacrifice his son without resort to any ethical universality, implies the existence of absolute responsibility.[38]

However apt the comparison with Kierkegaard, his aristocratic morality sits uneasily with Gandhi's concern for those elements of everyday life that also escape universality. One way we can understand these elements is by looking at what Gandhi is willing to bear responsibility for. In the passage quoted above, for example, he refuses to take responsibility for any violence that might result from the lack of mass discipline in non-co-operation, but claims complete responsibility for the violent deaths of up to a million disciplined people. Two years later, in 1922, the Mahatma calls off non-co-operation, much to the chagrin of his allies, because of mass violence at Chauri Chaura, for which he holds himself completely accountable. This action, which effectively ended the Khilafat Movement, illustrates more than Gandhi's mistrustful or paternalistic attitude towards mass politics. It demonstrates perhaps the Mahatma's attempt to become a political agent by laying claim to his very lack of agency, if this is defined as the control and ownership of an act, so that one becomes responsible only for what one possesses (as thing, act, or capacity) in some way. Indeed Gandhi performed penances throughout his career to expiate for instances of violence which he had not himself committed, in this way overturning

[35] Gandhi, 'Khilafat: Further Questions Answered', *Young India*, 2 June 1920, p. 171.

[36] S. Kierkegaard, *Fear and Trembling*, transl. Alastair Hanway (Harmondsworth: Penguin, 1985), p. 89.

[37] Ibid., p. 97.

[38] Ibid., p. 106.

the property and exchange-based nature of all relations based on juridical ideas of responsibility. Gandhi's claims to responsibility, rather, bore the mark of prejudice as friendship, for he claimed responsibility and did penance for another's acts.

In his effort to develop the inevitability of prejudice into friendship, Gandhi also emphasized the discriminating quality of sentiment, and this to such a degree that it became impossible to identify the commonality of a cause with the commonality of sentiment, as one would in an ideology of brotherhood, for instance: 'I can think out plans but execution must ever rest with Mussalman workers. The movement must be worked and led by them with the assistance of friends like me but also without, if need be. I must not be expected to make Non-co-operators; Mussalman leaders alone can make them. No amount of sacrifice on my part will produce in the Mussalman world the spirit of Non-co-operation, *i.e.*, sacrifice in a matter of religion.'[39]

Indeed his dislike of commonality prompted Gandhi also to abandon the notion of representation as suggesting some false and therefore potentially violent identification with a fraternity; thus his famous refusal to become even a four-anna member of the Indian National Congress, and thus his infuriating refusal to negotiate either with the British, or with the Indian minorities, as an authorized representative of this Congress:

> But I do not pretend to represent Mussalman opinion. I can only try to interpret it. I could not stand alone and expect to carry the Mussalman masses with me.[40]
>
> This Committee . . . has the least representative capacity. Shaukat Ali is an amiable man but a rabid fanatic carrying no weight with anybody, Hasrat Mohani a useless man who thinks of nothing but Swadeshi, Dr. Kitchlew a man of yesterday with no experience of the world outside Amritsar. Much the same may be said against the others. I am no doubt a superior person but after all a crank and an interloper at that. Any representation signed by it will carry little weight with the outside world in so as far as it depends upon the influence of the signatories.[41]

[39] Gandhi, 'The Non-Co-operation Committee', *Young India*, 23 June 1920, p. 200.

[40] Ibid., p. 198.

[41] Ibid., pp. 196–7.

But the discriminating friendship that one Indian might entertain for another was not dictated by the unpredictability of affection. For one thing, Gandhi required of Indians a certain investment in the ideal of friendship, which investment he thought could be made in suffering alone. This suffering, however, was neither the compassion that is as unpredictable as affection, nor the endurance of some common privation, but rather the deliberately independent selection of an experience whose positivity both invited and sustained friendship:

> Both the Mussalmans and the Hindus are on their trial. Is the humiliation of the Khilafat a matter of concern to the former? And if it is, are they prepared to exercise restraint, religiously refrain from violence and practice Non-co-operation without counting the material loss it may entail upon the community? Do the Hindus honestly feel for their Mahomedan brethren to the extent of sharing their sufferings to the fullest extent? The answer to these questions, and not the peace terms, will finally decide the fate of the Khilafat.[42]

> And to-day if I have thrown in my lot with the Mahomedans a large number of whom bear no friendly feelings towards the British, I have done so frankly as a friend of the British and with the object of gaining justice and of thereby showing the capacity of the British constitution to respond to every honest determination when it is coupled with suffering.[43]

The idealism of the Khilafat movement, in other words, was to be sustained by a personal investment in suffering which invited rather than gave friendship. The exquisite courtesy of such a relation being that it made one party available to another as a friend without either an offering or a taking, which, even if unconditional, could only form the mirror-image of contract as a mode of exchange. Gandhian suffering, moreover, radicalized the so-called bond of history as an experience-which-unifies-beyond-thought by reproducing its effect wilfully, in a way that untied experience as an imperative from history as a memory; which is to say by rejecting the supposed memory of some common historical experience making for brotherly obligation. In its making available of friendship on the entirely uncommon ground, or rather non-ground, of a willfully solitary experience, then,

[42] Gandhi, 'Pledges Broken', *Young India*, 19 May 1920, p. 162.

[43] Gandhi, 'How to Work Non-co-operation', *Young India*, 5 May 1920, p. 193.

suffering operated prejudicially, indeed even by brinkmanship, as when the spectacle of Gandhi's own suffering so often forced rivals to parley. Thus suffering in this sense made for a friendship that was neither affection nor agreement, but perhaps a relation of desires that diverged and were even opposed, and that yet desired one another. What this might mean we can see in Gandhi's accounting for the friendship of Hindus and Muslims in Khilafat. This is what he has to say, for example, about the Muslim reasons for such a friendship:

> I do not know that I have a right to arrogate greater purity for myself than for our Mussalman brethren. But I do admit that they do not believe in my doctrine of non-violence to the full extent. For them it is a weapon of the weak, an expedient. They consider Non-co-operation without violence to be the only thing open to them in the war of direct action. I know that, if some of them could offer successful violence, they would do to-day. But they are convinced that, humanly speaking, it is an impossibility. For them, therefore, Non-co-operation is a matter not merely of duty but also of revenge. . . . Although therefore their view-point is different from mine, I do not hesitate to associate with them and invite them to give my method a trial, for, I believe that the use of a pure weapon even from a mistaken motive does not fail to produce some good, even as the telling of truth, if only because for the time being it is the best policy, is at least so much to the good.[44]

And here are what Gandhi deems to be the Hindu reasons for Muslim friendship:

> But I would not go with the Mussalmans in any campaign of violence. I could not help them in promoting, for instance, an invasion of India through Afghanistan or otherwise for the purpose of forcing better peace terms. It is, I hold, the duty of every Hindu to resist any inroad on India even for the purpose specified as it is his duty to help his Mussalman brethren to satisfy their just demands by means of Non-co-operation or other form of suffering, no matter how great, so long as it does not involve loss of India's liberty or inflicting violence on any person. And I have thrown myself whole-heartedly into the Non-co-operation movement if only because I want to prevent any such armed conflict.[45]

[44] Gandhi, 'Khilafat: Further Questions Answered', *Young India*, 2 June 1920, pp. 172–3.

[45] Gandhi, 'The Non-Co-operation Committee', *Young India*, 23 June 1920, pp. 201–2.

These thoroughly prejudiced accounts, of accounts equally prejudiced, reveal for Gandhi a friendship that is interested but is not an interest. For this friendship involves no *quid pro quo*, only a desire for the friend in both senses of the phrase; a desire *for* the friend (that he should do such and such) and a desire for the *friend* (that he should be such and such). And it is in this 'desire for', which is removed from the placidity both of contractual and brotherly agreement, where Gandhi seems finally to place friendship: 'My goal is friendship with the world, and I can combine the greatest love with the greatest opposition to wrong.'[46]

Now Gandhi can and indeed has been accused of promoting his particular brand of friendship only to preserve the privileges of a specifically Hindu discrimination in all relations of caste and religion.[47] Such as it is, however, this discrimination is theorized coherently enough to leave no hypocritical gap between prejudice and friendship, so that Gandhi's discourse only becomes false when he falls, as he does now and then, into the language of interest or brotherhood. Of these lapses, the former is less offensive, interest already having received Gandhi's assent as a liberal imperium which friendship might oppose but cannot displace. The relation between interest and friendship here being conceived of as oppositional and, indeed, prejudiced, without the universalizing possibility of mediation.

Brotherhood of the egalitarian nationalist sort, however, remains un-thought, for it can be thought outside simple given-ness only as an interest to be destroyed back into the un-thought. But then this was not the only language of brotherhood available to Gandhi. Still possible even today is the old hierarchical notion of brotherhood, in whose terms the Muslim is defined as the Hindu's younger brother (and so also his sexual rival), a notion that is set up for betrayal and violence, complete with evocations of the division of a paternal inheritance. This inheritance, India, is curiously conceived as the mother of both by Gandhi as by other nationalists. So Gandhi's famous description of the partition of India as the vivisection of a mother by her sons, an

[46] Gandhi, 'The Question of Questions', *Young India*, 10 March 1920, p. 150.

[47] The classic account here is B.R. Ambedkar's *What Congress and Gandhi Have Done to the Untouchables* (Bombay: Thacker, 1946).

interesting reversal of the Solomonic parable, where it is the son who is to be partitioned between two mothers.

The idea of brotherhood Gandhi did frequently use, however, was, I think, a specifically Gujarati one, in which language the term brother (*bhai*) and indeed sister (*ben*) are routinely appended to all proper names, whether of relatives or strangers. In fact there are situations where even husbands and wives might call each other brother and sister, thus undoing any monolithic familial interpretation of these terms. Brotherhood here works in a nominalist and performative way, with no naturalist or even nationalist connotations attached. Thus Gandhi's use, in English and Gujarati, of 'Brother Jinnah' to name his greatest political rival, also a Gujarati.

Perhaps it was because Gandhi faced a choice between the violence of national brotherhood and the violence of liberal interest that he felt compelled to speak of friendship as something irreducible to either. Friendship, indeed, as a relation that did not merely align itself along given boundaries, like those dividing Hindus and Muslims, but that found itself within such boundaries as well. Apart from the primacy of neighbourliness, therefore, Gandhi did not differentiate between various kinds of friendship: 'My personal religion however allows me to serve my countrymen without hurting Englishmen or for that matter anybody else. What I am not prepared to do to my blood-brother I would not do to an Englishman. I would withdraw co-operation from him if it became necessary, as I had withdrawn from my own brother (now deceased) when it became necessary. I serve the Empire by refusing to partake in its wrong.'[48]

I have cited this text not to illustrate Gandhi's even-handedness so much as to point out that his translation of fraternal given-ness into the politics of friendship introduces rather than dissipates antagonism in such a relation. For if friendship is not the given, if it is always to be worked out, then a friend is a friend because potentially always a stranger, if not an enemy. In fact it might well be the latter possibility, of enmity, that finally gives friendship meaning: friendship not as an effort to pre-empt enmity, but enmity as friendship's very condition of possibility. After all, ethical life in general can only reveal itself in the

[48] Gandhi, 'How to Work Non-co-operation', 5 May 1920, p. 192.

face of enmity, not in that of inclination. This might be why the fraught relationship between Hindus and Muslims became for Gandhi the exemplum of any ethical relation. Whatever the reasons, then, for the rise and fall of the Khilafat Movement, it did provide Gandhi with his boldest experiment in such an ethics of enmity, an experiment whose problem can still be posed: how is a politics of friendship possible?

CHAPTER 4

The Anomaly of Kabir

Caste and Canonicity in Indian Modernity

MILIND WAKANKAR

Introduction: Kabir in Hindi Modernity

The name 'Kabir' is associated with a proliferating set of songs composed over the past five hundred years in North India, sung to this day in gatherings (*bhajan-mandalis*) of low-caste peasants and landless labourers.[1] They are also chanted in the monastic orders of Kabirpanthis set up by latterday followers of Kabir.[2] It has been remarked that human and divine language differs in one significant way, in that while God's names apply properly to each individual thing, human language tends to 'over-name' things.[3] The corpus bearing the signature of Kabir is a singular instance of this Adamite curse,

[1] The influence of Parita Mukta's seminal book on Mirabai will be apparent in this sentence. I am particularly struck by her attempt to draw on the social history of performance to understand Mirabai's politics, rather than solely on scholarly gloss and commentary. See *Upholding the Common Life: The Community of Mirabai* (Delhi: Oxford University Press, 1994).

[2] I rely here on David Lorenzen's accounts of Kabirpanthi practice. See especially 'Rituals of the Kabir Panth', in *Praises to a Formless God: Nirguni Texts from North India* (Albany: State University of New York Press, 1996), pp. 225–56; 'The Kabir Panth: Heretics to Hindus', in Lorenzen (ed.), *Religious Change and Cultural Domination* (Mexico: El Colegio de México, 1981), pp. 151–71; 'The Kabir Panth and Social Protest', in Karine Schomer and W.H. McLeod (eds), *The Sants* (Delhi: Motilal Banarsidass, 1987), pp. 281–304; 'The Historical Vicissitudes of Bhakti Religion', in Lorenzen (ed.), *Bhakti Religion in North India* (Albany: State University of New York Press, 1995), pp. 1–32.

[3] Walter Benjamin, 'On Language as Such and on the Language of Man', *Reflection: Essays, Aphorisms, Autobiographical* (New York: Schocken Books, 1978),

which conveys the secret both of creative expression and of the loss of original meaning. 'Kabir' points us to the idiomatic core of a language's history, where there is a ceaseless struggle between competing claims for nation in such terms as tradition, history and community. By the same token, Kabir draws our attention to that recalcitrant strain in language in general which, by refusing to remain still, helps turn the act of speech and the movement of writing into an untimely resource for marginalized groups such as Untouchables, who describe themselves today as Dalits ('the downtrodden'), and tribals. Couched in the many ways in which Kabir is sung, his Word (*shabd*) rises like a vast rumour from the western to the eastern reaches of North India and garners in this way new signatures, verses, and meanings. Suffice it to say there has never been a more adaptable body of work than Kabir's in the caste-riven society of the North, giving it an afterlife in popular song and cult very much like that of the ceaselessly manipulable epics and romances of old.

The facts about the historical Kabir (?–1518) are sketchy and have been gleaned in contrary ways from his poems themselves.[4] Kabir often describes himself as an Untouchable or Dalit weaver of Banaras—since the middle ages the North Indian citadel of upper-caste Hindu (brahmanical) scholasticism and caste hierarchy. He belonged to the weaver community of converts to Islam who still call themselves Julahas.[5] His dates are uncertain, but it is probable that he lived, working at his loom and composing his verse, at some point in the fifteenth

---

pp. 314–32: 'Things have no proper names except in God. For in his creative word, God called them into being, calling them by their proper names. In the language of man, however, they are over-named. There is, in the relation of human language to that of things, something that can approximately be described as "over-naming" [*Ueberbenennung*]: over-naming as the deepest linguistic reason for all melancholy and (from the point of view of the thing) of all deliberate muteness (330).' For the German, see Benjamin, *Sprache und Geschichte* (Stuttgart: Reclam, 1992), p. 47. 'Over-naming' is Benjamin's figure for translation as the profusion of meaning.

[4] For a discussion of Kabir's dates, see David Lorenzen, *Kabir Legends and Ananta-Das's Kabir Parachai* (Albany: SUNY Press, 1991), p. 18.

[5] For an analysis of communal (governmental) notions of Julaha culture in colonial sociology, notions that described them as 'bigoted' Muslims, see Gyanendra Pandey, 'The Bigoted Julaha', in his *The Construction of Communism in Colonial North India* (Delhi: Oxford University Press, 1992), pp. 66–108.

century. The face of early modern artisanal culture that Kabir presents to us—for which the craftsman's prehensile relation to tools is the tenor and the mystic poet's act of speaking the vehicle—compels us to imagine Kabir time and again as a living personality of enormous charisma and personal courage. This relation between 'work' and speech is also, as we shall see, the face of caste oppression and conversion. Yet the idea of Kabir that comes to us after centuries of hagiographic accounts, sectarian glosses, modern commentary, and the more recent appropriation within the Untouchable movement, remains a schizoid one.[6] The icon of Kabir in currency today has two dimensions. There is on the one hand the sceptic Kabir who negates everything, belongs to no one, affirms no identity. On the other hand there is Kabir the Dalit god who affirms everything by negating it. In the larger work of which this essay is a part, one of my aims has been to show how these two ideas of Kabir as a defiant romantic individualist and as a Dalit god are mutually incommensurable.[7]

[6] The standard text for the 'Western Recension' of Kabir is now Charlotte Vaudeville's *Kabir-Vani* (Pondicherry: Institut Français D'Indologie, 1982). Vaudeville's text brings together the sectarian recensions gleaned from the Dadu Panthi (founded by Dadu Dayal [1554–1603]) and Niranjani sects in Rajasthan and the Sikh Panth (the *Guru Granth*) in Punjab. The Rajasthani texts were first put together by Shyam Sundar Das, a leading Hindi activist of the Nagaripracharini Sabha and Ramchandra Shukla's mentor, collaborator on the *Kosh*, and colleague at the first Hindi department at Banaras Hindu University (BHU) in the 1920s. Das's edition, known as the *Kabir Granthavali* (Banaras: Nagari Pracharini Sabha, 1928), has been the canonical text of Kabir in Hindi departments to this day. The standard text for the 'Eastern' or Kabir Panthi recension, compiled in eastern Uttar Pradesh and/or Bihar in the late nineteenth century, is the one edited by Sukhdev Singh (Allahabad: Nilabh Prakashan, 1972). See the English translation by Linda Hess, *The Bijak of Kabir* (San Francisco: North Point Press, 1983). Large sections of these 'sectarian' recensions are now considered by philologists to be 'spurious' (inauthentically Kabir's). In the second edition of her translation of the Western Recension, after a reappraisal of the original manuscripts, Vaudeville has drastically reduced the number of poems attributed to Kabir. See her *A Weaver Named Kabir* (Delhi: Oxford University Press, 1993). It is worth noting from this archive that the Kabir 'corpus' is almost entirely a 'sectarian' corpus. Access to an authentic Kabir poem remains unavailable, save for those Vaudeville claims to have isolated on the basis of textual scholarship.

[7] See 'The Prehistory of the Popular: Caste and Canonicity in Indian Modernity' (Unpublished dissertation, Columbia University, 2002).

Who then is Kabir? We know merely that there is a mode of speaking associated with Kabir that has been endemic in subaltern cultural practice in North India for hundreds of years, one that holds together in one instance the act of saying 'Yes' and the act of saying 'No'. If nothing else, 'Kabir' is doubly comported in a posture of affirmation and negation towards the world and the deity.

Beyond this 'Kabir' is moot. Yet in the canon of Hindi literature, in the history of 'medieval' Indian religion, and in the annals of the secular vision of history on which the Indian state bases its idea of what it is to be modern, Kabir's place is a pre-eminent one. The pall of obscurity surrounding the historical Kabir has given way in the modern period to the light of controversy and debate. The name 'Kabir' has today become synonymous with a typically postcolonial question in India: can there be an indigenous modernity, indebted to but at the same time different from the idea of Europe? The historical energies that have since the time of nationalism continued to delve into the past, in an attempt to uncover the hidden bases for what Partha Chatterjee has called 'our modern', clutch again and again at the handful of things that are Kabir's—his apparently simple but powerful verses, his lowly background and his position as a convert.[8]

It is worth our while to try and understand why. Kabir's central place in the debate over the modern in India should recall us to the nature of Indian historical perception itself. History here in the modern era has been the vocation of missionaries, colonial bureaucrats, Orientalist scholars (indigenous and European), and bourgeois nationalists, both liberal and Marxist; it has very rarely been written by those who belong to the vast majority of Untouchables, peasants, women, and tribals. The latter appear instead as subjects in what can be called the 'history of the popular', a whole genre of elite writing that,

[8] Chatterjee distinguishes the movement within this modern itself as one that looks to the past as a means of 'escaping from the present'. We cannot, he writes, be the producers of our own modernity, for the 'bitter truth about our present is our subjection, our inability to be subjects in our own right.' And yet, he goes on to argue, 'it is because we want to be modern that our desire to be independent is transposed on to our past . . . we construct it only to mark the difference posed by the present.' Partha Chatterjee, 'Our Modernity', in *The Present History of West Bengal* (Delhi: Oxford University Press, 1997), pp. 209–10.

beginning in the late nineteenth century, drew both scholar and dilettante to the dense archive of popular practice in ritual, religion, and belief, extending as far back as antiquity. This archive was available to those among the colonial bureaucracy who practised a kind of ethnography by classifying for the purposes of the census the vast array of castes and religions.[9] And it was also of interest to two groups who played a central role in helping shape colonial policy with regard to language and education in the late colonial period. These comprised amateur scholars among colonial bureaucrats and European Orientalists on the one hand, and nationalist writers, critics, and indigenous Orientalists on the other. Both sets of scholars had begun to lay great store by the idea that a nation's distinctive traits could be discerned in the lived, everyday practices of the mass, as opposed to what seemed to be the often more eclectic and esoteric cultural practices of the elite. The notion of the popular implicit in their work was that of a complex 'life-world' comprising ritual, custom, and practice that could serve as a valuable index of the deep roots and extraordinary diversity of an authentically 'Indian' culture. The word 'lok', for instance, recurred often in debates on the popular in Hindi and other North Indian languages, and referred to 'the people' as well as to 'the worldly'. That is to say, it exemplified the greatly enhanced scope of the idea of culture implicit in the popular.

Why read the text of history for the popular? The colonial mission, with which such antiquarianism was complicit, was of necessity invested in gaining greater control over its subjects with the facility of greater ethnographic and historical insight into their varied cultures. For such scholars, complex religious formations, such as the worship of the Hindu god Vishnu, also known as Vaishnavism and widespread

[9] Nicholas Dirks's groundbreaking analysis of what he calls the 'enthnographic state' provides a crucial account of this effective governmentalization of the colonial state by means of caste. See Dirks, *Castes of Mind* (Princeton: Princeton University Press, 2001). In 'The Prehistory of the Popular', I describe this notion of the popular within the schema of a 'crytonymic' manoeuvre whereby the more intransigent aspects of the popular were sought by nationalist critics to be kept alive 'inside' the tradition. Within and without this inner crypt, the popular was to be posited as an object of ceaseless fascination by dint of its esoteric, secret aspects, yet kept alive paradoxically as dead.

in North India, provided the ground on which to establish 'scientifically' via philological and historical method a relation between Hinduism, for them the dominant faith in the land, and Christianity. Kabir, for instance, already drawn by European scholars into this Vaishnav tradition, seemed to them to be comparable to Luther, while his verses had the power of the Gospel of John.[10]

What drew indigenous scholars and thinkers to the inexhaustible archive of popular religion was the idea that had begun to establish itself of the nation as an age-old community of many faiths and creeds. India's heterogeneity of tradition appeared as a great barrier to national unity and was lamented by reformists from Ram Mohan Roy in the early decades of the nineteenth century to Dayanand Saraswati, founder in 1875 of the rationalist Arya Samaj, which strove to return to the original message of the ancient scriptures of Hinduism, the Vedas, by debunking popular myth and idol-worship.[11] By then, a newly emergent bourgeois nationalism, still in the process of asserting its claim to the nation as a whole, had found in the idea of 'one culture' a convenient bulwark both against the powerful intellectual legacy of the West introduced in India by colonial rule, and against all those 'fragments' of the imaginary nation (sects, castes, tribes, localities) that seemed resistant to the call to unity. The history of the popular was thus the point from which to seek in the distant past the origins of the greater national community that was to be reinstituted in the future, when foreign rule would be brought to an end.

This ecumenical project of Indian nationalism thus had its own goal, which was to derive from the popular in its many practices, precepts, and doctrines that primitive accord between subaltern and elite, hard to come by in the present, that would hold Indian society together. The attempt to read the text of the popular for this ancient affinity was of the greatest moment in the colonial formation of

[10] For an account of the European recovery of Kabir from the nineteenth century onwards, see Charlotte Vaudeville, *Kabir: Volume One* (London: Oxford University Press, 1974), pp. 3–36. For an exhaustive analysis of both the European and the nationalist project for a greater Vaishnavism as the resource for India's unity, see Vasudha Dalmia, *The Nationalization of Hindu Traditions: Bharatendu Harishchandra and Nineteenth-century Banaras* (Delhi: Oxford University Press, 1997), pp. 338–424.

[11] See Dalmia, *Nationalization*, p. 383.

disciplines, in that it gave rise to a new field in the cultural project of nationalism, which is to say, *criticism*. Why did criticism become the central force field in which the ideological strife over the soul of the nation would come to be waged? The answer has to do with the very significant fact that the rise of criticism in the modern Indian languages was contemporaneous with the growing interest in the history of the popular. While the role of criticism in the nationalist frame was to discover in the newly canonized literature of the past and the present the key to a new idea of community, it was the task of antiquarian research by nationalists (very much in sync with European Orientalists) to forge a new definition of religion.

The two projects often came together in the same scholar. So that one can imagine the great influence exercised in the evolving nationalist public sphere in the early 1900s by a strange hybrid, a combination of literary critic (or historian) and historian of religion, whom we can call the 'historian of the popular'. This was because the literary canon the former was helping to construct via commentary and critical edition overlapped to a considerable degree with the canon of religious texts from the vernacular middle ages that the latter, the historian of religion, was attempting to establish at the core of Indian religion. In his vision of the modern, this historian remained compelled by the pull of the Indian past, seeking by the labour of critical practice in texts that were at once 'literary' and 'religious' to transmit the obscure seed of the popular to the soil of a nascent nationalist project. The latter could now base on strong archival grounds its claim to speak for the nation as a whole, which is to say for 'the popular' itself shorn of its complex history. This will to interpretation of nationalist criticism directed itself towards clearing the space of the popular for an elite public ideal of tradition and meaning, a process that involved pushing aside the more obscure and opaque aspects of the popular itself, and ignoring its origins in radical low-caste protest and resistance. It is hard to understand the growth of criticism in the modern Indian languages without the mediating function of this specific kind of thinker and writer, who brought together moreover the esoteric strains of Orientalist research and the popular local traditions (themselves in the process of construction) of which the emerging indigenous literary canons seemed natural offshoots.

The Hindi critic Ramchandra Shukla's reading of Kabir in the 1930s is an illuminating instance of this coincidence of aims. Whether as a critic of literature intent on establishing Hindi's claim to the popular North Indian tradition, or a historian of religion invested in the legacy of Hinduism to the nation, Shukla invariably had recourse to the corpus of 'embodiments' that has come to be known as 'Bhakti' ('devotion').[12] For the idea of Bhakti as a 'tradition' is itself a symptom of its historical elaboration as an 'embodying' of devotion. This was arguably a process that began with the excursus on Bhakti in the *Gita*, found its modulation in the earliest Bhakti poets of sixth century southern India, and continued to influence modern accounts of the Bhakti period.[13] Which is to say that the insistence on reading bhakti as 'participation' in the secular life of the community of devotees was already, as far back as late antiquity, a function of a 'representation' of Bhakti.[14] This has three crucial implications for our understanding of

[12] For a conventional account of Bhakti that portrays it as a medieval upsurge of Hindu devotionalism, see Karine Schomer's 'Introduction' to Schomer and W.H. McLeod, eds, *The Sants: Studies in a Devotional Tradition*, pp. 1–20. For an extensive bibliography, see the appendices to *The Sants*, pp. 433–50.

[13] See Karen Pechelis Prentiss's *The Embodiment of Bhakti* (New York: Oxford University Press, 1999), p. 6. Paraphrasing a definition of *bhakti* by John Carman, Prentiss suggests that the 'term *bhakti* is used specifically to describe the human response to God and never to characterize God's response to human beings. In actively encouraging participation (which is a root meaning of bhakti), the poets [in the regional languages] represent bhakti as a theology of embodiment. Their thesis is that engagement with (or participation in) God should inform all of one's activities in worldly life. The poets encourage a diversity of activities, not limiting bhakti to established modes of worship—indeed some poets harshly criticize such modes—but instead making it the foundation of human life and activity in the world. As a theology of embodiment, bhakti is embedded in the details of human life.' The reference to Carman is to his entry on 'Bhakti' in *The Encyclopaedia of Religion: Volume Two*, ed. Mircea Eliade (New York: Macmillan, 1987).

[14] Prentiss goes on to make the following observation: 'The *Gita* is the first text we know of that uses the term bhakti as a technical term to designate a religious path. In its earliest usage, the term encompasses meanings of affection and attachment, but the *Gita* transformed the word into a technical religious term, specifying a religious path that encouraged active participation in worship without the sense of material and familial attachment that had characterized earlier uses of the word. Through comparison with traditional religious paths, the *Gita* distinguished bhakti and endowed it with autonomy as its own religious path; in the

the history of Bhakti. First, where 'bhakti' may have once referred merely to the localized worship of hearth-gods, it soon began to assume the 'technical' meaning of Bhakti as 'participation', a meaning that had already been put in place as early as the composition of the *Gita* in the first centuries CE. Secondly, the work of Bhakti has since the *Gita* come to mean a certain notion of the 'everyday', one amenable to the practices and techniques of 'participation.' One might even say that the secularization of Bhakti went along with its 'technical' appropriation in the *Gita*. And thirdly, the task of the Bhakti poets of the early modern era, from roughly the sixth to the sixteenth centuries, was to install a new 'dynamic' at the core of Bhakti, which is to say the bringing together of the transcendent and the local within poetic utterance. The last feature of Bhakti is reminiscent of a central tenet of 'vernacular' expression, which is the use of idioms of plurality to draw attention to the persistent asymmetry between the transcendent and the local. We can go so far as to say that the vocation of Bhakti was to introduce the idea of heterogeneity into the transcendentalized secularism of the *Gita*;[15] in short, the calling of the Bhakti poets was

---

Gita, bhakti denotes a method of religious experience that leads to liberation. As many scholars have noted, the *Gita* can be understood as a response to widespread Indian religious perspectives that view the body negatively. For the *Gita* the field of worship is coextensive with the field of ordinary human activity, if one's mind is focused upon God. Unlike classical law books, which sought to legislate correct human action, and unlike formalized prayers and ritual manuals, which located worship in a specific time and place, bhakti is represented in the *Gita* as a religious perspective that can inform all actions, at any time and in any place. This technical meaning of the *Gita* became authoritative, and the *Gita* was considered one of the three foundational texts (*prasthanatraya*) for Hindu religious commentary by the great philosophers Shankara and Ramanuja, as well as in later Sanskrit philosophical tradition. . . . Although the *Gita* and the [*bhakti*] poems in regional languages share [the thesis of embodiment] . . . the *Gita* is a teaching text in the question-and-answer format, in which the protagonist (Arjuna) learns—at times painfuly slowly—about bhakti. In contrast, the regional language poems presuppose that the author has bhakti . . . The bhakti authors detail their response to God and their response to their poems. There is an important dynamic at work in the poems, as the authors join together transcendent and local themes. The poems are personal, yet the authors encourage others to participate in their worldview; similarly, God is transcendent, yet he is concerned locally.'

[15] The structure of this transcendentalized secularism, in its staged foreclosure

necessarily, and with greater or lesser success, that of a detranscendentalization of Bhakti via the experience of the 'local.' It is in the interstices of this chequered history of detranscendentalization in the dominant strains of Bhakti that we should locate both the 'mystical' utterance of such poets as Kabir as well as, in the same gesture, the mystery or secret of caste subalternity (as the irreducible but always foreclosed trace of the local).[16]

As we move to a discussion of representations of Bhakti in the colonial period, therefore, we cannot assume that Bhakti was ever at any point in history a function of an ecstatic communion somewhere in the archaic past, prior to representation. Indeed, in this sense the history of the embodiment of Bhakti extended well into precolonial times. The point is, however, that the colonial period inaugurated a

---

of the concrete present, is the subject of the remarkable reading of the *Gita* in Gayatri Chakravorty Spivak's *A Critique of Postcolonial Reason* (Cambridge: Mass: Harvard University Press, 1999), p. 56, where she writes: 'Through the grotesquely phenomenal representation (by Arjuna) of Krishna masticating [in his *vishwarupadarshan*, or vision of the universal form] the details of the immediately perceptible phenomenal reality in time and space, the authority of the here and now is undermined and, in the reaction (by Arjuna), the phenomenality of affect is denied and produced as excuse.'

[16] 'Detranscendentalization' as such is always an incomplete project, for it implies a relentless 'working-through'. The Bhakti poets strove to obey the injunction of a persistently changing, unknowable and irreducible idea of the local or of the everyday (both of which are figures of otherness in Bhakti); but their attempt to abide by the injunction of the local/everyday was constantly stymied by the procedures of 'participation' that they inherited as part of the hegemonic rationality of embodiment in Bhakti first inaugurated by the *Gita*. When they invoked (willy-nilly, as a trace in the textual weave of their writings) the radical otherness of the local/everyday, they were in the moment of 'detranscendentalization'; but when they followed the script of 'participation' in the deity, they invariably 'transcendentalized' the other as an extra-subjective authority. Between the two moments (themselves irreducible, recuperable only analytically), Bhakti in the bhashas represented a highly enabling and productive failure to 'detranscendentalize'. If we understand the 'vernacular' less as a language than as an ethic of plurality implicit in the practical everyday ethics of caste subalternity, we get a sense of the unprecedented interweaving of the two moments in the work of the Bhakti poet with the greatest commitment to the vernacular, 'Kabir', and even more so in the successive authors of the Kabir recensions.

new moment in the history of 'criticism' in the Indian languages, one determined in reductive ways by the imagined community of the nation. For this reason, all three of the historical features of Bhakti, along with its apparatus of techniques outlined above, became subject to a reinscription in colonial modernity. First, as part of this momentous transition in the representational framework of Indian nationalism, the technical meaning of Bhakti as 'participation' was further refined to include the new subjectal techniques of being-affected (*bhavukta*): if Bhakti had once meant the cognition of the One by means of the Many, via a variety of localized modes of cognition, it now became the cognition of the One through the undifferentiated, homogeneous mass of devotees/nationalists. The common sets of assumptions guiding both Indian and European Orientalists in their search for a popular Hinduism of 'love' that attempted in the Bhakti period to 'reform' the brahmanical apparatus of legalized ritual and norms, have been extensively documented by Vasudha Dalmia and Karen Prentiss, among others.[17] Scholars such as Shukla, as Prentiss reminds us, were the first to privilege the affective worship of the embodied God (the *sagunatmak* Bhakti of Tulsidas and Surdas) over the worship of a disembodied God without attributes (the *nirgunatmak* Bhakti of Kabir), establishing as critical commonplaces about popular religion, distinctions that are today increasingly held to be tendentious and untenable.[18] Secondly, the notion of an 'everyday' Bhakti was extended to include the entire range of popular practice in a univocal manner (hence the valence of 'the popular' in nationalist discourse). And

[17] See also Krishna Sharma's *Bhakti and the Bhakti Movement: A New Perspective* (New Delhi: Munshiram Manoharlal, 1987).

[18] Thus Prentiss: 'The early orientalists had opposed jnana to bhakti, just as they had implicitly opposed two theistic perspectives, pantheism (*advaita*) and monotheism (*Bhakti*), whereas scholars [such as Shukla] now distinguish[ed] nirgun and sagun perspectives within Bhakti. Thus, in the contemporary understanding of Bhakti through poets' images of God, scholars include elements that the orientalists tended to distance, yet the opposition between knowledge and emotion is retained [in however sublated a form]', p. 21. For a critique of the distinction itself as a product of hagiographic/sectarian interpretation, see John Stratton Hawley, 'The Nirgun/Sagun Distinction in Early Manuscript Anthologies of Hindi Devotion', in David N. Lorenzen, ed., *Bhakti Religion in North India* (Albany: State University of New York Press, 1995).

thirdly, the practice of the detranscendentalization of Bhakti via locality was replaced by a transcendent and highly exclusive notion of the nation as community.

Likewise, for Shukla the 'modernity' of Bhakti, which is to say its place in nationalism's story of its own hoary origins, lay not in its tone of radical upheaval, its vernacular intransigence, but in its claim to an 'Indian' tradition. This idea of tradition, itself an outcrop of the turn in the history of representations of Bhakti consequent upon colonial modernity, became the touchstone for what was truly worth preserving in literature and religion. Responding in an implicit way to the missionary and Hindu reformist blitz against the so-called 'irrational' practices of popular religion, committed to the rational Enlightenment ideal of social transparency and discipline, and influenced by the European Orientalist attempt to assimilate Bhakti to Christianity, Shukla sought in Bhakti the seeds for an enlightened national idea of devotion to a greater cause. As I have suggested elsewhere,[19] the roots of an 'Indian' responsibility lay for Shukla in Bhakti's traditional devotionalism, which was in effect a Bhakti shorn of its popular roots, and relentlessly 'rationalized'.

It was while trying to read into the text of the popular precisely this idea of tradition that Shukla came up against the problem of Kabir. Shukla's peculiar interpretation of Kabir is a thread running through the entire range of his literary historical and his longer polemical essays. The interpretive ambition that underlay Shukla's poetics of responsibility will be easier to comprehend if we take this concrete, and in fact very representative, instance of his critical discrimination. Shukla's Bhakti poets of choice had been Surdas (1478–?) and Tulsidas (1532–1623), the critical editions of whose works he had, as I have mentioned, begun to prepare in the 1920s.[20] Representing the

[19] See 'The Moment of Criticism in Nationalist Thought: Ramchandra Shukla and the Poetics of a Hindu Responsibility', in Saurabh Dube, ed., 'Enduring Enchantments', a Special Issue of *South Atlantic Quarterly*, 101:4 (Fall 2002), pp. 987–1014.

[20] For a fuller account of their poetry, see Ronald Stuart McGregor, *Hindi Literature from its Beginnings to the Nineteenth Century*, pp. 76–80, 109–17. Shukla's introduction, 'Goswami Tulsidas', to his edition of the *Tulsi Granthavali* was published in 1923, the introduction to his *Jayasi Granthavali* in 1924, both by the Sabha. His edition of Surdas's *Bhramar-git Sar* was published in 1925.

tradition of worshipping a god with attributes, known as *sagun* ('determinate') Bhakti, the late-fifteenth-century poetry of Surdas drew an idyllic picture of the childhood of the Vishnu avatar Krishna. While the late-sixteenth-century poetry of Tulsidas extolled the grace and valour of the other Vishnu avatar Ram in his relations with his wife and family, and in his battle against the demon-king of Lanka, Ravan. Both poets drew their protagonists from the popular epic traditions in ancient Sanskrit (Ram and Krishna figure prominently in the *Ramayana* and the *Mahabharata*). Their storylines were the stuff of legend. Their ideals rested in the hollow of a pan-Indian spirit of love, amity, and courage. And their poetry, written in the Brajbhasha and Avadhi dialects of modern Hindi, could serve as a compelling argument for the long ancestry of Hindi traced back to the early middle ages, a time that saw the extraordinary flowering of regional literatures in India.[21] Here then were two poets who brought Hindi in line with the most widely disseminated traditions of Bhakti in north India, and who at the same time brought Indian religion, exemplified in Bhakti, in tune with the ideal of a rationalized and natural theology directed towards the soul of the modern nationalist subject. Here too was evidence that modern Hindi's (or Khari Boli's) roots lay in the flourishing dialects of Avadhi and Brajbhasha in which poetry continued to be composed up until the late nineteenth century, before the rise of modern Hindi itself. Here, moreover, was proof that the kind of immediate embrace of a manifest god represented by the still dominant traditions of Ram- and Krishna-Bhakti was far from being what European Orientalists and missionaries thought was a vulgar and mostly arcane mode of fetishism, one whose philosophical origins lay in high Hindu abstraction. It found instead its strongest expression in the popular legends and lore from which Surdas and Tulsidas derived their storylines.

And therein, in truth, lay the problem with Kabir. For the religious, linguistic and literary idiom of this early-fifteenth-century poet of low-caste origins, placed him at a great and seemingly unbridgeable distance from the later poetry of Surdas and Tulsidas. The latter was closer to the dominant (mostly upper-caste) traditions of North India

[21] For an account of the rise of a standardized Khari Boli Hindi, see Alok Rai, 'The Heroic Agenda', in *Hindi Nationalism* (Delhi: Orient Longman, 2000), pp. 65–92.

in terms of literary technique, religious aspiration and language. Whereas the 'crude' unfinished verses of Kabir, written in a mixed dialect that was straightforwardly neither Brajbhasha nor Avadhi, and nor Bhojpuri, Punjabi or Rajasthani belonged in tone and texture to what was known as 'Hindavi'.[22] The latter was the popular language spoken widely in medieval northern India up until modern times, before colonial bureaucrats and language nationalists in the nineteenth century began to promote the idea of two separate languages (with two distinct scripts), Urdu and Hindi, derived artificially from the common Perso-Arabic and Sanskritic fund of spoken Hindavi. The conflict between Urdu and Hindi had by Shukla's time become synonymous with the colonial and nationalist commonplace that the Urdu-speaking Muslims and the Hindi-speaking Hindus represented two distinct and incommensurable cultural and national streams in northern India. So that from Shukla's perspective in the 1930s, Kabir's idiom, redolent of the cosmopolitan era of medieval Hindavi when the modern idea of a homogeneous (Hindu) national tradition had not been current, and still bearing traces of ecumenical Sufi and Islamic influence, seemed suspiciously 'mystical' and 'foreign' to the generally accessible, more 'Hindu' (and therefore more 'Indian') values enshrined in the work of Surdas and Tulsidas.

Moreover, Kabir's god was not a determinate (*sagun*) avatar of Vaishnav Bhakti such as Ram or Krishna, accessible collectively through

[22] For the emergence of Hindi out of a colonial contest with Urdu, see Rai above; also Dalmia, 'Hindi as the National Language of the Hindus', *Nationalization*, pp. 146–221. See Mahendra's analysis of these heterogeneous registers in Kabir in his *Kabir ki Bhasha* (Delhi: 1969). Comparing the linguistic analyses of Mahendra with those of M. Jayaswal and B.P. Dube, Vaudeville writes: 'the three authors have come to quite different conclusions: for Jayaswal, the basic language of Kabir's verses is old Khari Boli [standardized Hindi] and the mixture of dialects it exhibits simply reflect the *rashtrabhasha* ('national language') of his time . . . Bhagavan Dube, on the other hand draws the conclusion that the basic language of Kabir's verses is Braj—but the Braj-bhakha [*bhasha*] of his time was not "pure", it was influenced by other dialects, principally by Khari Boli, but also by Punjabi, Rajasthani and Avadhi. For Mahendra, Kabir's language is a mix of Avadhi, Braj and Khari Boli, with some Rajasthani, Bhojpuri and Punjabi . . .', p. 68. On the narrative achievements of the Hindavi tradition in the early modern period, see the seminal forthcoming work of Aditya Behl.

love and devotion in a narrative and ritual mode, but was an indeterminate (*nirgun*) god lacking in attributes, who could be reached individually by casting aside doubt (*bhram*) and embracing knowledge (*gyan*).[23] More intolerable for Shukla was the fact that Kabir was clearly under the influence of older traditions of Shiva worship in yoga (especially those practised by the 'Nathpanthi' sect) and Tantra, which in their obscure metaphysics and sexual symbolism appeared arcane, illicit and otherworldly to the rationalist historian of the popular, representing marginal currents of belief and ritual that (for Shukla) had long since been superseded in the north by the dominant traditions of Ram and Krishna worship. Kabir's modern adherents moreover were low-caste groups, mostly peasants and tribals, whereas Tulsidas and Surdas were the favoured saint-poets of the landed proprietor class in his native north-west provinces whom Shukla saw as the nation's Kshatriya or 'warrior-caste' in the fight against the British. And most significantly, though rarely referred to explicitly by Shukla, there was the incontrovertible fact that Kabir himself belonged to the weaver (Julaha) caste of converts to Islam, placing him outside the pale both of the identifiably Hindu and the Muslim world.

Bearing this triple stigma of the foreign, the esoteric, and the subalternity of caste, Kabir's corpus understandably did not fare well in the canonical stakes of the Hindi enlightenment. Shukla returned to the problem of Kabir in essay after essay, and sought to derive his own highly complex idea of the popular from the texts of Surdas and Tulsidas, using Kabir very much as a counterfoil. Shukla's polemical attitude towards Kabir informed his reading and reconstruction of the Hindi 'tradition' as a whole. The object of his ire was always the current of popular enthusiasm and mystery in the past—one that ran from Yogic mysticism of the ancient Nathpanthis, of which he found telltale

[23] David Lorenzen argues in the course of his work on the Kabirpanthi sects that the *nirgun* tradition is more commonly associated with the 'ideological resistance' of the subaltern classes, while the *sagun* Bhakti tradition has often articulated 'a social ideology intended to serve as a sort of psychological glue that helps preserve both the harmony and privilege within the religious community and within society as whole (including its subordinate communities). ' The *sagun* tradition remains in this sense the dominant tradition of north India. See 'The Historical Vicissitudes of Bhakti Religion', p. 13.

echoes in the medieval poetry of Kabir, through to Sufism, and extending well into his own time in the guise of the Indian romanticism of Chhayavad ('chiaruscuro'), represented by the poetry of Suryakant Tripathi Nirala, Sumitranandan Pant, Jayshankar Prasad and Mahadevi Verma.[24] For Shukla, Chhayavad was merely a symptom of a pernicious current in Western thought, that of a kind of aestheticist individualism (*vyakti-vaichitryavad*) that he detected in Blake, in the work of the Decadents, and in Benedetto Croce's theory of expressionism.

Kabir's resurgence in the history of the popular, and his rehabilitation in the Hindi canon would have to wait until Hazariprasad Dwivedi's *Kabir* (1942), a book that with great passion and sheer force of argument, backed by an impressive knowledge of the high Hindu as well as the popular tradition, catapulted Kabir to the centre of the Hindi canon. Long considered the finest scholarly monograph in Hindi, it has since established Dwivedi's own reputation as the chronicler of an 'alternative' tradition. The latter had the virtue of being able to link the vast corpus of ancient and medieval lore of popular thought and practice with the democratic strains underlying much of the new kind of writing in Hindi. The novel, which Premchand had established as a mode of social critique by from the 1910s onwards, and the Indian Romanticism of the so-called Chhayavadi ('chiarascuro') school of poets in the 1930s, were powerful instances of these new trends. The Marxist account of Indian history in Hindi criticism, which had drawn for at least three decades after Shukla's death in 1941 on his vision of a radical community of devotee-subjects of Bhakti, working to rid the nation of foreign yoke, now needed to be revised.

Yet the most eloquent and powerful plea for such a rethinking of the Hindi canon, one that used Dwivedi's *Kabir* as its point of departure, would come almost forty years later, shortly after Dwivedi's death in 1979. The renewal of the debate around Kabir was precipitated by the publication in 1983 of a seminal work by Namvar Singh. Singh's book, *Dusri Parampara ki Khoj* (In Search of the Other Tradition) became

[24] For a history of the Chhayavad movement, see Karine Schomer, *Mahadevi Varma*. The classic account in Hindi of this variegated movement which emphasized a uniquely new relation to nature, seen as a passing and mysterious phenomenon of universal pathos, one that could be experienced only by the lone poet, see Namvar Singh's *Chhayavad*.

a touchstone for serious attempts to critique the history of canon-formation in Hindi, building on the history of what Singh referred to as the communitarian ('*jatiya*') tradition in the Hindi-speaking region of north India.[25] The book undertook moreover a wide-ranging critique of the Marxist tradition in Hindi criticism, and sought to revive all those aspects of the Hindi canon that Shukla had declared off limits. More crucially, Singh sought to underscore the importance of Dwivedi's research into the popular for the Hindi tradition as a whole.

What precisely was so new and strikingly original in Dwivedi's reading of Kabir? There had after all been signs of awakened interest in Kabir in scholarly circles as far back as 1916 when the poet 'Hariaudh' published the first selection of Kabir poems in Hindi. And in 1928, the venerable Hindi academic Shyamsundar Das had written a long critical introduction to his edition of the western Indian manuscripts of Kabir, the *Kabir Granthavali*.[26] However, a tone of upper-caste disdain and a condescending attitude to the quality of Kabir's verse considerably marred the critical fallout of these collections. Nevertheless, in the climate of increased nationwide violence in the 1930s between Hindus and Muslims, it was not long before Kabir was claimed by the left-leaning sections of the Indian National Congress, and by writers associated with the Progressive Writers Movement, as a symbol of 'communal' amity and peace between the two religious communities, referring the national tradition back to its syncretic and tolerant roots in antiquity. Yet Kabir's growing role as a political icon for the Congress's ideal of a secular nationalism that could speak for the majority Hindu as well as the minority Muslim community, did not alter the status quo in the centres of canonical debate in Hindi, Banaras and Allahabad, where Surdas and Tulsidas remained the quintessential saint-poets of the dominant North Indian tradition.

Born to a high Brahmin family in Ballia, the easternmost of the north-west provinces, and educated at the conservative bastion of Hindi studies, the Banaras Hindu University (established in 1916), Dwivedi's affective and intellectual roots had also been nourished in this tradition. His first book, *Sur-Sahitya* (The Literature of Surdas),

25 *Dusri Parampara ki Khoj* (Delhi: Rajkamal Prakashan, 1983).

26 See the introduction to Babu Shyam Sundar Das, ed., *Kabir Granthavali* (Banaras: Nagari Pracharani Sabha, 1968), pp. 7–51.

written in 1936 when he was twenty-nine, had attempted to reinterpet the ethical tradition in Bhakti in the Hindi-speaking North in terms of the message of love (*prem*), in Surdas which (unlike in Tulsidas's more conservative account of the social) sought the radical transcendence of social barriers.[27] Reading Kabir's work very much within the tradition of Surdas, but finding in the former the qualities of abandon, play and social intransigence that were (for Dwivedi) the essence of the radical popular tradition inaugurated by Bhakti in the North, Dwivedi sought to argue for the idea of Kabir as a romantic rebel, a sceptic for all seasons, one who like Diogenes could brook no false word, affirm no false doctrine and could be identified with no given tradition, sect or creed. Dwivedi wrote: 'Why people should want to think of Kabir as a syncretist (*sarva-dharm-samanvayakari*) of the Hindu and Muslim religions is hard to fathom. Kabir's own path was quite clear. He wasn't one to merely bring together these faiths by paying each a token tribute. He was more like the revolutionary who tore through the web of ritualized conduct and custom. Compromise was by no means his path.'[28] Dwivedi's Kabir, then, stood in an antipodal relation to the notion of secular tolerance for all faiths endorsed by Indian nationalism's vision, formulated most influentially in the writings of Jawaharlal Nehru, for the independent secular state of the future. Instead, Kabir (in Dwivedi's estimation) referred his readers to longstanding subaltern traditions of dissent and resistance in Indian society. As a figurehead for this radical undercurrent in the popular, Dwivedi's Kabir represented rebellion, protest, and the task of a radical upheaval in moribund social norms. Juxtaposed against the Nehruvian idea of the modern Indian nation as an imagined comity of faiths (so that for Nehru Hindu–Muslim riots could only be vestiges of pre-modern habits of mind), Kabir's Word stood instead for a relentless criticism of all tradition and conduct, and implied a kind of freedom of belief that refused to affirm anything but its own ideal of an indeterminate (nirgun) god. It should be said that Dwivedi's own transformed understanding of Kabir and Bhakti as a whole was indebted to the extraordinary energies being directed towards research into the history of the

[27] See *Sur-Sahitya* (Delhi: Rajkamal Prakashan, 1973 [1936]).

[28] *Kabir* (*Kabir ke vyaktitva, sahitya and darshanik vicharon ki alochana*) (Delhi: Rajkamal Prakashan, 1993 [orig. 1942]), p. 147. Hereafter *Kabir*. All translations from this essay are mine.

popular at Tagore's university at Shantiniketan (near Calcutta), known as Vishwa Bharati, which Dwivedi joined as a Hindi instructor and scholar-at-large in 1930.[29] The ecumenical pan-Indian thrust of research at Shantiniketan, working under the inspiration of Tagore, had already attracted a whole cross-section of European philologists and historians of religion and art such as Sylvain Levi and Stella Kramrisch. Tagore's close associate Kshitimohan Sen had brought out a four-volume critical edition in 1910 of Kabir songs taken from the Bengali oral recension of the Vaishnavism-inflected western Indian tradition of Kabir. And Tagore himself translated into English a selection from this edition, which remains the most widely available edition of Kabir in the West, *One Hundred Poems of Kabir* (1914), with a critical introduction by Evelyn Underhill, an authority on Western mysticism.[30] Openly acknowledging his debt to Tagore, Dwivedi's *Kabir* often had recourse to the former's poetry and ideas, and in this way followed Tagore in opening the history of the popular to marginal and sub-cultural forms of social protest in the past.

Posited as this principle of radical autonomy in the tradition, Dwivedi's Kabir could not easily be assimilated to the dominant traditions of protest and historical action in North India. For where earlier scholars such as Shukla had looked in the work of Surdas and Tulsidas for the ideal of a national community in action, Dwivedi pushed Hindi criticism's nationalist investment in socially purposive literature in the direction of the radical individual, the singular and 'dangerous' instance to whose specific protest the ideal of national community

[29] Dwivedi spent the most productive twenty years of his life at Shantiniketan, moving to Banaras Hindu University in 1950 for a brief but troubled tenure as the head of its Hindi department. During his two decades at Shantiniketan, he edited the *Abhinav Bharati Granthmala* and the *Vishwa Bharati Patrika*. For these and other details of Dwivedi's career, see the Sahitya Akademi's short biographical volume, Vishwanath Prasad Tiwari, *Hazariprasad Dwivedi* (New Delhi: Sahitya Akademi, 1996), p. 13.

[30] It has been argued that Tagore's Kabir was very much an instance of his own fascination for the 'mystical' poetry of the later Yeats; Tagore moreover read into Kabir's *nirgun* ('indeterminate') god his cherished notion of a monotheistic God, inspired both by the rationalist ideas of the reformist Brahmo Samaj, and the traditions of popular Vaishnav religiosity inaugurated by Chaitanya in Bengal. See Vijay C. Mishra, 'Two Truths Told: Tagore's Kabir', in Karine Schomer and W. H. McLeod, eds, *The Sants*, pp. 167–80.

would have to respond, inaugurating a new ethics of the individual in nationalism. In this way, Dwivedi emphasized for the first time the 'personality' of Kabir himself, and argued forcefully for both the power of Kabir's verse (calling him famously a 'dictator with language'), and for Kabir's status less as a Vaishnav devotee like Surdas and Tulsidas, than a guru in his own right. To cite a well-known passage from the conclusion to *Kabir*, for Dwivedi

> Kabir was a religious guru [*dharmguru*]. Which is why the spiritual sap [*ras*] of his sayings should alone be savoured. Scholars, however, have used and studied Kabir in various ways, traditionally choosing to see him as a poet, social reformer, preacher of religious syncretism [*samanvay*], arbiter of Hindu–Muslim unity, upholder of a specific sect, and as a thinker and interpreter after the traditions of Indian philosophy that follow from the Vedanta . . . [They tend to forget that] there has never been a personality [*vyaktitva*] like Kabir in the thousand-year history of Hindi . . . Abandon [*masti*], a rebellious [*phakkarana*] spirit and the acuteness that comes with a castigation of all things, [such qualities] make Kabir the most singular individual [*advitiya vyakti*] in Hindi literature. What extends its spell over the range of his utterances is [the force of] this 'all-conquering personality'. (*Kabir*, p. 170)

I will return to the implications of this notion of a 'singular individual' in the next section. Here it should suffice for us to note the crucial relation implied between the historical project of Hindi and the idea of Kabir's unique personality ('there has never been a personality [*vyaktitva*] like Kabir in the thousand-year history of Hindi'). Which of the two terms serves as a basis for the other? It is clearly the inexhaustible depth of this personality in Kabir, its potential for interminable interpretation, that makes meaningful all of a sudden the Hindi millennium. That is to say that it is the force of Kabir, transformative in its goal and opening up an abyss in time, which makes the past history of Hindi understandable. Understandable, that is, *within the terms* of the interruption that Kabir represents. Dwivedi's quest for an insight into Kabir's 'personality' then has the hallmarks of both an interpretative and a historical agenda.

With Dwivedi the history of popular, which the new discipline of criticism had arrogated to itself as its chief and only object, can be seen as having entered a new stage, which we can call the stage of 'interpretation'. In Shukla the popular had been read in terms of its *proximity* to dominant longstanding ideas of belief and community; so that whatever eluded the 'discipline' of Shukla's rigour had to bear the brunt of his condescension: Kabir was one significant casualty of this (Shukla) phase in the history of the popular. His pioneering and still influential account of the popular had been 'disciplinary' in two senses. First, in the sense of laying the ground for a new area of knowledge ('criticism') in the colonial contest of disciplines, wherein nationalism sought to lay claim at once to a universal idea of knowledge and to objects of knowledge different from that of the West. (The idea of an 'Indian' history of the popular as the unique object of criticism takes precedence here.) And disciplinary too, in the sense that certain 'decisions' had had to be made with regard to what could and could not constitute the Hindi canon, especially since the latter was being forged in close adherence to an idea of a popular tradition (exemplified in Tulsidas and Surdas) in the North. To this process whereby the popular came to be disciplined, Dwivedi counterposed another practice, which was to read the popular in terms of its *irreducibility* to the mainstream. The divide between elite and subaltern, dominant and marginal became crucial here, and continues to inspire the progressive stream of Hindi criticism today. Here Dwivedi would rely on his romantic account of Kabir to argue that the popular was the locus of a carefree, uninhibited individuality. This version of 'the popular' now contained within itself the seed of what was seen to be an age-old Indian idea of freedom from social and personal restraint; Dwivedi's challenge was that the dominant national tradition in the North would have to revise its cultural assumptions in order to embrace a marginal tradition of transgressive and rebellious (*phakkar*) behaviour. Only then, argued Dwivedi, would a truly 'national' tradition emerge as the locus of the cherished primitive accord between subaltern and elite that remained compelling both to Dwivedi's nationalism and to critics who followed in his wake.

This momentous transition from a disciplinary to an interpretive idea of the popular had its own peculiar repercussions. Now that the popular had become the locus of an interpretive agenda, and had begun to be read for its opaque and obscure features, there was always the danger of 'over-interpretation'. Dwivedi's own investment in the marginal was after all propelled by an ideal that was strictly nationalist in two specific senses; it sought to assimilate to the Hindi tradition, and hence to the national tradition as a whole to which Hindi was now arrogated, vast areas of popular practice accessible only to the archivist, the philologist, and the historian of religion. Such a project was also nationalist in the sense that it sought to establish on the basis of the popular the grounds for one single homogeneous Hindu tradition, which could then serve as the religious core of national culture. The case of Kabir alone is enough to remind us that such an ambition is reductive in the extreme; for neither in terms of literary form, nor language, and certainly not in terms of religion, is it easy to write Kabir into any monolithic idea of 'literature' or of 'religion'. But it was because the popular had become an archive 'for' interpretation that such a conflation was possible in the first place.

It is precisely this tendency to underplay all that is truly unassimilable to the so-called 'religious' tradition, that is to say, aspects of the popular that represent a serious challenge to the dominant brahmanical tradition, that has made Dwivedi, and by the same token, the entire tradition of Kabir criticism, and of dominant traditions of criticism in Hindi as a whole, the target of a powerful recent critique by the Dalit scholar, Dr Dharmvir.[31] For Dharmvir, not only does Dwivedi assimilate Kabir to the high Hindu tradition that the latter worked against all his life, but he disregards the latter's truest achievement, which was to establish 'another religion', of which he was both god and messiah, and which he founded for Dalits alone.

[31] Dharmvir is a scholar-civil servant who has written books on the Dalit leader Bhimrao Ambedkar, the playwright Vishnu Prabhakar, and the saint-poet Raidas. The book that placed him in the centre of controversy was *Kabir ke Alochak* (New Delhi: Vani Prakashan, 1997), in which Dharmvir launched an attack on the entire tradition of critical writing in Hindi on Kabir, and accused it of 'brahmanizing' Kabir. The chapter on Dwivedi in this book, titled 'Surya par Pura Grahan' ('Total Eclipse of the Sun') has been translated into English by Priyadarshan, and published in the journal *Hindi* 1:1 (April–June 2000), pp. 188–207. Apart from the key chapter on Dwivedi in *Kabir ke Alochak*, we now have Dharmvir's extended three-volume engagement with Dwivedi's *Kabir*, entitled *Kabir: Nai Sadi Men* (*Kabir in the New Era*). The titles of the three volumes, all published in the same year, are as follows: *Kabir: Doctor Hazariprasad Dwivedi ka Prakshipt Chintan* (New Delhi: Vani Prakashan, 2000); *Kabir aur Ramanand: Kimvadantian*; *Kabir: Baj bhi, Kapot bhi, Papiha bhi*.

There are two highly provocative but related claims here. First, there is the allegation that Dwivedi remains a high Hindu (brahmanical) scholar wishing to assimilate Dalit thinking to the Hindu fold. This, despite the unfaltering rigour and astuteness of Dwivedi's analyses, and despite his caution both against reading Kabir in token secular or syncretic (*samanvayvadi*) terms. So that where Dwivedi's text on Kabir had seemed to radical left scholars such as Namvar Singh to inaugurate and unveil an alternative tradition in the Hindi-speaking region of the North, it is quite clear to Dharmvir that Dwivedi remains unmistakably within that dominant high Hindu tradition in which the histories of low-caste peoples rarely receive adequate attention. Dharmvir's second accusation, made against the backdrop of the increased mobilization along religious lines of what was until the mid 1980s a largely secular project for an Indian nationalism, is even more provocative. For to argue in the present political conjuncture in India for an alternative religion for Dalits, with Kabir at its head, is already to say that there is a genuine need for a 'religious' as opposed to a merely literary or literary-critical revival among Dalits.

We might well join Dharmvir's detractors in Hindi studies and the history of religions in putting to him the following set of questions. To begin with, is not Dharmvir's yet another attempt to read as 'religious' what is really the secular vocation of a great medieval poet? Kabir did after all work all his life as a weaver. His poems continue to be sung by low-caste landless peasant and tribal converts to the Kabirpanthi sect and are still part of the folk wisdom of agricultural peoples in huge swathes of North India including Gujarat, Rajasthan, Punjab, Bihar, and Uttar Pradesh. More so, his quite apparent aversion to religious bigotry and ritual of any kind establishes him as a modern and secular 'Indian' before his time. Does not Dharmvir's account of Kabir's religion derive its central tenets, in however negative and oppositional a way, from the very tradition that he seeks to estrange Kabir from? They will argue further: To detach the figure of Kabir from the dominant, high Hindu tradition is commendable, but does not the move to extricate him from the tradition as a whole—its dominant and radical tendencies included—forgo, in the attempt, the very possibility of a solidarity with marginalized popular traditions within the Hindu fold? What would be the shape of this radical Dalit religion, which would place itself at such an absolute and non-negotiable remove from the social history of the popular? Where then would this 'other' tradition situate itself, this tradition which would have to be understood now (*pace* Namvar Singh, who speaks of following Dwivedi in going *In Search of the Other Tradition*) as the other of the 'other tradition'? And how would one speak of/from it? What, in sum, is the notion of representation (in the sense of both speaking of and speaking for the other) implied in Dharmvir's thinking, and how does it extend the idea of a modern Dalit awakening in literature, social science, in the domain of affirmative policies, in employment and education and in electoral politics—to the domain of the theologico-political?

In order to address these questions, we will need to return to Dwivedi's *Kabir*, which apart from being *the* text on Kabir in the last century (there has not been a more forceful attempt in any Indian language to argue for Kabir's place in the national tradition), constitutes Dharmvir's own point of departure. The latter's method consists of reading *Kabir* for its relentless assimilation of Kabir to the high Hindu tradition. In this respect Dharmvir's is very much a Dalit polemic in the tradition of the Dalit leader and constitutionalist Bhimrao Ambedkar, in that it attempts to recover from the historical and cultural mainstream of national culture the wherewithal for an autonomous Dalit tradition. The possibility of the latter rests on the political fiction of an absolute opposition between the high 'brahmanical' and the low-caste 'Dalit' currents in Indian history. And the strategy of such a Dalit critique is first to expose the ideological means by which brahmanical thinking seeks to elide the reality of caste oppression, and then to provide an alternative account of the nation's history, one written from the point of view of Dalits. Where Ambedkar had turned to a philological rereading of the Buddhist and Hindu traditions (he was later to convert to Buddhism), Dharmvir stays with a close almost legalistic reading of the text, on the basis of which he seeks to indict Dwivedi for his brahmanism.

In this essay I will attempt to read Dwivedi's text in the spirit but not the letter of Dharmvir's critique. This is because my interest lies in what Dharmvir makes available to us, which is to say a wholly different reading of the ties between the nationalist project and the history of criticism. He makes it possible for us to read this critical tradition for its inability to account for the place of the Indian Muslim in the nationalist account of the past, and to draw a relation between this elision of Islam and the traditions of Dalit protest. I cannot follow Dharmvir's lead, which is arguably a politically necessary one, in seeking to establish a radical disjuncture between the 'brahmanical' and the Dalit tradition. For it is quite clear to me that any such Dalit tradition should have the means to relate productively with what is after all a shared fund (which need not be a 'national' or 'high Hindu' fund) of cultural and political references going back to the social history of practice and belief in antiquity and beyond.[32]

In seeking to read Kabir as a point of entry into a critique of the idea of community in nationalist criticism, and in drawing attention to the ways in which he constantly reminds us of the call of the marginalized and downtrodden, I have adopted for heuristic reasons the perspective of the 'convert'. Now conversion and Dalitness refer in the case of Kabir to the same marginal status: Kabir is indeed at once *a convert and a Dalit*. Yet my own use of the idea of 'conversion' is (after Gauri Viswanathan) akin to a critical device; I seek to read the text of Kabir for the subject-position of the convert, one who cannot assume a given religious, social or economic identity, and must remain temporally forever 'in-between' all ascriptions of place, location and identity.[33] It is the pathos of this unfinished aspect of the convert's journey that opens a breach in our given scripts for the future, offering us hope for a different idea of community, one that would argue for the radical autochthony of the Muslim and the Dalit in Indian history. In other words, closely

[32] This idea of a shared fund, a kind of inner maelstrom in emergent aspects of culture, is a reminder of the extraordinary analysis of the motives behind Gandhi's second fast during the crisis surrounding the Communal Award for Dalits and minorities, and his conflict with the Dalit leader, Bhimrao Ambedkar, in Nagaraj's *The Flaming Feet* (Bangalore: South Forum Press, 1993). 'The point is', Nagaraj concludes, 'that Gandhiji chose to ignore that [spiritual] dimension of Ambedkar's personality. According to Gandhiji, the materialist approach was the weakness of his adversary and for Ambedkar spirituality was the weakness of Gandhiji: apparently these exclusivist positions concealed the simultaneous existence of both materialist and spiritual viewpoints in both of them', p. 20.

[33] See Gauri Viswanathan, *Outside the Fold: Conversion, Modernity and Belief* (Princeton: Princeton University Press, 1998).

related and yet distinct (they merge in Kabir), the figure of the convert and the figure of the Dalit can be seen to intersect at a point of critical intensity that introduces a serious rupture in the idea of the nation. It is from this minimal and intermediate space inhabited by the convert that I shall negotiate the readings that follow.

Dwivedi's Kabir: Violence of the Event

We learnt in the previous section that the shifting place of Kabir in Hindi modernity has something like a relation to the history of the popular. Why Kabir? For it would be in Kabir's call for a radical negation of all identity and of all prescriptions for selfhood and community that Dwivedi would discover a principle of absolute transformation in history. Let us pause briefly to complicate our picture of this transformative project. Such a transformative vision of history can also be discerned in Shukla's idea of responsibility (*lok-mangal*). But in this instance the nature of historical enquiry was directed towards the end of intervening in the present by means of a reorientation of the faculty of the imagination. Dwivedi's notion of transformation is similarly attuned to transforming the present; it is for this reason that his work has been so enabling for the radical trend in Hindi criticism represented by Namvar Singh; it is also what makes Dwivedi's quest for an 'other' tradition in Hindi a 'political' one. Yet the difference between Dwivedi and the earlier historians of the popular such as Rajwade and Shukla is his recognition of the need not just for a principle of transformation in the present but also, more crucially, the necessity for an alternative account of historical change.

It is for this reason that the accent in *Kabir* is consistently on the notion of the 'unique personality' of Kabir himself. For Kabir is unique not just because there is no one in the Bhakti tradition like him. He is unique because he functions as the locus at once of self-transformation and of historical transformation. 'Historical transformation', or which is the same thing, the 'transformation of history': the latter phrase should be understood in its subjective and objective genitive sense. The transformation associated with Kabir is at once a transformation within history and a transformation *of* the idea of history itself. Such a transformation would be 'absolute' because it involved (for Dwivedi) at once a relentless scepticism towards every worldly tie and an unconditional surrender before an abstract God (Kabir's Ram). As a mode of being-fragile, this implied laying oneself open to the Love that was God's, a Love that was at once redemptive and excessive. Kabir's mode of self-transformation was therefore intensely personal and productive of a multiple range of effects within Kabir's highly elaborate physiognomy of the soul;[34] it nonetheless had the potential to bring about fundamental shifts in historical understanding. Dwivedi's 'Kabir' thus becomes the irreducible locus for a mode of historical critique that, by sheer dint of individual will, redefines the nature of historical understanding itself, and inaugurates an idea of history based on the necessary recurrence of such self-transformation. But for such a historically effective transformation to take place, Kabir would have to be placed on the historical stage. That is to say that his historical agency would have to be staged in a certain way as being in excess of history. For the emergence of Kabir in history is for Dwivedi at once a break with and a continuation of the past. 'History' itself needed to be staged and undone in *Kabir*; Kabir himself was both a historical actor and founder of a new idea of history. For this reason, I would argue that the centrepiece of Dwivedi's book is its historical chapter, called 'The Place of Kabir in India's Religious Quest' (*Bharatiya dharm-sadhana men Kabir ka sthan*), which deals with the advent of Islam in India. Where a great portion of *Kabir* is dedicated to a commentary on and explication of Kabir's central concepts by drawing on the vast archive of premodern practice and thought, the historical chapter seeks to define in the most authoritative manner the 'nature' of Kabir's historical mission. Who or what was this mission directed against? How did it succeed in producing a range of shifts at the personal, social and political level? In what follows I will examine at length the central arguments of this historical chapter of *Kabir*. My method will be to read closely a series of nearly consecutive passages so as to uncover Dwivedi's idea of history.

[34] In 'The Prehistory of the Popular' I discuss at length the Dalit reading of Kabir's idea of Love, drawing attention to the way in which this reading transforms in the most intimate way Dwivedi's notion, itself derived from a governmentalized idea of caste, of Kabir's Love as a kind of self-abjection before God. I have argued there that by dint of this reading, the Dalit critique will have inaugurated a new idea of community.

If my claim that the historical chapter in *Kabir* is its centrepiece is borne out by my analyses, then it should be possible to extend its implications to the varied and inexhaustible exposition of Kabir's religion that Dwivedi presents in his book taken as a whole.

I will begin at the start of the chapter, which quickly sets the stage for the advent of Kabir in Indian history. Here it becomes apparent that Kabir's advent is for Dwivedi a response to another prior advent, that of Islam. Dwivedi writes,

> The epoch of the emergence of Kabir was preceded by an unprecedented event [*abhutpurva ghatna ghati thi*] in the history of India [*bharatvarsh ke itihas men*]. This was the advent of the highly integrated creed [*susangathit sampradaya*] that was Islam. The event violently shook religious thought and social arrangements in India. [*Is ghatna ne bharatiya dharm-mat aur samaj-vyavastha ko buri tarah jhakjhor diya.*] Its supposedly unchanging caste system was dealt a heavy blow. The sense in India was one of being beside oneself with anxiety [*sankshubdha tha*]. The scholarly [*panditjan*] response was to look for the causes of this stupefaction and to find ways of handling [*sambhalne*] [this crisis in] Indian society and religious thinking. (*Kabir*, 136)

Dwivedi is then a historian because he thinks after 'the' event. To think after is, first, to come after in a temporal sense, so that one can say the event has passed by. By this token, Dwivedi will have located himself in the lateness (the posteriority) of his own moment, having arrived late on the scene of Kabir's advent. Yet his own late-coming is not enough to disqualify him for the role of chronicler of the event. For us this ought to give rise to a series of related questions. How can one demarcate this event, its beginning and its end? What makes it possible for Dwivedi to return to this event? Can he continue to inhabit the event *even as it passes* before him? Or can such a sense of the event 'as a whole' require the retroactive gaze that comes with being able to situate oneself in a point in time that is 'absolutely' posterior to the event in question? But to 'think after' is also to think the event itself; it is to wonder after the nature of this event, and 'its' own historical emergence. What makes Dwivedi a historian in this sense, which is to say a philosopher of history, is his asking here not just for the meaning of the event, but for the non-event that precedes this event of Islam—makes this event what it is, cannot be, will have been. What is this prehistory? Dwivedi himself has a stake in answering this question.

Let us understand how the very next passage in the historical chapter in *Kabir* lays the ground for this prehistory, for an account of the status quo prior to the disturbance of Islam. The passage is worth quoting at length, both for its complexity and because we will have occasion to return to it in the ensuing discussion.

> India is not some new country. Great empires have been interred in its soil, great religious proclamations have resonated in its skies, great civilizations have arisen and gone to seed in its every corner, and their traces [*smriti-chinha*] still stand lifeless, as though the yelping goddess of victory had been struck by lightning. Innumerable castes [*jatiyon*], tribes, lineages [*naslon*] and wandering nomads have come here in packs. For a while they unsettled [*vikshubdha bhi banaya hai*] the mood in the country, but in the end after their initial intrusion [*dakhal*], they would buckle down and find themselves revered like the older gods—and sometimes earn even greater respect than them. It has been a unique feature of Indian culture that the internal social order and religious beliefs of these castes, tribes, lineages were never interfered with [*hastkshep*] in any way, and were yet made entirely Indian. . . . In this way Indian culture has assented [*swikar kar liya*] to the entire gamut of castes, along with their peculiar features. But up to now no 'creed' [*mazhab*] had come at its door. It [Indian culture] did not have the strength to digest this [*hajam kar sakne ki shakti nahin rakhta tha*]. (pp. 136–7)

What is this event that gives rise to the need for the narrative of a prehistory, or the fiction of a past? It is the advent, we will recall, of the 'creed (*susangathit sampradaya*) that was Islam'. Placed next to Dwivedi's characterization of the old *bharatvarsh* as 'not new', this helps evoke an idea of India as loose, undifferentiated, unorganized, the very antithesis of a 'highly integrated' society. The accent that Dwivedi will give to this older vision of India is that of an extraordinary openness to the new, a quality that for him inheres in the old. Though the themes evoked in the passage recur often in the literature of Indian nationalism since Nehru's *Discovery of India*, Dwivedi's vision of this 'prehistoric' India is nonetheless significant for its use of a language of trauma. Dwivedi's deployment of the nearly synonymous terms, *sankshobh* and *vikshobh* to describe the nature of this trauma is particularly significant. For the psyche of India appears to Dwivedi to have undergone two kinds of crises with respect to Islam, closely related in kind, but different in degree. Dwivedi's initial characterization of India's plight is that of 'being beside oneself with anxiety', for which he uses the adjectival form of *sankshobh*, i.e., *sankshubdha*. This is the pressing situation that India's scholarly class (presumably the priesthood) sets about trying to 'get a handle on' (*sambhalna*). Yet clearly this initial description does not adequately comprehend the exact nature of the trauma that Dwivedi has in mind, for he then resorts to the word closely related to *sankshobh*, which is *vikshobh* and its adjectival form, *vikshubdha*. Now *vikshobh* refers more alarmingly to the upheaval associated with the very first encounter with the other; it is in fact the exacerbation of a merely 'anxious attending-to' (*sankshobh*). *Vikshobh* is a condition much worse, more unsettling, bordering on madness.[35] How is India to cope with this sudden experience of madness?

There have been times before this that the stranger or madman has been in the house. These lines from the passage quoted above delimit the possibilities of assimilation in Indian society: 'Innumerable castes (*jatiy[an]*), tribes, lineages (*nasl[en]*) and wandering nomads have come here in packs. For a while they unsettled (*vikshubdha bhi banaya hai*) the mood in the country, but in the end after their initial intrusion (*dakhal*), they would buckle down . . . (they) were never interfered with (*hastkshep*) in any way, and were yet turned entirely Indian' (*Kabir*, p. 136). But those occasions only serve to further illustrate for Dwivedi the assimilative embrace of Indian culture at large: 'Indian culture could absorb these guests (*atithiyon ko apna saki thi*) because its religious quest has from the beginning been subjective (*vaiyaktik*)' (*Kabir*, p. 136). Historical Islam is a threat precisely to this assimilative idea of individuality, one that had in the past enabled Indian/Hindu to recover quickly from outside intrusion, and to work through the trauma (*vikshobh*) of violation.

It is worth noting here that the notion of individuality that Dwivedi read into Kabir had its origins in the scholar's early studies of Surdas,

[35] Standard Hindi dictionaries unhelpfully equate *sankshobh* and *vikshobh*. Since Dwivedi's Hindi diction tends to abound in Sanskrit phrases, and given that he was something of a Sanskrit pandit, one could well turn to Carl Cappeller's *Sanskrit-Worterbuch* (Berlin: Walter de Gruyter and Company, 1955, pp. 465, 402), which glosses *sankshob* as 'Erschutterung' (shake severely) and *vikshob* quite differently as 'heftige Bewegung, Aufregung, Verwirrung' (confusion, bewilderment).

which culminated in his book, *Sur-Sahitya* (The Literature of Surdas), published in 1936, six years before *Kabir*. More crucially, as Namvar Singh points out in *Dusri Parampara ki Khoj*:

> The [early] search for the origins of Krishna-Bhakti [in Surdas] necessarily took Dwivedi in the direction of *tantra*-inspired practices. One motive for this detour in *tantra* may have been formulations about Bhakti by scholars such as Grierson, who wrote that it spread far afield all of a sudden 'like a flash of lightning,' and went so far as to ascribe its emergence to the advent of Christianity in India. To this Dwivedi's retort was that this so-called 'lightning flash' was preceded by the 'hundreds of years that it took for clouds to build up for it'. Moreover, he needed to show that the notions of evil in Christianity and in the beliefs of the Hindu *bhakt*s were radically different. In his words, 'Surdas and the other *bhakt*-poets believed that evil was heteronomous or exogenous (*bahya ya agantuk*), whereas among Christian *bhakt*'s evil lurked within the interiority [of their souls] as so fundamentally natural to man (i.e., autonomous) that it was deep-rooted, radical (*antar aur svabhavik*)'. The crux of [Dwivedi's] rejoinder is that 'Surdas among others did not ascribe any radical evil to his soul. [*Surdas adi apne apko svabhavtaha papatma nahin samajhte*]'. [*Dusri Parampara ki Khoj*, p. 63][36]

[36] The reference is to *Sur-Sahitya* (p. 71). The Grierson essay which Dwivedi particularly objected to was 'Modern Hinduism and its Debt to the Nestorians', *Journal of the Royal Asiatic Society* (1907), pp. 311–35. In her analysis of this article, Dalmia explains that Grierson had tried to argue that the third century Syrian Nestorian Christians had introduced the religion of love into Hinduism in south India, from which point it had been taken up in the Bhakti movement. The impulse behind this move was to insist that Bhakti was analogous to the Protestant Revolution in that it had revolted against the hegemony of high brahmanism by preaching a popular gospel of love. Grierson was one of the main exponents of the idea of a unified Vaishnav Hinduism that was at the same time 'monotheistic'. See the discussion of Grierson in Dalmia, *Nationalization*, pp. 401–8; the line that Dwivedi cites from the 'Nestorians' essay is also cited in Dalmia, p. 402; I have chosen to translate Dwivedi's version and not Grierson's original. George Abraham Grierson (1851–1941) was trained as a linguist and worked in many middle-level administrative positions in Bihar for a number of years. Before long, he developed an appreciation of Bhakti literature and of the *bhashas* in which it was written (and especially of Avadhi and Braj, which he understood as integral aspects of Hindi). His prolific output of grammars, vocabularies and studies of dialects culminated in the multi-volume *Linguistic Survey of India*, begun in 1898, of which he was

What Namvar Singh provides us here is an insight into the basic motivation of Dwivedi's researches. For Dwivedi's was clearly a search for the origins of Indian subjectivity, whose roots he wished to trace to before the devotional surge of Bhakti proper, so as to ensure its historical precedence over the advent of Christianity in India. (Like many Christianizing Orientalists and apologists of empire, Grierson had tried to show that medieval Bhakti could not but have had Christian roots and affiliations.)

More crucially, what Dwivedi derives from these earlier practices is the idea of an interiority that exceeds and in fact renders facile a Christianized post-Kantian hermeneutics of the soul. Given that Dwivedi's theme is Christian moralism, 'radical' seems preferable to 'natural' or 'spontaneous' as a translation of 'svabhavik' in this context. Radical evil would refer in a Kantian sense to the problem of man's propensity to choose an incorrect maxim of practical reason; in this case, 'radical' would refer to the peculiar coexistence in human conduct of a fundamental affirmation of the imperative of practical reason as well as an innate propensity to opt not to follow the otherwise insuperable dictates of that practical reason—this fateful coexistence of opposed propensities lends to the Kantian or post-Enlightenment Christian subject the melancholic cast of a perpetually fraught individuality. To this 'autonomous' and 'radical' (*antar* aur *svabhavik*) individuality, Dwivedi opposes another idea of 'Indian' individuality, a *svabhavikta* bearing the vicissitudes of the devotee's complex interface with his determinate deity, one that is sustained not by an inner tension but by an open and assuredly *spontaneous* encounter with an otherness (an alterity) now understood as 'heteronomous' and 'exogenous' ('*bahya* aur *agantuk*). By the same token, evil (in Dwivedi's reading of Surdas) originates from a point outside the sovereign consciousness of the devotee; the devotee's relation to such evil is marked by a sceptical and

---

editor-superintendent. But his most important contribution was his propagation of a monolithic idea of Bhakti in Orientalist circles. See Dalmia, *Nationalization*, pp. 139–40. See also Prentiss's exposition of Grierson's 1910 contribution to the *Encyclopaedia of Religion and Ethics* in which he defined Bhakti as 'adoration'. See *The Embodiment of Bhakti* (New York: Oxford University Press, 1999), pp. 14–15. Here Grierson argued that Bhakti had been a civilizing influence on the more animist strains of Dravidian religion.

critical distance. Here again the basis of Indian/Hindu scepticism is the ability to stand at a distance from social norms by embracing a certain marginality (both Surdas and Kabir were marginal figures in this sense) and to embrace the larger Hindu ecumene. Resting not on an introjected principle of radical evil but on an open scepticism—an extroverted, indeed 'extrojected' individuality—Indian subjectivity, it follows, is for Dwivedi the externalization of evil or otherness; evil by this account is always out there. What does this 'out there' (*bahya*) refer to? Presumably, the 'out there' can mean the array of superstitions and false beliefs which provoke the social critique of the Bhakti poet; but it can also mean every entity that threatens to disrupt the equanimity of Indian/Hindu life.

The Christian idea of radical evil generates in Dwivedi the notion of an open-ended scepticism, one that operates within the limits of Indian/Hindu religion. Where the book on Surdas had initiated a shift in Dwivedi's thinking towards the historicity of Bhakti, the book on Kabir brings out with astonishing power the message of love and critique implicit in the Bhakti tradition. For Dwivedi Surdas's message was that of an all-embracing love, whereas in Kabir he could see the unprecedented coming together of love and a much more sceptical attitude. The locus of this mediation is Kabir's 'unique personality', which resonates for Dwivedi with all that is spontaneous, authentic, and ultimately unimpeachable about the Indian/Hindu worldview in its embrace at once of change and continuity. Contrary to the inwardness of the Christian idea of radical evil, Dwivedi seems to say, Indian/Hindu culture upheld radical freedom and individuality in a social and worldly way, endowing it with an implicit openness that only further strengthened its (India or Hinduism's) historical project. Hence the extension of svabhavikta to mean not just naturalness but also spontaneity, which is to say the inner resilience, the essential self-recuperability of Hindu subjectivity.

An earlier moment in nationalist thought (of which the Bengali novelist Bankimchandra and the Arya Samaj's Dayanand are representative instances) had attempted to found a natural theology for Hinduism by relentlessly rationalizing it. Dwivedi's own recourse is instead to the popular origins of Bhakti in esoteric doctrine and practice, and to the notion that this gave rise in the end to Bhakti as a religion of the spirit, the essence of India's spiritual quest, *dharm-sadhana*. The idea of this religion is couched in the romantic idiom of protest and personal rebellion, but it is nonetheless the prolongation of the ideal of the rational thinking kind of Bhakti-*ras* that one sees in Shukla, extended now to the new theme of interiority that Dwivedi inaugurates with his reading of Surdas.[37] The theme of this other kind of interiority, derived from the 'unradical' spontaneity of svabhavikta, posited at a great remove both from the radical evil of Christian askesis and (as we will discover) from the proscriptive (*varjanatmak*) religion of Islam, is endlessly malleable, and lends to Dwivedi's 'Indian culture' the kind of resilience that is required for it to emerge unscathed from the historical encounter, extending back through colonialism and the accompanying proselytizing work by missionaries to the early middle ages, with the Peoples of the Book. Dwivedi suggests the idea of this triumphant suppleness in the tradition by deploying with the greatest ease and panache the word 'svabhav' (radical, natural, spontaneous, interior, inner, referring also to behaviour and character). *Svabhav* then works on the register of the individual as well as the collective, and refers to individuality, spontaneity, openness, and in the final instance, to the very basis of Indian/Hindu idea of the social. A passage from Dwivedi's *Background to Hindi Literature* (1940), which comes between *The Literature of Surdas* and *Kabir*, gives us a better idea of how spontaneity (svabhav) functions for Dwivedi as the quintessence of social individuality. Here Dwivedi reiterates a point made earlier in the book on Surdas about the authentic spontaneity of Indian individualism, but extends it in the direction of the social. Dwivedi states,

> The Indian scholarly world had already during the millennium after Christ begun to lean quite naturally [*svabhavtaha*] toward the popular [*lok*] in the realms of thought, conduct, and language. Even if the exceedingly important event that was the eminent growth of Islam had not taken place, it [the Indian scholarly world] would nonetheless have gone the way of the

[37] The extent of Dwivedi's familiarity with Shukla's work is moot, and one can therefore adduce merely a family resemblance in their thinking here. Shukla's late and most productive phase overlaps with Dwivedi's early youthful work leading up to *Kabir*, but since Dwivedi spent this period away from the Hindi-speaking region, which texts of Shukla may have come to his attention in faraway Shantiniketan is hard to ascertain. See Namvar Singh, *Dusri Parampara ki Khoj*, p. 17.

popular. It was its inner strength [*bhitar ki shakti*] that pushed it toward this natural [*svabhavik*] path.[38]

Clearly, what enables the greater tradition to survive the jolt that is Islam is its tendency, which had set in place long before the jolt itself, to incorporate the most radical elements of the popular. Commenting on this passage, Namvar Singh points out that the use of svabhav (natural) and *svabhavtaha* (*naturally*) both reflect a concern in Dwivedi for that which is essentially, authentically, and more crucially, spontaneously, the tradition's own. It is the 'own' of this 'ownmost' that is at work in the '*sva-* of Dwivedi's *svabhav*(*taha*)', and is expressly opposed to the idea of foreign (Islamic) influence. Clearly, as Namvar Singh notes, 'it is the force of the popular [*lokshakti*] that [for Dwivedi] impels this tendency in scholasticism [*shastra*] toward itself. And it is moreover quite apparent that it is the "inner strength" of the popular in its very force that propels Indian history to evolve in this way.'[39]

The primordial root of the spontaneity (svabhavikta) that bestirs and propels the tradition as a whole is then undoubtedly the popular. The latter becomes in Dwivedi's account the locus of a complete social whole, in which the singular individual and the larger socius appear as elements within the unity of caste Hindu society. The prehistory of the popular that Dwivedi attempts is made necessary by that other prehistory of crisis, dovetailing with a corresponding posthistory that is to manage the crisis, which is the prehistory of the Islamic 'intrusion' (dakhal). It is the strangest of paradoxes that the prehistory of the popular (*lokdharm, lokshakti*) can also be the prehistory of the elite! (Dwivedi makes reference to this elite alternately in terms of brahmanical scholasticism, scholars, intellectuals, Indian society, Indian culture [*shastra, panditjan, vidvatjan, bharatiya samaj, bharatiya sanskriti*], etc.). Arguably what saved mainstream India from cultural extinction was the great inner spontaneity of the popular.

If we were to think that this 'vital current' in Indian culture is opposed only to the radical evil preached by the Christian missionary in tandem with certain phases in the project of colonialism, we need only to return to the passage in question in *Kabir*. We discover there that the

[38] Dwivedi, *Hindi Sahitya ki Bhumika*. Cited in Namvar Singh, *Dusri Parampara ki Khoj*, p. 77.

[39] Namvar Singh, *Dusri Parampara ki Khoj*, p. 78.

agitated (vikshubdha) soul of India has very early found a way in the middle ages to distinguish and therefore protect itself from the interference of Islam. It is after all only returning the compliment:

> Before the coming of Islam, this vast populace had no name. Now it was given the appellation, 'Hindu'. Hindu, that is to say Indian, which is to say a non-Islamic creed. Clearly within this non-Islamic creed there were all manner of other creeds, some were followers of Brahma, some believed in the cycle of karma, some were Shaiva, some Vaishnava, some Shakta, some Smarta, and who knows what else. Ranging through a hundred initiatives, and spread out over a thousand years, the ideas and traditional beliefs of this populace stood like an expansive jungle. (*Kabir*, p. 138)

Since it was Islam, Dwivedi seems to say, that exercised its nominalistic regime over us by reducing the heterogeneous body of Hindu beliefs to one single idea, that of Hinduism, we the members of this loose populace (*jansamuha*), (but how loose can Hinduism be if it is still, in the final analysis, Hinduism?) we too will seek to name Islam. It is in this procedure of rigorous othering that the ideology of svabhav is put to use.

The effects of this procedure of contradistinction are dual in that they affect both the thing named and the subject doing the naming. But the elements of the argument had already been put in place earlier in the passage we have read, and which begs repetition here.

> Indian culture could assimilate these guests (*atithiyon ko apna saki thi*) because its religious quest has from the beginning been personal (*vaiyaktik*). Each person has the right to his own kind of spiritual seeking . . . every person is responsible (*jimmedar*) for himself. The most important thing is not the worship of any particular religious idea or god but purity of conduct and character (*achar-shuddhi aur charitrya*). If a man stands by the faith (*dharm*) of his forefathers, remains pure in character, doesn't care to emulate another caste or person's conduct but prefers to die for his own creed (*swadharm*) and is honest and truthful, he will most certainly have stature (*shreshtha hai*), whether he be from the lineage of Abhir or from the line of Pukkas.

The whole range of personological terms—personal, each person, his own, responsible for himself, purity of conduct, character, a man, pure, own creed, stature—are opposed here to the power of the collective, to its ability to cancel the individuality of the one in favour of the absolute power of the whole.

But not before Hinduism as the creed of the singular has been opposed to Islam as the tyranny of the general. What precisely bestirs Dwivedi here is the unprecedented need for a new alliance. We can recall here that in the passage from *Sur-Sahitya* cited by Namvar Singh, Dwivedi had sought to respond to the Orientalist scholar Grierson's characterization of Bhakti as an outcrop of the advent of Christianity in India. There Dwivedi had made an argument for Bhakti's antiquity (the whole of *Sur-Sahitya* is in fact a rejoinder to Grierson in this regard). But here in *Kabir*, six years later, why are the words of the Englishman repeated verbatim without comment, as if in endorsement? The words reappear in a passage that tries to determine the exact role of Bhakti, and especially Kabir's Bhakti, in India/Hinduism's response to Islam. Dwivedi writes, on the verge of raising the curtain prior to Kabir's entrance, and a mere couple of pages after the passage above— 'It was at this time that there was the advent in the south of Vedanta-inspired Bhakti, which spread from this end of this vast Indian subcontinent to the other. Dr Grierson has said, "Suddenly like a sudden flash of lightning, there came upon all this darkness a new idea. . . . This new idea was that of Bhakti" [*Kabir*, p. 139]. In the text on Surdas, Dwivedi had been quick to oppose Hinduism's notion of individuality to the idea of radical evil in Christianity. There (as expressed in Surdas's text and brought out in Dwivedi's reading) Hinduism's most significant quality was to have generated an open, rebellious notion of individuality that faced challenges in the world at large; this was a secular, worldly individuality, one that asserted the right to criticise, object, protest. Where the idea of individuality in Christianity was one given to intensive spiritual introspection, Indian/Hindu individuality was, by Dwivedi's account, strictly worldly, heteronomous (bahya) and exogenous (agantuk). What accounts then for the volte face whereby, by the time of the *Kabir* book six years later, Dwivedi quotes in unqualified approbation the very same passage from Grierson that he had been quick to object to in the Surdas book? There Hinduism had been the religion of the spirit where Christianity had been the religion of the soul; for the very same reason, Dwivedi had argued for the relative antiquity of Hinduism when compared to Christianity. But by the time *Kabir* was written—one could argue Dwivedi was also responding to the increasingly tense communal situation in Bengal—the distinction between Hinduism and Christianity, and the argument for the former's historical precedence had grown to be less crucial than the need to understand and comprehend the challenge presented by the historical mission of Islam. For when it comes to the encounter with Islam, it is not very difficult for the radical individualism of the Hindu and the missionary or Orientalist's Christian hermeneutic of radical evil to march in step. At this point, Hindu and Christian subjectivity join ranks (without merging into each other) in order to stand up to the new order of the subject inaugurated by Islam. This encounter (staged on the cusp of the premodern in India, as Islam began its inroads and Kabir rose to India/Hinduism's rescue) is a complex and multifaceted one. It is triangulated along the lines of a religion of the law (Islam), a religion of the soul (Christianity), and a religion of the spirit (Bhakti). In his book on Surdas, the threat of Christianity seamlessly produced its counterpoint in Dwivedi's notion of the secular individuality implicit in Surdas's Bhakti. When it is a matter of an encounter with this historical Christianity, such an antithesis between an inner (radical) evil and Hinduism's secular worldliness is entirely possible, even natural. But when it is a matter of the relation to Islam, such antinomies collapse into each other and produce another opposition altogether, this time between Hinduism and Christianity on the one hand, and Islam on the other. This is because with Islam the argument is compelled to move from the realm of interiority to the realm of the sociological. The debate with Christianity is conducted at the level of the heart; the debate with Islam at the level of the law. The latter is the very image for Dwivedi's Hindu of the stern Semitic law that governs the proselytizing tribe.

What follows then is a passage in which Dwivedi distinguishes between Hinduism and Islam; it is here that we come up on evidence of a momentous decision with regard to Islam. 'The Muslim religion [*dharm*] is a '*mazhab*'. In a simple act of translation, Dwivedi accomplishes a political gesture at once linguistic, philosophical, religious, and social, which tears 'Hindi' away from its shared ancestry with 'Urdu'. A basic divergence is implicitly announced here in what was the hybrid popular language of the medieval North, between the stream that flowed from Sanskrit into Hindi (reflected in the word, dharm), and that other stream flowing from Arabic into Urdu (the word, mazhab). This is already a strange tautology. Dwivedi does not mean to say merely that the Muslim religion is a religion. After all, he does not say, '*Islam bhi ek dharm hai*' ('Islam too is a religion'). The implication seems to be on the other hand that the Muslim religion is less a religion like any other, but is in fact a 'religion' ('mazhab') like no other in times past. For it is as though the simple naming of the Muslim religion as mazhab is not enough. Dwivedi's scare quotes around 'mazhab' indicate a much more fundamental foreclosure of the Muslim in our midst. The fact is that for him Islam cannot possess either an appropriate notion of the religious or that of the social. Neither one nor the other, Islam is a 'religious creed', a monstrous *dharm-mat*, whereas Hindu society-religion is bolstered by the existence within itself of that absolute unit of sociality, which is the *jati*, or caste. The latter is always, before any systematic development or structuring (*sanghatan*) already social (*samajik*); what has ensured that its religious quest (*sadhana*) has remained relentlessly social, has been its good fortune (*suyog*) to have had its life-blood eked from the vast body of the popular. It would seem as though Dwivedi needs to put mazhab in quotes because of the peculiar very specific meaning that he wants to give it. Given that the accent throughout this passage is on the idea that Islam is a *dharm-mat* (religious creed) and not a dharm (religion), the weight of this Dwivedean nuance is borne entirely by the word '*mat*' (creed). Hinduism and Islam as dharms are like two parallel lines that cross each other and diverge in the infinite time of history at a point of absolute difference, which is *mat*. Beyond that limit of commensurability between societies and between cultures that is *mat*, lies the death of the personal, and hence the bloodthirsty (or *nirdaya*, p. 138) justice of the group that is mazhab. Why must Islam consistently be labelled a creed or *mat*? So much appears to hang on this little monosyllabic word! Now the lexical drift of both 'creed' and '*mat*' is, as the *Oxford English Dictionary* tells us, in the direction of a certain systematicity. A creed or *mat* refers to 'a fundament of faith, a body of words that authoritatively sum up the belief of a faith.' It is clearly this systematic aspect that seems to Dwivedi to quite radically distinguish Islam from Hinduism.

Such a basis in doctrine or doxa is for Dwivedi anathema to Hindu society. For, he goes on to say, where Islamic society 'was proscriptive (*varjanshil*) in religious matters but accepting (*grahanshil*) in social matters, Hindu society was on the other hand accepting in religious terms but proscriptive in social matters' (*Kabir*, p. 138). What is the singular quality that makes Islam such a strong adversary (*pratidvandvi*)? It is of course the idea, a great problem for Dwivedi, that Islam was accepting at the level of the social where Hinduism was not. In the contest for acolytes, it mattered little in the final analysis if one religion believed in the individual right towards spiritual seeking, and the other believed in the religious creed of the group. At the level of religious seeking, the individual could well be opposed to the collective, the individual spirit opposed to the scorn of the group. Again and again, Dwivedi drives home the single idea that Hinduism's great strength lay in its firm belief in the power of the individual seeker after religion (dharm). The problem of course is that this is, for him, not enough. Could Hinduism come up with an idea of social acceptance or tolerance, as opposed to merely religious tolerance? Clearly, the answer to this is no. For if it had, its condition before the arrival of Kabir would not have been one of shock. And it is at the level of the social that we find Dwivedi's religio-spiritual edifice breaking down.

For what slips out in the encounter with Islam, in the great ethical project of other-directedness in Bhakti which commences (for Dwivedi) with the advent of Kabir, is the problem of caste oppression, the ineradicability of Hindu social sanction to which the poetic utterance of the convert Kabir is a response. Dwivedi seeks to read the text of Bhakti ethically for its response to Islam as historical adversary—*Kabir* is a monument to this effort—but what continues to interrupt this movement of Hindu ecumenicism is the essential wound (an absolutely different *chot* from the *virahagni* [pain of separation] of Ram- or Krishna-Bhakti) at the heart of Dwivedi's high Hindu society, which is caste and the spectre of conversion. This is because the opposition between religious quest (*dharm-sadhana*) and creed (*mat*), acceptance (*grahanshilta*) and proscription (*varjanshilta*), and individual (*vaiyaktik*) and social (*samajik*) in Dwivedi's text all privilege the ecumenicism of caste, but from within its closed bounds. The perennial achievement of Hindu society (for Dwivedi) was that it had subsumed the problem of the social within the principle of tolerance towards individual spiritual and religious seeking. So that what is finally being opposed to *mat* in Dwivedi is really the essential holism of the Indic metaphysics of caste, which is now the religious agglomeration (*sammishran*) of self-existing monads, all seeking God differently. It is this idea, involving the elision of the actual conditions of caste, which makes it possible for Dwivedi to attempt a 'prehistory' of Hinduism prior to the advent of Islam. The task of this prehistory is to efface once and for all the historical transcript of conversion and by the same token the mode and manner of critique implicit in the unprecedented Word of the convert.

CHAPTER 5

Death of a Kotwal

Injury and the Politics of Recognition[1]

ANUPAMA RAO

A Failure of Judgment?

On 17 August 1991 a dalit kotwal in the village of Pimpri-Deshmukh in Parbhani district, Maharashtra, was bludgeoned to death on the steps of a Hanuman temple. Ambadas Sawane was killed by villagers who claimed he had desecrated the temple by entering it. As police investigated the murder, Sawane's death was politicized by party activists and government functionaries who joined his family in demanding redress. The contentious, and often conflicted, readings of the murder had one point in common: except for

[1] Thanks to Partha Chatterjee, M.S.S. Pandian, and Gyan Prakash for critical feedback that allowed me to clarify and recast my arguments. Steven Pierce, Arvind Rajagopal, and Rajeswari Sunder Rajan offered careful criticism and support. Riyad Koya has read and commented on every word of this essay, challenging me to think rigorously about politics and prose. During my fieldwork in Marathwada, Wandana Sonalkar, Tulsi Parab, Daryan, and Ojas gave unstintingly of their love and affection. I especially thank Tulsi and Wandana for all they taught me about Marathwada. Earlier versions of this essay were presented as talks at Columbia University, November 1998, and New York University, March 1999. I am grateful to audiences at both institutions for their questions and comments, and to Professor Val Daniel, Faye Ginsburg, and Fred Myers for inviting me to present at those venues.

Note: I retain the term Bombay. To call it Mumbai would be anachronistic since the Shiv Sena had not yet renamed the city at the time period within the essay. Mumbai is used by the Marathi sources, however, and I have used this term whenever quoting directly from them. Official names, and names of the accused, have been changed.

the defence, almost everyone agreed Sawane was killed because he was a dalit. Sawane's murder generated a great deal of publicity because of its brutality and its symbolic resonance with earlier instances of *mandir pravesh* (temple entry). It was the first case in Maharashtra to be judged under the Prevention of Atrocities Against Scheduled Castes and Scheduled Tribes Act of 1989 (hereafter PoA Act), which prescribes stringent punishment for caste violence.[2]

In his judgment, delivered at the Parbhani Sessions Court, Justice Adharkar held that Sawane was the victim of a caste crime. Even though the immediate motive for the murder appeared to be upper-caste retaliation for Sawane's 'desecration' of their Hanuman temple, Adharkar focused instead on Sawane's attempts to install an Ambedkar statue in the village, drawing attention to how dalit politicization had affected the context of caste sociality. Out of ten accused, Adharkar found five individuals guilty of bludgeoning Sawane to death. He let them off lightly, arguing that intent to murder could not be established. Of the five men acquitted, two were functionaries of state who were accused of playing a critical role in Sawane's murder. The police *patil* was accused of inciting the violence, and the police *sarpanch* of the village was accused of being negligent in his duties. At the time of writing, the case was still under appeal.

It is important to recognize the political nature of Adharkar's verdict. His judgment addressed the murder as a caste crime, a compound of penal crime and the crime of untouchability, drawing attention to the murder's extraordinary legal status. Furthermore, Adharkar's judgment, discussed in greater detail later in this essay, revealed his sensitivity to socio-political forces in the village and of the changed context of caste crime.

Though Adharkar recognized Sawane's murder as a political crime, however, his judgment resorted to a kind of evidentiary formalism in order to contain evidence of police negligence. This revealed that the police and the judiciary were themselves embedded in a caste habitus that led to faulty procedures of gathering evidence, and an inability to recognize the full extent of caste violence. Thus the very forms of recognition enabled by a law such as the PoA Act could also be undercut by

[2] The PoA Act was preceded by the 1955 Untouchability Offences Act, amended and renamed in 1976 as the Protection of Civil Rights Act.

the interpretive and evidentiary labours of state apparatuses such as the police and judiciary.

Until the passage of the 1989 PoA Act, an 'atrocity' was not legally defined as the performance of a series of acts recognized by law as perpetuating untouchability. Nevertheless, the term had acquired the weight of common sense in defining violence against dalits, as *The Fifth Report of the Commission for Scheduled Castes and Scheduled Tribes* (April 1982, March 1983) noted. According to the Ministry of Home Affairs, the term implies offences under the Indian Penal Code perpetrated on Scheduled Castes and Scheduled Tribes. '[W]here the victims of crime are members of Scheduled Castes and the offenders do not belong to Scheduled Castes, caste considerations are really the root cause of crime, even though caste consciousness may not be the vivid and immediate motive for the crime.'[3]

The PoA Act implies that motives for caste atrocities are overdetermined, and acknowledges the vulnerability of *all* dalits to violence. One of the important effects of the term 'caste atrocity' is that it converts ritual or cultural forms of disability, e.g. prohibition from temple entry or derogatory caste names, into legally cognizable forms of harm or injury. States of being are thus transformed into cognizable injury by laws such as the PoA Act, and this is predicated on a model of dalits as citizen-subjects at risk. The 'caste atrocity' is a bureaucratic form of recognition that binds dalit identity to the body, and perpetuates the idea of physical vulnerability as a condition of dalit existence.[4] Therefore, I suggest, the passage of laws to protect dalits from caste violence

[3] S.K. Gupta, 'Violence Against Scheduled Castes: Parameters and Trends', *The Downtrodden India: Journal of Dalit and Bahujan Studies*, 1994: 23, and cited in S.K. Awasthi, *The Scheduled Castes and Scheduled Tribes (Prevention of Atrocities) Act, 1989* (Allahabad: Premier Publishing Company, 1994), p. 159.

[4] I use the term recognition to indicate that caste relations, or even violence—neither of which seems to address recognition as a mutually fulfilling, or even respectful process—are forms of cultural exchange, transactions that involve addressing the other's personhood (in howsoever distorted a form). I am trying to preserve the moment of violence in the Hegelian model of recognition, rather than supporting Charles Taylor's model of recognition as a form of reconciliation, which evacuates recognition of its agonistic aspect. I am also assuming that forms of recognition are bound up with a regime of rights, that appearing before the law or the state as a person belonging to a certain group, a specific population, enables

are as important as the more familiar discourse of reservations in producing a governmental discourse on untouchability, though as yet there has been little attempt to trace how these two sets of policies have intersected.

The postcolonial state has marked specific groups of citizens with an excess of visibility (e.g. dalits, women) to acknowledge their marginality. This excess in turn requires corrective action to equalize unequal identities. Such a politics of exceptionality characterizes legislation on caste crime, where the language of law must equalize subjects who appear to be the abject bearers of marks of difference.[5] In fact the category of the 'caste atrocity' is a new juridical form that constitutes dalits as vulnerable political subjects entitled to state protection. However, the consequences and political outcomes of this legal/discursive structure are neither given in advance, nor regulated solely within apparatuses of state. Rather, the attempt to use the category of the caste atrocity as a model of justice, as a way of righting historic wrongs, itself brings to crisis many of the assumptions that undergird it.

Through a reconstruction of Sawane's murder I examine how the legal form of the 'caste atrocity' produces specific ways of understanding caste sociality, thereby changing the conditions for realizing caste personhood. As my analysis of Sawane's murder reveals, however, the forms of personhood presumed by such laws are politically negotiated, thereby transforming their juridical effects. The first two sections of this essay rely on classified police documents, government reports, and press publicity to explore the representations of Sawane's death as a caste atrocity. The third section explores how the case judgment reveals the limits of a state-sanctioned sociology of untouchability. These

---

the demand for resources or protection. I will elaborate on this further in the course of my essay. A brilliant reading of the kind of juridical recognition I have in mind, one that governs through a philosophy of stigmatized or racialized personhood, is Saidiya Hartman's *Scenes of Subjection: Terror, Slavery, and Self-Making in Nineteenth-Century America* (New York: Oxford University Press, 1997), esp. Chapter Two, 'Seduction and the Ruse of Power'.

[5] Anupama Rao, 'Understanding *Sirasgaon*: Notes Towards Conceptualizing the Role of Law, Caste, and Gender in a Case of "Atrocity" ', in Rajeswari Sunder Rajan, ed., *Signposts: Gender Issues in Post-Independence India* (New Delhi: Kali for Women, 1998), pp. 204–47.

sections together explore the disjuncture between progressive laws on the one hand, and local caste relationships on the other, as a space of intense political negotiation. The last section explores in some theoretical detail the juridical category of the caste atrocity and the forms of legal subjectivity that it produces.

Legal language alternates between abstract calls for dignity and political worth, and concrete formulae for quantifying damage and restitution. The work of the law is therefore to produce objectified categories that are contested and thrown back into the legal arena, in a cycle of exchange that grounds acts of recognition. Together these sections explore how juridical assumptions about dalit vulnerability are refracted through political struggles that can unsettle the contexts and conventions of a governmental imagination of caste civility.

Zone of Contact: The Police Function

Sawane's death required that the police understand the daily encounters between dalits and upper castes (Marathas and Malis, in this instance) as related to, yet distinct from, his murder. This was a sociological requirement produced by the special nature of the crime, where the victim's social identity provoked the kind of violence he suffered. As the police struggled to produce an official narrative of the murder, they also had to negotiate the police chain of command, respond to government functionaries in Bombay, and negotiate with political activists and the media. In this section I address how internal correspondence within the police hierarchy betrays the manner in which investigators collaborated with perpetrators' version of the event and were themselves imbued with a sociology of untouchability that biased them towards upper castes.

On the night of 16 August, Sawane's family found him lying in a pool of blood outside the temple. His brother Kachru took him to Tadkalas, where the police outpost was located, by bullock cart. A police constable then took Sawane to the Primary Health Centre, from where he was referred to Parbhani's Civil Hospital due to his serious condition. Ambadas was taken by jeep to the Civil Hospital in Parbhani, 25 kilometers from Pimpri-Deshmukh. Sawane expired soon thereafter. The surgeon who conducted the post-mortem attributed Sawane's death to a fracture of the occipital bone.

On 17 August, Sawane's brother, Kachru, filed a First Information Report (FIR).[6] Though the FIR filed by Kachru had been critical in drawing attention to Sawane's murder, Adharkar later disregarded the FIR, saying:

> The First Information Report is an important document. It is to be proved in the criminal case. But the said document is not a substantive evidence, and therefore, it could not be used for contradicting or corroborating the complainant. Its chief purpose is to acquaint the court with the case which the prosecution has set out at the earliest stage. In this way the earliest information of the occurrence is highly useful for the purpose of corroborating or contradicting the prosecution version, but cannot itself be a substantive evidence . . .[7] (pp. 52–3)

The judge later rejected evidence gathered subsequent to the FIR, and treated the FIR precisely as substantive, thereby compromising the prosecution's case. Initially, however, Kachru's FIR brought his brother Ambadas's death to the attention of the law. On the basis of Kachru's FIR five men were taken into custody: Suresh Chintaman Dhamale (22), Balaji Mulje Chavan (28), Shankar Gangaram Pardeshi (32), Shivaji Vithal Dhamale (35), and Shivaji Gangaram Pardeshi (40). Two of the men were Marathas, and three were Malis. On 2 September, the Marathi newspaper *Loksatta* carried a short note that all five accused (who were by then in police custody) were Shiv Sena activists.

The FIR points to a moment of transaction, the point at which the police wrote up an event as a criminal case, and initiated an investigation that could culminate in a judicial pronouncement if the evidence supported the prosecution's claim. The FIR marked a place of exchange, a place where two narrative strategies negotiated for space: Kachru's own evaluation of the significance and motive behind the beating that led him to file a report, and the manner in which the police officer reported Kachru's complaint in the FIR. The FIR was the first

[6] A case proceeds as follows: (1) the FIR is filed and receives a CR [Crime Record] number; (2) the police categorize the account into the categories of A [where evidence has not been collected], B [registration of a false case], and C [no offence committed]; (3) the chargesheet is filed, and (4) the case receives a CC [Court Case] number once it is sent to the court.

[7] Further references from the 151-page judgment delivered by V.B. Adharkar in Special Case No. 11/91, delivered 18 June 1992, will just mention page numbers from the judgment.

in a set of *narrative repetitions* that framed Sawane's murder for the police establishment, government officials, political representatives, and the media. The repetitive structure of the police reports is a significant bureaucratic form, its iterations producing the effect of getting closer to the truth of the investigation, whereas in effect the police correspondence misrecognized the full significance of Sawane's murder.

By the time Ambadas's body was brought home on the 17th, at 10.30 p.m. the police had begun their investigation.[8] That morning, the Sub-Inspector from Tadkalas, Kolhapurkar, had gone to the murder scene to draw up the *panchnama* and collect evidence. He also interviewed key witnesses: Sawane's father, brother, a neighbour, his wife Rukminibai, and a cousin. The accused were taken into custody. Due to the severity of the crime, the Sub-Divisional Police Officer (SDPO), Gopalshetty, also arrived in the village that evening to aid in police interrogation, house searches, and so forth. On the 19th Sawane's death was recorded under Section 302 (attempt to murder) read with Section 3(x) of the Protection of Civil Rights (PCR) Act (1976). *The addition of this Section 3(x) of the PCR Act was mandatory since the case involved a dalit victim, and signalled that the case merited extra care.* However the police record of the murder did not mention the PoA Act.[9]

[8] Officers up to the level of Superintendent of Police are drawn from the Maharashtra State Police. Levels of Deputy Superintendent of Police (DySP) and beyond are drawn from the officers of the Indian Administrative Service who have opted for the Indian Police Service. This mimics the distinct two-tier hierarchy of the colonial police, though the latter were racially divided between native police and their British superiors. For arguments that the police mediate between the demands of governance and local ties of caste, kinship, and community, see Shahid Amin, *Event, Metaphor, Memory: Chauri Chaura, 1922–1992* (Berkeley: University of California Press, 1995); David Arnold, *Police Power and Colonial Rule. Madras 1859–1947* (Delhi: Oxford University Press, 1996); Raj Chandavarkar, *Imperial Power and Popular Politics* (Cambridge: Cambridge University Press, 1998), especially the chapter 'Police and Public Order in Mumbai 1880–1947', pp. 180–233; and Anupama Rao, 'Problems of Violence, States of Terror: Torture in Colonial India', *Interventions: A Journal of Postcolonial Studies*, vol. 3, no. 1, 2001, pp. 186–205.

[9] Atrocities are punishable with imprisonment for a term not less than six months and upto five years, along with payment of a fine. Section 7(1)(d) of the

On 28 August, the Deputy Inspector General of Police (DIGP), Protection of Civil Rights (PCR) wrote from Bombay, noting that 'One Kachru Sahebarao Sawane, brother of the deceased, was brought by Vivek Pandit [an activist] who says that the Police Patil of the village is the main accused in this case but is not shown as the accused. Similarly the harijans were not allowed to enter the said temple.'[10] The Protection of Civil Rights (PCR) Cell was formed in 1988 to deal vigilantly with caste and gender issues, and the DIGP-PCR sits in the Maharashtra State Police Headquarters, Bombay. This wireless from Bombay regarding the role of the police patil effected a change in the police investigation. Parchani's SDPO, Parab, took over the police investigation.

The wireless from Bombay provided the impetus for investigating the role of local functionaries in the murder. Of course Sawane himself was a village-level police functionary. Kotwals in Maharashtra have been drawn from the Mahar community, following their ritual function as *veskars*. *Molesworth's Marathi Dictionary* defines a *veskar* (m) as: 'The person appointed to keep the gate of a village. He is usually a Mahar.' The veskar's duties are drawn from his guarding of the *ves*, the symbolic entry point to a village. Even in his modern, bureaucratic manifestation the kotwal patrolled the village boundaries, and was subservient to both police patil and *sarpanch*. The police patil's central role in Sawane's murder revealed the political implications of the case—the involvement of a state functionary who also happened to be

---

Protection of Civil Rights Act of 1955 is often read along with Section 3, since the former covers an insult or an attempt to insult a member of the Scheduled Castes on the grounds of untouchability rather than the more restrictive Section 3(x) of the PoA Act, which only covers the case of insult or humiliation of a member of the Scheduled Castes or Scheduled Tribes *in public*.

[10] Vivek Pandit published *A Handbook on Prevention of Atrocities: Scheduled Castes and Scheduled Tribes* (Vidhayak Sansad Publication, 1995). This handbook is meant to aid activists in the intricacies of the PoA Act. In his introduction to the handbook Pandit writes 'On 16th August 1991, Ambadas Savane, a dalit Kotwal of Pimpri-Deshmukh village in Parbhani district of Marathwada, was stoned to death by the upper castes for taking shelter in the temple premises during a heavy shower. I read a small news item in a local newspaper about this gruesome death. I was deeply affected, and fought for justice on his behalf. I could pursue the case using the SC/ST (Prevention of Atrocities) Act.'

a Maratha of high status, using his position to try to protect himself from prosecution.[11]

The most important piece of evidence to emerge from the police investigation was produced by an SDPO from Parbhani, Parab, who conducted the investigation from 28 August 1991 to 28 October 1991. The Parbhani SDPO, Parab, found witnesses who said that the police patil, Kishore Marathe, had incited the villagers to kill Ambadas. Parab noted that according to witnesses, the police patil remained near Ambadas and refused to send for help once he was badly wounded. Sawane's father said that the patil had sneered, 'Why don't *you* take him home?' Sawane's father said he had had asked, 'How did this happen, son?' To which Sawane replied, 'They have killed me, Bapu', and revealed the names of his killers.[12]

Kishore Marathe was not arrested until 29 August. Parab's evidence made it clear that the Tadkalas Sub-Inspector, Kolhapurkar, had ignored the police patil's involvement in Sawane's murder, suggesting police mishandling of the case. Significantly, Parab's investigation provided new evidence that he recorded in supplementary statements to the original investigation conducted by Kolhapurkar. Parab's investigation revealed that Sawane's murder was imbricated in local relations of power that the police had initially ignored. If Sawane's murder was political violence, what was at stake, why did the patil have such animus against him?

Before this issue could be addressed, press reports revealed that police practices came under scrutiny because a police officer (SDPO Gopalshetty, see below) who had visited the scene of the crime had spoken to the media about this case, arguing that caste tensions had *not*

[11] In 'Suggestions for Effective Policing in Rural Areas', Onkar Sharma observed that the *patils* and *kotwals* were a decaying institution, falling prey to political machinations. He writes: 'The present set-up of the Village Police is only nominal and its utility nearly nil. This Village Police agency is not in a position to meet the policing requirements of the villages efficiently and satisfactorily' (p. 239). *Eighth Police Science Congress* (Hyderabad: 1970). Debates such as this by IPS officers about the penetration of the police function into the village are important because they recognize policing as an explicitly political issue.

[12] Reported in 'Who Killed Ambadas Savne?', *Illustrated Weekly*, 14 September 1991.

been at the root of Sawane's murder. This revelation, like the involvement of the police patil in Sawane's murder, forced the police to respond to a larger context of publicity that evaluated their handling of Sawane's murder, derailing their attempts to handle the murder as an unfortunate, isolated incident. A police wireless noted:

> 7. SDPO from Sailu, S.B. Gopalshetty visited the offence. After visit Gopalshetty saw me, and told me that the incident was not an outcome of casteism but it took place all of a sudden. *Gopalshetty also issued a press release which states that he met the witnesses, majority of whom were from Hindu community and that according to them, the incident took place all of a sudden and there is no communal past history to the village.* [my italics] The press note further states that the incident took place due to misunderstanding which resulted in exchange of hot words followed by attack on the kotwal by the aforesaid five accused, injuring him seriously. . . .
>
> 8. I feel that . . . [the SDPO] did hurry in issuing the press note which was contrary to the very contents of the FIR and also to the facts subsequently revealed during investigation. It was because of this press note that the Department and also the Govt. of Maharashtra were put in embarrassing position. Not only this, but it resulted in unnecessary criticism by press and various political leaders that the police was partial and hiding the truth. From a bare read of the press note, it would be seen that the contents of Para I indicate that the incident of assault/murder took place due to temple-entry by a Mahar, i.e., Dalit, whereas para. 2 of the note speaks out all together [*sic*] different story that the incident took place all of a sudden due to misunderstanding. . . . On the spot enquiry revealed that Gopalshetty did not place true picture of the incident before me . . . he admitted to not have stated the facts of temple entry by a Mahar kotwal resulting in his murder by caste Hindus [with] an intention of avoiding likely flaming of communal atmosphere and its repercussions.[13]

When Gopalshetty's statement became public, it suggested that the police had not registered the importance of Ambadas's murder. By making a problematic 'public' statement, in fact, Gopalshetty had brought an unwelcome degree of attention on police practices, thereby compromising them. Moreover, by going to the press to 'clarify' that

[13] No. 5023/DSB/91, 19 August 1991. Superintendent of Police, Parbhani, to the DIGP, Aurangabad.

a misunderstanding was at the root of the matter, Gopalshetty sidestepped the caste component of Sawane's homicide. The news reading public, however, could not have missed Sawane's dalit identity. Thus in addition to implicating Gopalshetty, the press report also produced a broader climate of suspicion about police investigation into social evils.

Gopalshetty had told his superior that if the homicide had been publicized as a caste crime, it would have politicized the police investigation to the same extent as his (Gopalshetty's) press statement. Gopalshetty argued that he had in fact protected the fragile social relations in the village by not admitting to the full story of how Sawane had died, knowledge that might have led to further violence in the village. Gopalshetty's statement and the attempts to discipline him reveal that the police understood Sawane's murder as a caste crime. Even before the investigation progressed, the circumstances of Sawane's murder on the steps of the temple had registered as an exceptional incident. Gopalshetty appears to have been working with an earlier model of the police investigation as one that occurred under the sign of secrecy. The changed legal and political context, however, necessitated that the police bureaucracy address the case as a caste atrocity.

What is significant in both instances is that most local of the information had to be 'discovered' and declared from the very top of the chain of command in Bombay for it to be acknowledged by the local police. Grassroots common knowledge could not necessarily feed into the bottom-up osmosis of the conventional discovery process, of facts turning into knowledge, owing to the enclosed and self-referential character of police hierarchy enmeshed in a particular caste habitus. In this case the failure of an effective governmental apparatus had to be compensated by a governmentalized imagination acting in a more centralized, top-down fashion. The DIGP-PCR's note was enabled by a field of publicity that cut across these events, providing information capable of interrupting the police hierarchy. This field of publicity was diverse and diffuse. Interactions between media, activists, government functionaries such as those from the National Commission of SC/ST and the state and central governments' Social Welfare Ministry, members of the Legislative Asssembly, and NGOs produced a political context within which the police hierarchy was embedded. Publicity did not necessarily respect the police hierarchy of information (that is, local police gathered information while their superiors disciplined them by enforcing obedience to bureaucratic procedure), and was therefore capable of unsettling the enclosed world of the police investigation. It is to this issue that I turn next.

Publicity and Police

As Sawane's murder expanded beyond its immediate context, many aspects of the initial case were put to serious review. As different agencies and offices claimed jurisdiction over the review of the case, Sawane's murder began to involve police superiors, state and national politicians, and produced a juridical reading of dalit vulnerability that both recognized the atrocity of Sawane's murder, yet could not address it, mired as it was in a state-sanctioned sociology of untouchability.[14] Processes of fact-finding and hierarchical review functioned in tandem; the contest over how to frame Sawane's murder was both an internal one between government officers, and an external battle of publicity. This revealed the complex circuitry of debate, exchange, and compromise between apparatuses of state and political pressures.

The police wireless is an important point of entry into the case. It illuminates the working of the state apparatus and exposes the politicized nature of bureaucratic knowledge. Commands about following proper procedure were meant to ensure that the police recognized the unique caste component of Sawane's murder. Procedural discussions illuminated the 'new' demands on the police to make caste crime visible. Thus the transactions between different levels of the police illustrate how procedural discussions also allowed the caste component of the killing to be foregrounded or avoided, depending on the political pressures on the police.

[14] For instance, the Bureau of Police Research and Development, Ministry of Home Affairs, sponsored *Enforcement of Untouchability (Offences) Act 1955—A Survey* (1976). The Sardar Vallabhbhai Patel National Police Academy (Hyderabad) that trains IPS officers produced a *Syndicate Study on Implementation of the Protection of Civil Rights Act* (1980). Produced as regional studies of the effectiveness of these acts, the reports reflect the perspective of highly placed administrators who trained and sensitized police officers to respond to caste violence. Both reports carry sociological accounts of the practice of untouchability, and represent the practice as a social evil that has existed 'since time immemorial'.

As wireless reports negotiated the broader socius, we see that the outcomes of state intervention were contingent, the product of debate and negotiation between apparatuses of state with divergent, often contradictory, interests. These bureaucratic debates about procedure were significant because they illuminate how caste categories anchored shared concerns horizontally across organizations and vertically within them. Caste sociality seemed to work as a kind of quilting point, what Zizek calls a *point de capiton*, linking different sets of exchanges but remaining opaque and repetitive. The language of crime and atrocity had removed untouchability from the realm of social domination, and turned it instead into an aspect of governance. A police sociology of untouchability is evident in the same wireless message that mentioned Gopalshetty's unfortunate public statement. An earlier section of the wireless reads as follows:

> 4. [. . .] Dalits in the village even now do not enter the temple. If they want to worship or to take 'Darshan' they offer it from the footsteps of the temple from the outside. It was raining in the village on the fatal night. Kotwal Ambadas according to the F.I.R. lodged by his brother Kachru Sahebrao Sawane at P.S. Tadkalas on August 17 at 0700 hours was taking round as per the directions of Police Patil Kishore Marathe. When he reached in front of temple, he had to take shelter from rains inside the temple. Since he entered the sanctum of the temple the people gathered there for singing 'Bhajan' got annoyed. Heated arguments were exchanged between kotwal Sawane and these villagers. . . .
>
> According to the complainant Kachru Sahebrao Sawane b/o [brother of] the victim, he along with [another] when they were going in the village towards the temple to locate Ambadas, heard cries of Ambadas, the victim, at about 1030 p.m. near Hanuman temple. Hence, they rushed there and saw aforesaid persons attacking Ambadas with lathis and stones. Out of fear they ran towards their house and informed of the incident to the father . . . [they] went to the spot and found Ambadas lying unconscious in a pool of blood near footsteps of the temple.
>
> . . . It may be mentioned that the accused were saying that Ambadas Mahar entered into their temple and hence they were beating.[15]

[15] No. 5023/DSB/91, 19 August 1991, Superintendent of Police, Parbhani, to DIGP, Aurangabad.

I quote this report in some detail because of what it reveals about bureaucratic reason. The police report focused attention on the spectacular circumstances of Ambadas's murder on the steps of a temple, allegedly due to *mandir pravesh*, or temple entry. For instance, the wireless report drew attention to Sawane's entry into the temple as a transgressive act—'[s]ince he entered the sanctum of the temple the people gathered there for singing Bhajan during Nag Panchami got annoyed'. The police report also mentioned the upper-caste villagers' explanations for why they had used violence against Ambadas—'Ambadas Mahar entered into their temple hence they were beating'. Finally, the report drew attention to local caste etiquette—'Dalits in the village even now do not enter the temple. If they want to worship or to take "Darshan" they offer it from the footsteps of the temple from the outside.' The Superintendent of Police (SP) reproduced an upper-caste perspective in recognizing Sawane's entry into the Hanuman temple as a sacrilegious act with consequences. The wireless report is an internal document that recognized Ambadas's killing as a caste crime, even as its elaborate attention to village customs and dalit–savarna relations is generated from an upper-caste perspective.

In opposition to this wireless, which suggests that Sawane's murder should be understood as a return to a seemingly archaic, ritualized observance of untouchability, the PCR Cell consistently demanded a more political reading of the murder. Querying the lack of context to Sawane's murder, the DIGP-PCR sent a wireless query on 20 August, asking why there was no information about a long-standing dispute in the village. That very day, a wireless reply from the SP's office in Parbhani to Aurangabad and Bombay noted:

> (1) No previous dispute between the parties uptil incident 2) The facts came to be known to the police after the incident 3) The incident took place suddenly hence no preventive action taken in the matter. [#3 is underlined and on top of the wireless is handwritten 'How does the SP say that this happened suddenly. Ask the SP for detailed report with a special messenger at once.']

The PCR Cell had handwritten on top of the letter that it seemed unlikely that the murder had taken place suddenly, that the SP should provide more information about how a case could be made for the sudden eruption of conflict in Pimpri-Deshmukh. By 30 August, the DIGP-PCR had sent another wireless message to the SP in Parbhani asking why Bombay was yet to receive a detailed report about the incident. The DIGP also asked why the note given to the press had mentioned a misunderstanding when the first wireless report clearly showed that the offense of murder was committed on caste consideration.[16] The wireless circuit between the DIGP-PCR and the local police in Marathwada exhibits the role of the former as a watchdog, monitoring the provision of justice to vulnerable minorities, dalits and women. The DIGP-PCR represented a bureaucratic impetus to register Sawane's murder as a caste atrocity, an impetus that came into conflict, ironically, with the reluctance of the general police hierarchy to categorize Sawane's murder as an atrocity.

The press during this period was printing information that forced the police to respond to the public. A detailed report of Sawane's murder appeared in *Loksatta* on 28 August 1991. On that very day the DIGP-PCR had written the wireless about the police patil's involvement, which Parab was investigating in Pimpri-Deshmukh.[17] The DIGP's wireless had also, like the wireless above, focused on Sawane's murder near the temple as symbolically significant. Due to the external pressure and publicity around this case, the Additional Director General of Police (Law and Order) wrote to the Additional Chief Secretary of the Home Department (state of Maharashtra) on 30 August 1991. That letter, titled 'Incident of murder of a kotwal belonging to a backward community in Parbhani District', had been written to convey how the police had handled the case, and revealed little of the internal wranglings. That letter elicited a series of notes from the Home Department handwritten onto the letter.

> [Questions written onto page.]
>
> (1) Press note seems to have been clumsily prepared, and contains material that need not have been there.
>
> (2) No indication whether deceased had taken a leading part in installation of Ambedkar bust and whether this was resented by caste Hindus.

[16] No. 4372/DSB/91, 19 August 1991.

[17] Thus a supplementary FIR was filed afterwards indicating that Kishore Marathe, the police *patil*, was involved in Ambadas's murder.

(3) Whether such resentment manifested into altercations, or otherwise generated tension.

(4) Were office bearers like sarpanch, police patil, etc. involved?

(5) When was village last visited and didn't police official come to know of differences/tensions?

(6) SP's comment that the incident blew up after 10 days—apparently there was some whispering campaign from both sides.

This note, written in the margins of a formal letter, with its revelation of police mishandling at the district and village levels, reveals a parallel circuit of information, publicity that competed with knowledge produced by the official wireless report. Written in Bombay, the comments revealed knowledge that was carefully kept out of the letter. Especially significant to note is Sawane's attempts to install an Ambedkar statue, a piece of evidence that began to compete with the initial representation of Sawane's murder as the result of his taking shelter on the steps of the Hanuman temple. The note also bears the imprint of local politics and tensions (were the police patil and sarpanch involved; when was the village last visited) that exposed the compromises between the administrative and policing functions at the village and district levels. By then, Parab had recorded evidence of the police patil's involvement in Sawane's murder. Thus the involvement of state functionaries in this 'crime' was of no surprise to the author of the letter. In addition, the note exposed the police chain of command, with queries regarding the behaviour of the police at various levels, and the knowledge (probably gleaned from Intelligence accounts) that there was a whispering campaign for ten days prior to the incident. Significantly, this note addressed the local political context in Pimpri-Deshmukh. Instead of focusing on the issue of Sawane's murder near the temple, and began to focus attention on Sawane's attempts to install an Ambedkar statue.

The focus on the Ambedkar statue is relevant, because the local police in Pimpri-Deshmukh had come up with six probable 'causes' for Sawane's murder after conducting an on-the-spot inquiry and interviewing witnesses. The causes included: (1) something vague and ambiguous called 'tradition', which explained why dalits could not enter the temple, and had to stand at the steps to take darshan;

(2) Sawane's involvement in attempts to install a statue of Ambedkar in the village; (3) Sawane's consumption of large quantities of alcohol, which made him loquacious, and gave him the courage to enter the temple and abuse the caste Hindus assembled there [no alcohol was found in the blood during the autopsy]; (4) an 'illicit relation' between Sawane and a woman from the same village, which led to his being fatally assaulted by the woman's two brothers; (5) allegations that Sawane abused the Maratha villagers as well as the police patil's wife; and (6) suggestions that the event was a pre-planned human sacrifice. The set of motives constructed by the police took rumours in the village at face value, and tallied with statements by various political party leaders in newspapers about their understanding of the event.

For instance Advocate Shri Bobde (MLA, Shiv Sena) had suggested that Ambadas was killed due to an illicit love affair; Dalit Panther leader Rameshbhai Pandagale suggested human sacrifice as the cause of Ambadas's murder in an interview with *The Indian Express*, a view that was also supported by his colleague and Dalit Panther leader Gangadhar Gade in the *Maharashtra Times* on 4 September; The *Dainik Prabha* and *The Indian Express* published a story about the Ambedkar statue on 1 and 5 September respectively; Devidas Yashwant Deshmukh who held a liquor licence had come forward to testify that he had served Ambadas alcohol twice in his [Dukre's] home; Vishwanath Ganpath Dukre, participating in bhajans, testified that Ambadas was abusing Marathas in filthy language and that he also insulted the patil's wife.[18] These motives for Sawane's murder illustrate the local dynamics of caste and sexual enmity within which Sawane's murder was contextualized for police as well as the public. Many of these rumours detracted from forms of caste sociality that the police knew about through periodic visits to 'sensitive' villages, for example.[19] As it became necessary for the police to negotiate the thickets of rumour and publicity, their initial attempts to suggest localized political enmity as

[18] This is also noted in No. 5023/DSB/91, sent from Parbhani to Dy-IGP, Aurangabad Range, on 19 September 1991.

[19] Even in 1971, according to a CID (Intelligence) secret document, Pimpri-Deshmukh had been classified as a sensitive village. Villages are classified as sensitive according to their history of caste and communal violence, as well as reports of 'terrorist' activity in the area.

the cause of Sawane's murder were reinterpreted. Political pressure and publicity in fact lifted Sawane's murder from its highly localized context, and reframed it as a more representative form of political violence. The struggle to install an Ambedkar statue became the dominant explanation for Sawane's murder during this time.

There is an inverse relation between the transmission of information from the local village context, and the centralized bureaucratic chain of command. As the details of Sawane's death traversed this bureaucratic hierarchy, we see two distinct modes of addressing his murder: (1) localized attempts to maintain the status quo in the village which, in effect, meant containing knowledge of the perpetuation of untouchability; and (2) a greater sensitivity amongst the upper echelons of the police to the publicity that could be generated through evidence of neglect and misconduct. Both sets of practices were politically motivated—Bombay headquarters were under surveillance by the Maharashtra State Government's Home Department as well as by representatives of political parties, while the local police were reacting to the balance of power in Pimpri-Deshmukh. The responses by Bombay and the local police taken together illustrate the multiple interests and pressures upon the police, and their refraction through the police hierarchy. This schism also opened up a productive space for political negotiation engaging different strata of the state, and revealed how contentious the categorization of Sawane's murder as a caste crime had become.

It also becomes clear from reading the wireless reports that media publicity about Sawane's murder had alerted members of the state government, who had demanded information from the Home Department, which in turn asked for information from the police. For instance on 19 August , the Lok Sabha discussed the issue of atrocities against Scheduled Castes and Scheduled Tribes.[20] On 31 September,

[20] *Lok Sabha Debates*, vol. 3, 19–22 August 1991, pp. 225–94, 'Motion re. Atrocities Being Committed on the Scheduled Castes and Scheduled Tribes and Other Weaker Sections in the country.' This debate took place for about four hours, and considered issues ranging from the socio-economic weakness of SC/ST communities, to arguments about the persistence of untouchability as a social practice, to debates about making laws more stringent and effective. Besides the eclectic speaking styles of some members, what stands out most clearly is the range

the prime minister had written to all chief ministers requesting them to monitor atrocity cases.[21] The Committee on the Welfare of the Scheduled Castes and Scheduled Tribes argued that these measures were taken because of 'an astounding increase in the number of crimes committed against Scheduled Castes and Scheduled Tribes even after the implementation of [the PoA Act]', and noted that ironically, the passage of the act had produced greater collusion between state functionaries and upper-caste leaders, who prevented use of the PoA Act. Thus the central and state governments who had some investment, one assumes, in using the Act as a deterrent, had to respond to the fact that the existence of the PoA Act was producing caste violence. On 2 September, the DIGP-PCR alluded to this when he wrote to SP Parbhani saying:

> You are aware that DIGP PCR is looking after this subject and is required to send reports to State Government as well as Central government. It is very disappointing that you failed to send a report to me till it was discussed in the Parliament though you had sent your report to other officials. Explain your failure. All Unit Commanders are again requested to keep this in mind and must endorse copy of their wireless message and reports whenever atrocities are committed on SC/STs. Similar section of PAA must repeat must be applied wherever necessary.[22]

On 3 September 1991 The *Maharashtra Times* and the *Times of India* (*TOI*) carried news about the persistence of untouchability in Marathwada's villages. The journalist Rajdeep Sardesai noted in the *Times* that an NGO based in Vasai and the Nirmala Niketan School of Social Work, Bombay, had conducted a survey between 6 May and

---

of 'evidence' that was mobilized by speakers. Such evidence ranged from: stories from the Mahabharata about Eklavya's sacrifice of his thumb to illustrate the historic oppression of dalits; invocations of Ambedkar and Gandhi's arguments against untouchability, social and political evidence regarding the failure to implement reservations effectively, and the destitute conditions under which most SC/STs lived. Speakers consistently highlighted society's 'lack of resolve', as one member put it.

[21] *Committee on the Welfare of Scheduled Castes and Scheduled Tribes, Tenth Lok Sabha Report, 'Atrocities on Scheduled Castes and Scheduled Tribes and Patterns of Social Crimes Towards Them', 1992–1993*, p. 13. The Prime Minister also convened a meeting of chief ministers in October to discuss the atrocities issue.

[22] No. PCR/M-6/Parbhani D/T 2-9-9.

26 May 1991. The survey had found that over 80 per sent dalits did not have the right to enter temples in Marathwada, that they were barred from common water sources, performed defiling labour, and faced political discrimination. Sardesai's report concludes by noting that the report's finding questioned Maharashtra's claim to being a progressive state, the region that had produced Phule and Ambedkar.

On 6 September, the DIG-PCR sent a note demanding that special police officers be sent to the villages mentioned in the *Maharashtra Times* and *TOI* reports to investigate untouchability in these areas.[23] As they responded to external demands for more information, the police were placed in the awkward position of accepting untouchability as the broader context within which their own practices were situated, though they did not acknowledge this in the way they gathered village-level information.

A different *Times of India* report of 3 September noted negligence by government functionaries:

> Not only the police but the people's representatives seem very indifferent to the dastardly murder. The minister in charge of the district Lakshmanrao Dhate stated that he had not visited the village only because there would be an impression that he was on the side of only the Dalits. The Shiv Sena MLA of Parbhani, Mr Datta Bagade, said that he had not visited the village 'only because it would create tension, for except the Dalits and the Muslims all the others are voters of the Shiv Sena.'

Both the politics of untouchability and the struggles over political power came to be highlighted in the press accounts.[24] As various governmental agencies began to articulate with growing newspaper coverage of the event, the local context of caste relations became important

[23] No. PCR/M-3/Aurangabad 91 D/T 6-9-91. The note was sent to all police stations in Marathwada (under the ranges of Beed, Latur, Nanded, Osmanabad, Parbhani), to the DIG of the Aurangabad Range, the DySP-PCR in Aurangabad, as well as the Special IGP (Crime, Pune).

[24] Two reports of The Maharashtra State Government's *Anusuchit Jati Kalyan Samiti* [SC Welfare Committee] also addressed Sawane's murder in their 1991–2 *Cautha Ahval* [Fourth Report] and 1995–6 *Pahila Ahval* [First Report]. The 1991–2 report mentioned that the Welfare Committee had conducted a survey of the dalits [*magasvargiya*, backward class, is the literal term that is used] in Pimpri-Deshmukh on a 'war footing' [*yuddha patalivar*] in order to propose welfare schemes to build their confidence [*athmavishwas vadhavinyasathi*] in government!

because they were understood to contain the sociological conditions of possibility for Sawane's murder.

The most significant demand that Sawane's murder be recognized as an atrocity came from the National Commissioner of Scheduled Castes and Scheduled Tribes, Ram Dhan, who wrote to Chief Minister Sudhakarrao Naik on 12 September 1991 about his visit to Pimpri-Deshmukh on 3 September 1991. Ram Dhan's report emphasized Sawane's murder as the murder of a dalit victim, and drew upon the structures of legal recognition that the PoA Act provided. Ram Dhan's report begins:

> A sensational news item appeared in the *Times of India* dated 28-8-91 to the effect that a Scheduled Caste (Mahar) Police Kotwal of village Pimpri-Deshmukh in Parbhani district was stoned to death by upper-caste residents on 16-8-91 for standing on the steps of a Hanuman temple in the the village. That such an incident should have taken place in the year of the birth centenary of Dr Babasaheb Ambedkar is a matter of extreme shame to the Indian society.

Recognizing the symbolic significance of Ambadas's murder on the Hanuman temple steps, Ram Dhan associated the villagers' ire against Ambadas with his status as 'a young and upcoming leader of the Mahars'. He noted Ambadas's (foiled) attempts to install a statue of Ambedkar on a piece of *gaothan* land, and that the village had not celebrated Ambedkar Jayanti that year though it was the Ambedkar centenary. Ram Dhan had also noted the questionable behaviour of the village sarpanch.

Drawing on this, on 5th September the *Indian Express* noted that caste Hindus had prevented a procession being taken out to celebrate Ambedkar's birthday, and that the sarpanch had opposed the installation of an Ambedkar statue in the village even though Sawane had collected money from the dalits in the village to mark the Ambedkar centenary.[25] The DIGP also sent a wireless to the effect that the sarpanch of the village had 'neglected the incident and failed to act in the

[25] Noted in Wireless No. 5023/DSB/91, sent on 19 September 1991 from Parbhani to Dy-IGP, Aurangabad Range. Significantly, Kachru did not mentioned the installation of the statue and the ensuing tension in his FIR, the supplementary information gathered on 30 August 1991, or in his deposition before the Judicial Magistrate First Class on 1 October 1991.

capacity of head of the gram panchayat' only on 5 June 1992. (The case was decided on 18 June 1992.) As the attempts to depoliticize Sawane's murder by hiding the involvement of government officials such as the police patil and the sarpanch was revealed, the police and the state government negotiated to contain the political fallout of Sawane's death. Though the administration appears to have believed the murder was committed 'on the grounds of untouchability', they consistently downplayed it in public since these charges involved identifying perpetrators in the village, themselves representatives of the state.

Ram Dhan's report was especially significant in drawing attention to the symbolic charge of the Ambedkar statue, one that had led to Sawane's entanglements with, and eventual murder by, the caste Hindus of Pimpri-Deshmukh, though the police tried to guard against the immediate politicization of Ambadas's murder. Both Ram Dhan and Vivek Pandit demanded that Sawane's murder be registered under the PoA Act. The police finally registered the case under the PoA Act on 30 October 1991. Other government officials and the media too, began to press for registering Sawane's death as an atrocity, so that the perpetrators received the stringent punishment the PoA Act provided. The BJP led a delegation to the chief minister's office to press him to visit the village, and on 9 September the Republican Party of India (Athavale) held a demonstration of dalits in front of the district collectorate. By providing a political account of Sawane's murder, Ram Dhan's report pushed the temple desecration issue into the background.

Ram Dhan's report emphasized the geography of violence, the extent to which public space is a contested category. The attempt to claim 'public' space had invited an act of retribution upon Ambadas, reproducing the spatial logic of untouchability. Arguing that Ambadas's murder had been preceded by a struggle over the social signification of space, Ram Dhan illuminated a critical axis of dalit politics, the contest over the spatial and bodily codes through which untouchability was legible to most people.

Even more significantly, Ram Dhan argued that tensions between dalits and upper castes had existed since the demand for renaming Marathwada University after Babasaheb Ambedkar, and the large-scale violence against dalits that the *namaantar* [renaming] movement had unleashed during 1977–8.[26] Thus Ram Dhan's report provided a political explanation for Sawane's murder, connecting this discrete instance of caste crime with a much broader upper-caste resentment against dalit militancy. His report interrupted the police narrative and its containment of Sawane's murder by reframing the account as an atrocity. As with the office of the DIGP-PCR, we see that Ram Dhan was both a part of the state apparatus and exposed the limits of its political imagination and bureaucratic implementation. Thus these disparate interests within the bureaucracy jockeyed to sensitize the police, convinced that Sawane's murder was an atrocity because he was a dalit. This was the mandate, in a sense, of both the Commissioner of SC/ST and the DIGP-PCR.[27]

[26] Even before the Shiv Sena came to power during the 1995 elections, the Congress government had agreed to repeal over 1,100 PoA Act cases across the state in exchange for the renaming of Marathwada University as 'The Babasaheb Ambedkar Marathwada University', which occurred on 14 January 1994. Thus the symbolic renaming also meant that dalits who had experienced violence in the aftermath of the 1994 renaming—much as they had during 1977 and 1978—were left without recourse to the progressive legislation of the PoA Act. There is a large literature on the *namaantar* struggle. The next section of this essay draws on much of this literature to construct a brief political history of the *namaantar* struggle. Some important examples of pamphlets and reports produced locally include: A more recent examination of the renaming struggle is Sudhir Gawhane, *Namaantar Ladha—Ek Shodhyatra* (The Namaantar Struggle, A Quest) (Mumbai: Parivartan Prakashan, 1996). Gawhane's book commemorates the renaming struggle. Other works include: *Asmitadarsh* (a literary journal with volumes from 1967, editor Professor Gangadhar Pantawane); Ashok M. Baile and Jayant M. Baile, *Marathwada Udrekacha Itihas* (Mumbai, n.d); P.T. Borale, *Segregation and Desegregation in India. A Socio-Legal Study* (Bombay: Manaktala, 1968); R.M. Biwalkar, and Z. Kamble. *Mahadacha Muktisangram* (Pune: Rajhans Prakashan, 1977); M.B. Chitnis, *Namantaraviruddha Atyachari Andolan* (Aurangabad); Gopal Guru, 'Dalit Killings in Marathwada', *Economic and Political Weekly*, 21 December 1991, and 'Hinduisation of Ambedkar in Maharashtra', *Economic and Political Weekly*,vol. XXVI, no. 7, Feb 1991; *Research Report on Holocaust in Marathwada, 1978* (School of Interdisciplinary Studies, Pune University). The last was produced by a group of independent investigators from Pune University. The Commission on the Welfare of Scheduled Castes and Scheduled Tribes produced a study of the riot situation in Marathwada, and presented it to Parliament on 30 April 1979.

[27] For an early piece about the lack of governmental bureaucratic resolve in empowering the Commissione of SC/ST, see Marguerite J. Fisher, 'Problems of

This should be set against a note from Parbhani to the Dy-IGP, Aurangabad Range on 19 September :

> The incidence of murder of a Mahar kotwal Ambadas Sawane by caste Hindus at village Pimpri in Parbhani District on 16-8-91 has attracted huge press publicity and also visits by various V.I.P.s including Social Welfare Minister Ramdas Athwale, Parbhani District Minister Shri Madhukarrao Ghate, Hon. Chief Minister of Maharashtra and Shri Ramdhan, Chairman SC/ST, Government of India, New Delhi followed by the visits of different political parties and social delegations led by Dalit Panther, B.J.P., S.K.P., Shiv Sena, Human Rights Association, 'Rachnatmak Sangarsh Samiti', etc. to the village. I was also present for supervising bandobast and security arrangements. The press, State Associations and even Parliament had brought the village under focus over the above incident.[28]

As the police investigation came to interact with other forms of publicity, not only did Sawane's murder increasingly come to be represented as a caste atrocity, but the question of what precisely constituted the practice of untouchability was interpreted differently. Some press reports in English and Marathi tended towards understanding his murder as a case of mandir pravesh, locating the atrocity in the barring of entry into the temple. Others like Ram Dhan focused on the struggles over the Ambedkar statue as a political struggle. Pratap Bhangar, an advocate and activist of the Janata Dal, made an important statement about party affiliation. 'The police patil and the sarpanch have been politically affiliated for 10 years. At that time Ambadas and Kachru, who are today actively involved with dalit politics, were also with them. In fact they were dependent on Ambadas. With the entry of the Shiv Sena two years ago, the first seeds of discord were sown.'[29] We know from another press report that the five men convicted of

---

Implementation of India's Office of the Commissioner of Scheduled Castes', *Western Political Quarterly*, vol. 23, pp. 715–32.

[28] No. 5023/DSB/91.

[29] 'Who Killed Ambadas Savne?' *Illustrated Weekly*, 14 September 1991. I met Bhangar on 27 July 1996, because he was knowledgeable about the workings of the PoA Act. Though a Janata Dal activist during the Sawane murder, he had switched to the Shiv Sena when I met him. His wife, who accompanied me on my first visit to Pimpri-Deshmukh, told me that Bhangar (an OBC himself) did not like the Sena ethos but had chosen to go with the party that gave him a ticket.

Sawane's murder were all Shiv Sena activists. Significantly, the Maharashtra State Welfare Committee noted that in their meeting with Kachru it had emerged that the Muslims in the village had tried to leave Pimpri-Deshmukh when the Shiv Sena came to power. Ambadas had stopped them.[30] Thus the political context of Sawane's murder was complicated, suggesting that beyond the many forms through which the practice of untouchability was perpetuated, there were personal/ political rivalries that were being played out.[31]

Counter-narratives

> The Milind campus in Aurangabad is now an educational and cultural centre, thanks to the efforts of Dr Babasaheb Ambedkar. We now want to convert it into a power centre.[32]

> *Ayushyaman Kamble, jar tumhala Shiv Sena parvadnaar nahi, (tar) Jai Bhim*!' [Dear Mr Kamble, if the Shiv Sena doesn't sit well with you, then Jai Bhim!][33]

> Busloads of people come from Aurangabad's environs to have *darshan* of the BAMU [Babasaheb Ambedkar Marathwada University] gate. The gate itself is in the shape of a *stupa*, to evoke the Buddhist sites in the region such as Ajanta and Ellora, plus the mass Dalit conversion in 1956. I am surprised that people often take *darshan* [glimpse of a ritually charged

[30] Maharashtra State Government *Anusuchit Jati Kalyan Samiti* [SC Welfare Committee] *Cautha Ahval* [Fourth Report], 1991–2, p. 6.

[31] For a recent account of Sena politics, see Thomas Blom Hansen, *Wages of Violence: Identity and Naming in Postcolonial Bombay* (Princeton: Princeton University Press, 2001).

[32] Anon., interviewed by the research team investigating the Marathwada riots.

[33] During fieldwork in Bombay an activist and *shahir* [singer of revolutionary ballads] told me that in Mantralaya, [the seat of the state government in Bombay] he had seen this graffiti in the men's lavatories reading '*Ayushyaman Kamble, zar tumhala Shiv Sena parvadnaar nahi tar Jai Bhim*!' [Dear Mr Kamble, if you do not support the Shiv Sena, then Jai Bhim]. Kamble is a 'typical' dalit name, and Jai Bhim the classic greeting amongst Ambedkarites. The graffiti alludes to the Shiv Sena's perception of the separate identity of Mahars as a constituency, and indicates their readiness to ignore them since they are perceived to be politically negligible. The virulent antagonism between dalits and the Shiv Sena during the 1970s is thus signalled (in this slogan) as a thing of the past, in the context of the current (late 1990s) hegemony of the Shiv Sena in Maharashtra.

object, idol] at the BAMU gate and leave an offering, as though the university is a pilgrimage site.[34]

I would like to take this opportunity to move away from the governmental context, within which I have been considering Sawane's murder, in order to draw attention to how Sawane's murder might articulate with the broader context of dalit political struggles in Maharashtra. Due to considerations of space, I will take up Ram Dhan's important suggestion that the namaantar movement, the struggle to rename Marathwada University in Aurangabad, was an important precursor that had enabled Ambadas's politicization.

Between 1974 and 1978/9 dalits attempted to mark out urban space in Bombay through the actions of a group of young militants called the Dalit Panthers, rename the regional university in Marathwada in honour of Bhimrao Ambedkar, and erect busts of Ambedkar and fly the blue flag [*nila jhanda*] across Marathwada's villages. So important was the proliferation of signs such as Ambedkar's bust or blue flags, that they changed the urban and rural landscape. These were important means of announcing a new dalit identity.

To dalits the namaantar riots have provided an alternative history of violence, enabling and constraining further narratives. The renaming was a critical conjuncture in the experience of violence. It politicized dalits across Maharashtra and gave them a sense of their collective vulnerability to upper-caste anger. At the same time, phenomena such as the Dalit Panthers and the outpouring of dalit literature provided a means of countering upper-caste violence and oppression actively.

In 1978 and 1979, a series of riots and acts of collective violence occurred in concentrated fashion for about two weeks in Marathwada.[35] These were unprecedented in scope and organization even in that region, which has a bloody history of caste, class, and religious strife. The riots were provoked initially by the namaantar agitation. The demand for renaming Marathwada University and the ensuing transactions between dalit activists of varying political persuasions, community leaders, and the government took place in the city of Aurangabad. But

[34] Fieldnotes (excerpted, shortened), 17 April 1996.

[35] Marathwada comprises Beed, Jalna, Nanded, Osmanabad, Parbhani, and Latur districts, all part of the Nizam's Hyderabad.

the fallout of the violence that began in July 1978 was experienced most intensely in rural areas where houses were torched, dalits burnt alive, property destroyed, and statues of Ambedkar and Buddha desecrated. Academic observers explained the riots as a result of the growing embourgeoisment and urbanization of dalits, and the emergence of a shift in dalit identity and consciousness.[36] Aurangabad city and Marathwada's rural hinterland were the centres of the namaantar agitation, and the Dalit Panthers played a key part in the agitation.[37]

The Dalit Panthers engaged in urban politics—political violence around election time, neighbourhood turf battles, and so forth. Their identity was a militant political group distinct from an older, more corrupt dalit political leadership. During the riots in 1974 in the Naigaon–B.D.D. chawls (tenements) in Bombay, for instance, the Panthers came into open conflict with the Shiv Sena for the first time, in what was referred to at the time as urban warfare. The Panthers emerged as a counter-force in localities such as the Naigaon-BDD chawls by engaging in violence that made use of everyday objects such as cycle chains, soda bottles, and tubelights.[38] The riots clarified the emerging

[36] This had to do partly with the militancy of educated dalit youth, and the support of respected intellectuals.

[37] The Dalit Panthers were inspired by the Black Panthers in the United States and took their name from them. The Panthers formed as a public group in 1973, as a reaction to large-scale corruption and factionalism within the Republican Party of India (hereafter RPI) and its co-optation by various forces within the Congress. More specifically, the Panthers had come together informally over countering a boycott of dalits in the village of Bavda in Pune District in 1972, after which they continued to press for a radical and violent stance towards atrocities committed against dalits, and the government's ineffectuality in containing them. The group of young male radicals had drawn attention to themselves through their vitriolic critiques of Hinduism, caste Hindus, and the RPI. The RPI was officially formed in 1957, one year after Ambedkar's death, to substantiate his vision for a political party that would fight for the rights of dalits and labouring classes. Though a national party, the RPI's influence has been strongest in Maharashtra, and that too as a party of Mahars. The RPI has been co-opted by the Congress, and tends to swing with that part of the Congress that offers RPI leaders a berth in the state government. Since its inception the RPI has been riven with factionalism, and breakaway groups.

[38] In all 70 (out of 121) chawls in Worli were affected by the violence. The mission of the Bombay City Improvement Trust, which built the chawls, was, among

contradictions between the Panthers and a growing regional political formation, the Shiv Sena, over the struggle for controlling city space and neighbourhoods, and access to political power.[39] Some of the strategies and tactics developed in the context of these urban struggles were transferred to the mobilization around namaantar. The crucial distinction was that the spread of violence in the Marathwada riots was more haphazard and did not (could not) follow the logic of targeting neighbourhoods and built spaces.

Panther self-identification through virulently anti-casteist political rhetoric, claims to city spaces such as slums as the site of both exploitation and radicalization, and the turn to 'lumpen' or criminalized lifestyles were all perceived as a threat by the state. The Panthers were kept under police surveillance. Dalitness also became a matter of metropolitan sensibility and aesthetic self-fashioning at this time. The Panthers made the namaantar struggle a crucial aspect of the militant, masculine urban politics they supported. The namaantar became a matter of importance to urban dalits, focusing policy towards the matter of reservations in jobs and schools, segregation in urban housing, and the presence of caste blocks in slums and chawls. The demand played out differently in Marathwada, however, because of that region's history.

Marathwada, which became a part of Bombay only in 1960, was considered a feudal, underdeveloped region. The People's Education Society [hereafter PES] was established in 1945 to support dalit education. In Aurangabad the PES had established the Dr Babasaheb Ambedkar College of Arts and Commerce, the Dr Ambedkar College

---

other things, 'constructing sanitary dwellings for the poor and the police'. The trust was begun in 1898. In J.P. Orr, *The Bombay City Improvement Trust from 1898 to 1909* (Bombay: Times Press, 1911). In the ensuing violence, stones were hurled from the terraces of the chawls, brick missiles taken from the walls of the chawls' bathrooms were used, and at one point a live electricity wire was used to separate two sections of the chawl. The state government commissioned the *Report of the Commission of Inquiry on the Worli and Naigaum B.D.D. Chawls Disturbances in Bombay* headed by Justice Bhasme.

39 The B.D.D. chawls are located in the mill area. The area was already radicalized, with a strong leftist trade union presence amongst the mill hands. Both upper-caste Hindus and dalits would have shared an identity as mill workers.

of Law, and Milind College on land provided by the Nizam of Hyderabad. Initially, however, only 200 of the 800 students at the PES institutions were dalits. This began to change during the 1960s, with dalits students from Nagpur constituting the new majority. Educational institutions in Aurangabad are segregated along caste lines to a far greater extent than in Bombay, certainly. The counter to the PES institutions is the Saraswati Bhavan College, upper caste in orientation.[40] An account of the Marathwada riots noted the caste segregation of educational institutions:

> Milind Mahavidyalaya's English initials M.M. are popularly taken to mean Mahar-Mang college. The students call Saraswati Bhavan the Shetji Bhatji [merchants and brahmins] college; Maulana Azad College is known as the Mohammedan College, and Vasant Rao Naik College is called Vanjari College [Naik's caste]. . . . When Babasaheb Ambedkar's follower Shankarrao Kharat [an eminent dalit writer] became the Chancellor of Marathwada University, the students disparagingly referred to it as Maharwada University.[41]

The namaantar agitation started in 1977, and gained momentum to culminate in the Long March of 6 December 1979 which brought activists from all over Maharashtra to participate in a civil disobedience movement that culminated in Aurangabad. Activists courted arrest along the way, and embarked on a *jail bharo* [fill the jails] programme. Over these two years Marathwada was under siege, and many random acts of violence, as well as highly planned acts of violence, arson, and looting were carried out with the connivance of local authorities. The violence in rural areas conflated the bodies of dalits and markers of dalit pride such as statues and flags. Houses were torched, in at least a few instances dalits were set on fire, and their property was looted. The namaantar agitation failed, and the university was known as Marathwada University until 1994/5 when the name was changed to the Babasaheb Ambedkar Marathwada University, as a compromise to upper-castes who were against losing the regional appellation of the institution.

The namaantar agitation by urban dalits led to a terrific backlash

[40] This is largely true, though this should not suggest that dalits do not ever attend Saraswati Bhuvan.

[41] Ashok M. Baile and Jayant M. Baile, *Marathwada Udrekacha Itihas* (Mumbai: n.d.), p. 16.

against rural dalits, far removed from the demands for renaming. The primary mode of violence during the riots was arson. House upon house was burnt, as were the *samaj mandirs* [community centres] located in the Maharwadas. Some examples from the Parliamentary Report will suffice.

> [In Akola village] The first house that was set on fire belonged to Shri Kashinath Borde, a police patil from New Buddhists who is owner of 14 acres of agricultural land in the village. He had installed a flour mill in the village and was quite well off. He was the main target of the fury of the caste Hindus because in his official capacity he had been reporting the cases of harassment of Scheduled Castes. . . . His bullock cart and household articles were burnt. . . . The attackers set fire to the house with Mashals [long torches].

In village Kandari Khurd '27 houses belonging to Scheduled Castes and Neo Buddhists were . . . burnt.' In Adgaon village a dalit was threatened: 'He should be burnt alive. There was a cattle shed nearby and it was also set on fire. All agricultural implements were burnt.' In Parbhani, the Study Group team held a meeting with officials from the *zilla parishad* (district) where they were told that in Parbhani the agitators had started stopping trains and buses, and cutting telephone lines from 17 July 1978. The police had done nothing, and after 30 July, dalit *bastis* (habitations) were targeted. Village Temburni, in Nanded District was the scene of a horrible act that has become a central part of dalit counter-history. Pochiram Kamble was chased, brought back to village Chouka, and burnt to death.

Justice R.R. Bhole, a retired judge who brought out a pamphlet on the violence in Marathwada, wrote:

> I have gone around with my friends and workers and visited many affected villages and found to my dismay that there was hardly any connection between the violence committed on poor Dalits and the renaming of Marathwada University as Dr Babasaheb Ambedkar Marathwada University. The poor villagers whose properties were destroyed and whose life and liberty were threatened did not even know what this University was and whether there was any proposal to change its name. . . .

In 1978, cases of violence were reported from places as far away as Nagpur and Pune. The reign of terror unleashed against dalits was sustained, with the most horrific instances of violence, such as Pochiram

Kamble's, being marked in dalits' memories either through the proper name or the geographical location.

The *namavistaar* (name enlarging) agitation in 1994 was as brutal, but more restricted in scope than previously, occurring mainly in the districts of Beed, Osmanabad, and Parbhani. This time, the state government accepted the demand to enlarge the name Marathwada University to 'Dr Babasaheb Ambedkar Marathwada University', while the Panthers worked out a deal with the then-ruling Congress, and its immediate successor the Shiv Sena, to remove atrocities cases filed under the PoA Act.[42] The Shiv Sena government's contention was that dalits had misused the act to carry out acts of revenge against the upper castes.

The politics of large-scale violence during the namaantar agitations indelibly marked dalit–savarna relations, as Ram Dhan noted in his account. The namaantar agitation led to caste riots and massacres of an order that Maharashtra certainly had not known, and dalit youth were politicized in response. More important, as this section indicates, was the political contradiction that brought Dalit Panthers into violent conflict with the Shiv Sena, equating caste conflict with political tensions with great consequence. This larger political history inflected Sawane's murder, yet it was so deeply integrated into the daily relations of caste sociality in Pimpri-Deshmukh, that it took a struggle over the Ambedkar statue to reveal the deeper symbolic politics at play. This at least is how I interpret Ram Dhan' sensitivity to the regional specificities of Sawane's murder. These political memories, however, fell completely outside the judicial narrative.

Pronouncement: Legal Structures of Recognition

> Acts of brutality and terror continue to be part of the atrocities perpetrated on the Dalits and other lower classes, the more so the more [*sic*] they become conscious of their rights and begin to assert themselves . . . No

[42] The *namavistaar* agreement occurred when Sharad Pawar was still in power, as Congress chief minister of the state. When the Shiv Sena came to power that year (1994), it announced it would begin to revoke 'false cases'. It is generally believed that the Congress and the Shiv Sena were bargaining with the RPI on similar terms regarding the revocation of atrocities cases, arguing that the stringent provisions of the 1991 Act had succeeded in alienating many people.

> doubt the more such assertion takes place, the more the backlash from the upper castes and well to do who find this rise of the masses—something they have never been used to—intolerable and the more the efforts to divide, confuse, and coopt the forces of change.[43]

> If the discourse of the broadsheet helps open up a path for crime to enter history, it is the function of judicial discourse as a genre to cut off that path by trapping crime in its specificity, by reducing its range of signification to a set of narrowly defined legalities, and by assimilating it to the existing order as one of its negative determinations.[44]

The first two sections of this essay traced the transformation of the raw intelligence gathered through police work into the repetitive narrative structure of the wireless report, illuminating how governmental knowledge is vulnerable to internal and external mechanisms of surveillance (the media, local activists, the upper echelons of the police). Ironically, judicial discourse is thoroughly embedded in the information produced through practices of policing. We might be at a disadvantage in understanding the structures of legality if we are not attentive to how judicial knowledge is itself contaminated by the political negotiations that discursively structure a criminal case such as Sawane's.[45]

In this section I illustrate that the discourse of caste violence is important in producing new forms of legal subjectivity and changed forms of caste embodiment. In the legislation of Sawane's murder, normalizing judicial-legislative frameworks of the postcolonial state articulated with a distinct form of subalternity, i.e. dalitness, to politicize dalit and upper-caste identities as those of victim and perpetrator. This changed the experiential forms of these identities. Rather than enforcing a return to the status quo, caste violence unsettled the

[43] Rajni Kothari, 'Rise of the Dalits and the Renewed Debate on Caste', in Partha Chatterjee, ed., *State and Politics in India* (Delhi: Oxford University Press, 1997), esp. pp. 439 and 441.

[44] Ranajit Guha, 'Chandra's Death', *Subaltern Studies V* (Delhi: Oxford University Press, 1995), p. 140.

[45] This enlarges upon Baxi's critique of the Subaltern Studies collective's failure to engage rigorously with the labours of law. Upendra Baxi, ' "The State's Emissary": The Place of Law in Subaltern Studies', *Subaltern Studies VII* (Delhi: Oxford University Press, 1992), pp. 247–64.

socius, functioning as a form of politics rather than a substitution for politics proper. [46]

I have examined how police procedure and bureaucratic hierarchies articulated with forms of critical publicity to force the police to recognize Sawane's murder as a caste crime. I now move to the manner in which the case was brought to judgment by exploring how Adharkar connected the narrative of historic caste tension in the village with his evidentiary findings regarding intent, how he brought history together with politics. As I argued earlier, Adharkar's judgment revealed an awareness of the socio-political context within which Sawane's murder took place, yet ignored how caste sociality inflected the police investigation and resultant publicity. In so doing, Adharkar's judgment failed to recognize the atrocity of murder. Partly there were problems with the PoA Act itself, which assumed untouchability as a ground for the commission of caste crime, yet demanded that judges follow standard judicial procedure in bringing criminal trials to closure. This produced a split in judicial reason between the recognition of a caste atrocity, and the inability to address it by punishing its perpetrators. But more revealing are the limits to Adharkar's state-sanctioned sociology of caste and untouchability.

The Special Judge, V. B. Adharkar passed his judgment on Special Case No. 11/91 in the Parbhani Sessions Court on18 June 1992.[47] Adharkar's judgment began with a description of the 'geographical situation' and the 'social structure' of the village before considering how Sawane was murdered. Adharkar's focus on the geography of the village and the way in which Sawane was murdered suggests his recognition of the changed, 'political' character of violence against dalits. The desecration of Ambedkar and Buddha statues, harm to dalits' livelihood by destroying property or expropriating land illegally, and the use of caste-based insults are the direct results of dalit politicization

[46] The 1999 Human Rights Watch report, *Broken People*, argues that political and economic assertion by dalits is one of the reasons for their vulnerability to physical and symbolic violence. For a critique of the report's trans-historical focus on violence, see my review in *The Bulletin of Concerned Asian Scholars*, 32: 3 (July–September 2000), pp. 65–7.

[47] The first court for atrocities cases is the Sessions Court, which functions as a Special Court and the judge as Special Judge.

and collective struggle. Adharkar understood Ambadas's political consciousness—visible to him in Ambadas's attempts to install an Ambedkar statue—to have led to his murder. Adharkar recognized two forms of violence in Sawane's murder: new and violent forms of caste sociality commensurate with broader socio-political shifts indicated by the the fact that the Ambedkar statue had become the focal point of struggles between dalits and savarnas, *and* retaliatory counter-violence that attempted to reproduce dalits' stigmatized status. The struggles to install the Ambedkar statue had caused counter-violence that attempted to replicate seemingly archaic forms of caste sociality. Adharkar understood Sawane's murder on the temple steps, i.e. the upper castes' maintenance of the temple's purity, as such a form of retaliatory violence that attempted to maintain caste privilege in the face of dalit militancy. Dalit political militancy was met with an anachronistic form of violence in order to bar entry into a temple. Adharkar mobilized this form of explanation in his judgment.

The judgment begins with a geographical description that is correlated with the structure of caste power:

> As per ancient custom the untouchables reside in a separate Wasti outside the village at a distance of 300 feet towards the North side. The said Wasti was previously known as Maharwada and now as Boudhwada. For the sake of convenience it is referred to as Maharwada. There is a way from the village to the Maharwada running East–West. The Maharwada is the north side of the road and a house of . . . a caste Hindu (Mali) is to the South of the road. The untouchables decided to install a statue of Dr Babasaheb Ambedkar near the house of the said [Hindu] (p. 3).

Later the judge noted: 'On this proposed site the untouchables made the construction of the basement for installation of the statue 1½ months before the incident. The said site is not in the Maharwada but in the village' (p. 6).

The sarpanch and the police patil had opposed the installation of the statue. In July, when Sawane had started construction of the plinth of the statue, the police patil threatened him with dire consequences, but this went unreported to the police. To Adharkar this highlighted dalit political consciousness that the installation of an Ambedkar statue constituted a challenge to the geography of untouchability. The judge focused on Sawane's efforts to install Ambedkar's statue in the main part of the village, not the Maharwada. He noted that the villagers had tried to bribe the dalits with Rs 500 if they installed the Ambedkar statue in the Maharwada. Adharkar noted: '[S]ometimes the police had to go there to maintain law and order, and to see that there should not be breach of peace.' The caste Hindus had also wanted to install a statue of Savata Mali, a Bhakti saint, on the same site that Sawane had claimed.

The installation of Ambedkar's statue in the caste Hindu section of the village was read as both spatial trespass and a challenge to the dominance of the Malis and Marathas in the village. Ambedkar's statue was also a symbol of a protracted struggle to resignify dalit access to public space, overturning the structures of power and privilege that enforced the distinction between Maharwada and village. It is important that the judgment refers to a political struggle over dalit identity that preceded Ambadas's death. Thus Adharkar's judgment draws attention to a form of commemoration that politicizes space in localities, whether in villages or urban slums, indicating dalit struggles for dignity and political recognition.

In his judgment, Adharkar also drew attention to another political geography, that of the temple. In fact his judgment moves from the Ambedkar statue to the events at the temple on 16 August. Though the temple was supposedly a 'public place', Adharkar's judgment also focused on the temple as a symbolically charged space.[48] Sawane's murder

[48] Arjun Appadurai, *Worship and Conflict under Colonial Rule: A South Indian Case* (Cambridge: Cambridge University Press, 1981); Granville Austin, *The Indian Constitution: Cornerstone of a Nation* (Oxford: Clarendon Press, 1966); Partha Chatterjee, 'Secularism and Tolerance', in Rajeev Bhargava, ed., *Secularism and Its Critics* (Delhi: Oxford University Press, 1998); Aravamuda G. Iyengar, *The Temple Entry by Harijans* (Nellore: Sanatana Dharma Printing Agency, 1935); L.T. Kikani, *Caste in Courts or Rights and Powers of Castes in Social and Religious Matters as Recognized by Indian Courts* (Rajkot: Ganatra Printing Works, 1912); Dilip Menon, *Caste, Nationalism and Communism in South India* (Cambridge: Cambridge University Press, 1994); Chidambaram P. Pillai, *Right of Temple-Entry* (Nagercoil: Alexandra Press, 1933); Anupama Rao, 'The Emergence of a Dalit Public', in *The Caste Question: Struggles for Rights and Recognition* (forthcoming); and Cornelia Sorabji, 'Temple Entry and Untouchability', *The Nineteenth Century and After*, vol. CXIII, January–June 1933, pp. 689–702.

on the steps of the temple was repeatedly read by Adharkar as an instance of *mandir pravesh*. The judge noted that untouchability was practised in the village because dalits were not allowed to enter the temple in the village. 'The untouchables were prohibited from making entry into the temple on the ground of untouchability. In this way the untouchability was observed in the village.' The judge mentioned a series of events that exemplified this politics of space: the upper castes had denied Sawane entry into the Maruti temple because he was a dalit, they had insulted him by calling him Mahardya, and they had assaulted him *on the steps of the temple*. In his judgment Adharkar emphasized that the defense had not even tried to prove that the upper castes did not practise untouchability (p. 86).

An atrocity is by its very definition a public act with witnesses who can testify to the caste crime. The spectacular nature of the violation must be reproduced if the legal apparatus is to intervene. The fact that Ambadas was brought outside the temple, and referred to as Mahardya while he was being assaulted, became a critical element of the judgment. In addition to the spatial logic of untouchability, Adharkar also relied on the use of the term Mahar or Mahardya by the crowd assembled outside the temple. When asked why Ambadas was being beaten, the crowd outside the temple had maintained that the 'temple has been dis-sacred'! (The wording of the English translation of the judgment produced by the Aurangabad High Court.) The police report stated that the crowd outside the temple said 'In our temple Ambadas Mahar had come and therefore we have been beating him' (p. 73). Oral evidence gathered in court claimed that the crowd outside the temple said to Ambadas's brother: 'Oh Mahardya, how did your brother enter into the temple? The temple has dis-sacred' (p. 73).

The prosecution maintained that the status of the word 'Mahardya' as a term of abuse for dalits was important, not the question of who was addressed by the insulting name. The defence maintained that it was unclear whether Ambadas or his brother was called Mahardya. Because the PoA Act considers a caste insult as a psychic wound approaching the severity of a physical injury, this dispute over names achieves some significance. But the defence also argued: 'Because the villagers knew that Ambadas was Mahar by caste, if such person was referred to as ' "Mahar Ambadas' or only "Ambadas" has no meaning at all', attempting to elide the issue of the case insult altogether. In effect the defence was arguing that because Ambadas was known to be a dalit, verbal confirmation of his identity should not constitute a hidden motive for the crime. Adharkar countered that the *substance* of the testimony indicated that Ambadas's presence had desecrated the temple, that the crowd had conflated Ambadas's dalitness with his pollution of the temple.

Though Adharkar took the caste insult seriously, proving that the accused had intended to kill Sawane became slightly trickier. Adharkar's hesitation in ruling that the villages had committed a caste atrocity had to do with his focus on *intent*. The judge argued that there was no way of proving that the accused had joined together with the intent of committing murder. The beatings might have been motivated by the support for untouchability but the murder was in excess of the intent to grievously hurt and injure Sawane, and therefore it was not premeditated. While protecting the temple from pollution was a common object, the nature of the violence was unplanned. The accused had used weapons at their disposal spontaneously—the stones that were lying in a heap outside, and the sticks [*kathi*] they usually carried when they went out at night. It should be noted that according to a strict intepretation of the PoA Act, the defence would have had to prove that the accused did not mean to murder Sawane.

Adharkar also opened up the issue of intent by drawing on testimony by a dalit witness about the prohibitions on temple entry. Some dalit boys who had come from out of town with a wedding party in either 1985 or 1986 had entered the Hanuman temple, and the dalits in the village had been threatened with dire consequences if the boys weren't disciplined (p. 84). Though the witness had offered this as evidence of proscriptions on temple entry, Adharkar argued that this proved that entering a temple itself could not have led to Sawane's murder! The judge argued that the accused had assault, rather than murder, as their object. Since Adharkar did not believe that the evidence proved that the villagers in the Hanuman temple had *planned* to murder Sawane, his death could not be characterized as murder due to caste atrocity. Moreover, since the assailant who threw the rock that fatally injured Sawane could not be identified, none of the men could be punished for murder. He writes: '[T]he sum and substance of the evidence is that deceased Ambadas sustained one fatal injury resulting in death but it could not [be] attributed to a particular accused person in this case.'

Having produced a narrative about the socio-political context, Adharkar chose to close the case by sticking narrowly to the issue of intent. Adharkar did not mention the issues of police negligence that had been publicized so heavily except to note that three policemen had investigated Sawane's murder, producing discrepant accounts. Those discrepancies themselves warranted neither comment nor contextualization, though the judge had noted the pressure on the police to address the murder with the seriousness it deserved when he noted that the police investigation seemed to have taken a different turn after Parab began his investigation. 'There is no evidence that the political leaders or the Ministers brought pressure or influence on the investigation officers, but the truth is, as can be seen from the facts stated earlier, the direction of the investigation had changed. . . .' (p. 40).

Though Parab seems to have relied on Sawane's dying declaration, which named his assailants, Adharkar later contested this account, noting that the severity of Sawane's injury meant that he would have been unconscious by the time Kachru and others arrived at the temple. In effect Adharkar ignored the 'new' evidence produced by Parab, that incriminated Kishore Marathe, the police patil. Adharkar noted, '[T]here is no provision of recording the supplementary statement in the Code of Criminal Procedure', especially as a pretext for recording 'fresh statements'. Adharkar noted that Kachru had neither provided evidence of the involvement of the police patil in his initial testimony nor in supplementary statements. Adharkar took this as a serious omission that cast suspicion on the patil's involvement, but never stopped to wonder whether Kachru might have been scared to make this allegation. Earlier, Adharkar had treated the FIR as a merely a preliminary document; now the first report had become the last.

Though Sawane's murder had generated huge controversy outside the courtroom, and the actions of the police had significantly inflected the structure of the case, the political negotiations between state functionaries and political activists were bracketed out of the judgment. Might those giving evidence of the police patil's involvement have been scared of retaliatory violence? What were the current political alliances in the village that had made it difficult for Kachru to mention the struggle over the Ambedkar statue? How had the Commissioner for SC/ST's demand for applying the PoA Act itself generated a procedural demand for new evidence? The judgment addresses none of these issues which inflected the presentation of the case in the courtroom. The resolution of Sawane's murder case produced a number of reactions.

(1) The judgment exposed the unspoken spatial codes that structured the village. Adharkar's verdict refracted these codes through the PoA. His 151-page judgment began with a lengthy sociological account of the village as a caste-divided zone, and proceeded to locate tensions due to the building of an Ambedkar statue as the event most proximate to the murder. Invisible motives became visible through a state-sanctioned cultural sociology spotlighting caste violence. Sociology was adequate to intuit the inspiration for dalit resistance but it failed, however, when it came to understanding what it was dalits resisted. Even criminals who had committed a caste crime for demonstrably casteist reasons had to be given the benefit of doubt. The motives for Sawane's murder remained invisible because the judge's own sociological commonsense could not make clear the cultural principles by which 'ordinary', i.e. caste-Hindu citizens, acted. The five accused received sentences for each aspect of their crime for which they had been convicted. The sentences ran concurrently, and the accused were eventually convicted for a seven-year sentence plus a Rs 2,000 fine.

(2) The prosecution and the defense appealed the judgment. When the prosecution filed their appeal in the Aurangabad High Court on 10 October 1992, they demanded that the accused be tried for attempted murder, S. 302 IPC. The prosecution also demanded that the five accused (including the police patil) who were acquitted for all offences be retried. The prosecution noted that the judge had not taken note of all the evidence produced by succeeding investigations. The prosecution also argued that the judge's ruling on intent was unreasonable, because in an unlawful assembly it was impossible to discover who was responsible for an action. That ought not to have been reason for downplaying the severity of the crime, the prosecution argued.

The defence filed their appeal on 22 February 1993. The defence argued that the judge's refusal of bail was causing hardship to the five men who were all agriculturalists, and that they were innocent. In addition, the defense argued that the original information of the crime was tainted since it had been tampered with to conform to the PCR and PoA Acts.

(3) Beyond issues of penal justice, Sawane's murder was also embroiled in issues of compensation that affected the living, rather than the dead. Juridical conceptions of human worth equate it with the physical integrity of the body, so any violation to the body is also understood to constitute a loss of dignity. At one point in his report, Ram Dhan had noted: 'At present many of the State Governments are sanctioning Rs 1 lakh as relief to the families of those who are killed in caste and communal riots. As compared to these cases, killing of SC/ST persons in cases of atrocities on them amounts to crime against humanity. Therefore the families of SC/ST persons who are killed in cases of atrocities . . . deserve an equal treatment if not a more sympathetic one.' Thus outside the courtroom Sawane's death attained closure through the compensation offered to Sawane's family. Rs 54,050 was collected from the Chief Minister's Fund, the Social Welfare Board, the Revenue Employees Welfare Fund, District Collector, and the village for Ambadas's next of kin. His wife, Rukminibai, was offered the kotwalship at a salary of Rs 900/month, and given a small plot of land in Pimpri-Deshmukh. Having failed to punish the perpetrators, compassion now assumed the guise of compensation and rehabilitation, commodifying dalit pain and suffering.

4) If the struggles over public space dictated Sawane's actions, his murder revealed how contentious a dalit politics of presence is, one that commemorates dalit struggles for humanity and social justice. In the aftermath of the namaantar struggles in Marathwada, statues of Ambedkar and the Buddha had dotted the rural landscape, reterritorializing the space marred by brutal upper-caste violence. In Pimpri-Deshmukh today, one sees a statue of Ambadas alongside a statue of B. R. Ambedkar. Ambedkar's militant politics, his inauguration of the dalit as a political subject, shares visual space with a local dalit martyr.

At the most immediate and relevant level, Adharkar's judgment was a miscarriage of justice. However, public representation of the murder unsettled and realigned the political balance of forces in a manner more broadly representative of all discrete events of violence. Sawane's politics seems to have motivated upper castes to take recourse to a seemingly archaic form of retribution when they killed him on the steps of the temple. But the changed context of party politics, especially the involvement of the Shiv Sena in mobilizing Marathas, Malis, and OBCs, suggested a thoroughly modern context within which caste relations were embedded. Caste violence thus became a diagnostic, a symptom, of caste sociality. It brought daily forms of interaction regulated by the embodied geographies of untouchability to the surface. In this next section, I further consider the work performed by this juridical form of visibility to draw out the broader relevance of the first three sections of this essay.

Conclusion: Stigma, Political Worth, and Protection

Ambadas Sawane's murder, along with cases such as the Chunduru and Karamchedu killings, marks a shift in the post-Mandal politics of caste and untouchability.[49] It raises the question of the relationship between violence and the politics of identity.

[49] The post-Mandal conjuncture illustrates a broader shift that is taking place towards analyses of rights, democracy, and issues of minoritarian representation; i.e. renewed debates about histories of 'the political'. Significant works on the post-Mandal conjuncture are too vast to cite here. For a very selective list, see Rajeev Dhavan, 'The Supreme Court as Problem Solver: The Mandal Controvesy', in V.P. Panandikar, *The Policies of Backwardness* (New Delhi: 1997), pp. 262–332. Nicholas Dirks, *Castes of Mind: Colonialism and the Making of Modern India* (Princeton: Princeton University Press, 2001); Gopal Guru, *Kanshi Ram Yanca Bahujanvad* (Pune: Samajvignan Academy, 1994) and 'Dalits in Pursuit of Modernity' in Romila Thapar, ed., *India: Another Millennium* (Delhi: Viking, 2000); Kancha Iliah, *Why I am Not A Hindu; A Sudra Critique of Hindutva Philosophy* (Calcutta: Samya Publication, 1996) and 'Toward the Dalitisation of the Nation', in *Wages of Freedom: Fifty Years of the Indian Nation-state*, ed. Partha Chatterjee (Delhi: Oxford University Press, 1998); Aditya Nigam, 'In Search of a Bourgeoisie: Dalit Politics Enters a New Phase', *Economic and Political Weekly*, 30 March 2002; Sharad Patil, 'Democracy: Brahminical and Non-Brahminical', *Frontier*, 30 September–21 October 1995, pp. 42–6; *Seminar*, 'Reserved Futures', no. 375, 1990; Ashutosh Varshney, 'Is India Becoming More Democratic', *Journal of Asian Studies*, vol. 59, no. 1, February 2000, pp. 3–25; Yogendra Yadav, 'Understanding the Second Democratic Upsurge: Trends of Bahujan Participation in Electoral Politics since the 1990s', in Francine Frankel, ed., *Transforming India: Social and Political Dynamics of Democracy* (Delhi: Oxford University Press, 2000).

I have argued in this essay that the legal arena is important for understanding contestations over dalit identity. In this conclusion, I want to ask more generally how laws meant to deter the commission of caste crime might in fact engender a new politics of presence. Gaining recognition for forms of historic discrimination through collective struggle is a political achievement. It has allowed dalits to argue that their identity is born of surviving many kinds of injury. (Dalit of course means 'crushed', 'ground down', 'broken to pieces'—a militant reclamation of histories of suffering and resistance.[50]) Legal mechanisms of recognition and protection in fact objectify such counter-histories into the injury of identity. Legal forms of recognition, of which the caste atrocity is one, suggest that in such laws *we also find a philosophy of personhood and political worth*. This philosophy of personhood, the notion of dalit vulnerability, rests on a sociology of untouchability.

In his influential work, Marc Galanter has examined the history of reservations in India, and the expansion of 'compensatory discrimination' to an ever larger population of victims of caste inequality.[51] Galanter focuses on how 'the equality of opportunity' could be produced through state policy. In his account, this steadily expanding circle of entitlement is seen as both the product of, and a catalyst for, the limited and perhaps short-sighted politics of upward mobility that set disenfranchised castes against each other in the context of a politics of scarcity. Galanter's study argues that caste disability needs to be converted into socio-economic 'backwardness' in order to be justiciable.[52]

[50] I am drawing on Wendy Brown's argument about the political status of injured identity. See *States of Injury: Power and Freedom in Late Modernity* (Princeton: Princeton University Press, 1995). Unlike Brown, I do not find this to be a form of *ressentiment*, a failure of radical politics, as she seems to imply in her book. Rather, I have in mind something like Upendra Baxi's readings of the Indian Constitution as a capacious, performative document, that can be read both with and against itself by the disenfranchised. See *Mambrino's Helmet? Human Rights for a Changing World* (New Delhi : Har-Anand Publications, 1994), and *Inhuman Wrongs and Human Rights: Unconventional Essays* (New Delhi: Har-Anand Publications, 1994).

[51] See *Competing Equalities: Law and the Backward Classes in India* (Delhi: Oxford University Press, 1984).

[52] Even this process of converting caste into a socio-economic indicator has

Backwardness is a conception of dalit persons as suffering disproportionately (and unjustly) from the inequalities produced by caste.

The interwoven discourses of backwardness and of 'protection' acknowledge the history of victimhood and injury that they seek to legislate out of existence. They indicate that the postcolonial state transforms the categories available for thinking about dalit personhood, that it has in fact produced new forms of recognition upon which demands for rights depend. But intentions alone do not determine the law's effects, and indeed intentions are never alone. They are subtended and delimited by conscious and unconscious inheritances from the past.

The postcolonial state's discourse on untouchability enables a new political imaginary that makes a critical break with the past.[53] This has meant that the civil rights regime instituted by 'the national state' (to use Partha Chatterjee's phrase) has understood its task as respecting the dignity of vulnerable citizen-subjects by protecting their physical integrity in *the present* in order to compensate for the wounds of history, those practices of stigmatization that have caused collective suffering. Thus the Constitution addresses that past as a history of hurt, and the future as one of equalizing or compensating for the past. Simultaneously, one might recognize that the Constitution serves as a surrogate for politics, that it functions as a form of political containment.[54] But such efforts at containment may still generate new political categories. To conceptualize caste relations as constituting dalit victims and upper-caste perpetrators might flatten the complexities of social reality, but it suggests that the caste relationship itself is being imagined and understood differently, as intrinsically agonistic. However, the sociology of victim and perpetrator cannot imagine the political stakes of caste violence, e.g. as with Ambadas's murder.

---

happened haphazardly, without recent statistical evidence, making it impossible to have a discourse about poverty as caste inequality. See Satish Deshpande, 'Caste Inequalities in India Today', in his *Contemporary India: A Sociological View* (New Delhi: Viking, 2003), pp. 98–124.

[53] See in this context Balibar's discussion of the Declaration of the Rights of Man in his *Masses, Classes, Ideas: Studies on Politics and Philosophy Before and After Marx* (New York: Routledge, 1994). See also Judith Butler and Ernesto Laclau, 'The Uses of Equality' [exchanges] *Diacritics*, Spring 1997, pp. 3–19.

[54] I thank Gyan Prakash for drawing my attention to this.

How did legal forms and procedures, definitions and categories, apprehend the practice of untouchability? Laws against untouchability had to be organized around a capacious definition to enable the state to see a family resemblance between the diverse acts performed 'on the grounds of untouchability'. For example, issues of temple entry and of the installation of an Ambedkar statue, although located in very different models of social and political behaviours, both indicated different symptoms of caste conflict.

Legislation against caste crime was enabled by a generous interpretation of Article 15(4) of the Indian Constitution, regarding 'special provision for the advancement' of Scheduled Castes and Scheduled Tribes.[55] These laws modify judicial procedure in order to address the banality (and invisibility) of caste (or gender) violence.[56] However, Parliamentary Debates reveal a broad consensus prior to the passage of the 1955 untouchability Offences Act that defining untouchability was seen to be yet another way of fostering an undesirable identity upon dalits.[57] The dilemma of how to understand untouchability can also be gleaned from early judgments that were concerned to limit the right to religious worship granted by Article 26 of the Constitution if it interfered with the spirit of Article 17:

[55] For debates about the provision of the PoA Act, see for example: Jai Singh *v.* Union of India, *AIR* 1993, Rajasthan 177; Mahesh Chandra Choubey *v.* M. M. Dubey, *AIR* 1994, MP 151; and State of M. P. *v.* Ram Kishna Balothia, (1995) 3 *SCC* 221.

[56] Like the provisions of PoTA and TADA, the PoA Act addresses exceptional circumstances that suspend legal procedure in the interests of justice. Though the former set of laws is *defensive*—while the PoTA Act is *reformist*—they share the structure of the legal exception. On the other hand, those provisions of the PoA Act that address the difficulty in proving a *general practice of prejudice*, i.e. upper-castes' investment in maintaining their status through the practice of untouchability, resembles legislation addressing gender discrimination. The laws governing domestic violence illustrate this, for example. Section 498A of the IPC recognized that husbands and relatives could perpetrate cruelty against women; Section 113 of the Evidence Act made it possible to infer 'abetment' to suicide, and Section 174 of the Criminal Procedure Code made postmortems compulsory for women who had died within seven years of marriage.

[57] For example, *Lok Sabha Debates*, 26 August 1954: 408; ibid., 27 August, 1954: 451; ibid., 31 August 1954: 709; ibid.,27 April 1955: 6608, 6664, 6650, 6660–1, 6668–9. See also Rochana Bajpai, 'Minority Rights in the Indian Constituent Assembly Debates, 1946–1950', *QEH Working Papers*, QEWPS30,

> It is to be noticed that the word 'Untouchability' occurs only in Art. 17 and is enclosed in inverted commas. This clearly indicates that the subject-matter of that Article is not Untouchability in its literal or grammatical sense but the practice as it has developed historically in this country . . .
>
> *Art. 17 which was intended to give effect to the decision to abolish the practice of untouchability, as mentioned above, does not define that term.* Nor is a definition contained anywhere else in the Constitution. *This omission would appear to be deliberate as the intention presumably was to leave no room or scope for the continuance of the practice in any shape or form* (para. 4, my emphasis).[58]

Similarly the Protection of Civil Rights Act mentions that 'civil rights' means any right accruing to a person by reason of the abolition of 'Untouchability' by Article 17 of the Constitution' indicating the production of the dalit citizen as a person with civil rights as a consequence of the abolition of untouchability. Drawing attention to the practice of untouchability by defining it was understood as a form of discrimination. It could also provide linguistic leverage for opponents of such legal reform, whereas leaving it undefined could allow the state greater freedom in locating and punishing it. The consequence of these laudable attempts to bring dalits within the domain of political modernity has meant, however, that the state constantly reinscribes the

December 1999; and G. Narayana, 'Rule Making for Scheduled Castes: An Analysis of Lok Sabha Debates, 1962–1971', *Economic and Political Weekly*, vol. 15, 1980, pp. 433–40.

[58] Devarajiah *v.* Padmanna, *AIR* 1958 Mysore 84. These cases indicate the slippage between Article 17's understanding of untouchability as an issue affecting dalits, and attempts by plaintiffs who made use of the guarantees of Article 26 to legitimate forms of Hindu sectarian exclusion including the ritually-induced impermanent state of untouchability. In dismissing this particular case, the court held that the temporary practice of social boycott [against a Jain petitioner, in this case] did not constitute a practice of untouchability, which was restricted to disabilities arising from birth. Contrarily, in Hadibandhu Behera *v.* Banamali Sahu, *AIR* 1961 Orissa 33 the court held that a person excommunicated from a high caste also counted as an 'untouchable'. For judgments upholding that Article 26 permits for excommunication as a right that cannot be denied by arguing that it poses a threat to the civil rights of members, see Chinamma *v.* D.P.I., *AIR* 1964 Andhra Pradesh 277; Venkataramana Devaru *v.* State of Mysore, AIR 1958 S.C. 255; Sarup Singh *v.* State of Punjab, *AIR* 1959 S. C. 860, and Saifuddin vs. State of Bombay, AIR 1962, S.C. 853 (869, 873, 875).

habitus of untouchability into its bureaucratic functioning without acknowledging it.

Thus preventive laws have focused on specific acts and effects rather than on abstract definition or imputed intent. An unintended consequence, however, is that acts that reproduce dalits' untouchable status are difficult to separate from those that prevent dalit social advancement; in other words, untouchability's ritual and political effects are intermixed.[59] A relationship between violence to the physical body and humiliation as a harm to identity and selfhood is also assumed. The PoA Act conflates physical injury, linguistic violation, and psychological hurt.[60] The state's attention to caste violence is clearly a surrogate for a broader and more complex understanding of caste sociality. As a result, *violence functions as a public mode of recognition* between upper castes and dalits, and the caste atrocity becomes a symptom of a broader politics of untouchability. The term vulnerability, we might say, indicates an ambiguous legal conception of personhood.

This essay is part of a broader genealogy of dalit citizenship.[61] I have argued in the preceding sections of this essay that the social life of this

[59] Section 3 of the PoA Act details what constitutes an atrocity, including in its list acts that would more properly be considered 'political', and as well, as symbolic forms of humiliation. Section 3(1) of the act entitled 'Punishments for offenses of atrocities' notes that acts of humiliation (use of the caste insult, forcing dalits to eat or drink noxious circumstances [e.g., urine, excreta], the denial of access to water sources, barring of access to public property and public thoroughfares, sexual violence against dalit women), economic dispossession such as forcing dalits from their land or demanding that they perform bonded labour, as well as attempts to deprive them of the vote or keep them from holding political office all count as 'atrocities'.

[60] Drawing on the philosopher J. L Austin and the legal theorist Robert Cover, Judith Butler has argued that linguistic performatives blur the distinction between word and deed. Indeed, performatives, as Austin argued, are words that behave as if they are deeds; these words produce physical effects simultaneously with their utterance. For Butler, hate crimes in the United States are one such powerful instance of what she calls 'linguistic vulnerability', when words harm people to the same extent as the infliction of a physical wound. *Excitable Speech: A Politics of the Performative* (New York: Routledge, 1997).

[61] Significant moments in this genealogy are: the secularization of untouchability during the 1920s and 1930s, when dalits engaged with two significant discourses, that of the 'political minority' and the 'purified' or 'reformed' Hindu;

juridical form, the caste atrocity, produces contradictory effects once it becomes a term in the sociological toolkit for apprehending untouchability. I have also tried to shift away from a model of unilinear causality—'when dalits get politicized they encounter violence', or, 'caste violence is a reflection of upper-caste frustration with the reservations regime'. Legislation does not merely prevent or enable socio-political transformation, but functions as a mediating term, shifting the conditions of possibility of knowledge. Thus I have drawn on three key terms to elaborate this process: untouchability, legality, and publicity. Legality tries to adjudicate the forms within which untouchability becomes public. As currently constituted, law focuses on the exception, while everyday life operates as its normative basis. If untouchability cannot be understood apart from the 'touchable' Hindu, publicity too cannot be understood in isolation from the private lives it speaks to; its visibility is still tied to the invisible but quotidian world of caste relations. As we try to navigate past a legalized caste habitus of victim and aggressor, we need to acknowledge that there has been a change from violence that *prevents* dalits from claiming political rights, to violence that *responds* to their political militancy. When 'hidden' or invisible forms of violence are rendered spectacular, as they were during Sawane's murder, new political struggles are organized around what such violence illuminates about a given political context. The productive efforts of focusing on a legal regime might rest in fighting for that distinction.

Sources

This essay is based on protected or restricted information. I should note that the presence of dalits and liberal upper-caste Maharashtrians in the administration, as well as a responsive bureaucratic culture in the Maharashtra state government greatly aided me in my research.

---

demands that the practice of untouchability be recognized a civic and political disability; the emergence of state measures to protect dalits as vulnerable minorities; and new forms of caste sociality in post-1990s India. Each of these phases brought dalit activists into engagement with the colonial (and later, postcolonial) state, and caste Hindus, and dalit politics questioned the very grounds of nationalist (and postcolonial) politics. My ms., 'The Caste Question', explores this history.

For seven weeks during October–November 1996, I worked in the Protection of Civil Rights Cell of the Maharashtra State Police Headquarters. I was greatly aided by the Deputy Inspector General of Police who was kindly disposed to researchers because, he told me, his brother taught sociology. I was told that I could sit in the PCR Cell and take handwritten notes on files. My notes were inspected before I went home during my first few days in the PCR Cell.

The administrative office itself was extremely small, consisting of about ten clerks and secretaries. The IGP-PCR sat in an attached cabin. I was given a part of a desk that belonged to a typist who was on leave. The office staff became very friendly and helpful after my first week there because they found that I spoke Marathi, and because they were intrigued by why I seemed to enjoy working under highly uncomfortable circumstances in the office. (Towards the end of my time there, I had even brought in a square piece of plywood and a few flat stones to prop it up to help me flip through the case files!)

I asked one of the clerks about a large stack of folders on an open wooden shelf in the office one day, and 'happened' to find details about Sawane's murder and another large riot that took place in 1987 (again in the Marathwada region) regarding dalit encroachment on *gayraan*, common grazing land. I spent about three and a half weeks copying notes furiously from these files. I was able to gather information about Sawane's murder because the office did not necessarily know what I was interested in. And until I found the files on these two atrocities, I had been unsure about what I would discover in the PCR Cell.

The details I had found in the PCR Cell sent me back to Marathwada, where I spent almost a week travelling between Pimpri-Deshmukh, Parbhani, and Aurangabad before learning that all the documents related to Sawane's murder were at the Aurangabad High Court, because the case was under appeal. Progressive dalit lawyers got me entrance into the High Court. A meeting with the registrar after many failed attempts allowed me to examine the case material. I had to file a notarized affidavit stating that the information I gathered would be used for purely academic purposes, before I was allowed to photocopy material.

CHAPTER 6

Framing Custom, Directing Practices

Authority, Property and Matriliny under Colonial Law in Nineteenth-century Malabar*

PRAVEENA KODOTH

> Action guided by a 'feel for the game' has all the appearances of the rational action that an impartial observer, endowed with all the necessary information and capable of mastering it rationally, would deduce. And yet it is not based on reason. You need only think of the impulsive decision made by the tennis player who runs up to the net, to understand that it has nothing in common with the learned construction that the coach, after analysis, draws up in order to explain it and deduce communicable lessons from it. The conditions of rational calculation are practically never given in practice: time is limited, information is restricted, etc. And yet agents *do* do, much more often than if they were behaving randomly, 'the only thing to do'. This is because, following the intuitions of a 'logic of practice' which is the product of a lasting exposure to conditions similar to those in which they are placed, they anticipate the necessity immanent in the way of the world.—Pierre Bourdieu[1]

By the close of the nineteenth century, British judges and jurists had built up a corpus of matrilineal custom in the Malabar and South Canara districts of the erstwhile Madras Presidency

*I am grateful for detailed comments and criticism on earlier versions of this paper from D. Narasimha Reddy, P.K. Micheal Tharakan, J. Devika, G.N. Rao, Achin Chakrabarthy and D. Narayana.

[1] *In Other Words: Essays Towards a Reflexive Sociology* (Cambridge: Polity Press, 1990), p. 11.

through legal theorizing, dispute arbitration, and precedents established by civil courts. In the legal discourse on matriliny, these customs were framed as real customs, i.e. as against those that had not stood the test of court procedure.[2] This essay is a critical analysis of the legal discourse from the standpoint of its own assumptions, i.e. the ideas and theory that shaped and governed it. Colonial administrators were agreed that customary practice, rather than any religious precepts embodied in written sources, was the source of personal/family law for matrilineal groups in this region.[3] Operationally, it was left to the civil courts to interpret, define, and administer custom as and when disputes were brought before them.[4] There having been no effort to collect and code custom, the courts sought to determine what constituted custom at the point of a dispute on the assumption that real practices could be filtered through from the context, regardless of the specificity of the dispute.[5] A perusal of case law on matrilineal customs suggests that customs were interpreted not on the basis of existing practices but

[2] By the legal discourse on matriliny, I refer to a specific mode of interpretation of matrilineal customs articulated through the administrative—specially legal and judicial—processes of the colonial state.

[3] In the words of William Logan, an administrator-historian with extensive experience of Malabar, 'if it were necessary to sum up in one word the law of the country . . . that word would undoubtedly be the word "*custom*". In Malayalam it would be "*Maryada*", "*Margam*", "*Acharam*" all signifying established rule and custom . . .' (emphasis in the original). William Logan, *Malabar Manual*, in two volumes, vol. I (New Delhi: Asian Educational Services, 1995), p. 111.

[4] The first general inquiry into customary practice in Malabar was undertaken by the Malabar Marriage Commission, set up in 1891, a full century after the East India Company wrested control from Tipu Sultan in 1792. Besides, this inquiry was more to assess the mood for change in the customary marriage practice than to codify custom on the basis of existing practices. Report of the Malabar Marriage Commission (henceforth RMMC), (Madras: Lawrence Asylum Press, 1891), I, p. 1.

[5] Consider further Cohn's observation that British modelling of the process of adjudication in the courts on that of British law courts of the period had implications for the nature of cases. For, disputes which had continuity (stretching back and forth in time) and complex contexts, were reduced to the specificity of a 'case'. Bernard Cohn, 'Some Notes on Law and Change in North India', in *An Anthropologist among the Historians and Other Essays* (New Delhi: Oxford University Press, 1987), pp. 568–74.

in terms of a theory of matrilineal law, itself shaped by the process of interpretation. P.R. Sundara Aiyar, a Madras High Court judge and an early-twentieth-century compiler of matrilineal law, seems keenly aware of this: '[w]hile the law of property among the marumakkatayis was based entirely on usages, British exponents of the law allowed little weight to the views of the people and were guided by their own notions of a perfect system of marumakkatayam law'.[6]

Central to the colonial theory of matrilineal law was a regulatory notion of custom—the principles of marumakkatayam or aliyasantana law.[7] In turn these principles were defined externally with reference to modern patrilineal frameworks of interpretation, i.e. informed by comparative legal and nineteenth-century anthropological theories from Europe and North America. By the middle of the nineteenth century, Lewis Henry Morgan had marshalled considerable if scattered evidence of cross-cultural kinship to stake a conjectural but influential history of the evolution of the family. He relegated matrilineal societies to the prehistory of patriarchal society. However, if Morgan had helped dispatch matriliny to antiquity, it was Henry Summer Maine's patriarchal theory that informed the detail of the legal understanding of the matrilineal family.[8] Nineteenth-century comparative legal perspectives made it possible to move easily between Roman and Hindu law and to interpret matrilineal families in terms of the patrilineal (whether Roman or Hindu), i.e. as the archaic form of the patriarchal family in

[6] *A Treatise on Malabar and Aliyasantana Law* (Madras: Madras Law Journal Office, 1922), p. 13. Marumakkatayam refers to the practice of inheritance by one's sister's children. Here 'ego' is necessarily male. Marumakkatayam, however, was understood in opposition to *makkatayam* (literally, inheritance to one's children, where again 'ego' is male), the lineage practice of the Nambudiris (Malayala Brahmins).

[7] Aliyasantana is a Kannada term for matriliny followed by certain Tulu-speaking castes in the erstwhile South Canara district of the Madras Presidency.

[8] Publishing before Morgan, Maine had posited the patriarchal theory, wherein the patriarchal family was at the 'primitive' stage. Morgan posits the patriarchal family at a much higher stage in the evolution of the family. The differences between Morgan and Maine, though wide, were of little importance to the legal discourse. For an insightful discussion of these differences as of the coming into being of kinship as a field, see Thomas R. Trautmann, *Lewis Henry Morgan and the Invention of Kinship* (Berkeley: University of California Press, 1987).

a linear evolutionist theory of society.[9] From this it became possible to identify with the matrilineal family characteristics associated with the patriarchal family in its archaic form, and matrilineal customs were interpreted by analogy with more familiar customs of patrilineal and patriarchal societies—both Western and 'Hindu'—albeit of another time.

This is not to suggest that there was no effort to collect information on customs. Apart from the cases made out by the litigants, when the judges of the High Court felt the need they sent for more information from the lower courts. Such information however was evaluated in terms of the theory. The judges denoted acceptable or 'authentic' custom in terms of certain characteristics. Foremost, customs had to be general and consistent. They had to be established on the basis of the 'clearest evidence' and 'proof' as against 'vague statements'. 'Evidence' in this sense was already inscribed by a theory.[10] As Neeladri Bhattacharya points out, it was assumed that the underlying principles of practices could be grasped through modern theories. 'Observed facts made sense only within such a framework of explanation . . . [O]nce the essential principles were understood, ambiguities and confusions could be ironed out and the real practices systematized into codified rules.'[11] In some cases, the weight of information was heavily against

[9] Maine's work, which set up a comparative legal perspective on evolution using Roman, Greek and Hindu law, was particularly influential. However, the study of Indo-European languages and Orientalist literature beginning in the late eighteenth century had already 'invented' a common base for Roman and Hindu societies/languages. Ibid.

[10] Neeladri Bhattacharya's reading of the project of codification of custom in colonial Punjab has been very useful in understanding the conception of custom deployed in legal discourse. In Punjab the government made efforts to codify custom on the basis of an extensive inquiry in the middle of the nineteenth century. The conception of custom that shaped this project was informed by a general theory of the evolution of Punjab society. 'Indian evidence had no constitutive power in the making of this theory; the theory provided the frame through which the evidence was understood and ordered.' Neeladri Bhattacharya, 'Remaking Custom: The Discourse and Practice of Colonial Codification', in R. Champakalakshmi and S. Gopal, eds, *Tradition, Dissent and Ideology: Essays in Honour of Romila Thapar* (Delhi: Oxford University Press, 1996), p. 26.

[11] Ibid., p. 38.

the dictates of the theory, certain practices were accepted as 'exceptions', a term used to suggest a movement away from the 'authentic' and 'original' customs towards altered forms.

However, there were more impetuous ways in which a patrilineal commonsense spoke through the colonial administration. Face to face with matriliny, British judges betrayed a sense of acute unease. They warned that the system was 'difficult', 'peculiar' and potentially anarchic, moving then to contain the difference that it marked through a tight enforcement of rules. This anxiety was particularly apparent when adjudicating on claims that contested the authority of the Karanavan, the senior male.

It is instructive that much of the direction and inflexibility regarding the rules of matrilineal law emanated from the higher courts, the District and High Courts. For instance, cases brought to court seeking the partition of taravads (matrilineal joint family)

> were constantly successful in the Provincial Courts, but were invariably foiled on appeal to the Sudder Court at Madras, the objection being frequently taken for the first time by an English Barrister. It so happened that . . . the Sudder Court possessed one or more Judges, who were thoroughly acquainted with Malabar custom, and by whom cases from the district were invariably heard.[12]

Family customs as well as land relations came up for arbitration increasingly in the second half of the nineteenth century, a time when the importance of control over property and other resources was

[12] Lewis Moore, *Malabar Law and Custom* (Madras: Higginbothams, 1905), p. 16. In a case under aliyasantana, Holloway held that, '[I]f this indisputable rule had been abrogated by decisions of the highest courts of appeal . . . how much so ever I should have lamented that Judges had overstepped their proper duty of declaring law, I should . . . have followed such decisions. Here, however, the only decisions pronounced are those of inferior Courts, evidently influenced by their view of expediency in the particular case before them . . . Decisions dividing the family property have also been passed in Malabar and it is one of the claims of our late colleague Mr Justice Strange . . . that he successfully resisted the attempts of lower courts . . . to introduce foreign admixtures into a law of which whatever may be thought of the policy *none can deny the consistency of the theory upon which it is based*' (emphasis added). Munda Chetti *v.* Timmaju Hensu, Madras High Court Reports (henceforth MHCR), vol. 1 (1862–3), p. 380.

becoming clear.[13] Besides, matriliny was coming under increasing moral censure for the 'non-conformative' sexual and property practices that it sanctioned. It is not unlikely then that the information collected was skewed against such practices, both consolidating patriarchal hold over property and resisting the censure of Victorian morality.[14]

And yet this was only one part of the determination of customs. Sections that stood to benefit from court interpretations disputed plural practices. This sometimes led to complications and, over time, the courts were forced to set new boundaries to earlier interpretations, which, however, did little to dispel the 'framework of rules'. But just how far did the colonial legal processes go to alter the plurality of practice? It is apparent from the cases that came to court in the late-nineteenth and early-twentieth centuries that plural practices continued to prevail. Precedents sent signals regarding what was acceptable 'according to the law' and opened up possibilities against variant practices.

The analysis here is not restricted to any one social group or form of matriliny. Marumakkatayam and aliyasantana were perceived as founded upon the same principles and hence partaking of the same customs. Deriving the validity of practices from abstractions of matriliny such as 'that system which vests property in the females of the family', or 'the rule of nephews' made the interpretation of practices of one form available to the other; it gave them a common base in the legal discourse.[15] The only major difference in interpretation lay in the

[13] Sharpening the struggle for land as property, this period saw a series of agrarian revolts by Mappilla tenants against the denial of their conventional land rights by upper-caste 'Hindu' *janmis*. K.N. Panikkar, *Against Lord and State: Religion and Peasant Uprising in Malabar, 1836–1921* (Delhi: Oxford University Press, 1989).

[14] Information regarding matrilineal customs was accessed invariably from upper-caste men (who were also the superior interest groups in land). This is a settled tendency by the time of the Malabar Marriage Commission, which states that, '[m]arumakkatayam possesses no code . . . Prior to the advent of the British there were no courts of justice to record case law; and the Nambudiri Brahmins monopolized the study of the Shastras and were the sole recognized repositories of the unwritten custom of the country.' RMMC, I, p. 9.

[15] For instance, aliyasantana was brought under the purview Malabar Marriage Act, 1898 and was removed only at the very last moment from the Madras

recognition of female heads of family as customary under aliyasantana law.[16] The framework of matrilineal law, evolved in the civil courts, was generalized for matrilineal groups in Malabar and South Canara. They included the marumakkatayam Tiyas and Nairs and the aliyasantana Bants and Billavas,[17] categorized as Hindu; and the marumakkatayam Mappillas, a Sunni Muslim group.[18] Initially the judges were hesitant to recognize that the Mappillas in North Malabar observed marumakkatayam and not Islamic rules. However, in a case in 1860 Judge William Holloway seems to have settled the issue, holding that '[t]he presumption of course is that the descent is that of nephews, as is the rule of north Malabar universally'.[19]

The taravad referred to relations of property (*mudal sambandham*) shared by a group tracing descent from a common ancestress. In fact,

---

Marumakkatayam Act, 1933. Judges took recourse frequently to cross-references. Refusal to grant legitimacy to customary marriage in aliyasantana was extended to marumakkatayam, while previously the judges used the incidents of marriage general among the Nairs of South Malabar/Central Kerala to assess the legal status of marriage under aliyasantana. For a discussion, see Praveena Kodoth, 'Courting Legitimacy or Delegitimising Custom? Sexuality, *Sambandham* and Marriage Reform in Late Nineteenth Century Malabar', *Modern Asian Studies*, vol. 35 (2), 2001.

[16] In Holloway's words, '[t]his system of inheritance differs only from that of Malabar in more consistently carrying out the doctrine that all rights to property are derived from the females'. Munda Chetty *v.* Timmaju Hensu, MHCR, 1 (1862–3), p. 380.

[17] The Tiyas of North Kerala and the Billavas observed similar forms of social and property organization and were predominantly small peasant and agricultural labour castes, who, with the benefit of colonial ethnography, were better known for the 'caste occupation' of toddy tapping. The Nairs, a 'middle' caste, were matrilineal throughout Kerala but their position in the land hierarchy varied regionally. The Bants were a principal land-'owning' and cultivating caste and in aspects of social and property organization were very like the Nairs of North Malabar.

[18] Mappillas in North Malabar were matrilineal and had considerable interests in land and trade. Also, their socio-economic profile was quite distinct from that of the Mappillas of South Malabar. Kathleen Gough, 'Mappillas, North Kerala', in David Schneider and Kathleen Gough, eds, *Matrilineal Kinship* (Berkeley: University of California Press, 1961), pp. 416–17.

[19] The decision in the case was affirmed by the Sudder Court in Madras. Mallile Uppanna Pallichi *v.* Telalkunata Musaliyar Avella, Moore, *Malabar Law,* p. 324.

this was the only sense in which the taravad was understood in the legal discourse. The outer boundary of taravads seems to have been defined by relations of pollution (*pula sambandham*), whereby a wider matrilineal kin group was knit by symbolic ties— prominently in sharing birth and death pollution and a memory of common descent.[20]

This essay is in five sections. Section two is an attempt to take up issues of administration of justice during the British period. In section three I critically review two very different approaches to matriliny that are found in anthropological literature, my attempt being to draw out their assumptions. Section four is a gendered analysis of the legal discourse on matriliny. The conclusion draws together the interplay of theory and 'commonsense' in gendering the colonial discourse on matriliny.

Administration of Justice

If the administration of civil justice through the courts of law was an important function of government, it was also a site of the articulation of colonial authority. The Joint Commissioners reporting on Malabar in 1792–3 are clearly aware of this:

> And with a view to opening the eyes of the natives to the real and effectual control of our government, in respect of the judicial as well as the other branches of administration, the 49th articles directs the courts to itinerate during the fair season, throughout their respective jurisdictions . . . to the end . . . that their judicial influence, powers and control, may as speedily and as effectually as possible, be felt and understood to pervade every branch of administration so as to secure everyone his just rights.[21]

Malabar was politically fragmented before the Mysorean regime sought to contain local rulers in the eighteenth century. There has been

[20] However, there are indications that when expediency demanded it, it was possible to break off pollution ties. C.H. Kunhappa illustrates this for the divisions that traced lineage to Ayilliam in Chirakkal taluk. Being a numerically large taravad, comprising a considerable section of the people of this territory, death and birth pollution spelt a great inconvenience. It had been decided to terminate pollution ties, even while the related groups continued to share a cremation ground C.H. Kunhappa, *Smaranakal Matram* (Autobiography) (Kozhikode: Mathrubhumi Press, 1981), p. 17.

[21] Reports of a Joint Commission from Bengal and Bombay, appointed to Inspect into the State and Condition of the Province of Malabar in the year 1792 and 1793 (Madras: Fort Saint George Gazette Press, 1862), p. 124.

little scholarly engagement with legal institutions and processes immediately preceding colonial rule in Malabar, but there are suggestions that they had clear regional and local dimensions. Kathleen Gough notes, almost in passing, that the greater proliferation of rulers and chieftains in North Kerala went along with less centralized judicial processes than in Central Kerala.[22] E.J. Miller goes on to suggest that political dominion (kingship) and legal jurisdictions did not necessarily coincide in North Kerala.[23] However, 'juridical authority neatly coincided with political authority and economic power and the political and juridical authority of headmen and chieftains was also buttressed by trusteeship of the chief temple in the area and in certain other ways.'[24] Miller argues that, in the absence of centralized political authority, territorial segmentation stressed the interdependence of castes/social groups at the level of smaller units such as *tara, desam* or *nadu* (local units of territory).[25] Much more widely, every caste had

[22] Kathleen Gough. 'Nayars: North Kerala', in Schneider and Gough, eds, *Matrilineal Kinship*, p. 386. See also C.A. Innes, *Malabar Gazetteer* (Trivandrum: Government Press, 1999), pp. 381–4. The undulating terrain, with mountains coming close to the sea and extensive forest cover, facilitated both scattered settlements and fragmentation of authority structures.

[23] Eric J. Miller, 'Caste and Territory in Malabar', *American Anthropologist*, vol. 56, 1954, pp. 415–16. See also his 'Village Structure in North Kerala', in M.N. Srinivas, ed., *India's Villages* (Bombay: Asia Publishing House. 1960).

[24] Miller. 'Village in North Kerala', p. 46, and 'Caste and Territory in Malabar', pp. 412–14. There is considerable evidence of the interlocking of religious-ritual and civil institutions in defining the functioning of justice. K.K.N. Kurup notes the role of local shrines (*kavu*), with dominant Nair taravads of a locality as controlling patrons, in punishing infringement of norms. Kurup, ed., *Koodali Granthavari*, Calicut University Historical Series (Calicut: Empire Press, 1995), pp. xiii, 24. In an account of Kottayam taluk, Kumaran points out that the position of a *tara karanavan* (a village elder) among the Tiyas was tied to responsibilities arising from local shrines. Murkkoth Kumaran, 'Atmakatha', in Murkkoth Kunhappa, ed., *Murkkoth Kumaran* (Kottayam: National Book Stall, 1985), p. 32.

[25] The *taras* were grouped into *desams* and further into a *nadu*. Padmanabha Menon points out that the elders or karanavar of a *tara, desavazhis* and *nadu vazhis* (chieftains) administered justice but not in the mode of paid officials. K.P. Padmanabha Menon, *History of Kerala* (Give publication details), vol. 2, p. 248. See also Thurston and Rangachari, *Caste and Tribes*, vol. 7, pp. 39–40.

some sort of internal territory-based organization through which disputes could be settled, and the higher castes could sometimes intercede in the dispute arbitration of lower castes.[26]

Significantly, caste intersected with region, defining distinctions in territorial jurisdictions for different groups. It is known that the Nambudiris had easy mobility throughout Kerala, being to some degree above territorial or political divisions.[27] This went along with greater uniformity of custom throughout Malabar/Kerala than among the lower castes.[28] Quite in contrast, the regional character of the Nairs was evident in the fine distinctions they sought to maintain. 'Class for class the Nayars of different localities will not associate together. Thus Nayars of Travancore or Cochin or South Malabar will not be permitted to mess or intermarry with the corresponding class of Nayars of North Malabar, who always pretend to be of higher caste than the others.'[29] It is fairly well known that the organization of marriage among the Nairs and Tiyas in the region north of the Korapuzha (the Kora river, about nine miles north of Calicut) was considerably different from that in South Malabar.[30] Even in the early twentieth

[26] Murkkoth Kumaran, 'Atmakatha', pp. 46–7. See also Padmanabha Menon, *History of Kerala*, p. 248.

[27] Gough, 'Nayars: Central Kerala', in Schneider and Gough, eds, *Matrilineal Kinship*, p. 306. Miller, 'Caste and Territory in Malabar', p. 416. This could be traced to a much earlier period. Narayanan and Veluthat suggest that Brahmin communal identity had developed across Kerala by the late Cera period but the interrelated and strong corporate character of Brahmin settlements declined with the disappearance of the Ceras and the rise of independent Brahmin chiefs. M.G.S. Narayanan and Kesavan Veluthat, 'A History of the Nambudiri Community', in Fritz Staal, ed., *Agni: The Vedic Ritual of the Fire Altar*, vol. 2, pp. 419, 431.

[28] Ibid.

[29] Padmanabha Menon, *History of Kerala*, vol. 3, p. 13. Distinctions in custom among the Nairs of North and South Malabar are documented extensively in RMMC, I and II.

[30] Miller has noted that Nair taravads in North Malabar were matrilineal with virilocal postmarital residence for at least 300 years preceding British rule. Cited in Dilip Menon, *Caste, Nationalism and Communism in South India, Malabar 1900–1940* (Cambridge: Cambridge University Press, 1994), p. 11. See also Miller, 'Caste and Territory in Malabar', p. 416. Gough, 'Nayars: North Kerala', p. 390.

century there were clear restrictions against Nair women from North Malabar marrying men from South Malabar.[31]

Two layers of legal institutions of the Tiyas have been documented: (a) for internal administration; and (b) with authority over specific lower castes.[32] There is evidence to suggest that in Kottayam taluk (North Malabar) authority to arbitrate disputes was vested in the *nattu karanavanmar* (caste elders), a right possessed by specific taravads for each locality, and the elders could constitute different kind of *sabhas* according to the nature of a complaint.[33] However, among the Tiyas of Chirakkal taluk, a Tiya *stani* (dignitary or holder of title) from the Muthedath Aramanakkal family had the authority to decide disputes within the caste and his jurisdiction was invoked on appeal.[34]

[31] In the nineteenth century the Korapuzha constituted a cultural boundary and social relations for the lower castes/social groups were to some extent restricted to the region, though it formed several political units. Miller, 'Caste and Territory in Malabar', p. 416. Ravindran Gopinath, 'Garden and Paddy Fields: Historical Implications of Agricultural Production Regimes in Colonial Malabar', in Mushirul Hasan and Narayani Gupta, eds, *India's Colonial Encounter: Essays in Memory of Eric Stokes* (Delhi: Manohar, 1993), p. 367. There is extensive discussion of this and local efforts to challenge it in the evidence collected by the Malabar Marriage Commission, RMMC, II. See also K.T. Chandu Nambiar, *Samudaya Chinta*, Address to the 2lst Session of the Uttara Kerala Nair Samajam (Tellicherry: 1932), p. 25 and S.J. Puthenkalam, *Marriage and Family in Kerala* (Calgary: Department of Sociology, University of Calgary, 1977), p. 55.

[32] An instance of the authority Tiya elders had over specific lower castes was in the regulation of *vannatimattu*, i.e. to break a spell of ritual pollution arising from death, birth or menstruation, the Tiyas and higher castes were required to receive a change of clothes from a Vannati (a woman of a caste lower than the Tiyas). Tiya elders could prevent the *mattu* (change of clothes) being presented to women even of higher castes. Denial of *mattu* was hard punishment prescribed against those who flouted caste regulations (*jatyacharam*).

[33] Kumaran calls them the *tara karanavanmar*, denoting the *tara* (very generally a village) corresponding broadly with three or four *amsams*. See also Deposition by Panangandan Raman, RMMC, II, Appendix IV, C.K. Revathiamma, *Sahasrapoornima* (Autobiography) (Tellicherry: Vidyavilasom Press, 1977), p. 101. Kottayam taluk was distinct in having a number of dominant Tiya taravads, who were *janmis* and village heads.

[34] Depositions by Muthedath Aramanakkal Kunyi Kelappan Mannanar, and K. Krishnan Vazhunavar. RMMC, II, Appendix IV. The family, with vast land holdings in the eastern hilly tracts of Chirakkal taluk, is noted to have given refuge

Clearly then, conflict resolution procedures were not defined centrally in relation to the state. Nor however were they exhausted over any single site—state, family, caste-based and cultural institutions. The complexity of this dispersal becomes evident if we take up the function of justice in relation to the ritualistic performative practice of *teyyam* (*daivam* or god) observed in Kasargod, Chirakkal and the northern part of Kottayam taluks.[35] The preparation for and performance of teyyam drew together different sections of local society through specific *avakasam* (an inseparable combination of privilege and responsibility associated with a service or status) or as a community of believers.[36] 'The teyyattam sought to create a moral community through the establishment of a sense of limits—thus far and no farther. By deification of victims, it created a collective imagination of what was just and unjust.'[37] As a teyyam, a 'performer' from specific lower castes could chastise people much higher in the caste hierarchy, as also people of local importance for misdeeds.[38] Several of the stories performed dealt with local tensions, injustice, and punishment in the context of day-to-day caste and family tensions; they retold time and again the dis-tinction between acceptable codes of behaviour and excess.

---

to *antarjanams*, Nambudiri women, who were declared outcastes in a *smartha-vicharam*, an inquiry held when an *antarajanam* was suspected of adultery. Logan, *Malabar*, vol. I, p. 126. Thurston and Rangachari, *Castes and Tribes*, p. 43.

35 There were numerous *teyyams*, with thematic categorizations corresponding broadly to eco-cultural zones, the eastern hilly region, midlands and coastal areas, though this did not prevent a teyyam observed mostly in the coastal areas from having its 'source' (*asthanam*) in or from tracing its story to places in the eastern hills. Teyyams and their stories crisscrossed over the different eco-cultural regions but retained a distinct flavour of one or other of them. Certain teyyams were associated primarily with one or other caste but drew in other castes as patrons, service providers or worshippers. I am indebted to K.K. Marar, a scholar from Tellicherry, who has done extensive research on teyyam, for this perspective.

36 Though the shrine festivals and teyyam performances in North Kerala were associated with the lower castes, in some instances the Nambudiris too, who in the region were few and far between, were drawn in as patrons.

37 Dilip M. Menon, 'The Moral Community of the Teyyattam: Popular Culture in Late Colonial Malabar', *Studies in History*, vol. 9, no. 2, 1993, p. 199.

38 Ibid., p. 199. Besides, teyyams continue even today to be called upon to intercede directly in dispute arbitration. I thank Rajesh Komath for drawing my attention to this.

It was against these severally layered processes of administration of law, informed by notions of territory, caste and gender, that the British set up the multi-tiered civil courts.[39] That the existing institutions would decline only gradually was anticipated by early officials.

> The regulations [for the administration of justice in civil cases] . . . went rather to secure to the inhabitants one certain Judicature where they might, if they found it necessary, apply and obtain justice than entirely to deprive and prohibit the different Rajas from the exercise of the full and general judicial powers which they themselves considered as inherently vested in them, . . . accompanied with this further precaution that Rajas inquiries and decisions on such reference were revisable by the said court in all cases in which either of the parties were dissatisfied with the results thereof . . .[40]

[39] As Marc Galanter notes, in undertaking to administer the law in government courts rather than merely supervising the administration of law, the British initiated a process of 'expropriation' of law. It gave the government the power to 'find, declare and apply' the law. Marc Galanter, *Law and Society in Modern India* (Delhi: Oxford University Press, 1994), p. 17. The physical structure of legal justice took clearer shape in 1845 with the establishment of the Civil and Sessions Courts at Tellicherry and Calicut, the Subordinate Court of Calicut and the Principal Sudr Amins' Courts (in 1875 the Principal Sudr Amins were designated Subordinate judges) at Tellicherry and Cochin. The District Munsiff's Court continued to function, while the Provincial courts and Zillah courts of the early nineteenth century were abolished. Reorganisation continued into the twentieth century. Innes, *Malabar Gazetteer*, p. 384.

[40] Reports of the Joint Commission, p. 124. Constituted hence in a higher appellate role, the courts could dispute the procedures of caste institutions without directly taking issue with the institutions. A decision of a *smarthavicharam* (inquiry-based effort to elicit a confession from an *antarjanam* suspected usually of adultery), excommunicating a woman and a man she had implicated, was taken to and overruled by the High Court in Madras on the grounds virtually that the *smarthavicharam* had not observed procedures acceptable to the civil courts. The High Court held that 'the plaintiff' [the excommunicated man] not having been charged, nor having had an opportunity to cross-examine the woman, or enter on his defence, and otherwise vindicate his character . . ., the defendants had not acted *bonafide* in making the declaration'. Indian Law Reports (Madras Series), 12, 1889, cited in Thurston and Rangachari, *Castes and Tribes*, p. 224. In an earlier instance where the court took on a supervisory role, O. Chandu Menon describes a caste-based procedure for determining guilt (an ordeal of the balance) that he witnessed at Calicut around 1876 when he was Sub-Judge of Canara. This was in connection with a suit before the Sub-Court at Calicut to determine whether a

The colonial regime also relied on and even concentrated authority in existing institutions as in the incorporation of village heads (as *adhikaris* or *patels*) in the lower rungs of administration.[41]

The pressures of social governance complicated the shift effected on the question of laws and customs. If the stated position was to administer existing custom, officials were predisposed to see the division of topics of law in terms of the contemporary English division.[42] A division in English law between private and public shaped the category of personal laws, which were to govern the 'private' realm of family, marriage and inheritance.[43] On these topics the courts were to go by the former laws of the people, whether *shastric* or customary.[44] Officials, in the greater part of India, took on the task of determining 'Hindu law' in accordance with the shastras, resorting variously to existing *smritis* or commentaries and to commentaries/codes developed by select pandits under government instruction.[45] Several scholars have pointed to the official presumption in favour of written/shastric law.[46]

Nambudiri, who was party to the suit, had lost caste for breach of some caste rule. The ordeal was well attended and ended in 'so much confusion and uproar that many officials including myself were unable to see how exactly the scales stood; but the judges [Brahman priests who officiated as judges] loudly and vehemently declared in favour of the poor accused.' Padmanabha Menon, *History of Kerala*, pp. 267–70. One of the last effective ones was conducted in 1918 under the sanction of the Raja of Cochin. A.M.N. Chakiar, *The Last Smarta Vicharam* (Tripunitara: 1998), p. 95.

41 The village heads selected were in most cases former hereditary authorities and they were vested with powers to try minor civil and criminal cases. In such cases 'the economic sanctions for his political and juridical authority nevertheless remain, and to these are added the sanctions issuing from his position in the modern administration.' Miller, 'Village in North Kerala', p. 49.

42 J. Duncan M. Derrett, *Religion, Law and the State in India* (rpntd. Delhi: Oxford University Press, 1999), p. 233.

43 Tanika Sarkar, 'Rhetoric against Age of Consent: Colonial Reason and Death of a Child Wife', *Economic and Political Weekly*, vol. 28 (26), 1993, p. 1869.

44 Derrett, *Religion, Law and the State*, p. 234; Sarkar, 'Rhetoric Against Age of Consent', p. 1870.

45 Derrett discusses the 'making' of colonial Hindu law and the elusive search for a definitive code: pp. 225–74.

46 Ibid., pp. 233–5; Lucy Carroll, 'Colonial Perceptions of Indian Society and the Emergence of Caste(s) Associations', *Journal of Asian Studies*, vol. 37, no. 2,

Where shastric law was recognized, this did away with the distinction between written law and custom.[47] However, textual authority was introduced in the interpretation of custom, not based on written sources as well.[48] In Malabar and South Canara, besides the textual authority ascribed to customary practices, written codes were to intrude into the interpretation of custom.[49] Derrett suggests the kind of influence that was earmarked for written sources in Malabar. 'Though the Malayalam *Vyavahara-mala* . . . says nothing about the British, it seems certain that it was written to provide a book-law for the Malayalam-speaking inhabitants of Malabar at a time when they returned to relative self-government after the East India Company acquired the Malabar District from Tipu Sultan . . . The Malayalam law-book was available in 1800.'[50] Noticing a considerable shastric element in the text, the bulk of which concerned contracts and customs relating to Malabar, or Kerala, he adds that

---

p. 237. It has been noted that the very general adoption of 'Hindu' (book) law led gradually to erosion of customary law. Lucy Carroll, 'Law, Custom and Statutory Social Reform: The Hindu Widows Remarriage Act of 1856', in I. Krishnamurthy, ed., *Women in Colonial India: Essays on Survival, Women and the State* (Madras: Oxford University Press, 1989), p. 2. Madhu Kishwar, 'Codified Hindu Law: Myth and Reality', *Economic and Political Weekly,* vol. 29, no. 33 (1994), p. 2145.

[47] Carroll, 'Law, Custom and Statutory Social Reform'. See also Kishwar's insightful discussion of how the authors of the *smritis* discuss the contingency, variability, and flexibility of the precepts they lay out and speak of the importance of custom as distinct from these precepts. 'Codified Hindu Law', pp. 2147–8.

[48] Significantly, the Punjab case was seen as closer to English common law and posed against the Bengal tradition of shastric law, which was based on written sources and clearly textual. British officials then drew upon the English common-law theorists and nineteenth-century anthropologists to develop a theory of the evolution of Punjab's society. Bhattacharya, 'Remaking Custom', p. 26.

[49] Notably, the Malabar Marriage Commission validates the resort to custom as if it were a consequence of the absence of written sources. Hence it has to first dismiss the claims of the *Kerala Mahatmayam,* a well-known text in Malabar. Ibid., p. 10. In an instructive variation, the *Aliya Santanada Kattu Kattale* was relied on as an authoritative account of matrilineal customs in South Canara until it was declared a fraud by the court. Several important decisions of the High Court were based on it, and, in a case in 1883, though the Chief Justice noted that its 'authority had been seriously impunged', he based his judgement on a precedent that relied on the book. Moore, *Malabar Law,* p. 83.

[50] Derrett, *Religion, Law and the State,* p. 262.

> [t]here is no likelihood that such a work would have been written but for the presence of the British rulers and their notions of how local law should be found out and administered. And the attempt to give the whole system, including maxims of wisdom, legal procedure, land-tenure and rent questions, was evidently based upon the theory that if local laws could be made out the rulers would have them applied. *And so in fact it turned out, by and large, in Malabar, more than in any other district of the Madras Presidency, though we cannot attribute this decisively to the law-book itself.*[51] (emphasis added)

Though the treatise was not drawn upon in arbitration of cases or legal theorizing, 'Malabar law' was incorporated into influential treatises of 'Hindu law' that found immediate reference with judges.[52]

Issues of Matrilineal Practice: A Critical Review

It is only in recent years that the scholarship on matriliny has addressed the interpretation of customs by the colonial civil courts as an aspect of the transformation of matriliny.[53] Much of the research on matriliny in Kerala has come from the discipline of anthropology.[54] Clearly

[51] 'Bengal works' of the shastras were copied and studied in Kerala, almost certainly in the early years of British rule 'before civil procedure had commenced on its Anglo-Indian path' and Jonathan Duncan, one of the Joint Commissioners who reported on Malabar, wanted the 'Gentoo Code', the first major colonial digest on Hindu law published in 1776, to be consulted in Malabar. Ibid., pp. 242, 257–63.

[52] John Mayne's *Hindu Law* and T.L. Strange's *Hindu Law* were referred to by judges and compilers of Malabar and aliyasantan law to bolster interpretations. See for instance Moore, *Malabar Law,* p. 27.

[53] K. Saradamoni, *Matriliny Transformed: Family, Law and Ideology in Twentieth Century Travancore* (New Delhi: 1999), pp. 66–70; G. Arunima, 'Multiple Meanings, Changing Conceptions of Matrilineal Kinship in Nineteenth- and Twentieth-Century Malabar', *The Indian Economic and Social History Review,* vol. 33 (3), 1996, pp. 283–307; and idem, 'A Vindication of the Rights of Women: Families and Legal Change in Nineteenth-Century Malabar', in Michael Anderson and Sumit Guha, eds, *Changing Concepts of Rights and Justice in South Asia* (New Delhi: Oxford University Press), 1998, pp. 114–39.

[54] The most extensive is the work of Kathleen Gough, who documents also regional and social group-based variations. See 'Nayar: Central Kerala'; 'Nayar: North Kerala'; 'Tiya: North Kerala'; 'Mappilas: North Kerala'; and The Modern Disintegration of Matrilineal Descent Groups', in Schneider and Gough, eds, *Matrilineal Kinship*; idem, 'Changing Kinship Usages in the Setting of Political

within a discursive frame, this literature tended to generalize a view of matriliny garnered from the socio-economic configuration of one region, Central Kerala. Nambudiri settlements were concentrated in Central Kerala and I have argued elsewhere that this factor shaped the Central Kerala experience of matriliny and land relations.[55] In the taluks of North Malabar (as also South Canara and southern Travancore), the nature of tenancy, cropping pattern and matriliny was different from the Central Kerala (South Malabar, Cochin and North Travancore) pattern.[56]

Importantly, Kathleen Gough is aware of these differences and analyses matriliny in North and Central Kerala separately.[57] Yet she fails to consider that these distinctions could have had important institutional implications. Hence she too is able to generalize matrilineal kinship in terms of the Central Kerala experience and posit a uniform trajectory of change, beginning with the entry of land into the market in the colonial period.[58]

Besides, Gough was retrieving 'traditional' matriliny, in the mid

---

and Economic Change among the Nayars of Malabar', *Journal of the Royal Anthropological Institute*, vol. 82, 1952; Joan Mencher, 'The Nayars of South Malabar', in M.F. Nimkoff, ed., *Comparative Family Systems* (Boston: Houghton Mifflin, 1965); C.J. Fuller, *The Nayars Today* (Cambridge: Cambridge University Press, 1976); Melinda Moore, 'Taravad: House, Land and Relationship in a Hindu Matrilineal Society', unpublished dissertation, Department of Anthropology, University of Chicago at Illinois, 1983.

[55] See Praveena Kodoth, 'Courting Legitimacy or Delegitimising Custom?', p. 10.

[56] There were only two settlements of Nambudiris in North Kerala in Payyanur (a matrilineal settlement) and Taliparamba in Chirakkal taluk. That their influence in the region was not comparable to South Malabar/Central Kerala is reflected in differences in land and marriage practices. See Praveena Kodoth, 'Women and Property Rights: A Study of Land Relations and Personal Law in Malabar, 1880–1940', Unpublished Ph.D. Dissertation, Department of Economics, University of Hyderabad, 1998, pp. 127–35. Variation in cultivation regimes and tenures of North and South Malabar is discussed in Ravindran Gopinath, 'Garden and Paddy Fields'.

[57] She points out that the failure to distinguish between regions had given rise to much confusion. 'Nayar: Central Kerala', p. 305.

[58] Gough, 'The Modern Disintegration of Matrilineal Descent Groups', p. 640.

twentieth century, when the influence of colonial definitions of custom in the local understanding of/author's retrieval of practices could not be underestimated. She tends to affirm the colonial legal position as law, accommodating departure from law/'rules' in a distinction between the 'formal' structure of 'traditional' matrilineal kinship and 'informal' practices. There are suggestions of an assumption of colonial interpretations as law. For instance, Gough writes that gifts of land, occasionally, by men in North Malabar to their wives and children, were known long before the colonial period, *although they were against the law.*[59] While the law on this point, long before the colo-nial period, is unclear and certainly not addressed by Gough, nineteenth-century colonial law permitted alienation of only 'separate' property and only during a person's lifetime.[60] Colonial law was also distinctly uneasy on the question of the transfer of property from husband and father to wife and children, a discomfort that Gough too displays in understanding such practice in a structural frame.[61] There are several such instances in her work where custom brushes uneasily against the law'.[62]

Gough's engagement with the significant authority that senior women seem to have had over property and kin is instructive. The senior woman, Gough indicates, was not necessarily determined by seniority and might well be the oldest competent woman, and yet seniority was a crucial factor in determining power relations between the karanavan and the senior woman.[63] If the karanavan was the son

[59] Gough, 'Nayars: North Kerala', pp. 391–2.

[60] This was until the Malabar Wills Act, 1898 and the Malabar Marriage Act, 1896 came into effect. Even prior to this, however, the courts were known to have upheld marumakkatayam wills. Moore, *Malabar Law*, p. 182.

[61] *Putravakasam,* which referred to certain claims that children had to their father's property, did not have the force of law but several respondents to the Malabar Marriage Commission attest to its prevalence particularly in North Malabar. RMMC, II, p. 271.

[62] Gough writes of North Kerala that when a junior man leased land on *kuzhikanam* (uncultivated waste or forest land taken on tenancy) from his taravad, the improvements that he made on it might *by custom although not by law* become the separate property of his mother's matrilineal descendants. 'Nayars: North Kerala', p. 391.

[63] Gough, 'Nayars: Central Kerala', pp. 338–41.

or younger brother of the senior woman, 'she might indeed be the *de facto* head of the group', keeping accounts in her own hands and counselling him; but were he the older brother of the senior woman, then she was subordinate to him.[64] Her account throws up several axes of authority—gender, generation, competence and proximity in kinship, the intersections of which could constitute the authority of women and men differently. Do we have a suggestion of the historical contingency of authority and practice?

More recently, Arunima has contented that matrilineal kinship needs to be historicized. She argues that the identifiers of matrilineal kinship in colonial law, such as residence, impartibility, and the inalienability of property, were not essential parts of customary practice in pre-colonial Malabar; that the colonial interpretation of matriliny often militated against the rights that were historically available, particularly to women and junior members, within the taravad.[65] However, she tends to affirm the premise of colonial law in limiting the notion of rights to the axis of divisibility, i.e. in the dichotomy of separate and collective, which were defined in relation to each other. That in some wealthy taravads lands were set aside for women as *stanum* (a special status) property or otherwise, over which they enjoyed varied claims, does not in any way suggest 'separate rights' or 'access to their own separate revenues and properties', as Arunima suggests they do.[66] There is even evidence of women having sold their share of taravad property in the pre-colonial period.[67] However, this provides little insight into the nature or dimensions of the ability to transfer land by taravads or their members separately. To suggest that women (or men) had separate rights could only have the perhaps unwarranted consequence of projecting back into the pre-colonial period a conception of rights that formed the basis of the colonial interpretation of matriliny.

Several of Arunima's inferences are questionable. Take for instance her claim that in early colonial North Malabar women had rights to

[64] Ibid., pp 341–2.

[65] Arunima, 'A Vindication of the Rights', pp. 116–19.

[66] Arunima, 'Multiple Meanings', p. 292.

[67] Deed no. 35 in Logan's collection refers to a transfer by sale in 1739 by two women, Kurikkalote Palakkal Mittalevittil Ummanga and Uchchira, of 'as far as their share of the Tara, kandam (fields) and swamps below their house'. Logan, *Malabar,* vol. II, p. cxlvii.

management of the taravad, where the 'evidence' that she cites reveals only that Nair women managed domestic affairs in their natal taravads.[68] As Bina Agarwal has noted, this much is evident from Gough—who documents the senior woman's decision-making role in the inner domain of larger taravads in Central and North Kerala.[69] Arunima also claims that by the eighteenth century most new taravads were set up by women, undermining her own later recognition of the several ways in which taravads were set up in the eighteenth—as against the provisions of colonial law in the nineteenth—century.[70] Gough and Melinda Moore document that taravads or *tavazhis* (branches of taravads) were set up in a number of ways. Moore also finds that it was comparatively rare for a remembered founder of a taravad to be a woman alone.[71]

[68] Arunima cites Francis Buchanan's early-nineteenth-century travelogue: Arunima, 'A Vindication of the Rights, p. 118. Contrary to twentieth-century anthropological wisdom, Buchanan records that a woman in North Malabar could return to take up permanent residence in her natal taravad only on the death of her husband or on having been turned out of her husband's taravad. On the other hand, a woman could not divorce her husband. Perhaps a crucial factor here is that the information was gleaned exclusively from some principal men of the area. Francis Buchanan, *A Journey from Madras through the Countries of Mysore, Canara and Malabar*, vol. II (Madras: Asian Educational Services, 1988), p. 513. The Joint Commissioners cite a report furnished by the Chirakkal Raja, which indicates that there were greater constraints on women in North Malabar in relation to marriage. Report of the Joint Commissioners, p. 234.

[69] Gough, 'Nayars: Central Kerala', pp. 337–41; and 'Nayars: North Kerala', p. 397; Bina Agarwal, *A Field of One's Own: Gender and Land Rights in South Asia* (Cambridge: Cambridge University Press, 1994), p. 113.

[70] Arunima, 'A Vindication of the Rights', p. 117; idem, 'Multiple Meanings', p. 291. She takes the establishment of the Nileswaram royal family, when 'a princess from the Samuthiri's family eloped with a prince from Kolathanad to establish her own dynasty', as an instance of 'the common enough strategy of establishing *taravads* through elopement or marriage'. In doing so, Arunima interprets rather drastically Sreedhara Menon's account of the establishment of the family prior to Portuguese arrival in 1498. For Menon writes that, as a consequence of the elopement, the princess and her descendants were denied the right to a share in the Samudiri's property and that the Samudiri used the threat of arms to force the Raja of Kolathanad to create a separate estate for the princess at Nileswaram. See A. Sreedhara Menon, *A Survey of Kerala History* (Kottayam: National Book Stall, 1970), p. 181.

[71] Gough, 'Nayars: North Kerala', pp. 391–3; Moore, 'Taravad: House, Land',

The crucial point, as Arunima too notes, lay in the fact that descent was traced from women. And it is perhaps because of having to reconcile this and the possibility of women's agency arising from this, with the 'structural' patriarchy of the karanavan, that the tensions so evident in Gough's work arise. It may also be noted that, besides the legal discourse, ethno-historical writing produced under colonial rule, and post-colonial ethnography, there is little to suggest that the senior male had absolute powers in the taravad. A critical reading of the above discourses underscores the possibility raised by Ehrenfels that, unlike in patrilineal families, there was more than one node of power and a plural authority structure.[72]

The Legal Discourse on Matriliny

> I adhere most strongly to the opinion that where a rule of law indisputably exists it is the duty of the judges not to fritter it away on the specious pretense of bringing rules of law into harmony with what they may consider the requirements of society. If they are wrong in their view of such requirement . . . the evil is unmixed, if right, the mischief still predominates over the good because it prevents that systemic reform from which alone good can result. Such systemic reform is for the legislature.—William Holloway[73]

It was in the second half of the nineteenth century that marumakkatayam began to take sharp legal contours, coeval with increasing conflict over legal interpretations. This section will look at the interpretation of specific customs that determined the nature and extent of women's and

pp. 121–39. Moore notes that branches may split off for different reasons including fall from caste, quarrels or the desire of a husband to endow his wife and children. Ibid., p. 145.

[72] The mother, as the centre of the family, the mother's brother, as legal adviser and representative to outsiders and the father as of psychological importance an honoured guest and outsider. U.R. von Ehrenfels, 'Matrilineal Joint Family Patterns in India', in George Kurien, ed., *The Family in India: A Regional View* (The Hague: Mouton, 1974), p. 95. Gough records the limited but important customary rights of the father in North Kerala. Gough, 'Nayars: North Kerala', pp. 400–2.

[73] Munda Chetti *v.* Timmaju Hensu, 1862–3, p. 383.

men's functions of authority and rights to property in the legal discourse. Interpretation of conventional marriage, very generally referred to as sambandham, has not been addressed here. Yet as differences in property rights are so closely associated with the organization of marriage, it bears mention that one of the reasons why the civil courts refused to recognize sambandham as marriage was that it did not establish property rights—the assumption of course being that the establishment of (patrilineal) property rights was a defining incident of marriage.[74]

The Right against *Partition*

Though a decision against partition of the taravad was confirmed as early as in 1814, the provincial courts continued to allow it until the mid nineteenth century, when the higher courts ruled against it.[75] Two seemingly divergent explanations were advanced for the 'right against partition'. The understanding of the taravad in analogy with the impartible 'archaic Hindu family' avoided any reference to matriliny, or to women. In his compilation of Hindu Law, John D. Mayne places the taravad at the stage corresponding to the 'antique Patriarchal form' of the modern Hindu family, whereby 'the doctrine that property was by birth—in a sense that each son was the equal of his father—had then no existence . . . The son was a mere appendage to his father, and had no rights to property as opposed to him.' This validated impartibility except by common consent, i.e. 'no one member, nor even all but one can enforce a division upon any who object.'[76] Hence, each one had a right to resist division—*an individual right*, in the last instance. The notion of collective rights, said to govern the taravad, was trapped conceptually in a polarization of rights between individual and collective rights, which (a) turned necessarily on a form of individual right; and (b) excluded the very possibility of different bases of claims.[77]

[74] The colonial interpretation of sambandham raises distinct and complex issues of sexuality, property and legitimacy that have been addressed in Praveena Kodoth, 'Courting Legitimacy or Delegitimising Custom?'

[75] Moore, *Malabar Law*, pp. 13, 16. Munda Chetti *v*. Timmaju Hensu, p. 380.

[76] Moore, *Malabar Law*, p. 17.

[77] Sundara Aiyar points out that the nature of the rule was due to the British

However, William Holloway who, along with Herbert Wigram, was a driving force in giving a sharp legal outline to the taravad, invoked matriliny and women as determining factors of the rule of impartibility. In a case that established impartibility as custom, the judges disallowed a plea for division under aliyasantana law, which had come up before the High Court in 1862.[78] The plaintiff, a woman, sought division and the District Munsiff ruled in her favour generally, but disallowed her claim to a piece of land on the grounds that it had been shown to be the self-acquisition of the second defendant. Both parties appealed against the decision and the Principal Sadr Amin awarded to the plaintiff the entire lands claimed in the plaint.

In a special appeal before the High Court, the appellants contended that under the rules of aliyasantana, division could not be legally enforced. Noting that neither the District Munsiff nor the Principal Sadr Amin had pronounced an opinion on this point, the High Court remitted the issue to the Civil Judge for evidence of existing usage. The Civil Judge observed that division of family property had been allowed in numerous suits since 1825. This, however, did not deter the judges, Frere and Holloway, from denying such usage.

Frere contended that division at the behest of individual members is 'undoubtedly at direct variance with the ancient law on the subject'. He goes on to consider whether the 'ancient law . . . had been superseded by any custom or usage which has by long prescription or usage acquired the form of law' and finds that the precedents submitted by the Civil Judge concerned division in favour of males, i.e. 'in none does the question of compulsory division between the females who alone are recognized as the proprietors of the family estate, appear to have been judicially tried and decided.'[79] Holloway, however, was decisive in rejecting the claim to division.

> The divisibility of family property in Canara is one of those propositions, which fall within the category of law taken for granted, and is found when examined to have no solid foundation . . . [I]t has not been disputed, as

---

courts for it was extremely unlikely that a single member should have been given the right against the will of the majority in the taravad to resist partition. *A Treatise on Malabar*, pp 11–13.

[78] Munda Chetti *v.* Timmaju Hensu, pp. 380–3.

[79] Ibid., p. 382.

> indeed it could not be, that the compulsory division of the family property is wholly opposed to the authorities upon which the Aliya Santana system of inheritance rests. *It is equally opposed to the principles of that system which vests property in the females of the family. . . .*[80] (emphasis added)

The rule against partition is seen as deriving from a system that vested property in women.[81] For we might also ask, as Sundara Aiyar does, how could it be said that non-division followed logically from succession through females? 'And even if it did the question is not logical plausibility or perfection but what were the usages among the communities who are governed by it?'[82] Clearly then, despite or precisely because of the implicit connection between women and matriliny, the colonial discourse on matriliny was not about matriliny or women but about what comprised 'authentic' custom.[83]

Targeting precisely the right *against* partition, the plaintiffs in a case in 1870 staked their claim to the property of another taravad with whom they shared descent.[84] The defendants maintained that while they had descended from a 'common stock', their taravad and the plaintiff's were distinct. Given the way matrilineal law was developed with the emphasis on denying partition, a decision against the plaintiff could have meant affirming partition. In denying the contention of the

[80] Ibid., p. 383.

[81] Against division, both judges cite the authority of the *Aliyasantanda Kattu Kattle* or Bhutala Pandya's Kattoo, later denounced as a forgery. The text asserted that if a disagreement took place between sisters, the eldest sister was to provide the younger sister with a separate house and its necessary apparatus, retaining the general managership and the performance of ceremonies. In his judgment, Holloway interpreted this to constitute far from a claim to division a 'positive authority against it'. Ibid.

[82] Sundara Aiyar, *A Treatise on Malabar*, p. 13.

[83] Lata Mani has argued that the debate on sati reconstituted tradition, such that all parties to the debate invoked the 'authenticity' of a particular corpus of texts—the shastras in defence of and against the practice of sati. Despite the intimate connection between women and tradition in the colonial discourse on sati, the debate was not about women but about what constituted authentic tradition. Lata Mani, 'Contentious Traditions: The Debate on Sati in Colonial India', in K. Sangari and S. Vaid, eds, *Recasting Women* (New Delhi: Kali for Women, 1989), pp. 88–126.

[84] Erambapalli Korapen Nayar *v.* Erambapalli Chenen Nayar, Regular Appeal no. 120 of 1870, MHCR, 4 (1870–1), p. 411.

plaintiff, holding it to be a case where one of several branches had become better off, and another, 'by virtue of ambiguity of a word' had sought to reap the benefits, Holloway argued that 'As in all Hindu law so in the archaic form of it, which exists in Malabar, the first conception of the family is of an indissoluble unit, a mere aggregate with no separate rights . . . In Malabar as elsewhere, the inconvenience of this state of things has made itself felt and families . . . have split into various branches.' To validate the existence of formerly partitioned taravads, however, he calls to his aid the local concepts of *mudal sambandham* (community of property) and *pula sambandham* (community of pollution) and contends that the movement from *mudal sambandham* to *pula sambandham* was one of divisions. Yet, acknowledging that divisions had occurred along *tavazhis* did not lead to a search for a different basis for partition or to questioning the doctrine of 'common consent'.[85] On the contrary, stipulations were set to identify formerly partitioned taravads. In a decree upheld by the High Court, forty years of separation was held as sufficient to prove effective partition, the burden of proof resting with those claiming common descent.[86]

[85] In the early decades of the twentieth century, demands for partition were along the lines of *tavazhis*. Making out a case for *tavazhi* partition, T. Vasudeva Raja pointed out that 'Malabar is merely suffering from arrested growth, and the administration of law by the courts constituted by the British government on principles recognized in English jurisprudence is in no small degree responsible for this stunting process.' Home (Judicial) Department, 60–2 (1912), National Archives of India, New Delhi. U.C.S. Bhatt, member of the Madras Legislative Council from South Canara, argued that it had been routine to partition taravads until the High Court ruled against it in the mid nineteenth century. Proceedings of the Madras Legislative Council, vol. 59 (10 January 1932), p. 205. Importantly, Melinda Moore studies several taravad histories to indicate that branches may split off for different reasons including fall from caste, quarrels or the desire of a husband to endow his wife and children. 'Taravad: House, Land', p. 145. See also an account of partition in a dispute stretching over four years and settled through the lower courts in 1856, in K.T. Gopindranath, *K.T. Chandu Nambiar* (Kannur: S.C. Printers, 1996), p. 85, and K.K.N. Kurup, ed., *Koodali Granthavari* (Calicut: Calicut University, 1995), p. xviii.

[86] Moore, *Malabar Law*, p. 19. In the early twentieth century it was held that in a proper case, in the interests of family peace and order, a partition may be supported as a family arrangement. Parakkateri *v.* Koran 1912, in Sundara Aiyar,

Residence and Maintenance

It was assumed that under matriliny women necessarily resided in their matrilineal homes even after entering into a marriage. In North Malabar and South Canara, however, women resided in the matrilineal homes of their husbands during the tenure of their marriage. This point was not taken to court and tried directly. However, in a case before the District Judge of North Malabar in 1878, a woman and her son claimed maintenance from the karanavan. The claim included maintenance for the wife and children of the son. The defendant, the karanavan, pleaded that the plaintiffs were not entitled to maintenance as they had declined to live in the house that he had allotted to them. The judge went on to disallow maintenance to the wife and children of the son on the grounds that it was against the 'principles of marumakkatayam law', a point that was not even at issue.[87] Previously, the Subordinate Judge, who did not take objection to the inclusion of the son's wife and children, had ruled in favour of the plaintiffs. He did so on the grounds that the house in question was already occupied by eleven members and had no spare accommodation. The plaintiffs took the case to the High Court, where the judge remitted the case to the lower court for more information. On the basis of information received, the judge held that the claim was a proper one. It was pointed out that even the first defendant did not object to the custom of wives and children of men living in the husband's/father's taravads. However the court upheld this in the mode of an exception.

> *Although it would seem inconsistent with the principles of the marumakkatayam law* that the taravad should contribute to the maintenance of the ladies with whom the male members cohabit and of the issue of such cohabitation, . . . it is urged in this Court that it is the practice of the country in North Malabar for females to reside during the whole year in the taravad of the male with whom they cohabit . . . (emphasis added)

A Treatise on Malabar, p. 15. Further, it was held in a case in 1916 that 'separate residence, separate assessment and separate management are the common indicators of partition'. Ibid., p. 17.

[87] Varikara Vadake Vittil Valiya Parvati *v.* Varikara Vadake Vittil Kamaran Nayar, Indian Law Reports (all references are to the Madras Series) (henceforth ILR), vol. 6 (1883), p. 341.

In a sweeping move, the practice of women residing in their natal taravads after marriage, specific to South Malabar, was generalized to matriliny itself.

More generally, the accent on co-residence and impartibility meant that legally the karanavan could refuse requests for separate maintenance, outside the allocated taravad house, or even flexible maintenance arrangements within the household. However, this is one area where over half a century the claims of junior members to maintenance found increasing support in the civil courts.[88]

Dismissing a suit for separate maintenance in the District Court in Tellicherry in 1858, the judge had observed that '[t]he junior members of the family are not entitled to be supported out of the family house from the family property . . . To give them a cause of action, they must have alleged, and to succeed, *they must have proved, that by the acts of their karanavan* they were deprived of subsistence in their own family house'[89] (emphasis added). By the 1880s suits for maintenance were more successful indicating not so much a change in the provisions of the law as the widening of the scope of disputes, the adjudication of which pushed at the boundaries of earlier interpretations. Pleas for separate maintenance were successful as 'rare exceptions . . . as the karanavan has been the cause of quarrels that necessitate the plaintiff leaving the family house.'[90] A judgment in 1882 directed that members were entitled to claim maintenance if there was no room for them in the taravad house.[91] In this case it was decided also that if the karanavan made insufficient allowance, members of the taravad could apply

[88] In 1881 when a senior woman of a taravad refused to give up her possession of a room in the house, the karanavan sued. He maintained that he had the right to redistribute rooms in the house and the judge held upheld his claim on the ground that the powers of the karanavan were absolute. Moore, *Malabar Law,* p. 121. However, in 1917, a woman living in a separate room in the family house owing to scruples about cooking fish, was allowed separate maintenance. It was held that, '[w]hen a state of things has gone on for a number of years without objection, it may be unreasonable on the part of the karanavan to terminate it arbitrarily'. Sundara Aiyar, *A Treatise on Malabar,* p. 139.

[89] Moore, *Malabar Law,* p. 124.

[90] The maintenance granted, namely, two rupees per mensem, it was stated, was intended to discourage such applications. Peru Nayar *v.* Ayappan Nayar, Moore, *Malabar Law,* p. 128.

[91] Moore, *Malahar Law,* p. 132.

to the court to determine what was sufficient in the context of family circumstances and to a raise in allowance when the family wealth increased.

The Rule of the Karanavan and Women's Rights to Manage Property

As the 'general' rule in Malabar, management and control of property was vested in the senior male of the taravad, against which management by women was framed as an 'exception'. Except in the case of the *kovilagams* (royal families), management by women was held to be 'opposed to the present usage of every other Nayar family in Malabar.'[92] In the karanavan, the eldest male of the taravad was 'vested actually (though in theory in the females), all the property movable and immovable belonging to the taravad.'[93] Taking the presumption in favour of men a step further, in matters such as sales of taravad property, where there was an adult anandiravan (junior male) his consent was required even when the sale was assented to by a female member and was shown to be for taravad necessity.[94]

As the legal executor of the taravad, the karanavan was seen to represent it in its relations with people outside the taravad, importantly tenants or possible buyers of property. Land was the most important form of property among matrilineal social groups in Malabar. Control over land also meant a degree of control over certain groups of people, tenants, labourers and service (artisan) castes. Possession, control, or management of land was understood in terms of the roles of landowners and/or tenants as *janmis, kanakkar* or *verumpattamkkar* (cultivating tenants) and facilitated, inevitably, their coming together with the karanavanmar of taravads.

The powers of the karanavan were seen as growing out of his position as 'head of family'. However, in assuming that the karanavan was indeed a 'head of family', it is evident that the legal discourse drew

[92] Moore, *Malabar Law*, p. 121. The right of the senior woman to management was recognized in the Calicut and Walluvanad *kovilagams*, each of which had separate estates attached to it. The senior woman of the family was entitled to its management. Ibid., pp. 343–5.

[93] Varankot Narayanan Nambudiri *v.* Varanakot Narayanan Nambudiri, ILR 2 (1878–81), p. 328.

[94] Sundara Aiyar, *A Treatise on Malabar*, p. 63.

upon a theory of law rather than on local practice. In a case before the High Court in 1872 in which the custody of a child was in dispute, Morgan and Holloway held that

> by the principles of the laws of Malabar, the mother herself, while alive, and her children too, were under the guardianship of the head of the family, the Karanavan. Their position was precisely analogous to that of the members of a Roman family under the patria potestas. The Karanavan is as much the guardian and representative, for all purposes of property, of every member within the taravad as the Roman father or grandfather.[95]

The Civil Judge had drawn upon criminal law, which required the father of a child unable to maintain it, and 'the natural equity found in positive law,' entitled the father to guardianship of his children. The High Court reversed the order on the grounds that it was 'wholly opposed to the very principles upon which Marumakkatayam depends'.[96] In a later case, Morgan and Holloway held that the 'person to whom the karanavan had the closest resemblance is the father of a Hindu family,' and that like the latter his position as head of family 'comes to him by birth'. The karanavan's 'office is not conferred by trust or contract but is the offspring of his natural condition.'[97] These cases laid the field for understanding the position of authority of the karanavan in relation to all other members of the taravad. Clearly, the karanavan's position was natural because he was in the position of the father. Further, both these judgments show that the authority of the karanavan was posed not as 'natural' or internal to matriliny but derived through an imputed relation with a 'patriarch' as 'head of family'.

The practice of setting aside property for the maintenance of women in Nair taravads, which property they were entitled to manage, was disallowed by the High Court in the middle of the nineteenth century.[98] Among the bigger taravads, property was sometimes set

[95] Thathu Baputty *v.* Chayakath Chathu, Civil Miscellaneous Regular Appeal no. 406 of 1872, MHCR, 7 (1871–4), p. 179.

[96] Ibid., p. 181.

[97] Eravanni Revivarman *v.* Ittapu Revivarman, ILR, 1 (1876–8), p. 153.

[98] Moore, *Malabar Law*, p. 347. Moore points out that the practice was adopted by certain Nair families of distinction until disallowed by the High Court in Kondi Menon *v.* Vadakentil Kunni Penna, where a distinction was claimed between property set apart for women and the common taravad property. The notion of *striswothu* (women's property) came up in arbitration and it was held to be 'known

aside specifically for the maintenance of women and children, though the arrangements differed from one family to another.[99] In a suit brought against the Kavalapara Valia Nair (also referred to as the Moopil or senior Nair) by his sister the Valia Kava Nethiar, in the 1850s, even the defendant and his witnesses maintained that it was the practice to set aside properties separately for the maintenance of women, which was under the control of the senior woman. If the senior woman found this inadequate and informed him, the Moopil Nair usually paid the deficit. It was pointed out that the senior woman also received 1000 *fanams* from the 16000 fanams received as *malikhana* by the Moopil Nair.[100]

The general presumption in favour of management by the senior male was all too often turned into an exclusion of women from managerial roles or used to exhaust women's claims. To establish a custom against the 'general' custom of management by the senior male, the 'evidence' produced had to conform to certain requirements. For instance, it was not enough to argue that, 'the woman has always been the manager. To establish a custom contrary to the general customs of the country, the clearest evidence is required.'[101] This implied that a defence of practice as practice could be dismissed as constituting 'vague statements' rather than 'proof'.[102]

But what constituted clear evidence? The turn of interpretation on this point is indicated in an appeal suit before Holloway in 1855 wherein the Munsiff had held that the authority over a *paramba*

---

to marumakkatayam and not invalid'. Only written evidence, however, could establish the right. Bivi Umah *v.* Keloth Chiriyath Kutti, S.A. no. 932 of 1894, Madras Weekly Notes (MWN) (1919), pp. 693–4. Puthelath Chatti Soopi *v.* C.V. Kannan Nair, MWN (1929), pp. 873–7.

[99] Commentators on custom have pointed out that a considerable portion of the *janmam* property of taravads was set aside for women and children and that women had access to the management of such property. For instance, see 'Stanaswothu', *Janmi, Edavam* (May–June), 1908.

[100] K.K.N. Kurup, ed., *Kavalappara Papers* (Calicut: Calicut University Press, 1984), pp. 20–4. The Moopil Nair had opposed his sister's claim to maintenance while she resided at one of the many family residences on the grounds that it was not the usual residence of the women of the family. Contrary to the stance of the courts in later years, the Valia Kava Nethiar was held entitled to her claim.

[101] Moore, *Malabar Law*, p. 121.

[102] Zillah Decisions, March 1857, in ibid.

(garden) resided in the female and not in the male members.[103] Looking at documents, including one dated 1822–3, Holloway pointed out that as the names had been obliterated it was not clear from them that the former karanavatti, Ittiyachi, had demised the paramba to the present tenant. But, he argues, even if this were clear 'it would indeed be a violent inference that therefore the authority resides in women only'. Not pausing to consider whether authority could have been more inclusive and contingent, he suggests that 'it may well be that from the incapacity of males from tender age the woman was karanavatti in her life-time.' According to him, the weight of the evidence clearly showed that the grantor of the *janmam,* Rama Panikar, had succeeded Ittiyachi. What was this force of evidence? Holloway inferred that since Rama Panikar had been paying revenue on the paramba he had authority over it. Such acts as the payment of revenue 'would carefully have been avoided if the truth were that in this family females had the management of some portions of the property and males of others. *The separation in all acts of ownership would have been most carefully enforced*' (emphasis added).[104] It could of course be asked whether payment of revenue was a determinate marker of control, indeed of 'ownership' itself. By the time the Malabar Marriage Commission took evidence in 1891, it is clear that tenants were paying part of the revenue on land 'owned' by the janmis.[105] The frame of reference adopted excluded fluidity regarding family management and the possibility of diverse arrangements regarding revenue payments, sharing of income, or management and control of property itself within a single family.

With the odds high against formal recognition of women in positions of authority, it was difficult to supply 'sufficient' proof. In an appeal suit before him in 1878, Wigram disagreed with the Munsiff's

[103] A.S. 299 of 1855, in ibid.

[104] Ibid.

[105] Malapurath Para Nambi, for instance pointed out that while his taravad paid Rs 500, his tenants paid Rs 10,000. RMMC, II, Appendix IV. An appeal suit in 1927 involved a *karar* made in 1876 by which taravad property was described as *striswothu* and it was agreed that government assessment and renewal demises would be in the name of the senior woman and that the senior male member would collect rents. Puthelath Chatti Soopi *v.* Kannan Nair, pp. 874–7.

finding of a custom of female management.[106] Acceding that the defendant had indeed shown that her mother had, during her lifetime, managed the affairs of the taravad, as even the plaintiff had admitted, as also that the defendant's mother had managed excellently for no less than thirty-five years he infers, almost tendentiously, that 'it may well be that the male members as they grew up should wish to leave the management in her hands', and further that the evidence of the defendant was 'perfectly consistent with her [the defendant's mother] having assumed the management because there were no males of age in the taravad.' He also cautioned that '[t]he management of a female, like the management of an Anandravan must (in my opinion) *always be presumed* to be with the consent of those on whom the law confers the right of management i.e., the senior male, and may at any time be resumed'[107] (emphasis added). Stipulating that in some taravads females were entrusted with the management with the consent of the males, Wigram contends that he had not yet heard of a case where headship was claimed as a *right* by a female. The decree was confirmed by the High Court.[108]

The presumption in favour of management by men in Malabar carried with it suspicion of managerial claims by women. In contrast in South Canara, the presumption was in favour of women.[109] Yet, a close

[106] S.A. 434 of 1878 in Moore, *Malabar Law,* p. 122.

[107] Ibid.

[108] Wigram is alert to the 'deceptive' potentials of claims of management by women. In his compilation on Malabar law, he takes objection to a High Court judge's decision to secure the rights of a minor girl to the taravad estate against efforts to enforce a lease of certain forests for ninety-nine years, entered into by the three surviving adult males of the taravad on familiar grounds—that, 'it assumes without sufficient proof that there was a valid custom in the family vesting the management in the females'. Besides, he warns that 'the experience of those best competent to judge tells them that, in nine cases out of ten, where a family arrangement has been made vesting the management in females, it has been done for the purpose of fraudulently delaying or defeating creditors'. Ibid., pp. 123–4.

[109] 'The legal right to the family property is vested in the female members of the family jointly, but for little other practical purpose than regulating the course of succession . . . [P]ossession and control of the property belongs exclusively to the *ejaman*, or manager, of the family, who is ordinarily the senior of the female

look at available evidence from two cases, less than ten years apart, from Malabar and South Canara respectively, suggests that judicial approach was more at ease with, and hence privileged, male authority. In a suit brought by the younger of two adult males in a taravad to remove the elder, who was karanavan, the latter's conduct was found to be such as to warrant his removal.[110] On appeal, Wigram, the acting District Judge, chose to appoint a Receiver rather than rule in favour of the plaintiff's claim to the position of karanavan.

Meanwhile a second suit was brought by the senior female in the taravad to remove the elder male and appoint her in his place. In fact Wigram was aware of the second suit and makes the following observation: 'I do not think it would be in the interests of the tarawad to allow young married females to manage the property and their interests will be amply protected by the course I propose to adopt.'[111] With both suits before them, the judges of the High Court, Morgan and Holloway came down strongly on 'the mischievous extension of the doctrine as to the removal of karanavans . . . *The state of families and property in Malabar will always create difficulties. Their solution will not be assisted by bringing in the anarchy and insecurity which will always follow upon any attempt to weaken the natural authority of the Karanavan*'[112] (emphasis added).

They categorized these as a new crop of litigation facilitated by the sympathies of judges who were themselves junior members of taravads. '[I]t has been exercised on the mistaken principle that a man can

members . . . [and members] individually have no right to anything beyond such support'. Ibid., p. 124.

[110] Eravanni Revivarman *v.* Ittapu Revivarman, p. 153.

[111] Ibid., p. 153.

[112] Ibid., p. 156. The need to protect the karanavan's powers in the interests of discipline was invoked elsewhere too. In a case the *de jure* karanavan had renounced his rights and the taravad had been managed as two *tavazhis* for seventy-eight years. On the right of a *tavazhi* karanavan to sue for recovery of property, the High Court held that no delegation of powers by the karanavan was irrevocable even by the delegator and still less by his successors. The judges cautioned that 'with so peculiar a condition of property as that of Malabar, it is most essential for the avoiding of complete anarchy and consequent ruin to maintain the distinct rule as to the Karanavan's powers.' Velia Kaimal *v.* Velluthedatha Shamy, SA no. 372 of 1870, MHCR 6 (1870–1), p. 401.

properly be removed whenever a single departure from his duty to act equally for the benefit of all can be proved against the karanavan . . . The plaintiff in the regular suit was really the Brahmin paramour of one of the women and a by no means desirable manager for a Malabar family.' They ruled that the question was *not whether a man was unworthy of his position as karanavan but whether the removal would benefit the family*, a position that suggests the expediency of the move.[113]

Quite in contrast to the Malabar case, the High Court on appeal overturned the South Canara District judge's decision against management by males.[114] Two women, Deyi and Ammu, sought to remove Devu Shetty, the senior male, from his position as yejamanan (karanavan) and to recover property belonging to the family. The plaintiff claimed that the senior woman was the yejamanan under aliyasantana law. Two questions were taken up for decision in the High Court: whether it was the senior male or female or only the senior female that is entitled to be the yejamanan and assuming the latter whether she is entitled to countermand a *karar* (written contract). The High Court judges concluded that the first question was still *res integra* but found that they were unable to concur with the District Judge's decision in favour of the plaintiff, and particularly with his observation that management by males was detrimental to the interests of the family, and that their natural instincts were in conflict with the duty which they owe to the family. They pointed out that '*the question was not merely one of expediency*', and that in neighbouring Malabar the general rule was in favour of management by males![115]

Conclusion

Anthropological literature on matriliny, read against the grain, could help contend with the historical contingency of and regional differences in practices and power relations in the matrilineal taravad. Quite

[113] Ibid.

[114] Devu *v.* Deyi, ILR, 8 (1885), pp. 358–61.

[115] Regarding the karar, where the District Judge found that it showed only a temporary arrangement made for separate enjoyment, the High Court judges held that '[t]he arrangement is in our opinion a family arrangement made by all its members . . . and even assuming that the senior respondent is the lawful yejaman, we do not think that the karar can be arbitrarily set aside by her'. Ibid., p. 361.

at odds with this picture, the legal discourse on matriliny insisted on a timeless and immutable frame for customs. Colonial administrators tended to interpret matrilineal customs as binaries of more familiar patrilineal customs. Matriliny itself was understood virtually as the absence of patriliny. This also gave rise to an idealized conception of matriliny, wherein the karanavan implied the absence of the father. By maintaining that the karanavan in a matrilineal joint family was in exactly the same position as the father in a Hindu family, the civil courts merely replaced the father (in the patrilineal mode) with the karanavan (also in the patrilineal mode of the father), exhausting the role, place and legitimacy of the father. That the karanavan as 'head of family' was also vested with guardianship of 'married' women (and of taravad property) made room for greater difficulty, for this constituted a breach of the sexual contract embedded in 'marriage'. The notion of 'marriage as a contract' endorsed by the courts (embedded in the European social contract theories) required the husband to assume these roles, in the absence of which it was argued there could be no legally valid notion of marriage![116]

The interpretations created asymmetrical possibilities along the axes of gender, generation and proximity to the nodes of power (a) by specifically ordering functions according to gender and generation and (b) by constituting positions of authority in a patriarchal and patrilineal mode. Hence the legal discourse, shaped by an absence of serious engagement with local expressions of matriliny, lent pace and direction to the homogenization of practices across regions and social groups.

Importantly, in patrilineal societies, authority and lineage/descent of property were seen to flow together or at least very substantially together among the same set of persons (among men). In contrast, in matrilineal societies—and when patriarchal as in the legal discourse in Malabar—authority descended through the senior males and lineage/descent through women. The legal discourse poses as potentially destructive the tension between lineage/descent of property in the female line and significant roles of authority/responsibility for men. Judges

[116] Typically, for instance, the Malabar Marriage Commission uses the notion of 'marriage as a contract' to conclude that 'the principles of Marumakkatayam law do not recognise the institution of marriage'. RMMC, I, p. 26.

were exhorted to 'maintain the distinct powers as to the karanavan' so as to avoid the anarchy that was only to be expected of a system so 'peculiar' and 'difficult', bringing up a patrilineal common sense acutely uneasy with difference.

CHAPTER 7

A Poetics of Resistance

Investigating the Rhetoric of the Bardic Historians of Rajasthan

RASHMI DUBE BHATNAGAR, RENU DUBE
AND REENA DUBE

This essay describes our discovery, quite by accident—in the course of researching our book-length study of the cultural and discursive history of female infanticide in colonial India—of references to a community of travelling craftsmen-poets in the desert state of Rajasthan, against whom British colonial administrators mounted a systematic campaign in the nineteenth century.[1] Approaching this historical event from the perspective of women's histories means that we unfold one set of colonial explanations concerning the practice of female infanticide in relation to another set of British representations, namely that the Bhats and Charans caused female infanticide in elite landowning clans in the princely states of Rajasthan.[2] Thus, as literary critics and rhetoricians, we interpret Ranajit Guha's vision—of a historiography wherein woman, as the subject of history, activates

[1] We use the term Rajasthan, as distinct from the term Rajvara or Rajpootana, in order to mark the fact that the British designated north-western India as Rajasthan in the nineteenth century.

[2] Our book on female infanticide (New York: SUNY Press, 2005) examines the coming together of feudal idioms with British colonial infanticide reform in this form of gendered violence. We argue that the postcolonial justification of femicide as population control is a discursive product of a specific indigenous idiom of upward mobility (property accumulation by denying daughter's property rights) and the discourses of colonial British reform which mapped Malthusian theories on the terrain of female infanticide. Together this feudal-colonial discourse posits daughters as valueless consumers of family wealth rather than as producers, and

the small voices that have historically been marginalized in the statist discourses of colonial, nationalist and Marxist historical accounts—as a call to rethink the disciplinary, cultural and political situating of women's histories. [3]

Although frequent incursions into the colonial history of female infanticide are intrinsic to our method here, in an important sense this essay is not about female infanticide; rather it explores how a history of violence against women can become the place of incision into history-writing and bardic literatures. Can one move outwards from the larger project of women's histories to study the poetics of bardic literature without instrumentalizing women's histories and subordinating women's issues to male concerns? The answer we found was in the affirmative: one of the gains in such a project is that the analysis of feudal-colonial patriarchies illuminates the lives of women in relation to other small voices of history.

Subalternity as a Relational Term in the Intersections between Women's Histories and Bardic History

While supporting careful discriminations about subalternity, we suggest that it is useful to consider in this instance the subaltern as a relational term rather than view subalternity as an essential or permanent feature of any one group. In our view contestations over which group (elite Rajput women of infanticidal clans or lower-caste Charans) occupies subaltern status, and which bardic community is more subaltern, is a futile debate. For instance, a nineteenth-century Rajput woman's subaltern status in terms of the violence visited on her through

---

thereby configure female children as a dispensable population. It is because these are booklength and chapterlength arguments, that we can only gesture at these arguments in the present essay.

[3] We wish to thank Shahid Amin, Gyan Pandey, Dipesh Chakrabarty and Shail Mayaram for their engaged, challenging, generous, and intellectually rigorous reading of earlier versions of this essay. Their comments are exemplars of the kind of conversations and collaborations we envision between historians and literary critics in this essay. Ranajit Guha, 'The Small Voice of History', *Subaltern Studies IX*, eds Shahid Amin and Dipesh Chakrabarty (Delhi: Oxford University Press, 1996), p. 11.

the killing of her daughters was a relational issue and therefore determined by her relation to class (the practice was not common among poor Rajputs).[4] An elite woman occupying the place of the subaltern depended on her relation to her natal and marital family, the function she served for her father and brother in the making and breaking of political alliances, her relation to power within the complex kinship systems of the Rajput clan, whether she was the first or second wife, her relation to the eldest male heir of her husband, and whether she was the mother of one or more sons.[5]

It is a marker of biologism to confer absolute subalternity on women and female children of an infanticidal clan. Instead we distinguish between the extreme violence of killing female children at birth on the one hand, and the patriarchal system of rewards for the childbearing woman who acquiesces in daughter-killing and produces one or more sons. Our point is that this process of violence is designed to make women accept the marks of her servitude and reproduce woman devaluation when and if she gains power within the kinship system in her

[4] At no time were all elite Rajputs found to be uniformly practising female infanticide. Furthermore, the Shekhawati and Kachhawaha Rajputs never practised female infanticide. The lack of uniformity is also indicated by the fact that often the Rajput clan which practised this violence in nineteenth-century Rajasthan had a family branch in Oudh which abhorred the practice. British colonial profiling of the infanticidal community was racialist. British reformers categorized the Rajputs as a race, and perpetrated the colonial fiction that the practice came about because of the dangers of abduction of Rajput women, and the perils of being a warrior race, which does not explain the productivity of this practice among elite clans, nor why this practice thrived among clans long after they had become settled, landowning, and politically powerful.

[5] The productivity of female infanticide in elite Rajput clans is best understood in relation to the function served by daughters in the idiom of power that historians name 'saga alliance' politics. Dirk H.A. Kolff notes: 'Sagai, i.e. the alliance network, represents a mature set of political norms in itself. . . in pre-Mughal Indian history'. See Kolff, *Naukar, Rajput and Sepoy: The Ethnohistory of the Military Labour Market in Hindustan, 1450–1850* (Cambridge: Cambridge University Press, 1990), p. 101. The term saga is not only crucial to an understanding of the feudal political idiom of elite Rajput clans, as Kolff suggests, but also illuminates how elite Rajput daughters were used for the purposes of expanding the portfolio of political allies for the father and brother. A full discussion of the relation between female infanticide and saga alliance politics can be found in our forthcoming book.

turn. Thus female infanticide is an idiom of violence that works, like other idioms of domination, through contradiction and arbitrary selection. The purpose is not simply to take the life of daughters but also to discipline the women of the family into internalizing woman devaluation.[6]

Intersecting nodes cannot be located freely at any point in history, otherwise the project of putting women's histories at the centre of the historiographical project can fall prey to Orientalist and Hindutva discourses. For example, Orientalist scholarship reads off bardic texts and performances with the assumption that the living oral epic traditions of Rajasthan can be recuperated as anthropological essences, in terms of trans-historical themes like popular Hinduism, renunciation, or the warrior ideal. We suggest that the modern scholar's access to surviving bardic performers must perforce take into account the mediations by the British colonial apparatus that recorded, codified, disempowered, and criminalized the Bhats and Charans.

The difficult and interesting methodological question is how the uneven and fitfully documented history of feudal-colonial violence on women around the practice of female infanticide can itself become the site or point of incision for an investigation of the specifically colonial violence on a bardic community, and how the latter investigation loops back to illuminate women's histories. Intersections between histories of men and women are best located at the very place where the historical narrative fails and comes to a halt before the marks of gendered violence like the practice of female infanticide. For instance, arguments concerning pro-woman dissent cannot be made without taking into account pre-British and pre-Muslim forms of domination, because rewritings of the past through communalist histories inflect all readings of historical arguments through the lens of Hindutva-style nativism.[7] In the absence of such vigilance, Hindutva nationalism may

[6] In this context we interpret the argument made by Veena Talwar Oldenberg through her study of the Punjab case, that birth-order determined the practice of female infanticide, as signifying that the productivity of the practice of female infanticide did not lie only in reducing the female children of the family but also in disciplining women into woman devaluation. See Veena Talwar Oldenberg, *Dowry Murder: The Imperial Origins of a Cultural Crime* (New York: Oxford University Press, 2003).

[7] Our location of dissent in medieval texts is not an alibi for nostalgia about the

seize on such arguments as proof that in feudal pre-British, pre-Muslim, or pre-Mughal times, India had its own highly developed technology of history-writing, women were the equal of men, and women were the subject of history in this glorious past.

In order to understand the colonial charge against the Bhats and Charans in nineteenth-century Rajasthan, one must first struggle with traces of colonialist analysis in the preconceptions we bring to the subject. The Hindutva model of cultural history builds on the traces of colonialist judgements by positing pro-woman dissent and resistance in history-writing so that feudal patriarchies can be washed clean. By positing a bardic caste that was purely oppositional, and a form of writing where the marks of dissent are accessible to us in an empirical form, or expecting homogeneity between male bardic writing and Rajasthani women's cultural forms, we fall into the paradigm propagated by Hindutva cultural history. This expectation of oppositionality assumes that feudal patriarchy operates like a self-correcting system. Furthermore, this paradigm of opposition seeks legitimation by association with a spurious empiricism. In our view positivist and empiricist paradigms are insufficient tools for judging questions concerning dissent and resistance, because dissent is produced through language, writing and speech, idioms, poetic and narrative genres, and conventions.

We should be unsurprised to find Charan accounts that are pro-elite Rajput, anti-woman, anti-Muslim, because the lessons of history have taught us that those are the accounts that survive through elite support. Moreover, dissent occurs unevenly at multiple sites.[8] In the

---

pre-British Indian past. Significant traditions of dissent in North India can be traced back to anti-Brahmanical medieval movements, poetic forms, art, and Muslim–Hindu cultural-religious synthesis. For two seminal essays which theorize dissent in the Indian past, see Romila Thapar, 'Dissent and Protest in the Early Indian Traditions', *Studies in History*, vol. 2, 1979, pp. 177–95; Ranajit Guha, 'Dominance without Hegemony and Its Historiography', *Subaltern Studies IV: Writings on South Asian History and Society*, ed. Ranajit Guha (Delhi: Oxford University Press, 1989), pp. 210–309.

[8] There cannot be better proof of the vibrant legacy of pro-woman dissent in Charan performances than in the critical energy displayed in the work of the postcolonial Charan Vijay Dan Detha. Detha's work in collecting and bringing attention to the dissenting voices of women in Rajasthani folklore has brought him

narrative we compose about Charan poetics, the exceptional political, social and economic power that accrued to the Charans in medieval-feudal Rajasthan through their close identification with elite Rajput clans, is the very thing that makes them a significant site for an examination of the rhetorical, poetic and oral-performative modes of articulating dissent. Dissent is born not only among the marginal and the dispossessed, but often flourishes among relatively privileged craftsmen.

It is because localist histories of clans and families, in contrast to monumental histories of nations and empires, hold greater possibilities for including the lives of women, that we ask: what are the spaces for negotiation, the structural possibility for manoeuvre and reversal, in the domain of the Charan's craft? This question neither sentimentalizes nor oversimplifies medieval feudalism. The bard can either interpret his vocation as the legitimating ideologue who transmits the story of domination from the point of view of the victors; or contrarily he can transmit the story of exploitation from the point of view of the dissenter. Alternatively, he can inflect the triumphant story of domination with elements of dissent.

For the purposes of our larger argument concerning the situating of women's histories, Charans function in this essay as the exemplar both for subalternity as a relational, shifting space in the balances and reassemblages of power, and for exploring more general questions concerning the attenuation of regionalist histories and cultural modes for articulating dissent. For this reason we foreground the notion that oppositional interpretations are possible, although not invariable, in the oral-performative bardic text. The social space of performance and orality is a flexible, contradictory, and fluid space for dissent. The reason is that there are politically transformative possibilities in the repeated, ritualized, temporary community in the singing/reciting of the bard, and in the messages that flow between audience and individual bard.

---

widespread acclaim from women's organizations like *Manushi*. See *The Dilemma and Other Stories*, trans. Ruth Vanita (New Delhi: Manushi Prakashan, 1997). See also our detailed discussion of this volume in chapter four of our forthcoming book, as well as Renu Dube's conference paper on the folktale in Detha's volume 'The Crow's Way', forthcoming in *Proceedings of the Fifth Annual Comparative Literature Conference, University of South Carolina, Columbia, 2003.*

The Colonial Charge against the Bhats and Charans in Nineteenth-century Rajasthan

The Charans' rise and fall from power and the colonial processes of subalternization have significance for us because of the social function performed by bardic castes, which is to enable a community to imagine themselves in myth and allegory. The composition of regionalist histories did not simply die out as an inevitable result of the advent of British colonialism and statist historiography. The distinctive feature of the British infanticide reform policy in the princely states of Rajasthan, unlike the 'Bombay system' of colonial infanticide reform followed in Gujarat, or the punitive system of surveillance and punishment in the North-West Provinces, was the criminalizing of Bhats and Charans, a campaign conducted by the East India Company with the cooperation of native rulers.

We do not look for empirical evidence to prove or disprove that the Bhats and Charans caused the practice of female infanticide, because the interpretive grid through which British colonial administrative reports were written, recorded, and codified was post-Enlightenment Lockean empiricism. Moreover, the empirical is a construct of the real that is designed to reflect those elements of reality that are skewed towards the interests of dominant groups. In our view, the truths of history are not isomorphic with empiricism. Therefore, instead of seeking empirical verification of the British colonial accusation we examine the rhetorics and poetics of bardic texts and foreground the connections between indigenous panegyric, origin tale, and traditional idioms about the rights of women.

The colonial writer in the passage below reproduces and amplifies the British colonialist view of the bardic castes of Rajasthan in order to show why they are responsible for female infanticide:

> The English reader must not then, picture to himself, as the concomitants of a Hindoo marriage, some venerable harper heading a group of brethren of the lyre . . . The Bhats and Charans-bards and heralds-alike prostitute their honorable office to the most mercenary ends. They gather together from miles around, like vultures on their prey, bringing with them all the idle and dissolute, who on such occasions, be they minstrels, dancers, buffoons, barbers, or beggars, all pass for Bhats and Charans. Such is the

> motley group that . . . flock around the house of the bride's father . . . and if some luckless giver of the feast be bold enough to resist such extortion, he must do it at the risk of personal indignity and insult, if not actual injury. He must be prepared to have his own name and his daughter's branded with every term of contumely and scorn . . . very few men are prepared for this . . . The poor man, whose daily wages rarely exceed four annas (six pence), cannot thus, to celebrate his daughter's marriage, scatter to the winds two or three hundred rupees . . . without rueing the day that his daughter was born.
>
> Under such a system, who can wonder that the Rajpoot, and more or less every Hindoo, 'mourns when a daughter is born to him, and rejoices when he has a son?'[9]

A number of mistakes are made by John Cave Brown in this passage. The custom of expensive and showy marriages did not originate in the demands made by the bards, but in the elite Rajput belief system of viewing the female household and daughters' marriages in terms of medieval-feudal conspicuous consumption. Modern studies of the bardic castes have verified that gifts to bards varied according to the father's status.[10] The shifting scale of remuneration dispels the myth that bards were extortionists. These errors are part of a larger set of mis-recognitions. Brown and other colonial writers interpret the bardic function, the client–patron relationship, the bard's social function, and his relationship to the community in a pre-industrial society, within the logic of British colonialism.

In other words, colonial writers monetize all forms of exchange and social relationships between the bard and the community in terms of the money economy. For instance, Brown distorts the patron–bard relationship by implying that rich patrons are subordinate to a service group even though in a feudal society rich patrons are rarely at the mercy of a service group. A comic opera was played out in the colonial representation of the client–patron relationship between Bhats and Charans and Rajput chiefs. Colonial officers like the Political Agent at Jodhpur, Captain J. Ludlow, recorded, classified, and systematized the

[9] John Cave Brown, *Indian Infanticide: Its Origins, Progress and Suppression* (London: W.H. Allen & Co., 1857), pp. 16–17.

[10] See A.M. Shah and R.G. Shroff, 'The Vahivanca Barots of Gujarat: A Caste of Genealogists and Mythographers', in *Traditional India: Structure and Change*, ed. Milton Singer (Philadelphia: The American Folklore Society, 1959).

amount of payments to the Charans by different Rajput clans. These records reveal that in most cases the payments were, as Ludlow noted, voluntary and not coerced by the bards. Ludlow was on the brink of discovering the commonsensical fact that the elite patrons were the agents, not the victims, of this practice. At this juncture pragmatism won. Ludlow's conversations with the Rajput chiefs and his correspondence with his superiors helped him see the light: namely, that it did not suit the Company to point the finger at the warlike Rajput chiefs who might instigate a revolt and from whose territories a large percentage of sepoys were recruited into Company forces. Thus, persuasion rather than pressure was adjudged the correct reform policy for the Rajput nobility of Marwar.[11]

Brown's passage diverts the reader from arriving at the commonsensical conclusion that it is the elite Rajput father who mourns the birth of his daughter, and who is responsible for sanctioning the practice of female infanticide. The diversionary tactic in the text lies in portraying a feudal world turned upside down. Through the rhetorical device of inversion, the writer urges the 'English reader' to realize that what he is about to read is not a normative feudal world: the 'venerable harper' does not sit at the feet of his overlord but is a vulture and prostitute-mercenary; the Rajput father who mourns the birth of a daughter, and kills her because she is female, is not a murderer but a fellow-victim. In fact, Brown goes even further to imply that the Rajput father deserves more compassion than his female victims. He misrepresents the infanticidal father as a poor man, in spite of the fact that British colonial records overwhelmingly attest to the fact that fathers who put their infant daughters to death were not poor Rajputs 'whose daily wages rarely exceed four annas', but men who owned land and ancestral wealth.

The truth about the bards' relation to female infanticide is less dramatic than Brown suggests in the extract. The stereotypical view of the Charan as a legitimating ideologue for elite Rajput males does not take into account that while the bards were not social activists in our sense of the term, they were social commentators, and the social commentary in Charan chronicles, or in encoded poetic narratives like

[11] Foreign and Political Consultations, no. 30 for the year 1834, and no. 294 for the year 1842, India Office Records (hereafter IOR).

Chand Bardai's *Prithvi Raj Raso*, did not always harmonize with the self-representation of elite Rajputs. A significant example of the way Charans spelt out the political interests that underlie the exploitation of daughters for hypergamous marriages can be found in the distinctions that Charan chroniclers make between alliances made through women (*saga*), and alliances made through men (*bhaibandhu*).[12]

The prerequisite for the bard's oppositional functions was geographical mobility; thus the bard's ability to perform social commentary depended in large part on travelling from place to place, and gaining access to individual homes in far-off villages. Even when he did not have direct access to the women of the village or clan, and only heard about them through gossip and rumour, the mobility required for performing his duties meant that the bard carried news about the treatment of women inside the home. 'The Bhats', observes Bishop Heber, 'protect nobody'.[13] This is not quite true. As itinerant travelling storytellers, sometimes the bard functioned as the voice of the natal family for the married woman; at other times he served as the conscience of the community and exhorted them to collectively ostracize and shame the man or family that oppresses women.

We suggest that there was a subtle correlation between the treatment of elite Rajput daughters and the treatment of bardic castes in Rajasthan. The bad faith in Brown's word-picture of a Rajput marriage inheres in portraying the father as bonding with his daughter on the occasion of her marriage while 'rueing' the event of her birth. In our view a distinctively different grouping obtains in the marriage scene of the elite Rajput daughter. In feudal Rajput society, daughters and bards

[12] The anthropologist Norman P. Ziegler notes that the seventeenth-century chronicles of Marvara written by Charans used the term *saga* to denote political alliances contracted through women, either the married daughters' clans or the natal family of the son's wife, and distinguished these saga alliances from *bhaibandhu* or close relations by male blood. 'The Seventeenth Century Chronicles of Marvara: A Study in the Evolution and Use of Oral Traditions in Western India', in *History in Africa*, vol. 3 (1976), pp. 127–53; and 'Marvari Historical Chronicles: Sources for the Social and Cultural History of Rajasthan', in *The Indian Economic and Social History Review*, vol. XII, no. 2, April–June 1976, pp. 219–50.

[13] Bishop Heber, *Narrative of a journey through the Upper Provinces of India* (1828), in *Selections from Heber's Journal*, ed. M.A. Laird (Cambridge: Cambridge University Press, 1971), p. 269.

enhanced the father's prestige: the former's marriage secured prestigious alliances for the father and the brother; the latter's presence at the marriage helped to circulate far and wide the news of the prestigious marriage spectacle through ballad and song. Traditionally, the hospitality and gifts meted out to the bard on the marriage occasion were not only part of the feudal obligation of gift-giving in *dana*, additionally it was also an index of fatherly benevolence towards his daughter. A handsome dowry to the daughter inevitably meant generous gifts to the assembled bards.

It was through this complex interdependence that the bard functioned as a watchdog for daughters' rights. The Bhats and Charans fulfilled their pro-daughter function through the bardic genre of memorizing and praising every item of the dower. Contrary to Brown's assertion, bardic satire is far more likely to satirize the father on behalf of the daughter. There is a curious symmetry between the increase of female infanticide in the nineteenth century and the obsolescence of the bardic function in Rajasthani communities. When daughters became disposable in elite Rajput clans, the bards also became inconvenient. Most of the Bhats and Charans abandoned their traditional work and went into colonial service through Western-style education. Regionalist histories were replaced by official elite history; the erasure of non-Western modes of history-writing facilitated the erasure of women.

The grounds on which Western scholars discredited bardic histories were that they lacked empirical value. L.P. Tessitori's influential judgement was that 'there is probably no bardic literature in any part of the world, in which truth is so masked by fiction, or so disfigured by hyperbole, as in the bardic literature of Rajputana'.[14] James Tod's comments in the passage below are more ambivalent:

> These chronicles dare utter truths, sometimes most unpalatable to their masters. The vis or poison of the bard is more dreaded by the Rajpoot than the steel of fire . . . their pen is free: the despotism of the Rajpoot princes does not extend to the poet's lay, which flows unconfined . . . On the other hand, there is a sort of compact or understanding between the bard and the prince, a barter of 'solid pudding against empty praise' whereby the fidelity

[14] L.P. Tessitori, 'Progress Report for the Work done during the Year 1917', *Journal of the Asiatic Society of Bengal* (1917), pp. 20–1.

> of the poetic chronicle is somewhat impaired. The sale of 'fame' . . . will continue until there shall arise in the community a class sufficiently enlightened and independent to look for no other recompense for literary labour than public distinction.[15]

The first part of the passage is at odds with the last part. Note the initial rhetorical gesture of heaping praise: in Tod's view the bardic histories state 'truths' even though those historical truths may be 'unpalatable' to the patron, and are 'dreaded' by the martial Rajput more than a blow by the sword.[16] Tod even goes so far as to say that the Bhats and Charans enjoy freedom of thought and expression, their 'pen is free' and their narratives are 'unconfined'. However this piling of praise is only a preamble for the rhetorical unmasking of the bardic historians: Tod suggests that these Bhats and Charans are bought by patrons through gifts of money.

The colonial historian does not seek to resolve the contradiction between his two statements, the free pen of the bard versus the barter of pudding for praise, for he is operating on innuendo and speculation. Readers are invited to resolve the contradiction themselves through the Orientalist concept of degeneracy in Asiatic societies: namely, that there was an earlier time when the Charan's pen was free, but the community degenerated into greedy sycophancy. The underlying suggestion is that the gap between the two representations of the Rajasthan bards is the gap between the ideal and the real. This suggestion is reinforced by Tod's tone of regret, his tone suggests that he would have liked to believe that the Bhats and Charans are truth-tellers, but is disappointed to find the reality. Tod evokes yet another convention of Orientalist scholarship, specifically that the native of the colony is a liar. He achieves this by reporting the claims made by Bhats and Charans in the first part of the passage, and reporting the truth behind their false claims in the latter half.

[15] *Annals and Antiquities of Rajasthan*, vol. I (London: Routledge & Kegan Paul Ltd., 1829), pp. xvi, 25, i, iii.

[16] We focus on Tod's writing, and the rhetorical strategies in his writing. We do not claim access to Tod the historical person or to his personal benevolence, because authorial intentionality cannot be inferred through the text, or the author's 'real-life' conversations and actions. For a critical analysis of Tod's continuing popularity among postcolonial scholars, see our forthcoming book.

Tod's judgement that the bards compromise themselves by a barter of solid pudding against empty praise was repeated, remembered, and transmitted by British and Indians alike. Tod's ambivalence about the bardic castes derives from his reliance on them for his own history of Rajasthan on the one hand, and his desire to supersede the Bhats and Charans as the English bard of Rajasthan on the other. The colonialist who wrote history in the service of empire describes himself as 'a class sufficiently enlightened and independent to look for no other recompense for literary labour than public distinction.'[17] Tod's critique of the bards is part and parcel of the English distrust of modes of history-writing that were popular rather than elite, oral-performative rather than writing-based, and that on occasion were critical of the Rajput man of property rather than collusive with the rich patron.

Historical Consciousness in Relation to Colonial-Nationalist Constructions of the Rhetorical Species of Bardic Panegyric

Our investigation of the bardic castes participates in the Subaltern Studies project outlined by Guha: 'But suppose there were a historiography that regarded "what the women were saying" as integral to its

[17] British attempts to supplant the indigenous patrons of the bardic castes, and pay them to write indigenized versions of British infanticide reform, is evident in the following story. A member of the Bombay Civil Service, Lancelot Wilkinson, commissioned a Brahmin named Omkar Bhatta to write a tract in Hindi and Brajbhasha, which was translated into Gujarati and 700 copies distributed by James Erskine, Political Agent in Kathiawar, in the 1840s. We have not been able to find a copy of this tract, therefore we read this bardic tract through the lens of the colonial document. (See the full text of Erskine's letter detailing the tract in Wilson's *History*; op. cit., pp. 230–1.) The tract begins with the characteristic rhetorical manoeuvre of bardic narratives: exhorting and reminding the Rajputs of Malwa of their original glory in contrast to their present downfall, evident in their killing of their female children. The tract harmonizes British-style reform and Rajput religion: Bhatta exhorts the Rajputs to reform their tribe by conforming to the true maxims and rules of religion. The British were successful in employing pandits to create textual hegemony from the Hindu scriptures concerning sati; however they failed to create a body of bardic literature that would propagate their argument concerning female infanticide.

project, what kind of history would it write?'[18] Guha warns that a certain disorderliness and interruption of the narrative is inevitable in such a history, and adds that in his view 'perhaps chronology itself, the sacred cow of historiography, will be sacrificed at the altar of a capricious, quasi-Puranic time, which is not ashamed of its cyclicity'.[19] The writing of history not only involves arguments about the past, historical writing enacts a gesture from which we learn how to approach the past. It is for this reason that we call attention to the gesture of willed openness and self-revision by the historian in this statement. The gesture is self-implicating: Guha does not directly refer to indigenous historical traditions, but he does speak of shame about the cyclical conception of time in indigenous histories, and he also advises the historian to be unashamed to sacrifice chronology for the cyclicity of indigenous historical traditions.

Gyanendra Pandey arrives at a project similar to Guha's by calling attention to indigenous histories of the community. Pandey's prose performs a gesture of attentiveness to the indigenous account; he writes: 'It is my submission that the real alternative to colonialist historiography in the nineteenth century is to be found in the historical memory and accounts of the "little community", an example of which is the text we examine here—Sheikh Muhammed Ali Hasan's *Waqeat-a-Hadesat: Qasba Mubarakpur*'.[20] He rejects the nationalist historian's contempt and manipulation of folk good sense and common sense, and enacts a practice of listening to popular memory. We call attention to the activity of listening in both historians' description of indigenous histories; the significance of these pre-nationalist or non-nationalist historical traditions lie in their subtle and complex conventions for reciting, listening, and participating.

The two statements by Guha and Pandey illuminate the need for a theory—of textuality, genre, poetic codes, styles of audience interaction, and the very notion of what is signified by the term oppositional historical traditions—that might inform the postcolonial historian's engagement with the indigenous bard's chronicle. The

[18] 'The Small Voice of History', op cit., p. 11.

[19] Ibid., p. 12.

[20] Gyanendra Pandey, *The Construction of Communalism in Colonial North India* (Delhi: Oxford University Press, 1990), p. 115.

gestural element in Guha's prose, and it is only one of the rhetorically reflexive gestures in his work, is a willingness to suspend preconceptions and cherished presuppositions. Such a gesture gains fullness of meaning against the backdrop of work, indeed the massiveness of work that Guha has performed in dismantling the grand narratives of colonial and nationalist historiography. Likewise, the practice of listening enacted by Pandey's work suggests that attentiveness to Hasan's historical imagination and conception of community does not silence the Subaltern historian. In Pandey's text the two modes of history-writing are not in competition. In fact the Subaltern historian becomes the writing subject in the very moment of listening to the indigenous chronicler.

In marking these two gestures of willed openness and attentive listening, we are vigilant about the charge that the desired model for history-writing derives from those strands of literary criticism that are post-structuralist and post-modernist.[21] By treating historical prose as a literary-rhetorical artifact, we are not thereby suggesting that post-structuralist theories can be simplified into a model for history-writing, or that the interpretive activity between the historian and his/her audiences can be reduced to predictable formulaes. In fact it is precisely because, in the craft practised by the bards, poetry, epic narrative, origin tale, and chronicle are on a continuum that there are no pre-existing models in post-modern and post-structuralist theory for the investigation of *kavya-itihaas* in non-Western forms of history-writing. Given our own model for history-writing as a project that depends on the coming together of poets, historians, rhetoricians, and literary critics, we are not interested in privileging our own set of tools, but argue for a dialogue with professional historians.

Nevertheless this question will continue to rear up, partly because we are literary critics and rhetoricians and therefore may be perceived as wedded to our disciplinary tools (or to a simplified representation of our disciplinary tools), and partly because the question concerning the implicit model in our essay enfolds another question. Is the historical consciousness we posit in these itinerant nomadic bards feudal-medieval, and therefore of no use to the postcolonial modernities in

[21] We refer here to the sparkling polemical criticism by Aijaz Ahmed: 'Literary Criticism, in Other Words, is the desired Model for the Writing of History', in *In Theory: Classes, Nations, Literatures* (London: Verso, 1992), p. 208.

which the Indian women's movements function? Firstly, we argue that historical consciousness is not a positivist entity but is imbricated in questions of rhetoric and genre. Consequently, it concerns our understanding of rhetoric and genre within which that historical consciousness is encoded.

Putting questions about historical consciousness on a philosophical register violates the fundamental orientation of these historians. The Charans saw themselves as craftsmen rather than priests and therefore were more oriented towards the *techne* of rhetoric.[22] Class analysis is more revelatory when combined with caste analysis, an examination of the modes of community and labour in craftsmen's groups, and the decentralized craftsman's relation to geographical location. For example, the bard's envisioning his cultural work in the codes of artisanal guilds, and his relation to spatial location as wandering nomadic craftsmen, as well as his orientation towards rural villages rather than the fortresses of Rajput power, affects the bard's ability to mobilize dissent.

Secondly, the distinction between feudal-medieval consciousness and postcolonial modernities involves an examination of the textual relations between the historian and the traditional chronicler. These relations must be scrutinized without the hidden arrogance and dogma inherent in the progressivist telos of modern history. The question of *their* historical consciousness always puts into crisis our own historical consciousness of our pasts. Thus the burden of proof for the bards' historical consciousness lies not in the oral and written texts of the bardic castes, but in understanding the blind spots and resistances we bring to the task of studying these bards, and in comprehending the nature of our difficulties in gaining access to these bardic idioms.

Although poststructuralist theories do not have pre-packaged models for bridging the hiatus between kavya and itihaas, at its best post-structuralism provides openings, and these openings can be deployed to cross-examine our own critical practice. That is why in Guha and Pandey's prose the subterranean rhetorical figure of the ear interests us. In Derrida's interpretation of Nietzsche, the part-whole

[22] The valence of this class/caste distinction lies in the fact that versified rhetorics of history are a *techne* or craft, while statist historiographies are inclined towards philosophy.

figure of synecdoche in which the ear signifies the activity of listening enables the Nietzschean opposition between listening either as 'long-eared asses' or 'with small, finely tuned ears'.[23] For instance, Guha radicalizes Heidegger's insight that listening is constitutive of discourse by taking it one step further, and arguing that the rhetorical figure of the ear for the activity of oppositional writing is a woman-centred trope.[24] Indeed, if we may be permitted a feminist reading of Guha's oeuvre, the activity and protocols of criticism in his work consist of subordinating the figure of the historian, and in its place foregrounding the critical apparatus of listening as a mode of reflection and self-criticism.

We seek those places in the Subaltern Studies project where their encounter with indigenous chroniclers can be staged or has already been staged. In Guha's work those places do not lie so much in the historian's authoritative judgements, because the particulars of evaluations are invariably vulnerable to time, but in the gesture of self-revision that is not outmoded even when academic fashions alter. It is on these grounds that we mark our distance from those readings of his work that either defend him by protesting too much, or the strident criticisms which reify his work into a set of doctrinal statements. The problem is not that there is any doubt about the claims made on his behalf, but rather that these constructions patriarchalize Guha's work by an overemphasis on the notion of the founder and authoritative pioneer, conjoined to an underemphasis on those aspects of his work that are tentative and self-implicating.

Therefore we anchor the question—what kind of literary-rhetorical practice will make visible the framing devices, modes of emplotment and tropological prefiguring of historical events in bardic texts— to an examination of that place in Guha's work where he defines panegyric in the discussion of the twelfth-century chronicler of Kashmir, Kalhana's *Rajatarangini*. We widen the sphere of inquiry by looking at how Guha's work is drawn on by the fellow-Subalternist Gyanendra

[23] Jacques Derrida, *The Ear of the Other: Autobiography, Transference, Translation*, ed. Christie McDonald trans. Peggy Kamuf (Lincoln: University of Nebraska Press, 1988), p. 35.

[24] Guha says, 'That is why speaking and listening between generations of women are a condition of solidarity which serves, in its turn, as the ground for a critique'. 'The Small Voice of History', op. cit., p. 9.

Pandey, in order to clarify Pandey's overt relation to Bharatendu Harishchandra and subterranean relation to Chand Bardai. Guha's writing acts out, or more accurately performs, a problem concerning the colonial and nationalist construction of bardic panegyric as flattery. In our view a text's enactment of a conflict is more interesting than politically correct judgements, because the text highlights a problem to which there is no simple resolution. That problem concerns the loss that occurs through the disconnection of bardic literary forms like the *raso* and oral epics, from bardic historical genres like the *khyat*, *vamsavalli* and *pidhiyavalli*, a loss that we map out in the postcolonial hist-orian's alienation from, and ambivalences about, the genre of panegyric.

In his brief discussion of Kalhana's chronicle, Guha elaborates his definition of panegyric. Our focus is not on his specific judgement of this work but the grounds of his evaluation. He is critical of the chronicle on the grounds that the medieval bard 'was often indistinguishable from the panegyrist'. Guha ventures further and explains why the genre of panegyric is antithetical to the genres of history-writing. He defines panegyric as 'the courtier and the apologist speaking for gods, kings and noblemen' and suggests that it is a historical discourse that cannot speak 'with judicial impartiality about royalty and aristocracy' and that its potential for criticism 'was confined within the bounds of a feudal consciousness'.[25] In a moment we will move to a text by Bharatendu Harishchandra which bears out Guha's evaluation. At this juncture we note that Guha articulates a specifically nineteenth-century colonialist and nationalist construction of the panegyrical mode of indigenous history-writing as flattery, sycophancy, loyalism, and political conservatism.

Genres are powerfully determined by the centre/periphery logic of empire. We interrogate the colonial rationality within which Bhats and Charans were designated flatterers, because the accusations were levelled by British historians who were themselves ideologues and employees of the East India Company. For example, in the following statement the colonial writer conflates the indigenous genre of panegyric with self-serving unctuousness: 'And we may be sure these men [Bhats and Charans] do their best to make their presence welcome by

[25] 'Dominance without Hegemony', op. cit., pp. 217–19.

bestowing a due amount of flattery on their patrons'.[26] The colonial judgement was influential enough to cause a semantic change. The word 'Bhat' is explained in the dictionary as 'a bard, a minstrel, a flatterer'.[27] Thus two competing definitions of the Bhat coexist in popular memory: the Bhat as a chronicler and poet of the people, and conversely the Bhat as the sycophant of the rich Rajput client. We draw attention to the operation of centre/periphery in this colonialist codification: at the imperial centre the literary forms that mark the high points of the English Enlightenment are social and political satires; at the periphery bardic satire composed by the Bhats is interpreted as blackmail and extortion; at the centre epideictic oratory is an esteemed form of rhetoric; at the periphery the Bhat's panegyric is read off as insincere flattery.

It would be a simplified understanding of the colonial processes if we deployed the depth metaphor of an underlying pure panegyric and a superimposed colonial judgement. Colonialism creates its own realities, ably assisted by its competitor and ally, elite nationalism. If the Guha-Kalhana relation illuminates the problem of reading the panegyrical impulse in historical writing outside the colonialist description of sycophancy, then it would be misleading for us to suggest that we can recover these indigenous genres, narratives, political languages, and rhetorical modes as essences without accounting for nationalist appropriations. It is precisely in naming the discourses and language-literatures that mediate our access to the panegyric that Gyanendra Pandey's analysis and translation of Bharatendu Harishchandra's 1884 lecture at Ballia, and the Chand Bardai reference in the Harishchandra text, assumes significance for us.

A brief word about the cultural matrices of these three figures—Kalhana, Harishchandra, Chand Bardai—in North Indian history will explain their status in our argument, and the true dimension of the contestations. Kalhana's twelfth-century chronicle of Kashmir, *Rajatarangini*, has been a puzzle for the modern historian. It provides a glimpse of a historical imagination that records and comments on

[26] Brown, op. cit., p. 15.

[27] R.C. Tiwari, R.S. Sharma, and Krishna Vakil, *Hindi-English Dictionary* (New York: Hippocrene Books, 1994), p. 187; John T. Platts, *A Dictionary of Urdu, Classical Hindi and English* (Delhi: Munshiram Manoharlal, 1997), p. 177.

several aspects of the political life of medieval Kashmir: the conflict between the Brahmanas and the king: the politicization of the office of the *purohita*: the upward mobility of the Kayastha caste. Yet historians have not felt comfortable in their access to the historical voice that speaks in this chronicle.

At the other end of the pole, Bharatendu Harishchandra represents a different problem. He is a nineteenth-century literary ideologue who emerges from classes and groups in Eastern UP which were loyalist to the British, and his literary-historical-political impulses culminate in the language revolution for which he is most well known, establishing the Hindi language in the Devanagri script.[28] Harishchandra's construction of standard Hindi as the new national language marginalized Hindi dialects as non-standard Hindi and deprivileged dialect literatures. An instance of the dialect literatures that are marginalized by state-sponsored Sanskritized Hindi is the oldest and most popular ballad of Rajasthan, Chand Bardai's twelfth-century ballad *Prithvi Raj Raso*. Thus, in the narrative that we are weaving—about the difficulties we face, as historians, rhetoricians, poets and literary critics, in gaining access to the intertextualities between kavya and itihaas—Harishchandra occupies the space of the nationalist ideologue who determines our access to versified histories.

A notable illustration of this problematic is Pandey's incisive analysis of Harishchandra's use of encomia. The text in question, Harishchandra' s public speech at Ballia in 1884, is a textbook example of how explicit loyalism for the colonial master is combined with its seeming opposite, rhetoric in the service of the discourses of elite nationalism. The speech begins with a comprobatio, praise for his audience, for the citizenry of Ballia, and for the British administrator Mr Roberts. Imperceptibly, the speech moves into the historical mode through the

[28] Instances of how pro-British loyalism in the political sphere went hand in hand with cultural nationalism are the following: Harishchandra concocted caste histories, wrote on *Rajatarangini* as part of the rewriting of history and culture by the nationalist elite, and constructed communalist myths about Aryanized Hindu castes. Harishchandra's language revolution laid the basis for the forcible separation of Hindi from Urdu by positing the former as the true indigenous mother-tongue and characterizing the latter as a foreign language brought in by Muslim invaders. This separation of two language-literatures provided Hindu communalists with a weapon for linguistic hegemony and monolinguality.

conventions of the rhetoric of eulogia, for example the British master is compared to Akbar, the most statesman-like emperor in the Mughal empire. Throughout the speech a steady vein of praise for England accomplishes the rhetorical objective of providing the exemplum for the normative model for colonial modernity.

It is in the combination of praise for the British and the satirist's lash for the common people of India that a specifically colonialist-nationalist panegyric emerges. Harishchandra combines the panegyrical mode with another rhetorical mode that had a distinctive function in bardic writings: satire. An infinitesimal change occurs in the speech from the imitation of bardic praise to the combination of lavish compliments and savage invective. By activating the conventions of praise, Harishchandra draws on the audience's expectations of the bardic recitation. However, he creates a mixed genre in which the bard's satire, which was sometimes directed against the ruling classes in order to make them recognize their political responsibilities, is addressed in the nationalist speech to the common people. The speech makes it amply clear which sections of society are the target of savage indignation. The class content of the satire is delineated by distinguishing 'the people of Hindustan' from the dominant classes, 'the Rajas, Maharajas, Nawabs and notables of Hindustan'.[29]

It is in the relations between the emergent nationalist genre of Harishchandra's speech and the residual genre of bardic praise and satire that we discern the making of a historical consciousness that is not so distant from us. Pandey comments on Harishchandra's wide-ranging interests in history and the dating of historical events, and notes how this view of history defines itself in terms of territoriality.[30] Harishchandra's interests in reading and writing about history is a gauge of an emergent historical consciousness that wishes to remake the Indian past, and join it to the triumphant present of England's empire, in order to insert the future of the Indian nation in European modernity.

Historical consciousness is trans-individual and shared by an entire epoch, but an individual's access to the historical consciousness of

[29] Pandey,. op.cit., Appendix II, p. 272. See also Vasudha Dalmia, *The Nationalization of Hindu Traditions: Bharatendu Harishchandra and Nineteenth-century Banaras* (Delhi: Oxford University Press, 1997).

[30] Pandey, op. cit., pp. 110–11.

his time is determined by his class and his politics. How could one be a pro-British loyalist and a cultural nationalist at the same time? Harishchandra's rhetoric provides the answer, panegyric comes to signify abject and obsequious genuflections towards people in power. Simultaneously, the parallel movement of lashing the subordinate classes is vitriolic and borders on the self-hatred endemic to the classes which profited from, and were proximate to, the British master. Nevertheless the satiric glass is not held up to reflect Harishchandra's own follies. In the final instance his speech situates the performance of self-hatred in the context of self-interest. The more he can persuade the audience to assent to satiric jokes, anecdotes and proverbs about the indolent Indian masses, the more he can mobilize and organize the audience as their leader.

Thus the 1884 speech is a perfect illustration of panegyric as only another name for the fawning, grovelling submissiveness, and enslaved mentality of those classes, groups, and individuals that were indigenous profiteers of empire. In this sense our own reading of the speech is in agreement with Pandey. In a careful reading of Guha's definition of panegyric as political loyalism, Pandey notes 'the extraordinary encomiums that Bharatendu showered on the British, the paeans of praise for the new opportunities brought by British rule, or as one might say, the evident loyalism of the text'.[31] The inevitable conclusion is that a canonical figure like Bharatendu Harishchandra, known to most Indian readers as the father of Hindi literature (a title that Pandey quotes with a tinge of irony), is a male forbear of the modern nationalist and communalist. His speech embodies a face of the past that is unacknowledged in a good deal of Third-Worldist nationalism.

Historical consciousness cannot be conceptualized as univocal. The place of hope in Pandey's book lies in the statement we quote at the start of this essay, that there are many faces of the past, that Bharatendu Harishchandra is not the only male forbear for midnight's children, that there were alternative historical memories and accounts of the little community. There would be a false pessimism if we formulate the problem as—is it true or false that indigenous panegyric is collaborationist and loyalist—without also considering the making of this colonialist rhetoric in terms of the traditions it draws on and

[31] Ibid., p. 217.

appropriates. There is a place in the Harishchandra speech where we can comprehend the processes at work in the separation of kavya and itihaas, in the apparent opposition between the subjective lyricism of poetic praise versus the objectivity of historical prose. Bharatendu Harishchandra is in the full sway of the satirist's savage diatribe against the common people: 'Pull up your socks yourselves. Stop being lazy. How long do you wish to be called primitive, uncivilized, ignorant and lazy?'[32] It is at this point that a literary reference erupts into the political text. The text alludes to the figure that it wishes to supersede, Chand Bardai the poet-historian known for the ur-panegyric in North Indian literatures, *Prithvi Raj Raso*.[33]

There is not one essential *Prithvi Raj Raso* text, nor one authoritative reading. Moreover the legend and popular contestations as well as dominant Hindutva reincarnations of the legend should not be conflated with the ballad itself, for the ballad is not a univocal text. Poetic and rhetorical conventions for dissent are erased in colonized societies, thus pre-nationalist panegyric appears as political conservatism precisely when its rhetorical and oral-performative dimensions are erased. The possibilities for dissenting narratives lies in the story Bardai tells of daughters' rights, the princess Sanjukta resists her father's plans to use her wedding to further his political ambitions by eloping with the Chauhan king Prithviraj Chauhan.

The close relation between dissent and panegyric in bardic texts is discernible in the Bardai text. It is a panegyric on the *swayamvara* (*swayam* or self choosing and *vara* or marriage partner) form of Rajput marriage, in which the daughter chooses her groom. Earlier versions of the raso deployed panegyric, sometimes to ratify the Rajput patron's claims to political and military dominance, and sometimes to create a space for dissent. In dissenting interpretations, *Prithvi Raj Raso* functioned as counter-hegemony to propaganda by the dominant Rajput

[32] Ibid., p. 274.

[33] Several known bards are associated with *Prithvi Raj Raso*: Chand Bardai, Jalha, Kedar and Madhukar, as well as generations of anonymous bards. The language of the poems is generally Brajbhasha with elements of Rajasthani dialects, although there are Sanskrit versions too. The *doha* and *chaupai* are characteristic verse forms in all the versions. We recommend the version edited by B.P. Sarma (Chandigarh: 1962); and the critical study by Namvar Singh, *Prithviraj-raso ki bhasa* (Banaras: 1956).

clans that hypergamy was the only permissible marriage custom. When the bard sang the raso, he did not invariably lull his audience to pleasant nostalgia about idealized visions of the chivalric past of Rajasthan. The bard stimulated audiences to ponder the question of values in relation to daughters' rights, and in relation to the true Rajput ideals for men and women. Epideictic oratory does not merely dispense praise, it dispenses praise and blame in order to construct, and debate the construction of a standard of values for the audience. Thus, far from simply functioning as a tool for flattering the patron, there is sternness and majesty in the praise poem at its best. The panegyric taps into the deepest needs of the community. Actual practices of the local community are judged by the best that was thought and imagined by their culture.[34]

We are attentive to nationalist appropriations of pro-woman spaces for dissent in the balladic text. Later versions of the ballad tended to subordinate Sanjukta and the pro-daughter theme to the Prithviraj figure by making her into a passive figure of male rescue and focusing on the part of the plot that could be used to glorify war and masculinist values. It is in the contentiousness between versions that emphasized the pro-Sanjukta theme and praised Prithviraj for honouring women, *versus* those versions that valorized Prithviraj for his martial valour and blamed his defeat and death at the hands of Muhammad Ghori on his support of Sanjukta, that the textual reference in Harishchandra's speech becomes intelligible. The literary reference is deceptively low key, as if the speaker is quoting a historical event from memory, although a good deal of Harishchandra's ideological message about anti-Muslim communalist Hindu nationalism is conveyed through it:

> When Prithviraj Chauhan was captured by the Ghors, then someone told Shahabuddin's brother, Ghiyasuddin, that he[Prithviraj] was accomplished at aiming arrows at a sound. A gathering was called one day, and seven

[34] See Suzanne Pinckney Stetkevych for how the panegyric ode in the classical Arabic tradition, the high Jahili *qasidat al-madh*, encoded and transmitted the ideology of Arabo-Islamic hegemony in the Umayyad period, accounting for the pre-eminence of this poetic genre in Arabic, Persian, Ottoman and other Islamicate literary traditions. 'Umayyad Panegyric and the Poetics of Islamic Hegemony: Al-Akhtal's *Khaffa Al-Qatinu* (—'Those the dwelt with you have left in haste'—*Journal of Arabic Literature*, vol. 28, 1997, pp. 89–122).

> iron shields placed in position to be broken by arrows. Prithviraj had already been blinded. Prithviraj was told that at Ghiyasuddin's command, he should shoot at the shields [which would be sounded]. The poet, Chand, was also a prisoner along with Prithviraj. Seeing the preparations, he recited this verse: 'The arrow that is strung now, may be the last you string: Let the Chauhan not err: one arrow, one target'. Prithviraj understood the poet's words, and when Ghiyasuddin gave the signal by a sound, Prithviraj shot Ghiyasuddin with his arrow.[35]

Note how Harishchandra deploys the bardic conventions of anecdotes for a discussion of values. The bardic recitation is not judged in terms of empirical veracity, but in terms of popular memory and anecdote. In Harishchandra's speech *Prithvi Raj Raso* has been renarrativized into a story that prefigures nineteenth-century colonialism and nationalism. The anecdote begins with the defeat of colonized people: 'When Prithviraj Chauhan was captured by the Ghors', and ends with nationalist resistance: 'Prithviraj shot Ghiyasuddin with his arrow'. Pro-woman dissent has disappeared from Harishchandra's version of the ballad. What has taken its place is an emphatically communalist version of the past, within which Prithviraj is the Hindu–Rajput patriot and his antagonist is the Muslim ruler.[36] Rajput–Muslim contests for power and territory are re-read as nationalist–communalist contests between the Hindu ruler and the Muslim outsider.

Harishchandra's representation of Chand Bardai is crucial to this ideological project. He is no longer the semi-autonomous historian who can dispense praise or blame to his royal patron.[37] Instead, the

[35] Pandey, op.cit., pp. 274–5.

[36] The political relevance of analysing the rhetorical stratagems by which Harishchandra communalizes the legend of Prithviraj Raso, is to gesture towards Hindutva appropriations of the Prithviraj legend and the Raso text through schoolbooks and memorials.

[37] A modern-day Charan writer Inder Dan Ratnu refers to the colonial representation of Charans as a modern misconception by fellow-Indians, thereby indicating the popularity and prestige of the British view in India: 'Many people in India use the word "Charan" as synonym of "sycophant".' Ratnu contests this view: ' the qualities of the Charans for which they were renowned and respected were not sycophancy and flattery but their determination to resist by non violent means'. Like many subaltern histories, Ratnu's evidence is culled from oral genres of anecdotes and popular memory. For instance, Ratnu recounts the anecdote of

bardic historian is turned into a loyalist in the image of Harishchandra. The speech reworks the relation between panegyric and dissent by sleight of hand. In earlier versions Bardai's celebrated verses reminded the community that, in the past, women like Sanjukta had the right of marital self-determination, and the heroism of Prithviraj Chauhan consisted in protecting that right. Contrarily, in the Harishchandra text Bardai's celebrated verses no longer dissent from the dominant practices of violence against daughters, instead the heroism of Prithviraj lies in killing the Muslim invader.

The oppositional possibilities in traditional forms of panegyric and satire is a means, although it is by no means the only one, by which to understand the historical consciousness of bardic idioms. Panegyric is one of the sites where the postcolonial historian and poet encounters the autobiographical element in their disciplinary writings. These autobiographical elements do not inhere in the personal details of the historian's life, but in the borderline between work and life, and in the story about his male and female forbears that the historian and rhetorician tells herself or himself. To articulate the autobiographical element in historical and poetic prose, one must think through the relations between history as the science of the dead, and therefore in the Neitzschean and Derridean reading the science of the father, and the non-Western chronicler.[38]

---

the Charan poet Kaviraja Karani Dan Kavia who was asked by the rulers of Jodhpur and Jaipur to decide which of them was the greater king. The fact that Charans were praised for telling their patrons unpalatable truths about the Rajput cult of violence and land accumulation is evident from Kavia's reply: 'One has killed his own father and the other his own son for the sake of gaining or retaining power. Difficult to under-rate either of you' (http://www.terraplanepub.com/worldview/india1.htm).

[38] Nietzsche articulates the role played by the mother-function and father-function in his autobiography in *Ecce Homo* (1888), trans. and ed. Walter Kaufmann (New York: Vintage Books, 1969). We pay tribute to, but also depart from, Derrida's characterization of the Nietzschean duality of father as the principle of death versus mother as the living feminine, as the fundamental opposition between death and life in the genre of autobiography in *The Ear of the Other*, op.cit. In our view the living feminine is not subordinate to, or dependent on the Bhat's craft, but an alliance is possible between women's dissenting idioms and woman-centered idioms developed by Bhats and Charans.

To the extent that the Subalternist acknowledges a genealogical link to Charans who were hounded by the colonial state and forced to give up their traditional craft, it is a relation to one of the unacknowledged male/female ancestors.[39] To the extent that the modern historian makes the admission that it is no longer possible to write history without engaging with women's histories, the autobiographical element also lies in the fractured and contradictory ways in which s/he experiences both English and dialect as his/her mother-tongues, and the 'living feminine' in the long duration of pro-woman dissent. This is the place to note the barely concealed trope of woman as shakti in Guha's statement quoted at the start of this section, in the notion that women's history has the power to activate other small voices of marginalized groups. Thus the problematic of historical consciousness lies in our practices of forgetting and remembering: the bardic castes put the professional historian, layman readers, cultural workers and filmmakers in touch with an ancestor who practices a craft and speaks an idiom that we have neither fully forgotten nor clearly remember.[40]

The Criminalizing of Bardic Historians in Nineteenth-century Rajasthan

If we arrive at the infanticide reform documents without an examination of the social and cultural functions served by bardic recitations, we fall prey to the progressivist narrative according to which British infanticide reform successfully wiped out the practice from the princely states of Rajasthan. In marked opposition to the progressivist narrative about female infanticide reform we construct a narrative, not in the literary conventions of a conspiracy, but in the far more mundane

[39] See R.K. Saxena, *Social Reforms* (New Delhi: Trimurti Publications, 1975).

[40] For example, the figure of the bard was mainstreamed by Hindi language Bombay industrial cinema in Raj Kapoor's *Jis Desh Mein Ganga Behti Hai* (1960). The central character is a Bhat who reforms a group of dacoits through his radical innocence, his love of music, and his pacifism. The film attempted to absorb the figure of the bard into the socialist nationalism associated with the Nehruvian era. Nevertheless the very fact that Raj Kapoor turned his attention to an indigenous tradition of cultural production is an instance of borrowings between postcolonial cinema and folk traditions.

account of a series of negotiations, pacts and accommodations between elite Rajput males and the British. This account is of open complicity rather than hidden conspiracy between the colonial power and the indigenous elite: the elite Rajput male colluded with the British administrator to shame, humiliate, and blame the bardic historians of Rajasthan for crimes committed by the former within his own home.

On the heels of Tod's history of Rajasthan a reform campaign was mounted by colonial reformer-administrators in order to make reality conform to their interpretations.[41] Englishmen did not construct this narrative alone; in fact the narrative was a product of collusion between East India Company officers in Rajasthan and the indigenous elites in the princely states of Rajasthan. The system of blaming and prosecuting the Bhats and Charans—termed the 'Marwar system' of infanticide reform by James Sutherland, the Governor-General's agent in Rajasthan—was, once the reports and dispatches are stripped to their bare essentials, a two-pronged policy: firstly, political collaboration between the East India Company and the ruling clans of Rajasthan; secondly, the British war on the bardic castes. The success of infanticide reform in Rajasthan was measured by the extent to which the Charan's craft was made obsolete.

The scholarly and administrative processes by which the English administrators blamed the Bhats and Charans for the high incidence of female infanticide in Rajasthan illuminates the colonial idiom of domination in relation to non-European literacies and literatures. Criminalizing historians and poets requires complicity from the indigenous elite. The scholarly codification of bardic literature followed in the aftermath of British treaties with the states of Rajasthan. By 1818 these princely states were brought under the East India Company while preserving their internally independent status. The British

[41] The correspondence between British administrators indicates that they were well aware that the bardic castes of Rajasthan upheld daughters' rights rather than attacked them. For instance James Sutherland expressed the hope that the Bhats and Charans would cooperate with the British government, for the simple reason that the bards' interests were better served by the preservation rather than by the destruction of daughters (Letter from Sutherland to C.A. Elliott, secy. to Govt. of India, 11 January 1848, in Indian Political and Foreign Consultations, 11 February 1848), p. 74, IOR.

eroded the social base of bardic history in the one area that most affected the politically powerful male elite of Rajasthan, namely, the genealogical function of the bards. In an unprecedented move British historians assumed that genealogical function, and by 1829–32 the publication of the two-volume British history of Rajasthan in James Tod's *Annals and Antiquities of Rajasthan* accomplished the colonial objective of information retrieval from indigenous sources, rendering obsolete the social functions of Bhats and Charans, and appeasing the politically useful elite Rajput men.

The colonialist strategy was to read Jodhpur's history and discover laws that seemed to echo British policy against the Bhats and Charans. In 1839 the Court of Directors of the East India Company approved the plan by the Political Agent, Sutherland, to concentrate reformist energies on extirpating the villainous bards. Infanticide reform began as part of the imperial discourse of better government. Sutherland and John Ludlow, along with the ruler and ministers of Marwar, framed a code of rules for better government of the state of Marwar. The 45th article of this code fixed the fees of the Charans according to the individual patron's income. Furthermore, Sutherland reported to his superiors that he had learnt of a proclamation passed by the ruler of Jodhpur in the year 1763 which regulated payments to the Bhats and Charans on the occasion of marriages. Thus the East India Company's interference between the patrons and the bardic castes was represented as simply the reactivation of a defunct native law. [42]

The Jodhpur ruler's regulation was part of the political tug of war between feudal rulers who wished to curb the growing political influence of clans in their princely state, and elite clans who made a bid for power and status by conspicuous consumption at marriages. The

[42] J. Sutherland's Note, 'Jodhpur Code of Rules', Art. 45, 3 January 1841, Parliamentary Papers ([1843), p. 57, IOR. A note by the Jodhpur vakil to the British Political Agent dated 2 June 1842 stated that the ruler of Jaipur had proclaimed in 1731 that his Rajput subjects should celebrate the marriage of their daughters in Jaipur, under the supervision of the state authorities, so that they would not be harassed by the Bhats and Charans. India Political Consultations, 28 December 1842, p. 295, IOR. The Court of Directors of the East India Company expressed satisfaction at Sutherland's Marwar system, and suggested that the Bombay system should follow Sutherland's scheme, however the Bombay government found the Marwar system impractical.

elite Rajput daughter's wedding was a social-political event of considerable significance if the father chose to make it so. Bardic accounts of the daughter's wedding helped disseminate the patron's influence far and wide as the itinerant Bhats and Charans travelled through Rajasthan, Gujarat, and Oudh. Therefore the patron's excessive expenditure, and the record of this in bardic narratives, constituted warning signs that the patron and his clan were readying themselves for a bid for political power.[43] This element in the Rajput idiom of power was wrenched from its political-cultural context and reinterpreted to signify that the root of the evil practice of female infanticide lay in the exorbitant demands made by Bhats and Charans.

In colonial discourse the discursive term for open complicity between the East India Company and the indigenous elite was 'native initiative'. An elaborate political minuet was danced between the rulers of Jaipur, Udaipur, Jodhpur, and the English Residents and Political Agents stationed in the princely states of the province. The native rulers would routinely appeal to the East India Company for help in controlling the avaricious demands of the Bhats and Charans at marriages, ostensibly as a way of reducing marriage expenditures, and thus encouraging parents to preserve their female children. The East India Company in turn would represent these appeals as a native initiative and come to the rescue of the rich and the powerful. The criminal profile of the Bhats and Charans was circulated and a consensus took shape to lay the blame for female infanticide squarely on the shoulders of these extortionists. For the latter half of the nineteenth century, the reformist issue that formed a regular part of the political conferences between English Residents and the rulers of Udaipur, Jaipur, Harowli, Bharatpur, Dholpur, and Kishengarh were co-operative efforts to prosecute Bhats and Charans.

The charges brought against the Bhats and Charans for causing female infanticide had a great deal to do with British judgements about

[43] For example, in 1848 at the height of the British-led programme for the disciplining of the Charans and counter-resistance by the Charans, the Thakur of Raipur flouted the authority of Marwar by a lavish wedding for his daughter and generous payments to the assembled Charans. This show of power was swiftly scotched by the Marwar ruler's punishment of the Thakur, with the approval of the East India Company. See Saxena op., cit., pp. 34–5.

bardic history. The Bhats and Charans had elaborated a written and oral tradition of history-writing that was in an advanced stage of development. The bias in British codification of the bardic literature of Rajasthan lay in the notion, popularized by colonial writers, that premodern bardic genres like the *vamsavalli,* the *pidhiyavalli* and the khyat concoct fictitious genealogies and origins in order to flatter the patron for money.[44] Bardic satiric genres like the *bhumd* were characterized as forms of blackmail through which the bard extorted money from his patron.[45] This colonial judgement of the Rajasthan bards is no longer unanimous. The bards of Rajasthan were not parasitic dependents but constituted a semi-autonomous caste of hereditary retainers. Scholars now believe that the partial autonomy of the bards derived, like all relationships in feudal societies, from a network of reciprocal duties and obligations between the community as a whole and a caste with traditions of literacy and service.[46]

Research on the bardic castes shows that historical writing and poetry were not the preserve of the upper castes in medieval north India. Historical evidence for the partial autonomy of the bard's social function lies in the linguistic change, as well as the change in class and caste hierarchy that occurs in history-writing in fourteenth-century Rajasthan. Language is a major indicator of social change, for example the language in which the Brahmanical Bhats composed historical

[44] From 1914 to 1919 the Asiatic Society of Bengal sponsored a series of surveys which systematically collected bardic poetry and published it in *Journal of the Asiatic Society of Bengal* under the title 'Bardic and Historical Survey of Rajputana'. These writings were collected and transcribed by James Tod, as well as by the Italian philologist L.P. Tessitori, for the Asiatic Society. In 1996 a joint Indian-Italian international conference was held in Bikaner, Rajasthan, on 'Tessitori in Rajasthan', which included papers by S.K. Kavia, 'The Contribution of Dr L.P. Tessitori to Bardic Literature', and G.S. Sharma, 'Tessitori's Contribution to Rajasthani Language and Literature'.

[45] For an independent-minded writer's criticism of bardic satire, see Bishop Heber, *Narrative of a Journey,* pp. 268–70.

[46] See C. von Fürer-Haimendorf, 'The Historical Value of Indian Bardic Literature', *Historians of India, Pakistan and Ceylon,* ed. C.H. Philips (London: 1967), pp. 80–90. Rajendra Joshi, 'Charans: The Contextual Dynamics of Caste in the Rajput System', *Religion, Ritual and Royalty,* ed. N.K. Singhi and Rajendra Joshi (New Delhi: Vedams, 1999).

literature shifted from Sanskrit to Brajbhasha. This change was accompanied by, and stimulated by, the inclusion of low-caste Charans.[47] This shift in class and caste composition of the poet-historians, as well as the shift from a learned language to the vernacular, is memorialized in a myth of origins. According to the myth, the Bhats were guardians of the sacred bull Nandi belonging to the deity Shiva. In the Charan myth, which poetically and mythically explains the percolation of knowledge and the craft of writing/recitation to the lower castes, it is only when the Brahmin Bhats could not protect the bull that Shiva created a courageous caste of Charans. We decode the myth as suggesting that the protection of the god's bull symbolizes the bard's vocation of protecting and preserving the community ideals of human reciprocity. The myth reminds Charans that the bard must be fearless rather than subservient to kings and landlords in history-writing.

It was precisely the bard's mobility and transmission of news from place to place that threatened colonial authorities since they wished to have absolute control over the flow of information. Therefore the bards' mobility was perceived as a threat to the political-administrative interests of the British colonial power. In 1844 the Jaipur Council of Regency asked for the aid of the British government to pass a rule

[47] The entry of the non-Brahmanical Charan caste into historical writing was part of a general movement of democratization of the craft of history-writing. John D. Smith writes, 'from the fifteenth century onwards a great mass of literature was produced; the bulk of it is the work of Charans'. With the subsequent decline of the Charans, bardic occupations were assumed by a variety of specialized lower castes. Thus for instance Smith finds that the epic poem 'Pabuji' is said to be 'first composed by the Carans' and then at some stage the Harijan caste of Nayaks became the bardic transmitters of the epic poem, *The Epic of Pabuji* (Cambridge: Cambridge University Press, 1991), pp. 3, 18. The distinguished folklorist Komal Kothari notes that the lower-caste perspective is incorporated into the bardic narrative through the caste origins of the central hero, 'The heroes of oral epics, however, are not of royal lineage and are often of low descent'. *Oral Epics in India*, ed. Stuart H. Blackburn, Peter J. Claus, Joyce B. Flueckiger, and Susan S. Wadley (Berkeley: University of California Press, 1989), p. 113. See also Stephen Fuchs' study of the Bhats affiliated to Harijan weavers in *The Children of Hari: Study of the Nimar Balahis in the Central Provinces* (New York: Praeger, 1951), pp. 172–84. Tribal societies also have bardic castes, for instance C. von Fürer-Haimendorf studied the Pardhan bards of Raj Gonds in Madhya Pradesh, in 'The Pardhans: The Bards of Raj Gond', *Eastern Anthropologist*, vol. 4 (1951), pp. 172–84.

whereby the Bhats and Charans of Rajasthan would be forbidden from attending marriages outside their own territories, and any infringements of this executive order would be punishable by the confiscation of their lands. It is noteworthy that the two states that took the lead in restricting the movement and fees of the Bhats and Charans, Jaipur and Jodhpur, had minors on the throne. Sutherland describes the political vacuum as offering 'the opportunity for the British Residents to assist the Councils of Regency in the work of administration. . . measures were enforced with greater success here'.[48]

One can gain some sense of the negotiations that took place between the colonial power and the ministers of the Jaipur state from the following story. Bardic castes of Rajasthan are Muslim as well as Hindu; nevertheless the British mistakenly believed that Bhats and Charans belonged exclusively to the Hindu community.[49] Ludlow suggested a communalist scheme of surveillance for the Bhats and Charans: namely, the hiring of Muslim intelligence agents to attend the marriage festivities of Rajput daughters in Jaipur state in order to report on the intrusion of Bhats and Charans from other parts of Rajasthan and north-west India. The Jaipur Council of Regency rejected this plan, perhaps because they felt that this scheme of spying went too far and would almost certainly invite retaliation from the Bhats and Charans.

The benefits of collaboration for the East India Company lay in learning from the elite natives how far to push the Bhats and Charans without incurring large-scale resistance. Conversely, the Rajput elite

[48] J. Sutherland to F. Currie, 10 March 1847, India Political and Foreign Consultations, 17 April 1847, p. 47, IOR.

[49] The Hindu–Muslim elements in bardic writings are relevant to the postcolonial understanding of historical traditions of India. Kothari observes: 'on the border areas of western Rajasthan and Pakistan many romantic epics are sung by Muslims known as *vat* and play a considerable role in the Sufi religion of that area'. *Oral Epics in India*, p. 108. C. von Fürer-Haimendorf notes that there were bards in the Muslim states of Junagadh (pp. 80–90). The exemplary study in this area is Shail Mayaram, 'Meos of Mewat: Synthesizing Hindu-Muslim Identities', in *Manushi*, No. 103, November–December, 1997), pp. 5–10 and idem, *Resisting Regimes: Myth, Memory and the Shaping of a Muslim Identity* (Delhi: Oxford University Press, 1997).

earned benefits from the Company and were not subject to the harassment and surveillance suffered by the Jhareja Rajputs of Kathiawar, or that was meted out by the imperial power in the post-1857 period to the Oudh Rajputs in the name of female infanticide reform. Ludlow's official letter records the Council's diplomatically worded objections: 'The only objection was that the Council of Regency at Jaipur did not wish to come forward to infringe a time-honored custom during the minority of their sovereign'.[50] Nevertheless, Ludlow asked the Political Agents of the princely states of Udaipur, Jodhpur, Harowli, and the durbars of Bharatpur, Dholpur, and Kishengarh to issue proclamations confining the movements of the Bhats and Charans to their own respective states on the occasion of marriages. The colonial representation of these restrictions cites native rulers as the original complainants, and portrays the restrictions as native initiative: 'the measure must be considered as the act of the native durbars and not of the British government'.[51] The burden of reform efforts in 1846 consisted of sifting through the stream of reports concerning the movements of the Bhats and Charans, especially rumours that the bards infiltrated into Rajasthan from the British-led provinces.

The Charan's conception of his social-political role was integral to bardic forms of resistance. It was the sacred part of his craft to guard his independence, and to resist when the conditions for his independence were removed. According to the feudal belief system in nineteenth-century Rajasthan, the person of the bard was magicalized; he could travel without being robbed by thieves and remain unharmed in the battlefield. The English claimed that they were repelled by the fact that the sacralized bard could enforce his power through self-immolation, and that the indigenous community, which interpreted bardic self-immolation as cursing the land with calamity, famine and barrenness, dreaded this extreme step.[52] An administrative report noted that

[50] J. Ludlow to C. Thoresby, 12 April 1844, India Political and Foreign Consultations, 30 November 1844, p. 152, IOR.

[51] India and Bengal Letters, 2 June 1845, para 19, IOR.

[52] Romila Thapar describes the bardic castes as having forged the mode of dharna or passive resistance by undertaking a fast at the door of the patron who disrespected them. 'Dissent and Protest in the Early Indian Traditions', *Studies in History*, vol. 1, no.2, 1979, p. 183. Thus what the English saw as barbaric practices

the extortionist Bhats and Charans—it was fairly routine for the colonial document to refer to the bardic modes of resistance as blackmail and extortion—included wounding themselves, committing suicide, or *traag* at the door of the patron.[53]

The years 1846–7 are crucial in the evolution of the discursive processes by which indigenous modes of dissent were criminalized. When their fundamental right to move from place to place was abrogated, the besieged Charans confronted their traditional patrons. Note how a Jaisalmer vakil characterizes bardic resistance: in 1846 he reports that a body of 'armed' Charans threaten human sacrifice if their demands are not met by the durbar of Jaisalmer. The report also characterizes the mobility of the Charans as a source of resistance to authority; it suggests that the Charans from Jaisalmer were able to resist and insist on their demands because they had sought and gained asylum in Jodhpur. In 1847 the Jaipur Council of Regency reports that some Charans caused disturbances in Jaipur and were punished by the Council.[54] The traditional idiom of resistance was discursively represented as 'disturbances' which threaten law and order; the community of poet-historians that was itself under attack was described as engaged in criminal activities. To those familiar with the colonial itinerary for

---

in the colony are now recognized as a mode of dissent adopted by Gandhian nationalism in the twentieth century. See also Denis Vidal, 'An Echo of Gandhi: Traditional Resistances in the Face of Colonialism' (*Cahiers Des Sciences Humanes*, vol. 28, no. 2, pp. 187–207), in which the author lists suicide threats by Bhats and Charans as customary methods of social protest.

[53] Greathead's report on Jodhpur for the year 1846, 11 September 1847, Indian Political Foreign Consultations, 24 December 1847, p. 144, IOR. The scale of bardic resistance can be gauged from the fact that in 1847 the number of protest suicides by Charans in Marwar totalled 200. The official report noted that this number of self-immolations or suicides committed by Charans was greater than the total number of satis reported for Marwar for that year. Indeed one does not have to be an advocate of sati (in fact we are not advocating female self-immolation) to make a distinction between the practice of sati in Rajasthan in support of the Hindu patriarchal ideal of female virtue and husband-worship, and the Charans' protest suicides, which are a traditional idiom of protest in South Asia.

[54] Note from Jaisalmer vakil, 1 July 1846, India Political Foreign Consultations, 8 August 1846, p. 67, India and Bengal Letters, 5 November 1847, p. 15, IOR.

resistance by tribals, peasants, craftsmen, and sepoys, the language of the reports by princely states carries the imprint of colonial discourse. In the Jaipur and Jodhpur reports the reference to armed Charans, the term 'disturbances', and the colonialist representation of protest suicides as 'human sacrifice', are an all too familiar sign that the colonial apparatus was readying itself for massive reprisals.

The reprisals came all too swiftly. In 1847 an act was passed by the ruler of Marwar declaring those Bhats and Charans who resorted to human sacrifice as guilty of murder.[55] The leaders of the Bhats and Charans of Rajasthan were imprisoned for seven years, and others banished from the territory. From the perspective of the East India Company, the disciplining of the Bhats and Charans effected the abolition of the practice of female infanticide in Rajasthan. For instance, the report of the Political Agent of Jaipur in 1863 declares that restrictions on the movements and fees of the Bhats and Charans has been very beneficial in reducing marriage expenses, and female infanticide is no longer a general occurrence.[56] By the end of the nineteenth century indigenous modes of history-writing were eclipsed and discredited by British administrators and historians.[57]

Rival Interpretations of the Purriar Meenas' Tale of Origins, and the Rhetoricity of the Bard's Recitation

The crucial difference between Graeco-Roman traditions of history-writing and the historical literature composed by the bardic castes lies

[55] James Sutherland to the Secretary to Govt. of India, 11 January 1848, India Political and Foreign Consultations, 11 February 1848, p. 74, IOR.

[56] Report of Political Agent, 8 December 1863, India Legislative Proceedings, 14 October 1865, p. 17, IOR.

[57] The disciplinization of the Charans of Mewar provides insight into how a traditional craft or *techne* which depended on elite patronage became extinct. In 1879 the Bhats and Charans of Mewar tried to survive by self-censorship. They fixed the *tyaag* payments and reported infringements. In return the Maharana of Udaipur utilized tyaag payments to fund a school for Charan boys in Udaipur, thus ensuring that future descendants abandon the traditional occupation. In 1888 the Walterkrit Rajputra Hitkarini Sabha was set up to regulate marriage expenses. In 1901 and 1907 the Mewar rulers forbade all Charans and Bhats of

in the religious idiom within which kavya-itihaas is articulated. The Western model of history as literary artefact does not make room for the notion that the middle term between history and literature in traditional Indian historical genres is religion. Religion is not simply an ideology, or false consciousness, or a mode of power and an apparatus for manipulation of the masses. For our purposes, religion is also a set of conventions, epistemologies and practices which are neither predictable nor politically simple and unidimensional. It provides a set of images and narratives, and the articulation of dissent through a reworking of religious tropes by the poet-historian. Indeed, it is noteworthy that the religious figure we encounter over and over again in bardic and British contestations about history-writing in Rajasthan is the Hindu god Shiva, and the sects and cults in his name in the region. In order to examine the multiple functions of religious tropes in non-Western history-writing, we interrogate the genre of the origin tale.

Since we are not doing a sociology of the Charan caste, nor is our agenda to assert the superiority of Charan writings over the recitations by other bardic castes, we do not confine our set of texts to origin tales by Charans. Our purpose is better served by an origin myth that does not belong among the more well-known and established Suryavanshi and Chandravanshi clans, nor does it belong in the repertoire of the Charan caste. Rather, it provides the view of bardic genres from below, namely, a view from the Purriar Meenas community of Rajasthan.[58] The question of how to determine the meaning of an origin tale becomes particularly significant in the case of a tale that returns us to our

---

other states from entering the princely state, and in 1916 the Udaipur ruler made the Bhats and Charans sign a deed swearing that they would not travel to territories outside Mewar, or allow their counterparts from other territories to enter Mewar. For a detailed account see Saxena, op. cit.

[58] See G.N. Sharma, *Rajasthan through the Ages 1300–1761 A.D.*, vol. II, Bikaner: Rajasthan State Archives (1990), p. 220. We are grateful to Shail Mayaram for bringing our attention to contestations about whether the Meenas should be called tribal or Rajput. Our own purpose in this essay is not to adjudicate this debate but to examine two texts, the colonial text of colonial infanticide reform as it constructs a narrative about the Purriar Meenas by recording the incidence of female infanticide in the community, and the several mediations through which we gain access to the Purriar Meenas origin tale.

place of incision, by connecting the clan's origins to female infanticide. It is in consonance with our method because we do not wish to unmoor questions concerning history-writing from the function of woman devaluation in narratives about the past. Therefore we highlight the violence that occurs on Meenas women as a result of the community's imitation of the norms and customs of the dominant Rajput castes of the region.[59]

Our turning to the bardic genre of the origin tale is also designed to highlight the colonialist legacy, in the aftermath of the criminalizing of the Bhats and Charans, which is discernible in a number of post-colonial historical studies of the origin myths of Rajasthan. The protocols of interpretation of these studies consists of identifying bardic history-writing exclusively with the genealogical functions of the bard, thus erasing the multiple social duties the bard performed in the life of the community. This interpretive procedure re-enacts the British colonialist preoccupation with the bards as genealogists. Once bardic writing is represented as feeding the Rajput's nostalgia for origins, the way is paved for discrediting bardic genealogies as fictitious and empirically inaccurate.

Colonial writers brought Lockean empiricism to bear on these genealogies; such an approach was weighted against the bard's craft because genealogies were rhetorical constructs designed for discussion. A narrative about a clan's origins was often a rhetorical occasion for a discussion of the clan's values. The bardic recitation of genealogies generated reimaginings, not only of the geographical and mythic origins of the patron's clan but of the values practised or violated by the clan's descendants. Truth-status cannot be exclusively claimed for the empirical methods of one historiographical tradition. The point is not

[59] Historically, pastoral-peasant and tribal populations faced two cultural choices, either they could retain their religious-social identity and way of life or they could mainstream themselves by Sanskritizing themselves. The former option entailed steady pauperization, as is evident in the case of the Bhils of Rajasthan who continue to live in south-western Rajasthan in a state of poverty. The latter option entailed a loss of religious belief systems, connection to the land and to the past; however, the gains lay in the opening up of economic opportunities over several generations. The latter option was chosen by the Meenas, who at one time ruled the area around Jaipur.

that the bards recited origin myths that were untrue; rather the question that needs to be posed is—what were the truths articulated and renewed by the bard's recital.

The final interpretive procedure in postcolonial historical studies of the Suryavanshi and Chandravanshi genealogies in Rajput clans is to interpret the political function of the bard's genealogies as ideologies of legitimation. The argument that the origin myths of Rajasthan are ideologies of legitimation is not wrong. It is however an incomplete argument because these legitimating myths were not fixed narratives of a static society. The fluid, strategic, rhetorically and poetically significant part of the bard's recitation of Rajput genealogies lay in the discussion guided by the bard on what it meant to be a true Rajput. The performance of the tale permits an enormous range of different and contradictory meanings. It is from the perspective of statist historiography that Rajput genealogies exclusively signify ideologies of legitimation without any room for dissenting narratives.

The particular ways in which the bard negotiated the switchings between poetic codes signalled his interpretation to his audience, and marked his oppositional stance as well. For instance, a critique of domination is articulated when the bard deploys his skills to modulate a narrative about war into an epic about non-violent resistance to tyranny and domination through conquest.[60] Although the poetic codes concerning war and nonviolence were not mutually exclusive, the bard could supplant the specific narrative pleasures belonging to a story about power, loss of power and the reclaiming of power—in which the plot turns on disputes between rulers about property and wealth—with the specific narrative pleasures of the wanderer who has no property, home or attachment.

[60] The stereotype that all Rajasthani oral epics are about male valour in war is disproved by the fact that many of them subvert the glorification of violence with episodes where the warrior renounces arms and follows the medieval *jogi* Gorakhnath in the life of renunciation. John Smith observes that the Rajasthani epic of Pabuji can be recited by the Nayak caste of performers in order to emphasize the theme of blood-feuds (*vair*) or contrarily the same hero can be described as an exemplar of ahimsa or non-violence. Smith simply lumps these contraries together as 'themes which are of central importance in the Hindu culture of western India' (op. cit., pp. 3, 4). We suggest that the dominant elite Rajput code of revenge and violence (*vair*) was contested by subaltern codes of resistance through activating the conventions of renunciation, or the poetics of pacifism (ahimsa).

Traditional tropes and figures for dissent were activated whenever the poet-historian switched the martial code in *virkavya* or war poetry to the tropes and codes of *vairagya* or renunciation.[61] For instance, a major intervention in sixteenth-century medieval historical interpretations of Rajput–Muslim history is achieved in Jaysi's *Padmavat* when a warlike Rajput king is described as a yogi. The lack of a singular, fixed meaning of the bardic text is exemplified by Jaysi's representation of the Padmani folk text: a tale whose elite decodings justify woman devaluation and self-immolation is transmogrified by Jaysi into a text about woman reimagined as Sufi guru.[62] Thus the same epic narrative can be reinterpreted to articulate women's subordination or women's freedom.[63]

Origin stories of Rajput clans were exigent. The reason is that origins had to be adapted in order to appeal to the constantly changing rulers of North India. Genre analysis facilitates the understanding that the origin story for a particular Rajput clan tells us, not so much where they came from and who they were, but rather indicates who they wish to be and what are the claims on land and power that they wish to make on the basis of their genealogy. That is why the tale of origins in the khyat, as a means for constant reinvention, does not have one function

61 We are grateful to Shahid Amin for pointing out that the conventional wisdom about medieval syncretism needs to be rethought, even though syncretism is the unexamined vocabulary within which Hindu–Muslim cultural assimilations are articulated. The reason is that India's vaunted syncretism disallows historical traditions that talk of difference, of conquest, both military and by Sufis over jogis. See also Charles Stewart and Rosalind Shaw, *Syncretism/Anti-syncretism* (New York: Routledge, 1994).

62 See the remarkable reading of communalist decodings and appropriations of a bardic text by Shantanu Phukan, 'None Mad as a Hindu Woman: Contesting Communal Readings of Padmavat', *Comparative Studies of South Asia, Africa and Middle East*, vol. XVI, no. 1 (1966), pp. 41–54.

63 The point is best demonstrated through the Lorik-Chanda epic. The same epic in the Chhattisgarh region of eastern Madhya Pradesh emphasizes pro-woman tribal customs like elopement, reflecting the greater freedom of the women in that region. There is also the Sufi version of the text in the fourteenth-century poem Maulana Daud's *Candayan* which subtly opposes the martial elements of the story with an emphasis on love and sacrifice. The fact that there is no essential meaning to any one bardic text is attested to by Stuart Blackburn who says 'there is no single text we can call the Lorik-Canda epic'. *Oral Epics in India*, op. cit., p. 6.

but several functions. Moreover the functions of the origin story keep changing, depending on how the claim to ruler status through ancestral rights is accepted by the dominant political players in North India. As live, oral-performative, and socially embedded writing, the Rajput origin tale is an unstable, flexible, and mobile text. It is precisely in the digressions, oral improvisations, as well as contextualizations that the bards perform a reflexive, critical, and oppositional critique of the dominant Rajput ideology.[64] Thus there is no essential meaning of the Rajput origin myths, they are responsive to the changing material conditions and political necessities of the community.

One section of the Meenas community, the Purriar Meenas, traditionally inhabit the tract in the vicinity of Deolia in Rajasthan. Their traditional occupation is agriculture and service, but gradually over generations they moved into the military and named themselves Rajputs.[65] The reason that this community came under official scrutiny in the nineteenth century was that they practised female infanticide. In 1844 the British census of eleven Purriar Meenas villages revealed the shocking sex ratio of 369 boys and only 87 girls, or 23.58 girls per hundred boys; sixteen years later, in 1860 it was 28.88.[66] Among the many oral legends documented in the 1865–7 'Report on the Political Administration of the Rajpootana States' British data collectors found a myth of origin that seemed to draw a direct connection between the Rajputs' worship of Shiva and the religious injunction to kill all female newborn.[67]

In the legend the ancestor of the Purriar Meenas, Shalla, prays to the god Shiva for as many sons as the hair on his head. Shalla beheads

[64] The Nayak bard recorded by John Smith names his improvisations as part of the prose declamatory *arthav* (op. cit., p. 27). The bard Ram Swarup recorded by Susan Wadley calls his explanations *samjhana* and describes improvisations as choosing a path: 'Ram Swarup identifies these shifts in content, delivery styles, songs, and tunes as shifts in 'path' (*rasta*) and claims that he must choose the right path, whether it be a story element or a mood symbolized in a song genre, in order to perform well'. *Oral Epics in India* op. cit., p. 91.

[65] T.S. Katiyar, *Social Life in Rajasthan: A Case Study* (Allahabad: Kitab Mahal, 1964).

[66] Saxena, op. cit., p. 4.

[67] Report on the Political Administration of the Rajpootana States (1865–7), Bikaner: Rajasthan State Archives, 318. Henceforth RAR.

himself after the god grants his wish. At that very moment Shalla's unnamed daughter enters the temple and her shadow falls on her father's headless trunk, unleashing the god's curse on Shalla. The legend ends with Shalla's descendants vowing to kill all newborn daughters of the community in perpetuity. In our view the Meenas legend is constructed like a riddle. The riddle is this: how to accomplish the impossible phenomenon of an entire clan ensuring that there are only sons born in their families. The answer to the riddle lies in the clansmen achieving through coercion and violence that which cannot be accomplished by nature. The riddle points towards human will rather than divine intervention. The human being does not go scot free, he is marked by the violence, he cannot represent himself as the founder of a clan or a father of many sons, he must also acknowledge the murder of many daughters.

The relations between gender and genre in the origin tale are flattened out in the colonialist written reconstruction of the legend, and gender becomes a static and essentialist entity instead of being dynamic and open to rhetorical shiftings and repositionings. Myths of origin were recorded, preserved, and retold by the historians of Rajasthan, who were affiliated to a family, clan or community. The oral component of the Purriar Meenas tale contains a reflexive social commentary about the unnaturalness of female infanticide. However the RAR document transcribes the origin story in such a way as to erase the bardic critique of men who sanction female infanticide. Genre analysis unravels the riddle about the justifications made by the Purriar Meenas to outsiders like the British, and insiders like the descendants of the community, concerning the killing of their newborn daughters.

The representation of gender in the Purriar Meenas text is mediated and produced by the genre conventions of the text. The literary form deployed by the Purriar Meenas tale is a khyat, which narrates the history of a clan. The historical truths in the khyat inhere not in facts or dates, but in the cultural values that are affirmed in the narration. The central historical truth that the khyat tells concerning the origins of Rajputs is that the word Rajput denotes not a specific group of people, but rather an idiom through which people of varied and diverse origins (foreign invaders, low castes, Muslims, tribals, traders, mixed-caste communities as well as Brahmins) constantly reinvent themselves in response to changing political circumstances.[68] The bards' use of the khyat suggests that at some point in history, the tribal community of the Purriar Meenas reinvented their origins. In the tale female infanticide stands metonymically for Rajputization. The Purriar Meenas tell this story about themselves because daughter killing and son preference represents the community's assumption of Rajput status by adopting the values and customs of infanticidal Rajput clans.

An important qualification needs to be noted here about gender and genre in the bardic myths of origin. Rajputization did not always represent violence on Rajput women. Women emerge in many of the origin stories as central historical agents in the process of reinvention and upward mobility. The earliest Rajput origin stories in Rajasthan refer to a man from a non-Kshatriya caste marrying a Kshatriya girl, and subsequently assuming his wife's caste status and founding a dynasty. Other stories describe a low-caste man marrying a Brahmin girl and founding a clan. In some cases the clan ancestor is portrayed in the origin story as migrating to Rajasthan and starting a new life there by marrying the king's daughter. In later versions of origin tales in Central India the female ancestor travels from Rajasthan for a pilgrimage to Madhya Pradesh and gives birth to a son who founds a dynasty there.[69] In all these origin stories the woman endows her husband with caste-status, occupation, or a dynasty-founding male heir.

Women's role loses much of its vitality in the written version of origin tales which metamorphose into a repetitive, male-centred and male-defined account of battles, warriors, and kings. Origin tales are not always about battles, warriors and kings. They are also tales about women's survival knowledges. For instance, origin tales narrate how the female ancestor ensured the preservation of the next generation. One such origin story is *Nainsi ri Khyata*, a seventeenth-century bardic chronicle about the origins of the Sisodiya Rajputs.[70] The written

[68] For the debate about Rajput origins, see B.D. Chattopadhyaya, 'Origins of the Rajputs: The Political, Economic Processes in Early Medieval Rajasthan', *The Indian Historical Review*, vols III, I (1976).

[69] Surajit Sinha, 'State Formation and Rajput Myth in Tribal Central India', *Man in India*, vol 42, no.1, January–March, 1962, pp. 5–80.

[70] Mumhata Nainsi, *Marvara ra Parganam ri Vigata*, trans. and ed. N.S. Bhati, in *Seventeenth Century Chronicles of Marvara*, vols 1 and 2 (Jodhpur: 1968–9). See

version tends to represent the role of the female ancestor as a passive transmitter of patriarchal values: she accompanies her husband for a pilgrimage because her husband wants a son; after her husband's death she gives birth to a son and commits sati. In the *Nainsi ri Khyata* the female ancestor's function in the story is not simply the begetting of a son.[71] She comes to life as a character after her husband's death. The khyat focuses largely on her actions and speeches as she takes refuge with some Brahmins and uses her resourcefulness and power of persuasion to convince the Brahmins to take care of her child after her death. This story of origin celebrates the survival knowledge of the female ancestor much more than the male founder of the Sisodiya clan, and indicates that the khyat was a genre in which women did not simply appear as passive daughters and son-bearing wives.[72]

We can appreciate the fluidity of the origin tale better if we compare the Purriar Meenas tale of origins with the three versions of the story of origins of the Sisodiyas of Mewar.[73] The thirteenth-century inscription casts the origins of the Sisodiyas in terms of the divine conferral

---

also another edition of the khyat in Badriprasad Sakariya, ed., *Muhata Nainasi ri khyata* (Jodhpur: Rajasthan Pracyavidya Prastisthan, 1960–2, 1964–7).

[71] There is a good deal of evidence of women's dissent and pro-woman male dissent in dialect literatures. For example the Rajasthani sacrificial epic narrative structure envisions a woman-centred code of resistance through sacrifice (*aahuti*). However, the sacrificial narrative can all too easily become a celebration of sati and *jauhar*. In spite of these appropriations and ambivalences, the Rajasthani oral epic permits a spectrum of oppositional codes.

[72] The predominance of strong female characters in the bardic narratives suggests that a women-centred perspective was present in the composition and transmission of these narratives. Kothari notes that in the performance of the Rajasthani oral epic, 'Some 60 to 80 per cent of the text is presented by the wife'. *Oral Epics*, op. cit., p. 103. For instance Smith notes that the agent in the Pabuji narrative is not the hero but the Charan goddess, 'it is Deval who makes the story happen'. *The Epic of Pabuji*, op. cit., p. 97. Kothari also observes that 'The leading female characters in Rajasthani oral epics in particular show other than model behavior. . . the women are dominant and cruel; the men are weak and fated'. Ibid., pp. 114–15.

[73] We focus on the Sisodiya clan of Rajputs because textual representations of this clan are the site of contestation between woman-centered and woman-authored dissent. For example Meera's poetic record of Sisodiya persecutions of

of Kshatriya status on the Sisodiyas, and these values were designed to appeal to the players in North Indian medieval politics.[74] The Sisodiya clan's beginnings are narrated somewhat differently in the seventeenth-century version recited by bards. The reason is that the same story has to be adapted to the concepts and values of the dominant imperial power at Delhi (the Mughals) by emphasizing illustrious lineage and claims on land based on ancestral right.[75] The nineteenth-century version concerning the Sisodiya ancestors is articulated by Tod, and this time the key elements are rewoven into a new version that

---

her as their daughter-in-law pre-dates James Tod's nineteenth century eulogistic history of the Sisodiyas in *Annals and Antiquities of Rajasthan* (1829) and is diametrically opposed to it. See our article on Meera in *boundary 2*, 31: 3 (2004), pp. 1–46.

[74] The Sisodiya inscription of the late tenth century says that their Guhilota ancestors may have been from the Brahmin caste and intermarried into Rajput clans, thereby exemplifying the convention in the origin narrative where women give caste status and occupation to the husband. A later inscription in 1285 describes how the clan ancestor, Bapa Ravala, Rajputized himself; the inscription alludes to the processes of Rajputization through the parable of Bapa Ravala's conquest of Mevara through the blessing of the god Siva. However there is evidence that the Sisodiyas conquered the territory from the tribal Bhils, their royal coat of arms depicts an armed Bhil male standing on one flank. The local legend in Udaipur is that the Guhilota ancestor befriended the Bhils and eventually became their chieftain. We decode the parable about Shiva's blessing Bapa Ravala as narrativizing the colonization of the Bhils by the Guhilota kingdom. There is a considerable bardic record of the Guhilota-Bhil interactions. See also D.C. Sirkar, *The Guhilas of Kiskindhi* (Calcutta: 1965), pp. 3–4.

[75] The seventeenth-century bardic chronicle *Nainsi ri Khyata* gives a markedly different twist to the Sisodiya myth of origin. The story is that the Sisodiya Guhilota ancestor was a ruler in South India. He went on a pilgrimage to Mevara with his wife in order to pray for a son but he died there, and his son was brought up by Brahmins. This story retains the thirteenth-century trope of Brahmin-Rajput intermarriage; however there is a subtle change in the seventeenth-century version—this time the Sisodiya claim to the Mevara kingdom is established through the suggestion that the ancestor, Bapa Ravala, was born a king, therefore he has an ancient right to rule. His claims to the place are established by the story of his adoption by a Brahmin family in Mevara, and by the fact that for ten generations his descendants lived in Mevara, thus acquiring a sense of belonging to the place. Moreover the Brahmin adoption signifies the sacralizing and legitimation of the Sisodiya claim to power.

is adapted to the British colonial concept of racial purity. In effect this version of the tale asserts that the Sisodiyas are the premier Rajput clan because they are the most pure-blooded and ancient race.[76] Thus the core values affirmed by the genre of the khyat are not engraved in stone; they are mobile, and flexible, adapting to changing political exigencies. Moreover, the several versions of the Sisodiya tale of origins demonstrate that a community's Rajputization did not always involve the practice of female infanticide.

For the bards the meaning of a narrative was profoundly intertextual. In a bardic text the multiple borrowings and references to the origin myths of other Rajput clans as well as to the Puranic myths allows the significance of the narrative to alter considerably. The Purriar Meenas legend telescopes motifs that are found in the three versions of the Sisodiya legend. Modern scholars of bardic literature note that this intertextuality 'appears to be the result of rather extensive and complex feedback from the literary traditions of other prominent ruling houses'.[77] As a case in point, the Meenas legend deploys the same motif found in the thirteenth-century Sisodiya legend, namely the god Shiva blessing the founder of the clan. Likewise the Meenas legend also shares the theme of son preference with the seventeenth-century version of the Sisodiya legend. The intertextual echoes between the third version of the Sisodiya legend and the Meenas legend are most prominent. The nineteenth-century version, transcribed by Tod, employs the euphemism of racial purity of the Sisodiyas to refer to the killing of daughters because they cannot be married into an impure Rajput clan. The subtle difference between the third version of the Sisodiya origin tale and the Meenas legend is that the latter does not employ euphemisms like impurity, it explicitly describes the crime and justifies it on the grounds that the practice has been going on from the time the community Rajputized itself.

The fact that Rajput myths are intertextual and continually borrowing from one another, as well as the fact that the genre can always be tailored to a new set of values, means that the bard has a good deal

[76] *Annals and Antiquities*, p. 15.

[77] 'The Seventeenth Century Chronicles of Marvara: A Study in the Evolution and Use of Oral Traditions in Western India', *History in Africa*, vol. 3 (1976), p. 152.

of manoeuvrability. For instance, the bard can make a digression and recite episodes from the Hindu epics, the *Ramayana* and the *Mahabharata*, in order to remind his audience that Kshatriya and Rajput values in the past meant the protection of daughters and the equal treatment of daughters and sons.[78] The bard can also link the Purriar Meenas story of origin to the origin tales of other clans in order to make the point that the founder of other Rajput clans were known for their use of arms to defend women and children rather than decimate them. Thus the bardic recitation does not always ratify the patron's claim that female infanticide has been going on from time immemorial.

The religious references in the rhetorical and oral-performative dimensions of the Purriar Meenas myth suggest that the practice of female infanticide is open to debate rather than limited to ratification. The historical events and players in the Purriar Meenas text clothe the significant mythic event, which exists in cyclical time. In keeping with Guha's observation that the historian must be unashamed about the cyclicity of Puranic histories, we caution against characterizations of the mytho-religious level of the text in essentialist terms. The mythic-religious realm does not always indicate the bard's escape from history and politics. Sometimes the mythic dimension allows the bard to critique the dominant classes and focus on the materiality of history and politics. For instance, a key difference between the written tale in the RAR document and the bard's oral recitation involves the question of human agency, whether it is the human being, Shalla, who causes the practice of female infanticide, or whether the god Shiva is perceived as causing/sanctioning the practice. British discourse about Indian religions identified religious actions with passivity. The written version of the legend tends to favour the conclusion that the Purriar Meenas community commit female infanticide because they are passive followers of a religious injunction that had been laid down in the lifetime of their ancestor Shalla.

[78] A digression was considered an important break from the high style of the panegyric in order to give the audience the opportunity to relax. In the case of the Bhats and Charans, an aside into the familiar and well-loved tales from the *Mahabharata* and the *Ramayana* would serve to not only give the audience some respite, but also to drive home the message by other means.

Human agency was always put in an evaluative framework in bardic history-writing. If we examine the complex ways in which the Purriar Meenas myth unfolds the causal logic of the practice of female infanticide, we find that the myth gestures unambiguously towards the human being Shalla as the desiring subject, as the agent whose desire and prayer sets the story in motion. According to the legend, no god, or natural calamity, or social pressure prompts the male ancestor of the community to wish for an infinite number of male progeny. The legend explicitly locates the human being as the causal agent: it is male patriarchal desire that begins the process, which ends in intergenerational daughter killing. In so doing the myth locates the origins of the practice of female infanticide in the secular patriarchal custom of son preference and the privileging of men over women.

It may be difficult for us to imagine that the bard would dare to tell such harsh truths to his patron. Many features of the genre indicate that these critical and subversive interventions were precisely the domain of the bardic recitation.[79] Modern anthropologists have noted that the bardic recitation contains a great deal of extra material. Shah and Shroff note, 'The plot of the story may be simple and brief, but the bard telling it stretches it out to last two or three nights.'[80] Colonial scholars commented on this extra material as improvisations by the bard that are not outside the main tale, but in fact determine its meaning: 'parts of the bardic accounts are not intelligible without oral explanation . . . and it was indeed the bards' practice to intersperse the recitation of family histories recorded in their vahi with extempore

[79] One reason that bardic writings contain traces of pro-woman dissent is that it may have been the work of women Charans. More work on the contributions of women Charans is needed. This kind of women's history is not accessible through traditional empirical tools but has to be gleaned from legends, temples, and the traces in modern practices of the *bhopi* or female singer of the Rajasthani epic. For example, the Karni Mata temple in Bikaner district honours a Charan female ascetic, and several Rajasthani epics have a dominant figure of a Charan goddess like Deval, indicating the canonization of prominent Charan women at some point in history. Furthermore, the influence of female Charan bards is discernible in modern Rajasthan in the performances of the Pabuji epic as well as the Devnarayan epic by the lower-caste Nayak community.

[80] 'The Vahivanca Barots of Gujarat', op. cit., p. 42.

explanations and amplifications.'[81] The excerpt calls bardic improvisations 'explanations', which implies that they were more than fillers and entertainers. A significant clue about the purpose of these oral explanations is that bardic recitations in elite Rajput houses were, as Zeigler observes, 'the primary media through which young Rajputs were traditionally educated', and as an educational tool the tales gave the community a sense of their history and 'schooled [them] in the moral values of their fathers; and tutored [them] in their future roles in society'.[82] Through the bard's improvisations and asides, and the audience's interjections, the full text of the legend becomes intelligible.

The reciprocity of the bard–community bond in the oral recitation is activated right at the start when the bard recounts how Shalla prays for an infinite number of sons. The father's desire for countless sons is enunciated in terms that, to anyone familiar with religious and folkloric utterance, denote an absurdity: as many sons as the hair on his head. The phrase warns the audience that the divine boon given to a human being is impossible to realize in human terms. The bard's retelling this legend also relies on his audience's recognition of the conventions for representation of the god Shiva and the genre in which the myth is verbally articulated. In this participatory mode the storyteller and the audience richly appreciate the fact that the Purriar Meenas' god violates the fundamental features of Shiva worship. The reason is quite simple. The desire expressed by Shalla for as many sons as hair on his head not only denotes the human being's desire that exceeds the proper limits of human life, Shalla's son preference also denotes the desire to disturb the gender balance in society by an all-male progeny.

Asking for countless sons is an inappropriate prayer for the Shaivite devotee because Shiva/Mahadeo is a Hindu deity who is conceived as the male principle in harmony with the female principle, never at war with the latter. The bard can make this point without referring to scriptural dogma, he can point instead to the lived practices in diverse Shaivite sects.[83] Shiva is heterogeneously configured in different

[81] A.K. Forbes, *Ras Mala, Hindu Annals of the Province of Goozerat in Western India*, ed. H.G. Rawlinson (London: 1924), p. 265.

[82] 'Seventeenth Century Chronicles of Marvara', op. cit., p. 129.

[83] More than any other deity Shiva embraces the dispossessed and the outcast; for example, in the Tantric worship of Shiva the female devotee is granted equality with the male devotee. In other forms of Shiva worship the god represents respect

Hindu sects as a deity harmonizing male and female cosmic principles, not as a divine sanction for woman hatred and gender imbalance. The written colonial version of the Purriar Meenas myth makes it appear that, in Rajasthan, Shiva is worshipped as a daughter-cursing god at war with women. However, we argue that the myth contains a religious parable. It is through this parable that the bards of Rajasthan reconcile the apparent contradiction between the Purriar Meenas' god and the Shiva who embodies harmony, and explain to their audience how the god Shiva has been put in a position where his power is harnessed for violence on women and female children. This mythological parable would be well known even to the children of the audience, and is the subject of rich comedy and verbal exchanges between the bard and his audience. In different variants of the same basic narrative it is the story of the innocent Shiva (Bholenath) granting a boon to a demon (*asura*). The source of the irony is that the god, whose dance signifies cosmic harmony, grants boons to evil men and demons who, time and time again, unleash cosmic and human disorder.

Through the laughter between the audience and the storyteller, the bard makes a serious statement concerning the problem of practical justice in society which is signified through the parable of Shiva granting inappropriate boons. For example, the bard can use the Purriar Meenas legend as a cautionary tale about the universal destruction that follows if the Shaivite principle of cosmic harmony is harnessed for causing gender imbalance through an exclusively male clan. The nineteenth-century Rajput audience could make a guess about what happens next in the narrative, because they knew how Shiva's dilemma *vis-à-vis* the unnatural desires of demons is ultimately resolved in other versions of the same parable, where Vishnu rescues Shiva and rights the wrong. The coming together of the two gods is not only represented in many Puranic tales; it is also celebrated in the Hari-Hara symbolism in Rajasthan and elsewhere in India.[84]

---

for woman as the complement to man in the androgynous figure of *Ardhnarishwera*. Moreover, Shiva's link to tribal deities is proved by the fact that he is always imaged in sculpture and dance in relation to one or other of the fertility goddesses. In other parts of India Shiva is the patron saint of matriarchal communities of women artists.

[84] The Hari-Hara or Harihar worship of Shiva and Vishnu is performed at the Harihareshvara temple in the village of Harihar in Karnataka, where the main

It is at this point that the bard makes a stunning critique of female infanticide without moving out of the protocols of the religious parable and the genre of the origin tale. Popular retellings of such unnatural desires by demons often portray the god Vishnu as appearing in female form to delude the demon and deflect his wish fulfilment. The bard has to tailor his improvisations by gauging the mood of his audience: he has been preparing for his critique all along by controlling the representation of the founder of the clan in the religio-mythic personae of the asura, and at this point he recalls for his audience the ways in which Vishnu assumes human incarnations whenever there is great social injustice. These mythological references are deleted by the RAR document, perhaps because they appear to be meaningless digressions. However, for the bard they are a vehicle to control the representation of female infanticide as the unnatural disturbance of gender harmony and sex ratio. The female victim appears as god, or god appears as the victim. Either way the oral legend emphasizes the point that the unwanted daughter of Shalla avenges herself through assuming the power of Vishnu.

The notion of the curse is alien to our modern secular imagination. We may find it difficult to imagine the potential for critique in the premodern language of the curse.[85] We juxtapose two texts which show that the folkloric idiom of the curse articulates the social condemnation of infanticidal Rajput clans by the rest of the community. The Purriar Meenas legend's placing of the curse is open to interpretation. British reformers were convinced that one of the answers to their reformist question—how can a noble Rajput race which honours its women commit the crime of female child murder?—is that religion forces Rajputs to suppress 'the sentiments of nature' towards their offspring.[86]

This colonialist reading of the legend's curse betrays an ignorance of the complex ways in which the curse functions in popular consciousness. The curse is a highly condensed metaphor for the logic of

sculpture combines the two gods. The worship of Vishnu in female form as Mahalasa is performed at the Mahalasa temple in the village of Mardol, Goa.

[85] For an excellent discussion on the function of the curse in pre-modern Europe, see Keith Thomas, *Religion and the Decline of Magic* (New York: Macmillan, 1971).

[86] Tod, op. cit., p. 505.

cause and effect. It is a metaphor that only works in a society where the oppressor and the oppressed share a common set of values, and the oppressed can rebuke the tyrant for departing from those shared values. In the folkloric imagination the power of the curse is given to the poor and the dispossessed, the threat of the curse gives a certain power to those who are powerless in every other way. The bardic representation of the curse can alter its meaning considerably. In certain parables in the Hindu religions, the god grants a boon to a human being, and if the human being's boon disturbs the social and natural order the boon is circumscribed by a curse. In many such tales the god Shiva, helpless to deny the unnatural wish, reserves the right to contain the boon with a curse.

Predictably in the Purriar Meenas legend, a woman enters the temple as soon as the wish is granted. At a signal from Shalla's daughter who is also Vishnu in female form, Shiva swings into action. Shiva's curse is directed towards the male ancestor Shalla, not towards Shalla's daughter. Shiva's curse makes manifest the causal logic of the unnatural wish for innumerable sons. The result of wishing for an infinite number of male children is disappointment when a female child is born. In the infanticidal clan this patriarchal wish results in killing all female newborn and preserving male infants. The legend positions the unwanted daughter as possessing the power to frustrate her father's boon when she is powerless in every other way. In the bardic version it is not Shiva who hates all female children, it is Shalla's son preference that causes daughter killing.

Our second example for textualizing the curse as a condensed folkloric oppositional idiom to gender violence is a conversation recorded in the administrative travelogue of Oudh written by W. H. Sleeman. Colonel Sleeman interrogates his fellow traveller and native informant, Raja Bakhtawar Sing, as they travel through the Oudh countryside. In the course of this conversation Sleeman indicts the Oudh Rajputs who confess that they commit female infanticide, not in legal-judicial language but in the religious discourse pasted together by the British in which the Hindu religious sanctions (*hooka pani band*) were invoked against the infanticidal family. Bakhtawar Sing neither practises female infanticide nor approves of it.[87] Sing is goaded by the

[87] Rajah Bakhtawar Sing of Shahgunge began his career in the 8th Regiment of the Company's Light Cavalry and while at home on furlough, secured the

English sahib to provide an explanation of the practice, and he wishes to please Sleeman. Bakhtawar Sing is a figure of some significance in the colonial text. He is an example of the native informant who benefits from Muslim imperialism as well as British colonialism by first serving as a trooper in the Company's army and also securing the patronage of the sixth Nawab of Oudh. At the time of Sleeman's travels through the Oudh countryside, Sing is an old man who serves as Sleeman's Quartermaster-General while still attached to the Oudh court.

Serving two masters, Sing occupies the subject position of the native informant who translates the idioms of one culture to another by drawing on the folkloric and bardic language of the curse on the infanticidal clans.[88] We excerpt this explanation from Sleeman's diary because it spells out the cause-and-effect logic of gender imbalance, a point that the Purriar Meenas legend makes through the conventions of the religious parable:

> They are all punished in this world; and will, no doubt, be punished still more in the next—scarcely any of the heads of these landed aristocracy are the legitimate sons of their predecessors—they are all adopted, or born of women of inferior grade—the heads of families who commit or tolerate such atrocities, become leprous, blind, deaf or dumb, or are carried off in early life, or by some terrible disease—hardly any of them attain a good old age—nor can they boast of an untainted line of ancestors like other men—if they get sons they commonly die young. They unite themselves to women of inferior castes for want of daughters in families of their own ranks; and there is hardly a family among these proud Rajpoots, unstained by

---

patronage of the Oudh ruler, Saadut Allee Khan, and became responsible for land management as well as acquired zamindari rights in Shahgunge and Faizabad. See *A Journey Through The Kingdom Of Oude, in 1849–1850,* vol. I (London: Richard Bentley, 1858), p. 151.

[88] Sing's relation to the bardic genre of alhas recording the people's version of the insurgency of 1857 is worth noting. His nephew Man Singh, unlike his uncle, could not continue to serve two masters: till February 1858 he fought against the British by aligning himself with Begum Hazrat Mahal, the wife of the deposed ruler of Oudh, Nawab Wajid Ali Shah. However his nerve failed, he retreated to his fort, which was besieged by the Begum's troops, and this narrative of cowardice and desertion became the leit motif of the alhas. Also see Amaresh Misra, *Lucknow: Fire of Grace: The Story of its Revolution, Renaissance and the Aftermath* (Delhi: HarperCollins, 1998), p. 67.

> such connexions . . . the curse of God is upon them, sir, for the murder of their own innocent children! . . . When men murder their own children, how can they scruple to murder other people. The curse of God is upon them, sir.[89]

In our modern secular language we would say that selective female infant killing causes an imbalanced sex ratio. The folkloric idiom may not have recourse to scientific data to show the long-term effects of female infanticide on the sex ratio, but it has accumulated generations of experience for naming the long-term effects of gender imbalance in a household, clan or society. Bakhtawar Sing names these consequences as a curse; he observes: 'The curse of God is upon them, sir'. The text of the curse, in Sing's reported conversation, signifies intergenerational sterility, a high infant mortality rate, and the spread of the cycle of violence from elite women to lower-caste women.

Note that neither Sing nor the bard reciting the Purriar Meenas tale openly and directly defend the right to life of the female child through the vehicle of the curse. Instead their rhetorical manoeuvre is to expose the desire for upward mobility and its frustration. For example, the bard subverts the Meenas' claims to Rajput status by showing that the boon turns into a curse; similarly the Oudh Rajputs' claims on land and power on the basis of their 'boast of an untainted line of ancestors' is frustrated by disease, early death and sterility in their families. Most importantly, Bakhtawar Sing comments on the larger social repercussions: infanticidal families prey on women of lower castes, the cycle of violence spreads beyond elite women and encompasses women of lower castes who are brought in as wives, mistresses, or daughters-in-law to revitalize the family's ability to reproduce itself. There is a commonsensical logic in Sing's curse. He refers to nurture: a household in which there are no traditions of protecting a female child in the first few years of her life, will not be able to construct a selective nurturing process for male children. Thus the textual function of the curse exemplifies the opposition between written history and oral-performative bardic recitations. The curse functions in the Purriar Meenas tale, and in Sing's observations about female infanticide, not as irrational superstition but rather as folkloric articulation of the social disaster of a declining sex ratio.

[89] A Journey Through the Kingdom of Oude, p. 170.

To the extent that woman as subject, as audience, and as female singer are included under the sign of history, the bard's recitation carries the possibility of illuminating the lives of women and addressing their specific concerns. By placing the protection of daughters' rights at the centre of the historian's duties and sense of his vocation, we mark our distance from the scholarship that frames Indian women in colonial and liberal-nationalist discourses without taking into account the long history of dissent in India. If there is one site where this essay asserts hope, it is in rethinking the life of an idiom of dissent. We argue that indigenous pre-colonial modes of dissent are inherited from the medieval-feudal period, and continue to re-emerge in disparate and discontinuous forms in colonial and postcolonial times. Women-centred histories cannot obey and adhere to a chronology—that has been rightly suspected of being an unexamined colonial heritage—of medieval, British, and postcolonial periods. That is why Guha's insight that chronology will have to be rethought in a woman-centred historiography is pertinent to this essay. Bardic idioms of dissent have reinvented themselves in postcolonial literatures of protest, despite assaults by the dominant upper classes in north India, and in spite of the codification and dismantling of these forms by colonial and nationalist writers.[90]

In postcolonial societies historical arguments have a politically explosive role to play in the public sphere, partly because the postcolonial state is premised on and legitimated by nationalist historiography, and partly because fundamentalist governments are intimately concerned with the history books brought out by state institutions.[91] In order to

[90] A good example of postcolonial revivals of bardic writings as literatures of protest is Raghuvanshi Krishnamurti, Veerendra and Narendra Kumar's *The Ballad of Budhni*, trans. Vasantha Surya (Calcutta: Writer's Workshop, 1992). Here the traditional North Indian bardic genre of the *alha* is used to write, in the dialect of Bundeli, a protest narrative against the police attack on the village of Budhni in 1988. For a postmodern recuperation of the oral epic tradition see Jean-Francois Lyotard, *The Postmodern Condition: A Report on Knowledge*, trans. Geoff Bennington and Brian Massumi (Minneapolis: University of Minnesota Press, 1984).

[91] The postcolonial analogue for the war declared on indigenous historians in nineteenth-century Rajasthan is the marginalizing of historians who do not follow the Hindutva model of Indian history by the BJP government. This essay is, in

recover religion as a middle term between literature and history, and discredit communalist and statist Indian histories, a dialogue between historians and literary critics is necessary. The poets and historians of a society are the vehicles of popular memory and they have the power to foment discontent. Consequently the separation of itihaas and kavya impoverishes culture and cripples dissent. As long as bardic literary forms like the raso and oral epics are studied independently of bardic historical genres like the khyat, vamsavalli and pidhiyavalli instead of being seen on a continuum, we will not have extricated ourselves from colonialist analysis of idioms of dissent against the practices of daughter devaluation in north-west India.

---

part, inspired by the debate among the Indian intelligentsia in the aftermath of the withdrawal of the two volumes written by K.N. Panikkar and Sumit Sarkar in the Towards Freedom multi-volume project by the Indian Council of Historical Research. For more details on this controversy, see Harsh Sethi, 'Debating History', *Economic and Political Weekly*, 11–17 March 2000; and A.G. Noorani, 'Freedom Movement in 1938', *Economic and Political Weekly*, 1–7 April 2000.

CHAPTER 8

The Work of Imagination

Temporality and Nationhood in Colonial Bengal*

PRATHAMA BANERJEE

> The world has long possessed the dream of a matter, of which it must only possess the consciousness in order to possess it in reality.
> —Karl Marx[1]

The use of the word 'imagination'—in the sense of 'imagined communities' or 'imaginary institutions' or even 'social imaginaries'—has changed the face of South Asian historiography since the 1980s. Especially after Benedict Anderson came out, in 1983, with his analysis of nations as contingently imagined political entities, there was no going back from the lesson that nations were constructed things, and not naturally given, as we were once prone to believing.[2] Yet the word 'imagination' itself remains curiously undertheorized—as if it is a self-evident working of the mind, a naturally given form of human reflexivity. There are, of course, some insightful studies which

*Discussions with Dipesh Chakrabarty, Gautam Bhadra, Partha Chatterjee and others at the Centre for Studies in Social Sciences, Calcutta, have helped me write this essay. I am also particularly indebted to Ajay Skaria for sharing his work with me and for his incisive questions, not all of which, I realize, I have been able to answer.

[1] Marx, letter to Ruge, quoted in Ernst Bloch, *The Principle of Hope* (Cambridge, Mass.: MIT Press, 1986), p. 156.

[2] Benedict Anderson, *Imagined Communities: Reflections on the Origin and Spread of Nationalism* (London: Verso, 1991).

contextualize imagination as a social act,[3] just as there is philosophical work which understands imagination as a mechanism for the invention of society.[4] Yet, we are still to politicize our everyday uses of the word 'imagination', and still to fully apprehend the political import of imagination as an act, an act which invests our sensibilities of the not-yet with a strong materiality. Recently, Dipesh Chakrabarty has deepened our political understanding of colonialism and postcoloniality by his project of 'provincializing Europe'. And significantly, an analysis of imagination as a category forms a central part of this project.[5] Chakrabarty shows that imagination in early-twentieth-century Bengal worked neither as a mentalist category, as in mainstream traditions of European romanticism, nor purely through a disciplining of the mind by technologies of print and census enumeration, as Anderson would have it. Imagination worked through the redeployment of traditional modes of envisioning, *darshan*, through which the nation, like the otherwise formless deity, appeared as manifest and concrete at different times and in different ways. In this, imagination was less a working of the human mind than a shared mode of 'embodiment', a set of everyday practices which gave body or form to the idea of the nation, as it were. The crucial imperative of nationalism—pride, love and adoration of one's nation—was made possible precisely by this imagination, which created the nation, rather than by purely discursive acts which constructed it as an object of scientific knowledge and historical analysis. My essay is inspired by a reading of works such as this, which seek to understand acts of imagination not in terms of discourses of realism or its opposite, but in terms of the politics of how reality comes to be in the first place, with all its materiality, concreteness, and apparent inescapability.

[3] J.M. Cocking, *Imagination: A Study in the History of Ideas* (London: Routledge, 1991); George Frederickson, *Comparative Imagination in the Histories of Racism, Nationalism, Social Movements* (Berkeley: University of California Press, 2000); P. Miller, *Dreams in Late Antiquity* (Princeton, Princeton University Press, 1997); J. Smith, *Fact and Feeling* (Wisconsin: University of Wisconsin Press, 1994).

[4] Cornelius Castoriadis, *World in Fragments: Writings on Politics, Society, Psychoanalysis, and the Imagination* (Stanford: Stanford University Press, 1997).

[5] Dipesh Chakrabarty, 'Nation and Imagination', *Studies in History*, 15:2 (July–December 1999), pp. 177–208.

In this essay I argue that to understand the full significance of the work of imagination we must go beyond the common assumption that imagination refers, ultimately, to our capacities for visualization or practices of seeing. A context such as colonial Bengal helps us do this—for here, by the late nineteenth and early twentieth century, imagination as a practice came across not only as a mode of visualization but more crucially as a practice of acting with and upon time. I shall argue that Bengali nationalist writings of the early twentieth century were using the word imagination by translating it as *kalpana*—a Sanskrit word which, apart from implying the act of imaging, also implied the sensibility of a creative temporality. This sense of imagination as kalpana drew on early Indian traditions of aesthetics and grammar and redeployed these traditions in the context of colonial-modern theories of history and memory. Since the chronological time of colonial modernity was profoundly implicated in the fabrication of notions of 'primitiveness' and 'backwardness', the Bengali educated classes, uneasy with their own claims of historicity, had to supplement history with what was consciously undertaken as the work of kalpana, a creative deployment of time which would allow the colonized to nullify their sense of a perpetual lag in the time of progress. Also, by the early twentieth century in colonial Bengal, imagination itself began to be written as the sign of the 'primitive'. This ascribed to the word imagination a different temporal dimension, which was simultaneous to but went beyond its usage as kalpana. 'Primitives' were definitionally attributed the capacity for mythmaking and storytelling, the capacity for breaking out of the prison of representation, as it were. The Bengali *bhadrolok* felt that they had abdicated precisely this capacity to 'tribes' like the Santals, in their desire for positivism and historicism. Hence the alacrity with which the Bengali educated classes sought to understand and use 'primitive' symbols—as if such a reclamation of 'primitive' imagination would resurrect the colonized's claim to a future more desirable and more contemporary than that which was being offered by dreams of modernity.

In other words, I shall argue that if modernity was a way of judging in terms of time and temporal positioning—modern *vs.* primitive, advanced *vs.* backward etc.—imagination in colonial Bengal emerged as a way of redeploying time itself. Imagination was invoked not only to interrogate the self-evidence of chronology, it was also invoked as the radical undoing of the 'primitive'–historical binary upon which the regime of modernity was founded. It was by the mobilization of imagination that the 'primitive' seemed to strike back at history, and the colonized intellectual—also implicated in the textualization of history in contrast with 'primitiveness'—had to own up 'primitiveness' itself as the sign of his own difference and identity. (I also hope to show that this mobilization of imagination, in the name of kalpana and under the sign of the 'primitive', had to be somewhat different from modern European literary and artistic traditions of romanticism and 'primitivism'—after all, the colonized could not simply take recourse to the 'primordial' and the 'natural' in his critique of modernity, for he was accused of being always already located there.) In colonial Bengal, therefore, imagination did not just work to implode the narrative closures of history. It also worked to reconvene temporality itself in favour of the colonized, by mobilizing practices of kalpana—kalpana being a word with a strong temporal sense, a sense which is deemphasized if we read the word singularly, as we do these days, as a translated equivalent of the word imagination. It would seem, therefore, that as an intrinsically temporal act, imagination worked with the same imperative as that of history and history-writing, even though as a discipline, with a claim upon the 'real', history repeatedly sought to exile imagination to the domain of the literary. In other words, the colonial condition compels us to remember that there is more to the work of imagination than the lesson that imagined things like the nation are constructed and not natural, and that fact and fiction are never neat opposites. In fact, the colonial condition shows that understanding imagination as an act is not merely a matter of deconstructing the fact–fiction problematic. In the colonial condition it becomes part of the problematic of time and politics. As Abanindranath Thakur said explicitly in early twentieth-century Bengal, 'imagination is the breath of the not-yet'.[6]

Imagination and History

Imagination is directly translated as kalpana in contemporary Bengali language. Only one of the lexical meanings of the root word—*kalpa*—shares the sense of vision with the English word imagination, as when

[6] Abanindranath Thakur, 'Antar Bahir', *Bageswari Silpa Prabandhabali* (Calcutta: Rupa, 1962), p. 102.

used in association with other terms like *chitrakalpa* (imagination of a picture) or when in an earlier usage kalpana implied embellishment (a *kalpak* was a barber, kalpana was the decoration of an elephant to be mounted by the king). However, as the masterly Bengali encyclopaedia of Nagendranath Basu, put together between 1886 and 1911, shows, a central meaning of the term remains temporal—kalpana is the power to invent a new thing.[7] The root word, kalpa, stands for a day of the creator, Brahma, or for two thousand epochs of the gods. It implies the temporality of the creation and the passing of the world. Kalpa also stands for the cataclysm that is supposed to visit the earth at the end of each such creative day, the destruction after which the world is built anew. *Sankalpa* or resolve is a power that is indestructible by time—yet kalpa is a duration which can erode even the solidity of sankalpa. Accordingly, kalpana may mean conjecture or creation or, at times, even desire—terms indicating modes of apprehending the future and bringing about things which are as yet non-existent. [8]

An earlier Bengali lexicon—published in 1831, which sought to translate and popularize through print the classical Sanskrit lexicon *Amarkosa*—lists the term kalpa under the rubric of heavenly names or *swarga varga*. Having listed the names or synonyms of gods, of the ancestors and of Brahma, the text classifies kalpa as the 'name of time'. This continuum of names/words is also inhabited by, apart from gods and ancestors, the categories of causality, origin, veda-s, *itihas* (later used as the translation of the word 'history'), logic, economics, puranas, and speech, in that order.[9] I mention this early text in order to indicate the semantic neighbourhood which the word kalpa inhabited before it became a synonym of the word imagination as we know it today. This location gives us clues to understanding the differences with which imagination or kalpana might have worked in our particular context of colonial Bengal.[10]

[7] Nagendranath Basu, *Biswakosh*, III (Delhi: B.R. Pub. Corp., reprint, 1988), p. 317.

[8] Ibid. Also see Benimadhab Das, *Sabdarthamuktabali* (Calcutta: author, 1866).

[9] Jagannath Prasad Mullick, *Sabdakalpalatika* (Srirampur: Mission Press, 1831), pp. 17–33.

[10] Before proceeding further, I must make a few clarifications about the uses that I may appear to make of etymology, in the context of writing a history of

Without trying to reconstruct a semantic history of the word kalpana, which I am not competent to do, let me briefly make a few references to its earlier usages in order to show that the word kalpana, even in earlier non-colonial traditions, was known to strain against the

---

colonial Bengal. When I refer to meanings of the word kalpana, meanings other than the meaning we assign to it when we read the word as exactly a synonym of the word 'imagination', I am not by any means referring to any foundational sense of it. In that sense, it is not a Heideggarian search for the 'primordiality' of the phenomenon called imagination/kalpana. It is not even an etymological argument—harking back to the 'origin' of the word. All that I am trying to show is that once put into translation, the word kalpana lost its otherwise potent temporal intentions and became tied to the sense of vision and envisioning as in the English word 'imagination'. Translation, in other words, was as much a whittling down of meaning as a multiplication of it. The same act of translation also put it in the field of a certain poetics, familiar to us by the rubric of European romanticism and by the names of Wordsworth and Coleridge. In fact, this tradition remains popular with the educated Bengali middle classes—Wordsworth, Coleridge, etc. are mandatory reading even today in school syllabuses, and lay readers of Rabindranath, for instance, approach the ideas of nature and imagination in Rabindranath in the same 'romantic' fashion today. References to kalpana as a word different from the word 'imagination' are thus intended to remind us that this act of translation was also contingent, that the word kalpana, even in early twentieth century, was mobilized in ways other than that of the word 'imagination', in traditions other than that of romanticism. The point is to highlight the specificities of the colonial condition and what these implied for the act called imagination. There are certain historiographical risks that such semantic references face. For one, late eighteenth–early nineteenth century philological/ethnological traditions approached word-meanings as synonymous to the conceptual apparatus of a culture. Collecting the vocabulary of a foreign language was supposed to be the way of mapping the mental horizon of a foreign people, who could then be put in comparison to Europe in terms of 'objective' linguistic and therefore mentalist skills. Discussing semantics often raises the fear that one is falling into this early Orientalist trap. For the other, in context of the cultural politics of today's India, referring to Sanskrit or Brahmanical texts to make sense of colonial modernity raises the fear of ideological conflation with the upper-caste Hindu right—who have cornered and appropriated early Indian texts for their sectarian political purposes. It is important therefore, that I emphasize at the very outset that my referring, in a limited fashion, to Sanskrit philosophical and poetic traditions is an act of contingent and contemporary interpretation. My argument does not depend on finding meanings that are either chronologically originary or culturally authentic. My logic is limited to the purpose of making sense of some important texts of late-nineteenth

representational imperative of knowledge. In classical Sanskrit philosophy, for instance, Bimal Krishna Matilal shows, *vikalpa* or kalpana, was a highly contested category. Kalpana meant relentless verbal/ conceptual proliferation, at times even hypothetical alternatives. Buddhists, Naiyayikas and others debated continuously upon the possibility of *sa-* and *nir-vikalpa pratakshya,* i.e. of direct and concept-loaded perception. What is interesting for us is that, just as Hume described imagination as a 'magical faculty', Buddhist philosophers too found kalpana or verbal proliferation to be an obsession residing in humans from the 'beginning of time'. In other words, imagination or kalpana was admitted in these classical theories of perception as philosophically unaccountable. In ordinary Sanskrit usages, the word kalpana implied what the poet undertook in order to invoke *rasa* or moods/feelings in his audience.[11] In this tradition too, rasa, in the association of which kalpana appeared, was understood as something which inhabited the domain of the undefinable. In other words, even in classical scholarship, both philosophical and literary, kalpana resided at the margins of the domain of epistemology—as an act not fully explicable in terms of theories and modes of knowledge. And it was precisely this defiant nature of the word, as we shall see, which made its use so significant in later contexts of colonial modernity.

In classical Indian poetics, imagination or kalpana, which invoked rasa, was known to be eminently untheorizable. This was because language itself appeared, in some versions of classical grammar, as something which went beyond structures of referentiality and meaning. In these traditions, language was recognized by its exclusive power of 'suggestion' or *vyanjana*—a power which necessarily became palpable at the interface of the speaker and the audience, and went beyond the realist intent of linguistic articulation. This suggestiveness or vyanjana was inexplicable in terms of lexical meanings or even in terms of figures of speech and *alamkaras* or embellishments. It was simply *dhvani*, a word which in Bengali is understood to merely mean 'sound'.

---

and early-twentieth-century Bengal, in order to expand the semantic possibilities of a word which appears to have acquired, by now, a singular and uncontested meaning through translation into English.

[11] Bimal Krishna Matilal, *Perception: An Essay on Classical Indian Theories of Knowledge* (Oxford: Clarendon Press, 1986), pp. 309–13.

It was this power which put language beyond all other modes of articulation, be it paint, lime, marble or even drama.[12] And it was this power—rather than any positive referentiality—which activated the imagination of the audience. It was imagination, in turn, which permitted the audience to experience rasa, and rasa, it was said, was unsayable—being neither a given, a priori thing nor a consequence, a result of anything, nor produced out of the logic of *pramanas* or proofs. Rasa, invoked by kalpana, 'was an act, yet not an act, known yet not knowable, eternal yet not eternal'.[13]

I mention all this in order to note the texture that kalpana had acquired in its association with early Indian rasa theories. Rasa invoked *basana*—perhaps inexactly translatable as desire—which, it was said, was an experience that existed neither in memory nor in tradition nor in habit (was it a kind of ontological orientation towards the future?). It appeared to reside deep within the self, and was the originary condition of life, thought, work and knowledge. The fullness of this mode of apprehension was in that it could admit contradictions between two forms of knowledge and even between the literal and the suggested meaning of a single formulation.[14] This sensibility—as Abhinavagupta, the most famous of classical aestheticians, believed—was neither produced out of mimesis, the form of speaking which denies that one speaks *for* and insists that one speaks *as* (in the way that Bharata's dramaturgy defined successful poetic representation as an effective simulation of reality) nor produced out of the audience's experience of poetic representation as the author/poet's original and authentic creation (in the way that we have learnt to do in modern times). Portrayal of fear, for instance, would produce indifference if the audience experienced it as another's, i.e. as the poet's, singular and inimitable construction. It would produce debilitating fear itself if experienced as reality. In neither case could fear be imagined as a rasa. To Abhinavagupta, therefore, rasa was truly invoked when fear was experienced by the audience as neither the self's nor the other's, but as generalized. This

[12] Kanti Chandra Pandey, *Comparative Aesthetics I* (Varanasi: Chowkhamba, 2nd edn, 1959), pp 257–8, 490.

[13] Abantikumar Sanyal, *Abhinavagupter Rasabhasya* (Bardhaman & Calcutta: Vidyabhavan, 1963), p. xvi.

[14] Ibid., pp. 45–6, 58.

generalization was neither the audience experiencing the poet's work as real nor an experience of illusion created out of displacement and suspension of disbelief, neither the experience of metaphor nor of mimesis, neither the immediate transportation caused by magic nor the gradual reception of ideas by the audience in a pedagogical relation to the poet. It was rather a generalization which produced a commonality of desire and togetherness in society. And it was precisely this generalization which was the work of imagination.[15] (Is it significant that this experience of a shared fate and location was caused by the audience's immersion in the poetic work, an immersion produced by the exercise of kalpana which was very different from the perspectival distance required by imagination when understood as a mode of viewing and visualization?) It is this history of the word imagination—where it was understood as the condition of generality across speakers and listeners—which is important to us in our following analysis. This is not to say that this semantic history was an uninterrupted continuum in which colonial Bengal participated unproblematically. In fact, as we shall see later, if both kalpana and rasa became important references in certain kinds of writings about the nation in colonial Bengal, they were radically displaced into a political field, as they began to function as supplements to sensibilities of history and historicism in colonial modernity.

It was in the late nineteenth century that the word kalpana reappeared in Bengali middle-class discourses as an antithesis to historical consciousness. Faced with the colonial accusation that Bengalis/Indians had no history of their own, Bankimchandra Chattopadhyay—later canonized as the 'father' of modern Bengali language and literature—fired the imagination of his contemporaries by a call to everyone to write history.[16] A central part of this project was the reclamation and cleaning up of early Indian texts and their transformation into texts of authentic and factual history. Bankimchandra himself made great

[15] Ibid., pp. 91–4.

[16] Ranajit Guha, *An Indian Historiography of India: A Nineteenth-century Agenda and Its Implication* (Calcutta: K.P. Bagchi, 1988); Partha Chatterjee, *The Nation and Its Fragments* (Princeton: Princeton University Press, 1993); and Sudipta Kaviraj, *The Unhappy Consciousness: Bankimchandra Chattopadhyay and the Formation of Nationalist Discourse in India* (Delhi: Oxford University Press, 1995).

efforts, for instance, to prove that Krishna was a real-historical and not fictional character, by trying to weed out the kalpanik or imaginary elements from the empirical narrative of the epic *Mahabharata*.[17] Not only did he ask that imagination be eliminated from historical texts, he also sought to subsume literary imagination itself to the laws of history. Thus, the love poetry of Bengal was explained away as the historical effect of a fertile and abundant land which fed a sedentary and secure tradition of conjugal affection and tender domesticity.[18] Evidently, it was important to Bankimchandra to show that '[e]verything is a consequence of laws. Even literature is a consequence of laws'.[19] Akshay Kumar Datta, one of the earliest historians of Bengal, famous for his treatise *Sea-voyage and Commerce of the Ancient Hindus* (1901), wrote in 1851 that, in order to understand the operation of natural laws, the human mind must be understood in its perfect correspondence to nature, to the object of its analysis.[20] In his own interpretation of a certain Hegelian version of the progress of world history, Bankimchandra too legislated that perfect knowledge required the perfect identity of the Subject and the Object. He critiqued poets like Wordsworth for being absurdly idealistic—for portraying the human mind as if it existed beyond the 'shadow' of worldly reality. And blamed 'erotic' poets like Jayadeva for being purely sensuous, for narrating the world as if it could exist except in the 'shadow' of human interiors. That is, to Bankimchandra, neither the imagination of European romantics nor the imagination of Bengali bhakti poets could be called valid modes of imagination.[21] It was from this epistemological position, based on the perfect correspondence of mind and matter and seemingly cleared of all that was imaginary and 'unnatural', that Bankim and his peers sought to claim historicity—for their own writings, for early Indian texts and for Bengal itself. When Bankim acknowledged the importance of the poetic intent, it was because he saw poetic

[17] Bankimchandra, 'Krishna Charitra', in *Bankim Rachanavali II*, ed. Jogeshchandra Bagal (Calcutta: Sahitya Samsad, 1954), pp. 560–84.

[18] Bankimchandra, 'Bibidha Prabandha, Bidyapati o Jaydev', in *Bankim Rachanavali II*, pp. 190–1.

[19] Bankimchandra, 'Manas Bikash', in *Bankim Rachanavali II*, p. 886.

[20] Akshay Datta, *Bahya Vastur sange Manav Prakritir Sambandha Vichar* (Calcutta: Tattvabodhini Press, 1851).

[21] Bankimchandra, 'Bibidha Prabandha, Bidyapati o Jaydev', p. 192.

imagination as a means of 'purifying' human interiors, perhaps making it more capable of perfect correspondence with the world and therefore, of knowledge. When he exclaimed that a bad poet, like a thief, should be sentenced to corporeal punishment he seemed to imply that words *were* indeed things, to be regulated by the same laws and codes which governed the world of objects to be possessed.[22]

However, already in the late years of the century there was an emergent critique of this historicist claim on the real. Rabindranath Thakur claimed in 1902 that he who had never read history was ill-fated, but less so than he who had never read poetry;[23] and in 1896 he wrote that the epic *Mahabharata* was not poetic history at all, it was, if anything, historical poetry. Rabindranath argued that by eliminating imaginary elements from the *Mahabharata*, Bankimchandra had merely demonstrated what history was not. He had completely failed to show what history really was.[24] In fact, Rabindranath categorically stated that, apart from the nine rasas set out by classical Indian poetics, there were other shades of rasas which had remained unnamed in classical texts. Historicity was precisely one such hitherto undetermined rasa.[25] To name historicity as a rasa was not only to place it in the domain of imagination (and not in the field of evidences and scientific knowledge), it was also to understand history-writing, on the lines of classical rasa theory, as a mode of achieving a generality of mood/feeling across a community. In his introduction to the first issue of the historical journal, *Aitihasik Chitra*, edited by historian Akshay Kumar Maitra, Rabindranath wrote precisely this.

> The principle of oneness is like the life-principle. It cannot remain contained like an inanimate thing. . . . If it can radiate across space, it wants to diffuse through time as well. If it can undo the distinction between the far and the near, it also tries to end the distinction between the past and the future. . . . *This force of oneness is so inexorable, that it invokes imagination [kalpana] to compensate for the lacks of history, and thus makes history itself futile.*[26] (emphasis mine)

[22] Bankimchandra, 'Dharmatattva', in *Bankim Rachanavali II*, pp. 668–70.

[23] Rabindranath Thakur, 'Aitihasik Upanyas', in *Rabindra Rachanavali* [hereafter *RR*], XIII (Calcutta, West Bengal Government, 1962), p. 821.

[24] Rabindranath Thakur, 'Krishnacharitra', in *RR XIII*, pp. 926, 931.

[25] Rabindranath Thakur, 'Aitihasik Upanyas', p. 818.

[26] Rabindranath Thakur, 'Aitihasik Chitra', in *RR XIII*, pp. 478–9.

By the turn of the century, it must be remembered, history too was no longer understood in Bengal as Bankim's 'history for and by all'. In 1914, the most well-known historian of the times, Akshay Kumar Maitra, had announced that Bankim's time of encouraging everyone to write and think history was over. What was needed now was to practise 'correct and worthy history'.[27] In his speech to the history session of the seventh Bangiya Sahitya Parishat conference, Maitra complained that there was as yet no consensus in India on what history was and therefore no correct methodology of doing history. He suggested that education should henceforth be oriented towards a training in 'discovering, collecting, preserving and assessing levels of evidence', and in the 'suspension of community or national interests'. For, he said, 'truth was a greater ideal than patriotism and the ethics of practice'.[28] Thus disciplined, history had become, by the early years of the twentieth century, a genre of knowledge—rather than a national practice, as Bankimchandra had wanted it to be in the late nineteenth century.

And, not surprisingly, it was this disciplining of history that caused the bringing in of imagination from the backdoor, as it were. Pramatha Mukhopadhyay, for instance, argued that empirical/chronological time fragmented existence into the discrete moments of past, present and future. This not only disabled creative practice but also failed to identify the desire which called for history-writing in the first place. Real or 'originary' time, on the other hand, was able to generate intuition or *pragnya* when it intersected with practical time. It was this pragnya, more than just *gnyan* or knowledge, that allowed one to imagine the long past and the unarrived future right in the present.[29] The desire for history was born precisely out of this non-chronological time, in the time of articulation (*abhivyakti*) and it was precisely this desire which was the rasa of history—the rasa of *ananda*/bliss and of its other variation, pain.[30] Pramatha Choudhury too, critiquing Akshay Maitra's speech on scientific history, warned that the loss of poetic imagination from history-writing would disable practical creativity:

[27] 'Aitihasik racana koutuk', *Sahitya*, 2(vii), 1914.

[28] Speech by Akshay Maitra, in *Sahitya*, 25(i),1914, pp. 42–54.

[29] Pramathanath Mukhopadhyay, *Itihas o Abhibyakti* (Jadavpur: Jatiya Sikshaparishad Granthavali, 1929), pp. 39, 299.

[30] Ibid., p. 63.

'Science is the knowledge of pre-given substances. The account of new creations is not to be found in the book of science.'[31]

This face-off between imagination and historicism reached its peak in the early decades of the twentieth century, in the debate between historian Akshay Kumar Maitra and painter-storyteller Abanindranath Tagore.[32] Maitra claimed that in contemporary India, while there was relentless discussion on aesthetics, there was no credible history of art. To him, this lack of history meant a lack of knowledge about the evolution of Indian art, and therefore a lack of predictive competence which could apprehend in the colonial present what the future held for the nation.[33] To Maitra, the historical characteristic of Indian aesthetics was that it was determined by a well-defined system of laws, where nothing was left to chance. Those artists, like Abanindranath, who disavowed these laws in the name of newness and creativity were, if anything, not Indian.[34] Maitra even went on to assert that '[a]esthetics/art is part of the science of man. Imagination has no right to it. . . . The laws of evidence which found [historical] judgement, must also found aesthetics'.[35] To this historicism, Abanindranath retorted that the right to imagination had to be earned anew every time in practice, that this was never passed down like history through the laws of inheritance.[36]

It was in the course of similar face-offs between historicism and poetics that knowledge and imagination came to be concretized in Bengal as two contraries, with imagination being interpreted as a predominantly *practical* and therefore, *futural* imperative. Rabindranath

[31] 'Review of Sahityasammelan' (*jaishtha* 1914), in *Prabandhasamgraha,* Pramatha Choudhury (Calcutta: Visva Bharati, 1952), p. 55.

[32] Internal to the discipline of history, a similar debate was also going on between Haraprasad Shastri, Rameshchandra Majumdar and Rakhaldas Bandopadhyay on the relevance of history to cultural nationalism. I shall concentrate on the painter-historian debate here because the sensibility of imagination was more explicitly talked about in the this context.

[33] Akshay Maitra, 'Bharatsilper Varnaparichay', 1912, in *Bharatsilpa Katha,* Akshay Maitra (Calcutta: Sahityalok, reprint, 1982), p. 10.

[34] Akshay Maitra, 'Bharatsilpacharchar Nababidhan', 1912, in *Bharatsilpa Katha,* p. 15.

[35] Akshay Maitra, 'Bharatsilpa Tattva', 1922, in *Bharatsilpa Katha*, pp. 33–4.

[36] Abanindranath Thakur, 'Silpe Anadhikar', in *Bageshwari Silpa Prabandhabali,* p. 11.

Thakur, for instance, argued that imagination worked with a logic fundamentally different from that of knowledge. He said that to know something was a once-and-for-all act, when one knew something one knew it for ever. The shared emotional state produced by kalpana, however, deepened with the practice of reiteration—with its passage through time and through memories of generations, through repetition and differentiation. He also believed that, while knowledge had to be proven, *bhav* had to be disseminated. Even though knowledge was meant to be spread amongst more and more people, its not being generalized did not take away from the truth of such knowledge. Imagination, however, had no existence, without practices of sharing and generalizations.[37] In fact, to Rabindranath it was the reality of the nation which showed this beyond everything else—that the necessity that drove the work of imagination was different from the necessity which drove the production of knowledge.

To be born in a particular nation was an accident, Rabindranath argued; one neither earned nor deserved it. The territorial nation, therefore, itself could never become the true subject of history. The true subject of history was the nation that one imagined.[38] If people like Bankimchandra had believed that historical truth was sufficient in itself to reclaim the glory of the nation, they also had to admit that in history not everything was glorious. Yet, if in all its defeats and humiliations, the nation appeared beautiful and lovable, it was because the nation was necessarily created through kalpana (imagination) and *sahanubhuti* (shared feelings). Precisely, therefore, the nation could never acquire an identity through a knowledge of it, however scientific such knowledge might be. In any case, if it was a matter of merely finding the truth, then it would be irrelevant who wrote the history of a nation. It was precisely because the nation was imagined—and imagined together—that we ourselves must write its history. Even Bankim had had to admit that.[39]

This imagination (kalpana) which worked to create the nation, Rabindranath said, was analogous to the act of divine creation—thus resonating the semantic history of the word kalpana which came from

[37] Rabindranath Thakur, 'Sahityer Samagri', 1903, *RR XIII*, p. 743.

[38] Rabindranath Thakur, 'Sahitya Parishat', 1906, *RR XIII*, p. 884.

[39] Rabindranath Thakur, 'Aitihasik Chitra', *RR XIII*, pp. 480–1.

the root kalpa, meaning a day of creation/destruction by the supreme deity Brahma. The sense of this analogy, to Rabindranath, lay in the understanding that imagination claimed no necessity, at least of the kind that we are used to in the context of scientific proofs and historical progress. Perhaps even God could not apprehend the work of creative imagination in the mode of knowledge—'(w)ho knows from what all this occurred. Where does creation come from, was it somebody who created all this or was it not? The one who oversaw creation from above, knows this, or *does not know*'[40] (emphasis mine). In other words, like the nation, Rabindranath argued, the work of imagination itself, which created the nation, was arbitrary and contingent. It operated beyond the limits of historical laws and scientific explanations, which founded our sensibilities of knowledge. And yet if imagination, and the nation, were no less true for that, this truth was fundamentally different from the truth-claims of what we understood as knowledge.

The truth produced by the work of imagination was the truth of dreams. As Rabindranath argued, scholars had tried to prove that the world was a lie; that there was no self-evident reality available to direct perception or vision. But all they ended up proving was really that nothing was truer than the so-called lie, than the dream.[41] Rabindranath was not alone in this formulation of the truth of dreams. It must be remembered that numerous texts of 'dream histories' were already being published in late-nineteenth- and early-twentieth-century Bengal. These texts constituted a new genre of history-writing which sought to utter all that disciplined histories could not. Thus Rajnarayan Basu, while contemplating the contemporary history of Bengal with its modern amenities but with its bondage and unfreedom, claimed to have dreamt up a clear vision of the Pala regime of Bengal. Circumventing the present, these memories directly led to the 'dream future'—when Bengal was completely free, and had overtaken England in progress.[42] Though this dream-reality was never present, except as a potential, and was therefore unrepresentable in the disciplinary

[40] Rabindranath Thakur, 'Vividha Prasanga', *RR XIV*, p. 577.

[41] Rabindranath Thakur, 'Loksahitya: Chhele Bhulano Chhara', *RR XIII*, p. 669.

[42] Rajnarayan Basu, 'Ascharya Svapna', in *Vividha Prabandha I* (Calcutta: Oriental Publishing Estb.,1882), pp. 94–7.

mode, it was nevertheless a real though abandoned dimension of the past.

These seemingly 'absurd' possibilities were intended as no less 'actual' than the empirical. Dreams possessed an ethical imperative, for dreams could not lie in the way that consciously fabricated narratives, including histories, could. Dreamt in the isolation of sleep or of lonely contemplation, these dreams could also be dreamt without fear and inhibition and could be written by anybody and everybody who dared to transgress the given limits of the present. It was only in the form of dreams that one could write about the bloodless war by Bengalis who, tired of their clerical routine in colonial offices, gathered bamboos from the Bengal and Assam forests, made them into spray-tubes and, scattering chilli-water, defeated the entire colonial army.[43] The 'truth' of dreams was thus harnessed against the 'truth' of facts. In the colonial present, where truth was submerged in the conflict of many opinions, in the dazzle of novelty and above all in the limiting experience of unfreedom, truth could only be activated by a release of 'imagination' from the prison of representation and mimesis, i.e. from the prison of reality. Dwijendranath Thakur, in the early twentieth century, wrote how imagination had been suppressed by the over-use of irony in nineteenth-century historical thought. So he withdrew into dreams to find the true path that ran precariously through the antagonisms and contradictions of everyday life.[44] Pramathanath Raychoudhury too sought to banish 'the clever, satirical ones . . . the wrinkled in mind, the pauper at heart', who disowned the truth of dreams.[45]

In other words, imagination in colonial Bengal was seen as not only working beyond the limits imposed by historicism and its version of factual and finished pasts, but also working out a terrain beyond the limits of knowledge itself. The truth that the work of imagination produced was not a 'fact'—i.e. not something that was 'known' to be true, and could thus function as the basis of predictions and lessons for the future. Imagination produced a dreamlike truth that would have to be made true in the future, by generalization and by practice. On the surface, the history–kalpana face-off might seem quite like the science/

[43] Ramdas Sharma, *Bharat Uddhar* (Calcutta: Canning Library, 1878).

[44] *Svapnaprayan* (Allahabad: Indian Press, 1914), p. 214.

[45] *Svapna* (Calcutta: Purnacharan Das, 1906), pp. 1–2.

art or fact/fiction problematic familiarized to us by traditions of Western modernity and its epistemological double-binds. In fact, it can easily be shown that some of the authors discussed above were influenced and provoked by debates internal to European philosophy and criticism. What makes the history-kalpana face-off crucially different, however, is that it can be understood as a particular moment in the life of the colonized (Bengali) intellectual where imagination came to be invoked not just as an epistemological issue nor merely as an ontological matter, but as a manifesto for practice.

This was the moment of imagination's critical interface with the political. (Of course, this was also one of the most tragically failed moments of Indian/Bengali nationalism, but more about that later.) The mark of this moment was that history and kalpana—even as they engaged in an intense face-off—never really developed into a counterpoise in the writings of the authors discussed above, in the way that science/art or fact/fiction did in European traditions; that is, until this face-off was displaced by mid twentieth century by the antagonism, more conventional to modernism, between the poet and the realist. Desperate proponents of kalpana, like Rabindranath, repeatedly sought to make history their own, paradoxically in the very name of a critique of history-writing. And dream-narratives, we have seen, had to sell themselves as texts of history.

This was because in the colonial context, history-writing had a very specific, perhaps 'anti-historical' function. History, definitionally, demonstrates succession and continuity through time—which is why 'transition' has always been a central problematic in historiography. For the colonized, however, even as history demonstrated the continuity in the present of ancient glories of the nation, history also had to thematize a constitutive rupture—the phenomenon of colonialism itself. For the colonized, therefore, the past of history had to be more than a moment in the story of the cumulative and incremental progress of mankind. It also had to be more than a moment of 'origin'. Against the logic of the apparent continuity of chronology, history had to reconvene the past, precisely in mismatch to the present, in order to expose the limits and the arbitrariness of the colonized times. After all, despite critiquing history as a discipline, no one could forget that Bankimchandra's claim to historicity was primarily a claim to the memory of an unsubjugated and free past, a claim to the possibility of a future, which ought-to-have-been, but for the contingency of colonialism. Bankim's historical past was meant to expose the colonial present as unnatural to, undeserved by, and somewhat out of joint with the otherwise hopeful history of the land. Imagination or kalpana, therefore, even as it struggled against the prison of historicism, had to harness this history itself if it had to provisionalize the colonial present, as a time somewhat alien, imposed and unprecedented, and thus open it up for intervention. Imagination, hence, could not function in full counterpoise to history, imagination had to harness history itself in its practices for the future. It was this which made imagination question, not just on its own but on history's behalf, the sensibility of knowledge itself. It was also this which prevented the kalpana–history face-off from becoming a self-contained problematic of epistemology. And it was this formulation of imagination as practice, as something which began where knowledge reached its limit, which made the relation between memory, in fact time, and imagination into the central problematic of Bengali nationalism. Finally, it was also this which, in Bengal, prevented discussions about art and aesthetics from becoming an autonomous terrain, as they continuously slipped into general discussions about history, identity and nationhood in a way which modern aestheticians would surely consider to be an overpoliticization of art.

Time and Imagination

Abanindranath claimed that kalpana or imagination was the 'breath of the non-yet'—a futural imperative, a mode in which what was not yet given could be created for the first time. But in the same breath, he also claimed that kalpana meant nothing except in association with *smriti*, memory. There was no point in an imagination which did not pervade memory.[46] To Abanindranath, 'brave is the one who can hold the immensity of imagination in memory, he is the king of both the formed

[46] Satyajit Choudhury argues that it was precisely this articulation of imagination with memory which distinguished Abanindranath's imagination from, say, the imagination of Coleridge and Wordsworth, poets whom many twentieth-century Bengalis were otherwise extremely fond of. Satyajit Choudhury, *Abanindra-Nandantattva* (Calcutta: Sanyal Publications, 1977), pp. 61–3.

and the formless, he is the brave, the poet, the artist, the sage, the discoverer, the virtuous, the creator'.[47] Rabindranath distinguished between two kinds of imagination: one, an impoverished imagination which grasped novelties as newness in and for itself; and two, a creative imagination which grasped newness in its relation to memory.[48] In other words, it was a limited imagination which represented a new thing as unprecedented. Creative imagination was precisely that which could articulate the unprecedented with memory and history, i.e. articulate future and unarrived possibilities as potentials of the past. The definition of a new thing as merely new, because it replaces the old, Rabindranath said, proved nothing beyond the succession of temporal moments. Even though history as a discipline defined itself primarily in terms of the principle of succession, this claim to mere succession failed to account for the desire for history itself.[49]

According to Rabindranath, it was precisely the desire for history which called for kalpana—because kalpana worked not merely to envision other times; it worked to put a relationship in place between times, between the past and the future, just as between peoples. To Rabindranath, *sahitya*—the Bengali word for literature, which comes out of the word *sahit*, meaning 'together with'—reflected this imperative of imagination, the imperative of putting peoples and times together.[50] Rabindranath argued that it was only because, in the name of historicism, there was a 'civil war' between truth and imagination that relations of togetherness had become suspended in the nation in colonial modernity.[51] If togetherness was the work of imagination, it was not accidental that Rabindranath's writings were replete with references to rasa as that which created a unity between times and peoples. We have already mentioned an element in classical rasa theories, which defined rasa as exactly that which produced a generality of mood in society. We have also noted that Rabindranath himself believed historicity to be one of the many rasas which had remained unstated in classical texts. For our purposes, it is this matter of coming together,

[47] Abanindranath Thakur, 'Antar Bahir', in *Bageshwari*, p. 105.
[48] Rabindranath Thakur, 'Kabir Abhibhasan', *RR XIV*, p. 395.
[49] Rabindranath Thakur, 'Sahityarup', *RR XIV*, p. 399.
[50] Rabindranath Thakur, 'Bangla Jatiya Sahitya', 1894, *RR XIII*, p. 798.
[51] Rabindranath Thakur, 'Aitihasik Upanyas', 1902, *RR XIII*, p. 817.

of putting in place a relationship between peoples and between times, which makes the invocation of kalpana and rasa by Rabindranath and his colleagues interesting.

When authors like Rabindranath made kalpana and rasa part of the same problematic as that of history and history-writing, imagination seemed to become, at least for a while, the radical clue in the formulation of what we would today cryptically call the Self–Other problematic of colonial modernity. In the rest of this essay, I shall try to understand this crucial displacement of what would otherwise appear to be a literary imperative—that of imagination—into the domain of the political. I shall argue that imagination was invoked in colonial Bengal, by authors like Rabindranath and others, in order to negotiate not only social and cultural but also temporal otherness within the nation. I shall show that this was done by authors simultaneously invoking imagination and the 'primitive', with the intention of moving beyond the knowledge-imperative and into the realm of an alternative futural practice. I shall, of course, also try to understand the ultimate failure of this undoubtedly ingenious move—on the grounds that proponents of imagination abdicated the possibility of an alternative practice by misrecognizing the so-called 'primitive' herself, and by thus removing the act of kalpana from the time of the everyday and reconfiguring it under the realm of the poetic and the regime of the authorial.

Like Bankimchandra and others of his time, Rabindranath too saw the nation as a difficult and unprecedented coming together of 'outsiders' (read Muslims) and 'primitives' (often called non-Aryans) with ancient and 'civilized' Hindus/Bengalis. It was the interior 'otherness' of these 'outside' and 'primitive' elements which made the Indian nation singular, defined by a unique coming together of different and, most importantly, non-contemporary communities. In any case, the colonial condition itself implied that the present appeared as an other to the 'authentic' past of the nation. At the same time, this present appeared as non-contemporary to the present of Europe, to the modern and the truly contemporary subject of history. The fundamental imperative of nation-building, therefore, had to be the resolution of these internal non-contemporaneities, the bringing of other times and other peoples together with the present and with the self. In fact, the bringing together of different peoples was almost synonymous to the bringing together of different times, different stages of history. Nation-building, therefore, was not merely a matter of negotiating cultural and political differences, it was a matter of negotiating temporal mismatches.

Rabindranath argued that this coming together of times could be achieved only through creative imagination, and not in the aggregative mode of classificatory knowledge of the nation. Unity was produced out of the practice of imagining one's singular self as differentiated—like God, man recognized himself in multiple senses and multiple rasas in his creations.[52] And behind this practice of differentiation, there lay no greater cause than the play (*lila*) of imagination itself, no greater necessity which explained or justified its contingencies and fortuities.[53] Rabindranath's argument was that knowledge merely allowed one to find identity in terms exclusively of the self—that was how the object of knowledge was constituted as self-sufficient and self-evident. The Indian nation, however, could never be sufficiently characterized in terms of such a self-identity. The Indian nation, by its very nature, had to be a matter of *anubhav*, the fundamental mode of apprehending rasa—for anubhav was to identify oneself in terms of something else, in terms of others.[54] To apprehend rasa was to make particular the things which were found to exist in commonness and generality.[55] Imagination was precisely this practice which made the common appear as one's own, and reproduced that which was intimately one's own as common to all peoples and all times.[56] Bankimchandra would have argued that a national literary imagination was the product of a historical oneness within the nation. But Rabindranath argued quite the reverse—that oneness in the nation was primarily created out of the work of a national imagination.[57] For imagination was precisely that which worked out a togetherness, not only across peoples but also

[52] Rabindranath Thakur, letter to Amiya Chakravarty, 1936, in *RR XIV*, p. 292.

[53] Rabindranath Thakur, 'Kabir Kaifiyat', 1915, *RR XIV*. Also, 'Sahityatattva', 1933, *RR XIV*, pp. 353–61.

[54] Rabindranath Thakur, 'Sahityatattva', 1933, *RR XIV*, p. 353.

[55] Rabindranath Thakur, 'Sahitye Tatparya', 1934, *RR XIV*, p. 373.

[56] Rabindranath Thakur, 'Sahityer Samagri', 1903, *RR XIII*, p. 743.

[57] Rabindranath Thakur, 'Sahitye Gourav', 1894, *RR III*, p. 867.

across past, present and future, across the archaic, the 'primitive' and the possible, the dream.

Unlike in texts of classical times, Rabindranath said, rasa could no longer be defined as that which was unsayable.[58] This was perhaps evident in the numerous references, definitions and explanations Rabindranath had to make in order to establish, discursively, the working of rasa as the mark of difference of the Indian nation. Perhaps this was also because in colonial modernity the work of imagination had to claim the same domain of articulation as the work of history—which was undoubtedly and primarily defined as a discursive field. Yet it was precisely this discursiveness which thinkers like Rabindranath had to critique in order to imagine a 'coming together', a coming together different from the classificatory and enumerative aggregation which the knowledge of the nation proposed, an aggregation which tended to fall apart in practice so very often and so very predictably. Rabindranath, therefore, continued to define poetic imagination as that which tied together the said with the unsayable. He argued that the generality effected by the work of imagination was a generality achieved not just by the meanings intended by speech. It was a generality which was achieved through the continuing resonance of dhvani or the sound of language, i.e. through the power of language to create vyanjana, to suggest things beyond meaning. For this resonance was more easily generalizable than meaning itself, which after all remained contextual and often local.[59] Moreover, this resonance possessed a duration, which was not exhausted by the instant of its utterance. It was this persisting resonance, independent of contextual, lexical and even figurative meaning, that created a temporality which was not fragmented in terms of contexts and of historical stages. This resonance could remain common to two different linguistic groups within the nation just as it could be shared by two times—the past and the future—of the nation. The work of imagination operated in this continuous temporality which was not fractured into ancient and modern, 'primitive' and advanced—for rasa worked not with intended meanings but with 'incomplete signs' which inhabited nature and

[58] Rabindranath Thakur, 'Kabir Kaifiyat', 1915, *RR XIV*, pp. 301–2.

[59] Rabindranath Thakur, 'Kabye Gadyariti', 1932, *RR XIV*, 520; 'Gadyakabya', August 1939, *RR XIV*, p. 528.

language.[60] It was precisely the unfinished and therefore the suggestive nature of signs which allowed different peoples and different times to share them and yet articulate them differently in different contexts and at different moments. (It is interesting how such a formulation can easily fit a political-rhetorical sensibility—where speech is made to work as meaning different things to different audiences. It is another matter, however, that for Rabindranath to admit his own formulation as 'political' would also be to admit the instability and contingency of the practical act of coming together as a nation—a contingency inadmissible, as we shall see, to the sense of temporality which imagination was made to inhabit by him and his colleagues.)

The temporality enunciated by this imagination was a non-substantive time, Rabindranath argued; but it was not the empty, homogeneous, abstract time which marked historical chronology. Nor was it the substantive temporality of historical evolution and progress. This was a time which not only critiqued the historicist understanding of chronological and unilinear time, but also displaced the location of History itself. Once the nation was understood as the coming together of different times and different peoples, Rabindranath explicitly wrote, its history could no longer be written a priori as 'our' history. In fact, 'we' were seeking to belong to what we identified as the desired and desirable history of India.[61] Indeed, Rabindranath was making a radical political claim in the name of imagination here—for he was arguing that the temporality of the history of our imagination was not derivative of the biography of the subject-nation, the locus of this history was not the community. The task therefore was not just to write this history, but also to create the appropriate subject-agent who would deserve this history and post facto make this history intimately his/her own. In other words, the movement of historical time was not founded upon the essential constant of a 'we the nation', 'we' were supposed to apprehend time and generalize ourselves across time if we had to claim this history at all.[62] Only thus could the collective, known as the nation, be created.

[60] Rabindranath Thakur, 'Rupasilpa', 1939, *RR XIV*, p. 428.
[61] Rabindranath Thakur, 'Purva o Paschim', 1908, *RR XIII*, p. 53.
[62] Ibid.

The 'Primitive' and Imagination

It was not just Rabindranath who conceptualized imagination as a clue to the resolution of the Self-Other problematic of colonial modernity, nor was he the only one to note a temporal intent behind the act of imagination itself. Accusing Bankimhcandra of 'over-historicism', Benoy Sarkar stated that 'primitives' were ignored by history, at its own peril, because by doing so 'historicism' failed to harness the 'creative intelligence of man'.[63] By contrasting itself with the 'primitive' condition, scientific historicism abdicated to its other what was crucial to human development—the working of creative imagination. That is, by claiming to be rational and historical, the nation had given up the right of imagination in favour of the 'irrational' and 'myth-oriented' 'primitive'. Sarkar insisted that it was not 'demonstrable anthropologically or psychologically that imagination belong[ed] to the primitive mind and preceded ratiocination and concrete experience'.[64] The historical nation could, therefore, reclaim this power to imagine from what it had othered as 'primitive' and archaic, by banishing the 'poetic' from historical texts like the epics and the puranas. Only by incorporating the 'primitive' and the creative temporality that s/he represented, could the nation achieve 'totality'—for history was 'incomplete and quite unable to guess the future destiny of mankind . . . so long as it [did] not concern itself with the whole of human life and its thousand and one manifestations'.[65] Benoy Sarkar taught philosophy at Calcutta University, chaired the Malda education council from 1907, ran an institute of economic study from 1927, and one of sociology from 1931 and published the monthly journal *Arthik Unnati* (Economic Development).[66] He emphasized that national unity was possible only through the study of 'folk culture' via 'anthropology,

[63] 'The Acceptable and the Unacceptable in Bankim's Social Philosophy', *Calcutta Review* (August 1938), p.123.

[64] Benoy Sarkar, *The Positive Background of Hindu Sociology*, quoted in Flora, *The Evolution of Positivism* (Naples: Instituto Universitario Orientale, 1993), p. 46.

[65] Benoy Sarkar, *The Science of History and the Hope of Mankind* (London: 1912), pp. 12, 17–18.

[66] Ida Sarkar, *My Life with Professor Benoykumar Sarkar* (Calcutta: 1977).

sociology, ethnology and philosophical history'. His mentor was Brajendranath Seal, who had not only written about the poetic epochs of the Indian civilization, he had also attended the 1911 Race Congress in London University. In his address to the Mythic Society, Seal had rejected the conventional ethnological techniques of 'static comparisons' and 'analogical induction', and proposed a 'historical-genetive' method which could uncover the originary and the creative temporality of a nation.[67]

In one of his late poems, Rabindranath figured his desired freedom as the freedom of forest-people. He wished to create 'free verse forests which implod[ed] all limits', by which he could 'liberate creation from the prison of the unending, unmoving present/the endless arrivals of the not-yets'.[68] Living in Birbhum, in the vicinity of Santal settlements, Rabindranath recognized in his 'tribal' *palki*-bearer, the 'god carved of black stone', 'the beauty of the farthest of times and distance'.[69] In the Santal youngster playing the flute he recognized 'the call of time'.[70] In the Santal young woman, working on a construction site, he marked the 'black bird, made of cloud and lightning, wings hidden within'.[71] And in a remarkable prose-poem, Rabindranath figured the river Kopai that ran through Birbhum as a Santal woman. It is worth quoting, because it invests the 'primitive' woman with a poetic language that made freedom possible even in subordination, poverty and colonial unfreedom.

> She lacks the distinction of ancient lineage. The primitive name of hers is mixed up with the loud laughing prattle of the Santal woman of countless ages. . . .
>
> Kopai in her pulsation finds its semblance in the rhythm of my poet's verse, the rhythm that has formed its comradeship with the language rich in

[67] 'Definition of Race, Tribe and Nation', paper presented at Universal Race Congress, London University, July 1911, reprinted in *Modern Review*, 36, 1924, pp. 696–7.

[68] Poem 39, *Sesh Saptak* (1935; reprint, Calcutta: 1989), p. 137.

[69] Poem 15-1, *Sesh Saptak*, p. 55.

[70] 'Ogo Saontali Chhele', *RR IV*, p. 367.

[71] 'Saontali Meye', *RR III*, pp. 294–6.

music and that, which is crowded with the jarring trivialities of the work-a-day hours.[72]

'Tribal' and 'folk' tales by now had become a necessary part of national education. Shyamacharan Dey compiled Bengali folktales, Kashmiri folktales, and Bhil, Kuki, Chakma, Paharia and Santal creation stories for the study of middle-class Bengali children.[73] Encouraged by Rabindranath, Asit Halder wrote, in simple Bengali without conjoined letters, Santal tales of how in the olden days, rabbits could scare tigers. The famous painter of Shantiniketan, Nandalal Basu, illustrated these Santal stories.[74] The Sishutosh Series of texts for children included Santal stories too, presented through the voice of the old Santal Udol, who spent every evening chatting with young boys and girls. The author called upon every Bengali parent to let this Santal into his or her home.[75]

Pramatha Choudhury mocked Western anthropology because it feared to admit the 'primordial' or the *adim* to its own time. He found it ironic that the West pushed the 'primitive' to distant lands and then 'discovered' them post facto, with guns in one hand and clothes in the other—as if violence and shame were actually not signs of 'barbarism' in modernity.[76] He insisted, against the historicist claims of some of his contemporaries, that the practice of nation-building called not so much for a sense of the past, but for a sense of the future—the 'playground of imagination'. In this future, unity would appear not as an exclusive Aryan unity, as many historians had argued, but as the unity of popular dharma, a unity of which the 'primitive' must as much be a part as the Bengali intellectual himself.[77] Choudhury saw the practice of poetics rather than the practice of karma, as Bankim had written, as the ideal historical practice—for poetics was the metonym of what we understand as historical civilization. In these practico-poetic terms,

[72] 'The Kopai', *Visvabharati Quarterly* (hereafter *VQ*), (1), new series, 1935, pp. 31–3.

[73] *Anaryer Upakatha* (Calcutta: 1914–15).

[74] *Buno Gappo* [*Wild Tales*] (Allahabad: 1922).

[75] Nagendranath Gangopadhyay, *Udol Buror Saontali Gappo* (Calcutta: 1921), preface, pp. 4–5.

[76] 'Primordial Man', in *Sabuj Patra* (*sravan* 1920), pp. 246–67.

[77] 'The Unity of India', 1914, *Prabandhasamgraha II*, pp. 5–7.

Greece appeared as dramatic, Rome as epic, Italy as sonnet, and the Jewish nation as lyric. The Indian civilization, he said, appeared as a fairy tale, with a bold and unrestrained imagination, 'which conceptual and scientific knowledge [could] never discover, because it [was] the *postulate of active life, not a passive axiom of knowledge*'[78] (emphasis mine).

Authors like Rabindranath, Pramatha Choudhury, Benoy Sarkar and others, thus, invoked the need for imagination and the need for the 'primitive' in the same breath. This concurrence of the notion of the 'primitive' and the notion of imagination is what is crucial to our understanding of imagination itself as a temporal-political act—as an act which is primarily that of re-establishing intimacy with the non-contemporary, with another time just as with another people. By itself, this concurrence is not unique to colonial Bengal. In Europe too, traditions of painting and poetry have invoked the 'primitive' in defiance of the grip of modernism. Philosophically too, the 'primordial' has been invoked in order to mark, with the anterior presence of the subject, what would otherwise simply appear as the relentless flow of time. Early-twentieth-century thinkers in Bengal were obviously familiar with some of these European searches—as apparent from the pages of the journal from Shantiniketan, *Visvabharati Quarterly*. What was specific to colonial Bengal, however, was the intellectuals' concrete and everyday experience of proximity to the 'primitive'. The colonial discourses and technologies, which—in the course of the eighteenth and nineteenth centuries—materially constituted some peoples as 'tribes' and 'aborigines', also made the inalienable presence of the 'primitive' within the nation a problem for identity formation. This experience of the 'primitive *within*' did not allow an anthropological/conceptual distance between the 'primitive' and the colonial-modern nation-subject (after all, the Bengali too was 'primitive' compared to the European). Recuperation of the 'primitive' was, therefore, always also a contamination of the self, and so dangerous. In other words, the experience of the 'primitive' *within* posed a peculiar political problem—the non-contemporaneity of internal constituents disabled their

[78] 'Is India Civilised?', 1918, *Prabandhasamgraha I*, pp. 19–20.

coming face-to-face with the contemporary subject of history, thus making impossible the practical creation of solidarity in a coming together of peoples of the nation, in and at the same moment in time. Such non-contemporary peoples seemed to appear in the present as literally an absence, and therefore as only and solely representable by someone else.

To my mind, the work of imagination was intended to neutralize precisely this temporal estrangement, an estrangement caused not just by differences and antagonisms between communities, but by pure and seemingly unsurpassable non-contemporaneity *within* the body politic. Therefore, when Pramatha Choudhury imagined the Indian nation as a fairy tale or when Rabindranath sought in the 'primitive' a language that did not make itself redundant by reducing itself to a transparent mirror of reality, they were not merely reinviting the non-contemporary into the present, denying Bengali historiography's originary and recurring act of counterpoising the historical with the 'primitive', the Aryan with the non-Aryan. I believe they were also trying to hint at the limits of representation itself—representation being that act of knowledge (and of politics) which was grounded in a prior temporal estrangement of peoples and times, that act which claimed to bring forward into the present peoples and things which definitionally belonged to another, more 'primitive' era.

Representation—as a technique of knowledge as well as a technique of making present those who were literally absent from the time of the present—presumes that the subject-agent has a direct and positive access to the peoples he seeks to represent. This is a claim for knowledge. Colonial-modern knowledge systems were produced precisely on the basis of such a claim. It was the colonial ruler/author who claimed the earliest and the keenest of such access, backed by technologies of exploration, surveys, fact-gathering, fieldwork and administration. The colonized's counter-claim, that a people knew its own self better than an outsider ever did, did not contest but merely displaced this principle—of direct access and proximity—of representational knowledge. In the formulation by some Bengali intellectuals—that imagination was something which was given over to the 'primitive' and could therefore never be accessed directly by modes of knowledge—

we find, however, the realization that ready representation might not always be possible. This realization about the limits of representation, it seems, emerged out of the apparent analogy between the subject-agent's relationship with the act of imagination and the nation's relationship with the 'primitive'.

There seem to be two aspects to the working of this analogy. We know that—even though late-nineteenth-century Bengali historiography was grounded on the absolute counterpoise of the Aryan with the non-Aryan, rewritten as the counterpoise between the civilizational and the 'primitive'—the colonized could not, like the colonizer, ethnologically transport the 'primitive' to another time and another land. Nationhood, therefore, had to be enunciated in terms of the problematic of the 'primitive *within*'—even Bankimchandra had had to admit that this was the 'first question' of national history.[79] This meant that, in the last instance, it was precisely the 'primitive within' who seemed to become the sign of difference of the colonized with the colonizer. The 'primitive'—and his/her defining trait, imagination—thus, appeared as the last site within the nation, which remained, by definition, inappropriable by colonizer's the homogenizing intent. The 'primitive within' and the poet's kalpana appeared as the only surplus to modernity and to modernity's representational competence, which the colonized could work with in his effort to undo the universality of historicism.

But then, since both the 'primitive' and imagination were othered, in nineteenth-century Bengal, by the same act of knowledge—that is, by history-writing—it seemed that neither of them could be owned up in the mode of 'knowing' the nation. Both imagination and the 'primitive' called for the building of a relationship, where the possibility of a relationship itself appeared actively destroyed—as colonial modernity transported the 'primitive', along with his/her imaginative competence, to utter non-contemporaneity. Indeed, it was this destruction which appeared as the precondition to historicity itself. Imagination, therefore, had to be reclaimed from not only a marginalized space, but from a different time altogether. This different time was not merely the past of history-writing, but a past—like the 'primitive'—which, if written historically, would appear to have no future. Not only because

[79] Bankimchandra, 'Bangalir Utpatti', *Bangadarshan* (*poush* 1880).

this past could not be fully recalled, this was also because sensibilities of modernity and progress had necessarily severed the nation's relationship with this past just as it had with the 'primitive'. Re-establishing a relationship here, therefore, required a novel practice—because it was knowledge itself which had caused this severance.

As we have already mentioned above, Pramatha Choudhury clearly stated that the act of imagination found in the fairy tale, the metonym of Indian civilization, was a principle, not of knowledge, but of practical life. Rabindranath too argued that historical knowledge—based on the principle of succession—was inadequate in the undoing of our colonial-modern alienation to our ancestral times. To him, it was the fundamental error of history as a discipline to believe that traces of our past would simply become accessible and representable if we cleared the air between the new and the old, removed the cobwebs blocking our vision, and dug up and polished monuments of the past.[80] According to Rabindranath, this error was based on the modern disciplinarian's discomfort with temporality itself. Because the present appeared as transient and the future unimaginable, historians took resort to a sense of memory wherein time appeared consolidated, apprehensible and therefore, fully representable. They refused to admit that even the past was as inaccessible to us as the future, that our memory was nothing in comparison to our forgetfulness.[81] To Rabindranath, therefore, other times—whether the past or the future—could only be owned up through acts of imagination, never through positive and representational knowledge.

Under the sign of the 'primitive', therefore, Rabindranath and his colleagues of early-twentieth-century Bengal tried to reclaim imagination as a practice—and primarily a practice—of harnessing different times. This was seen as fundamentally different from the historian's ambition of writing a full account of the past. For the work of imagination, it was said, valued incompleteness—the incompleteness and openness that marked practices for the future and which the historian wished away in the name of exhaustive research and representation of the past. Rabindranath argued that the historian's dream of knowing everything about the past was a debilitating desire which refused to

[80] Rabindranath Thakur, 'Bangla Jatiya Sahitya', 1894, *RR XIII*, p. 798.

[81] Rabindranath Thakur, 'Bismriti', *RR XIV*, p. 598.

admit that the end, where imagination ceased, was a closure which was never not arbitrary.[82] To him, this claim to know everything was to admit a cessation of practice in the name of complete knowledge. This was a forced closure which denied temporality itself and which neither our memory nor our sensibilities of the future could really ever admit.

Now, the question to ask would be: did this harnessing of kalpana, in the name of the ongoing *practice* of nation-building (as opposed to the *knowledge* of a pre-existing nation), emerge then as an effective critique of representation, in all its political import? Did this critique of representational knowledge suggest a political agenda other than the pedagogically founded nationalist politics of progress, reform and modernization? Evidently, it did not. I would argue that this was because Bengali intellectuals—even as they identified practice as that temporal imperative which colonial modern knowledge-systems sought to deny—ended up conflating practice itself to a certain notion of poetics. It was this conflation of practice and poetics which removed their notion of practical and creative time from their sensibility of the everyday, and prevented their notion of imagination from becoming politicized in the process. This becomes clear once we ask the critical question—if by giving over imagination to the 'primitive', some thinkers in colonial Bengal turned imagination itself into an act of temporalizing, how did such thinkers make sense of the materiality of their real-life 'primitive' neighbours, the so-called 'tribes' like the Santals, who worked as construction workers and landless labour in Rabindranath's Birbhum and passed as indentured coolies through the markets of Calcutta? What was it in the Santal, for instance, which inspired the Bengali educated classes to find their sense of practice in him/her? And what did all this do to their sensibility of practice itself?

A detour through some of the ethnological writings of early-twentieth-century Bengal is revealing. A crucial figure here would be William Archer who endlessly collected empirical evidence of the Santals as a people who, despite their poverty and misery, seemed to make sense of the world through songs and poetry. A typical figure of the administrator-ethnologist who spent a long time in the Santal Parganas, in order to collect and codify Santal customary law, Archer,

[82] Rabindranath Thakur, 'Nana Katha', 1885, *RR XIV*, pp. 719–20.

significantly, went on to become a historian of Indian art. Archer's favoured status amongst Bengali intellectuals did not derive from his well-known sympathy for the marginalized 'aborigine'—after all Verrier Elwin was strongly criticized by Bengalis for protecting and preserving 'primitives' as anthropological specimens. Archer was liked because he invoked the 'primitive' in the context of a certain discourse about poetic imagination. Archer's personal notes show his alliance with Bengali authors like Rabindranath, Sudhin Ghosh, Rathin Mitra, Gopal Ghosh, Tarashankar, Bishnu Dey, and with painters like Nandalal Basu and Jamini Roy—who according to Archer, showed a 'warm appreciation' of this conflation of poetic and anthropological thinking.[83] In fact, it is quite possible that the Bengali intellectuals' conflation of practice and poetics was made possible by their transactions, perhaps via figures like Archer, with traditions of 'primitivism' in European art and literature. It is significant that while in their many writings, authors like Rabindranath invoked the performative and the suggestive in language (vyanjana)—the idea that had marked their borrowings from classical rasa theories and which had given them, in the first place, an opening into experiences beyond the discursive—in their interpretive practices, they, like in European traditions of criticism, often preferred to stay with the textuality of tropological and figural analysis.

Archer confirmed, in the language of literary criticism, what many colonial ethnologists had already observed in the 'primitive'—the 'fact' that the 'primitive' possessed a primarily metaphorical mind. Thus, the missionary Reverend MacPhail had written that '[among] the Santals, a spade is called anything but a spade, and a man is almost never addressed by a [proper] name. Relationship is universally assumed to avoid the necessity of doing so.'[84] The Santal worldview was, thus, seen as that of symbolic plenitude and cross-references—articulated not in a structural mode like knowledge, but in the work and slippage of metaphors, by which far-fetched things seemed able to insinuate each other. In a manner almost reminiscent of Umberto Eco's fascinating character Padre Emanuele—who said 'Metaphor, setting our mind flying betwixt one Genus and another, allows us to

[83] Archer Private Papers, MssEur F 236 (hereafter AP), p. 73.

[84] *The Story of the Santal* (Calcutta: 1922), p. 10.

discern in a single Word more than one Object'[85] —Archer made copious notes of Santal dreams, riddles and poetry in search of unthinkable and outrageous comparisons.[86] In this, the realm of dreams, poetry and anthropology became coterminous to Archer.[87] If Freud saw dreams as clues to an individual's most secret private world, Archer claimed that the symbols of 'primitive' dreams were clues to society's most 'originary', hidden—often inarticulate—imaginations. Interpreting 'primitive' dreams was therefore the most radical act of anamnesis. His argument was that, unlike the romanticized 'savage', produced by the European imagination to fit the desires of European poets, the anthropologist's very real 'tribe' and its capacity of symbolization offered to the world 'the shock of new images'. And the wholly unfamiliar, and we may add, non-contemporary world that the 'primitives' brought to attention liberated the mind from the prison of the present—'a tribal system brings together objects and actions which are alien to a civilized consciousness and these actual connections in tribal life induce an excitement which is parallel to the charge in a poem.'[88] The anthropologist-poet apparently created a similar charge and excitement by bringing two irreconcilable times together—the time of the 'primordial', originary yet never past, and the time of imagination, not yet present, yet not far in the future either. The articulation of these two times exploded the constraining and contextualizing presence of the historical and the empirical, and simulated an escape from the prison of representation.

The symbol—the figure common to poetry and anthropology—was also invoked by Bengalis contemporary to Archer. Radhakamal Mukherjee, for instance, who described Indian society as 'permeated by the aboriginal element from top to bottom',[89] also claimed that the symbol was the most useful figure that could be used to narrate the nation. A symbol could stand for multiple referents—i.e. capture

[85] *The Island of the Day Before* (London: 1996), p. 90.

[86] AP/181.

[87] AP/72.

[88] Ibid.

[89] 'Race Elements in the Indian Village Constitution', *Man in India*, 3 (1–2), 1923, p.1.

'infinity in a concrete form'—and at the same time a concrete symbol could be unpacked to reveal a many-layered reality.[90] In other words, in early-twentieth-century Bengal, the symbol was being formulated as a kind of narrative device useful both for anthropology and for poetics—because it could capture the work of imagination. It must be kept in mind that the figure of the symbol itself had had a very specific history in European thought. Hegel had argued in *On Aesthetics* that symbolism represented 'primitive' art, where form and content were irreducible and accidental to each other, where there was no unity of origin and expression, where the spectator could only remain doubtful about the 'meaning' and intent of art. Modern art, on the other hand, expressed the inner unity of form and content.[91] More than a century later, Georg Simmel similarly invoked the symbol to distinguish modern from 'primitive' minds. To Simmel, 'primitive' symbolism was 'nebulous' and represented the lack of the mind's 'direct' access to reality. If the modern mind used symbols at all, they were highly developed abstract signs, like money, which could mediate complex exchanges and processes. As Simmel said, '[s]ymbolism, which at a lower cultural stage often means detours and waste of energy, is expedient and saves energy at the higher stages'.[92]

In an inversion of these progressivist mentions of the symbol, Archer and Mukherjee conceptualized the symbol as the 'primordial' capacity of the human mind to effect a multiplicity of meanings in one single gesture. As Mukherjee said, symbolization was 'the process of substituting relatively simple and concrete images for far more complex and abstract ones'.[93] The famous linguist Suniti Chattopadhyay invoked symbolization as the originary act of art, where nature was manifested through emblems and icons rather than through mimesis and representation.[94] The symbol was a unit with multiple meanings, the perfect trope for a nation of 'unity in diversity'. Jamini Sen quoted

[90] 'Symbols of Religion', *VQ*, 7 (1929–30), p. 269.

[91] Johannes Fabian, *Time and the Other: How Anthropology Makes Its Object* (New York: Columbia University Press, 1983), pp. 126–31.

[92] *The Philosophy of Money* (London: 1990), p. 149.

[93] 'Symbols of Religion', p. 263.

[94] 'Some Problems in the Origin of Art and Culture in India', *VQ*, 8 (1930–1), p. 275.

Nietzsche against what he called the Socratic tradition of pure intellectualism, to show that India began its culture, not in mimesis and representation, but in symbolization, in the form of the first deification of life. This *achintya bhedabheda* implied that 'in the unity of our vision is involved a diversity of outlook [which] makes us, at every moment of our life, players in an expressional drama that never denies the multiplanar being of man'.[95] The West, it was said, must borrow from India a dose of this originary expressionism, if it had to recover from the trap of defining itself negatively, in terms of what it was not (the other) and what it was no longer (after the original fall).[96]

There was, of course, a crucial difference between Archer's use of 'primitive' symbols and the Bengali authors' use of it—for the latter had to necessarily invest a certain temporality in the work of symbolization. In talking of 'primitive' symbolism, Archer predominantly used the image of painting. After all, an appearance of simultaneous presence of multiple images was more easily painted, i.e. spatially configured, than textualized. Even though Archer collected and published numerous Santal poems, his imagination of 'primitive' life was more in the nature of a 'depiction' than an enunciation. And when he wanted to convert his field-notes from the Santal Parganas into a book about Santal traditions of love and poetry—he called his book a 'portrait' of the 'primitives'.[97] For the colonized, however, imagining the nation as a portrait/painting could pose obvious problems. After all, it was too close to the colonial image of indigenous society as a static collection or museum of races. A portrait or a collection, even as it painted shades and classified difference, could not engage with temporality. As Rabindranath explicitly said, if painting gave form to the Idea, it was only the temporal phenomenon of music which could give life and animation to it.[98] Bengali poetics therefore had to make use of the symbol somewhat differently from Archer's use of it. If the latter posited the symbol as a spatial/synecdochic embodiment, literally, of a complex

[95] 'The Philosophic Background of Eastern and Western Culture', *VQ*, 5 (1928), p. 350.

[96] Ibid., pp. 353–6.

[97] *The Hill of Flutes, Life, Love and Poetry in Tribal India: A Portrait of the Santals* (London: 1974). These field notes were taken during the period 1942–6.

[98] 'The Function of Literature', *VQ*, 1(1), new series (1935), p. 77.

whole, the Bengali needed the symbol to delineate and mediate time, and history.

Thus, Dhurjati Prasad Mukhopadhyay, himself known for his expertise on music, said that the symbol was the form in which the past appeared in the present. The past lent itself to reuse and reinstation in contemporary times as a symbol. It was for this reason that the time of history was non-linear.[99] In fact, in early twentieth-century Bengal, the debate about art often took the form of a debate on the nature of the time of history. We have already referred to the painter-historian debate above. Abanindranath Thakur criticized Orientalist schools of painting because they formulated the nation's temporality in the archaeological mode, as static and synchronically structured.[100] In a remarkable essay on Aryan and non-Aryan art, Abanindranath Thakur made the chiaroscuro, the play of light and dark, into a symbol of known and unknown, far and near epochs blending into each other.[101] To him, the 'primitive' *anarya* appeared as the 'seed in the fruit' of art, 'which even though rejected while tasting the flesh, was the precondition of the fruit in the first place'.[102] The linguist Suniti Chattopadhyay described the contemporary art scene in Bengal as frequently using 'primitive' symbols, the most important of which tried to depict Santal music, drum and dance, the 'vision of colour and throbbing life'.[103] As evident, the Santals themselves were taken as a symbol of the temporality of life—-the rhythm of music and dance centrally defined the Bengali impression of 'primitive' existence—even in traditions of painting. It was in this sense that the 'primitive' was seen to offer to the colonized the capacity for symbolization—a capacity which aided the nation not only to effect multiple meanings in a single gesture, but also to imagine an everyday perpetually marked by the dynamic temporality of music and dance and poetry. Even though this was a congested and unfree everyday, it was nevertheless an everyday alleviated by the

[99] 'Progress and Personality', *VQ*, 8 (1930–1), p. 65.

[100] Tapati Guha-Thakurta, *The Making of a New Indian Art, c. 1850–1920* (Cambridge: 1992), p. 220.

[101] 'Arya o Anarya Shilpa', *Bageshwari Shilpa PrabandhabaliI* (1941, Calcutta: 1988), pp. 284–5.

[102] Ibid., p. 289.

[103] 'Our Elder Brothers, the Kol people', *VQ*, 2(1) (1924), p. 30.

temporality of the relentless work of imagination, which seemed to turn life itself into a poet's unceasing creative practice.

Conclusion

I have argued that in a context such as colonial Bengal, the work of imagination must be understood at two levels. First, at the level where imagination was explicitly called for not only as counterpoise and supplement to historicism, but also as a way of taking history beyond the knowledge imperative itself. Imagination was understood at this level as a practical imperative which even the fullest of knowledge systems could not replace. Second, at the level where imagination became not only a mode for envisioning the not-yet, but also a mode by which one could go beyond the need for visualization itself, i.e. go beyond the claim of knowledge systems to foresee the future. At this level, imagination was understood as an engagement with temporality. I have tried to show that imagination as a practical/temporal imperative was formulated in colonial Bengal on two simultaneous registers. On the one hand was the harnessing of earlier traditions of rasa and kalpana—which not only utilized the sensibility of creative time inherent in the word *kalpa* but also articulated, in the name of rasa, a non-discursive plane of social togetherness, where it was not the meaning of a word but the performative and allusive vyanjana of language which was seen to be the shared ground across peoples and times. On the other hand was the theoretical putting together of notions of imagination and the 'primitive', such that imagination itself became a practical mode of re-establishing proximity to non-contemporary times and of borrowing from the real-life 'primitive' an everyday temporality of unceasing poetic practice. In this, imagination was seen as a way of nullifying the temporal estrangement and hierarchy which colonial modernity had instituted between different peoples of the nation.

In other words, in early-twentieth-century Bengal, the work of imagination was being seen by many as an alternative way of conceiving the nation, which, in historical terms, appeared as 'backward' to the West and which, being a disorderly conglomeration of modern and 'primitive' elements, seemed to defy every attempt at unification. It was said that the work of imagination, if so deployed, could generate togetherness across times and peoples. But this togetherness would be one that was not founded on a commonality of meaning/spirit/essence—a commonality which escapes Indian politics even today and which appears more often than not as a coercive imposition of a majority culture and history on minority and subaltern groups. This would be a togetherness that realized itself in terms of a generality of idiom, mood and performative competence, which neither derived from nor led to a monolithic Indian 'culture' but which could be used in the articulation of different ways and modes of being at home in the nation.[104]

Why, despite the incredible popularity of at least Rabindranath, did this proposed work of imagination never take off? Why was the idea of togetherness across differences so easily reduced to the empty state slogan of 'unity within diversity'? And why, after all, did this sensibility of togetherness—not in meaning but in performance—become reduced to a culturalist understanding the nation? To my mind, this was because the temporality proposed by the work of imagination could never acquire the political force which the temporality of progress (e.g. of the Nehruvian Congress), or its supplement, the temporality of political revivalism (e.g. of the Hindu right), did. And this, in turn, was because the Bengali educated classes' sensibility of imagination—as that which was given over to the 'primitive'—was based on a crucial miscognition of what they called the 'primitive's metaphorical mind'.

The Bengali middle classes, and ethnologists like Archer, discovered poetry amongst the Santals, collected 'tribal' metaphors, dreams, verses, etc., in order to prove that 'primitives' made sense of life through the practice of a certain poetics. But in listing 'tribal' symbols

[104] It was not incidental, therefore, that Rabindranath himself, being one of the most articulate proponents of this power of kalpana, would imagine the nation to be a world unto itself—an embodiment of difference and wonderment, built out of the coming home of endless waves of strangers and outsiders. Nor was it incidental that Rabindranath, in his very conceptualisation of the nation, would see through the agenda of nationalism as something already played out in the West and as having already reached its historical limit. To him, the nation was neither the desirable nor the logical end to the human experiment—for it was after all, an imprisoned subjectivity which had to finally strain against arbitrary and territorialized national boundaries. For an elaboration of this aspect of Rabindranath's thought, see Ashis Nandy, *Rabindranath Tagore and the Illegitimacy of Nationalism* (Delhi: Oxford University Press, 1994).

and metaphors as constitutive of a 'poetic' imagination, they missed the strategic insight that the Santals might have had to offer to contemporary Bengali sensibilities of practice. Bengali intellectuals did not find it important that so many of the symbolic associations found amongst the Santals actually operated as riddles. These were riddles meant in principle to be cracked—and presumed a moment of collective discussion and commentary on the Santal's everyday life. In fact, riddles were very common amongst the Santals of the time; it was the ability to make sense of riddles which was supposed to demonstrate an individual Santal's wisdom and was, for instance, an important part of dealings between the bride's and the groom's families, where judging each other's insights into life was important. Thus, there was the story of Kora, a seemingly poor and stupid man, who spoke strangely and therefore was known to be mad. It was only that rare young woman, whose father had incidentally brought Kora home, who finally understood Kora's strange utterances for what they were. They were riddles, she said, and cracked all of them. Everybody in the village agreed that she and Kora were meant to marry each other.[105]

Santal stories, recorded in the late nineteenth and early twentieth centuries, are replete with tales of misunderstandings and misapprehensions, where riddles become instrumental in resolving troublesome issues and everyday double-binds. There was, thus, the story of a man who asked his son-in-law why he had not dammed the outlets from his paddy field. The young man was surprised, for he had indeed done so and the water was standing well under the rice crop. But later, when the son-in-law lost most of his crop to the moneylender, the wise old man explained that this was precisely what he was hinting at, when he had asked earlier why the son-in-law had not built enough dams on his land. And 'the son-in-law admitted that he was right and that his words had had a meaning.'[106] In other words, when s/he made symbolic associations, the Santal did not claim to become a poet, an author.

[105] 'The Bridegroom who Spoke in Riddles', in *Folklore of the Santal Parganas*, Cecil Henry Bompas (Delhi: Gyan Prakashan, reprint, 2001), pp. 174–6.

[106] 'The Father-in-law's Visit', in Bompas, *Folklore*, pp. 227–8; also see the stories 'Enigmas', pp. 239–40, and 'The Goala's Daughter', p. 242, in the same collection.

The Santal did not, by the act of symbolization, seek to configure the rest of the community as a readership, who could only post facto and only tentatively interpret the author's symbolic associations, try to recover the author's intention and make sense of the author's metaphors in terms of their own specific contexts. Instead, here the speaker's words were meant to produce a moment of discourse, such that a meaning, otherwise concealed under the apparent self-evidence of reality, could be made manifest to all. In saying the riddle, the speaker caused himself and his audience to come together, in unravelling the so-called metaphorical association at almost the very moment of making the association itself. In other words, the act of making and cracking a riddle appeared here as a transparent and, in the last instance, collective act, which was deliberately meant to create the contingent situation of coming together in understanding.

Riddles, it must be remembered, not only anticipate the concurrence of two incongruous or heteronomous things but also make explicit the concrete act of making them appear concurrent. That is the point of solving a riddle—the unpacking of an apparently mysterious or impossible or even absurd association. An 'original' and hitherto unthought of metaphor—when read as poetry—makes the claim of stretching the limits of language, of rendering false the realist and representational intention behind language's function of referentiality. An unusual association—when intended as riddle—however, makes the claim of demystifying the self-evidence of reality itself. On the one hand, by finding sense in extraordinary associations, Santali riddles, for instance, unpacked the strangeness and oddity of common and everyday reality, as when Santals referred to excretion as 'paying the moneylender', to eating watered rice during their annual hunger period as 'looking at the stars', to the coconut as the 'brown sahib of Calcutta with hair on his bones'.[107] On the other hand, by making extraordinary associations, Santali riddles offered the possibility that in everyday life, theoretically distant things could and did appear practically proximate and confrontational. It was not just that in riddles, as in metaphor, far-fetched and disconnected experiences could stand in for each other, but also that what were apparently far-fetched

[107] AP/ 181.

could, in the practice of coming together and creating understanding, become proximate and mutually relevant and/or confrontational. The critique of representation and referentiality that this practice of making and cracking riddles offered could, thus, become an everyday, and not a poetic, critique. As the Santal stories demonstrated, the operation of riddles showed that the wise one with an understanding of everyday things and acts could, in practice, bring both differing people and disparate judgements together in an act of resolution.

In reading Santali riddles as merely literary figuration, Bengali intellectuals missed this everyday and practical nature of Santal acts of metaphorization. In fact, Bengali poetics of early twentieth century categorically sought to remove itself from the time of the everyday, the time of quotidian lives and the time of the nitty-gritty of politics. Since the everyday was felt to be mired in colonial unfreedom and the compromises which a subaltern existence called for, Rabindranath, for instance, categorically stated that it was the 'width of leisure' which was the location of poetic practice, thus wishing such practice away from the everyday and the ordinary time of life and labour.[108] In its confinement within what was called 'leisure', the practice of kalpana, therefore, stopped short of becoming a political strategy of resistance to universal forms of knowledge and representation. The time of imagination—despite its critique of knowledge—did not inform practical time, for it shared with knowledge the othering of the time of the everyday. It can even be said that the creative time of kalpana did not become the time of practice precisely because it tried to become its surrogate. And in historical and political terms, the nation was allowed to subsume creative time itself as, ironically, one of its many essential and timeless traits.

In allowing the nation to subsume kalpana as one of its timeless traits, Rabindranath himself nullified his own, perhaps risky, formulation—that in the practice of imagination even the nation could and did appear as contingent. This contingency of the nation had to be admitted, because imagination signified a future beyond the familiar, beyond what one was equipped by knowledge to anticipate. But it had also to be admitted because imagination, unlike knowledge, could

[108] 'The Philosophy of Leisure', *VQ*, 7 (1929–30), p. 8.

never be slotted as a particular trait or competence in possession of some and not others. Everybody—even the 'primitive' and primarily the 'primitive', as Benoy Sarkar said—could claim imagination. Imagination, therefore, did not offer an uncontested or self-evident vision of an agent, a leader, a subjectivity with a natural and inherent right to the exercise of it—not even the nation, as Rabindranath had to admit for a moment, could particularly claim imagination as its own special trait. After all, imagination was open to appropriation by anybody because it could only be claimed as one's own in practice, never through an a priori theoretical justification. Kalpana, therefore, appeared as a practice which not only questioned the representational adequacy of knowledge, but also had the potential to question the conventional understanding of what a political subject-agent was. After all, whether it was the prince of Machiavelli, the state of Hegel, the proletariat of Marx or the nation of historicism, politics has always appeared, in modernity, as the special competence of an exclusive subject, who could claim access to something which others could never have, whether it be skill, knowledge, nationality or the virtue of 'having nothing to lose'. Such a subject-agent is, always already, in a pedagogical relationship with the masses he must mobilize—because his crucial competence appears as something akin to a knowledge which others lack. In fact, the place of 'politics' in modernity can be understood precisely in terms of this constitutive paradox—that the moment of the 'political', the moment of the truly contingent, always takes the political subject by surprise, for his claim to political agency had been really a claim to prior knowledge. The mobilization of kalpana, however, would have required an alternative vision of political agency itself, since by definition it defied possession by an exclusive and knowledgeable subject—i.e. until imagination and its temporal creativity was subsumed as the nation's exclusive competence, which was what was done in twentieth-century Bengal.

In terms of everyday political practice, therefore, proponents of 'progress' and proponents of creative temporality seemed to agree with each other—that for the sake of the nation, the unquestionable political subject, 'primitives' must, in the last instance, be educated and 'Hinduized'. Even Rabindranath, the theorizer par excellence of creative and non-linear temporality, accepted that, however tolerant

India was, society must in the last instance 'improve' and to do so, refuse to 'preserve the grotesque just for th e *anarya*'. After all, '*tamasikata* [indulgence of dark and immoral vices of the flesh] could never be a truly Indian substance'.[109] Thus, despite the poetic insight—that 'primitives' were the last inappropriable location in colonial modernity—even Rabindranath continued to hope that, while India would assert the principle of difference in confronting colonialism, it would relinquish difference itself in its own mobilization. After all, how else could the concept of a singular and self-possessed political subject be enunciated? In other words, poetics made difference—between its internal constituents, between creative time and progressional time, between the colonizer and the colonized—into a metaphor of the nation. It failed to make difference into a ground for practical negotiations. Because it did not lend difference to strategic and political use, poetics' own difference to historical practice remained neutralized. In practical terms, like the farthest outpost of the nation, the rebellious poet and the sensuous and free 'primordial' of his imagination awaited their mobilization by mainstream nationalist politics, without being able to intervene in it.

[109] 'Bharatbarsher Itihaser Dhara', 1911, in *RR XVIII*, pp. 450–1.